. . . AND
COMMUNICATIONS FOR ALL

. . . AND COMMUNICATIONS FOR ALL

A Policy Agenda for a New Administration

Edited by
Amit M. Schejter

LEXINGTON BOOKS

A DIVISION OF

ROWMAN & LITTLEFIELD PUBLISHERS, INC.

Lanham • Boulder • New York • Toronto • Plymouth, UK

LEXINGTON BOOKS

A division of Rowman & Littlefield Publishers, Inc.
A wholly owned subsidary of The Rowman & Littlefield Publishing Group, Inc.
4501 Forbes Boulevard, Suite 200
Lanham, MD 20706

Estover Road
Plymouth PL6 7PY
United Kingdom

This volume is the product of the Future of American Communications (FACT) Working
Group assembled at the Institute for Information Policy (IIP) at the Pennsylvania State
University in December 2007, with a supporting grant provided by the Media Democracy
Fund (MDF). The editing was done by Judy Maltz, and the project coordinator was
Jonathan Obar.

British Library Cataloguing in Publication Information Available

Library of Congress Cataloging-in-Publication Data
—And communications for all : a policy agenda for a new administration / edited by
Amit M. Schejter.
    p. cm.
  Includes index.
  ISBN-13: 978-0-7391-2919-7 (cloth : alk. paper)
  ISBN-10: 0-7391-2919-8 (cloth : alk. paper)
  ISBN-13: 978-0-7391-2920-3 (pbk. : alk. paper)
  ISBN-10: 0-7391-2920-1 (pbk. : alk. paper)
  ISBN-13: 978-0-7391-3483-2 (electronic)
  ISBN-10: 0-7391-3483-3 (electronic)
  1. Telecommunication policy—United States. I. Schejter, Amit.
  HE7781.A75 2009
  384.0973—dc22   2008044657

Printed in the United States of America

∞™ The paper used in this publication meets the minimum requirements of American
National Standard for Information Sciences—Permanence of Paper for Printed Library
Materials, ANSI/NISO Z39.48–1992.

Contents

Preface

A Second Chance

IT IS RARE THAT POLICYMAKERS GET a second chance, but today, they may be fortunate enough to have such an opportunity. As this book goes to press in the fall of 2008, it is aimed to assist the new administration that will be elected this fall to seize the opportunity, learn from past mistakes, and design a communications policy that will be forward-looking, make information technologies available to all, enhance their contribution to a more vibrant democratic sphere, to a greater sense of social responsibility, and to an improved quality of life for all Americans.

Twelve years after the landmark Telecommunications Act of 1996 was passed, the media and telecommunications industries in the United States are more concentrated and less competitive than they were beforehand. Fewer Americans are taking advantage of new technologies in comparison to their peers in other industrialized countries; the technologies available to them are inferior, yet at the same time they are required to pay more for them. The combination of shortsighted, though well-intended, policies and the tendency to cater to the powerful interests of incumbent industries—telephone, cable, and broadcasting companies—has led to disastrous results.

Half a century ago, the United States was light years ahead of the rest of the world when it came to providing its citizens with access to communication networks and when it came to the sophistication of these networks. Today, it lags behind most of the developed and some developing nations on both counts. Even worse, evidence suggests that in the absence of dramatic policy changes, this trend will only intensify.

The policy agenda set down in these pages was prepared by a group of sixteen scholars of eleven major American universities. Media and communications studies scholars, economists, legal scholars, public policy scholars, education researchers, engineers, and social scientists from various disciplines, they joined together to form the Future of American Communications Working Group under the auspices of the Institute for Information Policy at Penn State University. Their work was supported by a generous grant from the Media Democracy Fund. Each member of the working group enjoyed a free hand in drawing up his or her recommendations, and no vote or unanimous agreement regarding each recommendation was taken. In this sort of interdisciplinary work, it is our belief that the whole is greater than the sum of its parts.

The policy prescriptions we offer take into account the current crisis plaguing U.S. communications policy, as policymakers strive to support a future in which the United States will reclaim its position as a world leader in the field. Indeed, policy alone will not suffice, but it is an indispensable tool in this effort. While each chapter represents solely the views of its author, some common threads are evident throughout, among them the following:

- The United States should adopt a comprehensive and pro-active national information policy that promotes social inclusion as well as ubiquitous, high-quality, open Internet service.
- The policy should be technologically neutral, embracing all communications technologies and redefining the breadth and scope of longstanding corrective policies.
- The policy should address the four Cs of access: connectivity, capability, content, and context. The goal of connectivity, at the heart of most policies that aspire to increase access and/or bridge the digital divide, represents but a first step toward functional access and empowerment. Capability, content, and context must be woven into any strategy seeking to achieve a better informational future for all.
- A balance needs to be struck between measures that are market-led and measures that are government-led.
- National policy should recognize that a vibrant national broadband network is comprised of both public goods and consumer products and that it is designed to promote the former and create truly competitive markets for the emergence of the latter.

Our recommendations are based on a consensus that all communications services, including interactive, information, and entertainment services, will eventually be provided over broadband. At the same time, we believe that the

Internet reduces uncertainty for users in important contexts, encourages civic engagement, enables the creation of social capital, and is shaped through user-generated content.

Our national goal, therefore, should be making broadband ubiquitous. All policies and rules adopted in the next several years should be viewed as transitional, their objective being the smooth transition to a national, content-rich, nondiscriminatory broadband network. But even if the Internet is kept open and broadband becomes inexpensive and ubiquitous—two huge policy challenges—that alone will not resolve all the key issues. Derailing hypercommercialism, creating vibrant noncommercial zones, and protecting privacy are other important goals to be addressed in these pages.

The forward-looking policy we propose stems from a vision of how the industry should look in the future, and mid-range policy measures are recommended to take us there.

The recommendations of the working group members are outlined in the following chapter, the introduction and summary. More detailed descriptions are provided in the individual chapters. Following the summary, the book is divided into four sections. In section I, *Frameworks*, Jorge Reina Schement of Rutgers University discusses the new contract for universal access in the twenty-first century; Ernest J. Wilson III of the University of Southern California Annenberg School for Communications urges us to revisit the traditional perspectives for viewing the media industries; Robert W. McChesney of the University of Illinois argues that scholars of all disciplines need to engage in the policy debate, and Amit M. Schejter of Penn State provides a comparison of communications policies across the globe that sheds light on where the United States has erred.

The recommendations outlined in the introduction are discussed in further detail in section II—*Infrastructures and Industries*. Marvin Ammori of the University of Nebraska College of Law discusses the *wireline industry* for delivering high-speed Internet access and the means by which to make it more competitive; Richard D. Taylor of Penn State prescribes the way the *cable industry* should be prepared for the transition to an all-broadband network; Jon M. Peha of Carnegie Mellon offers a middle ground in *spectrum management* that balances between property claims and the call for a spectrum commons, and proposes the launching of a national emergency communications system; Rob Frieden of Penn State discusses the *wireless industry* and prescribes ways by which to increase competition among wireless operators for the benefit of consumers; and Philip M. Napoli of Fordham proposes a new framework to guide the debate on *ownership in the media industries*. In section III—*Access*—Krishna Jayakar of Penn State lays the foundation for a new approach to *universal service*; Sharon L. Strover of the University of Texas proposes a strategy to confront the unique challenges facing *rural communities*; Andrea H. Tapia of Penn State outlines the focus for *municipalities* planning on providing broadband services; and Heather E. Hudson of the University of San Francisco identifies the key components for efficient and innovative distribution of the *E-rate*. In section IV—*Content*—Ellen P. Goodman of the Rutgers School of Law Camden discusses the future of *public broadcasting* as it becomes public service media in the digital age; Kathryn Montgomery of American University presents the challenges for *protecting young audiences* in the digital future, in particular the overlooked teenage demographic; and Leonard M. Baynes of St. John's University School of Law addresses the challenges of increasing *minority representation* in both traditional and new media in light of the sharp decline in minority ownership in the past decade.

The book targets many different audiences—scholars, students, policymakers, and activists. It is also quite a unique project in that it is the collective work of sixteen independent scholars motivated solely by a commitment to serve the public interest. Unlike much scholarship in telecommunications debates, none of the scholars accepted or solicited corporate funding for this project. The book is also comprehensive, addressing as wide a variety of pertinent issues as possible. Each recommendation presented here stands on its own logic and represents the views of its author alone. It should be noted, however, that at various stages of the process, various proposals outlined here were scrutinized and challenged by members of the working group.

The working group meetings and the writing of the different chapters took place during the first nine months of 2008 and went to press in the fall just as we learned that Barack Obama will lead the new administration. We believe that the challenges we identify and the route we each offer provide an essential roadmap for his new administration as it confronts the twenty-first-century challenge of ensuring a ubiquitous, reliable, nondiscriminatory, and innovative communications network for all.

University Park, PA, November 2008

Introduction

Summary of Recommendations

Part I: General Recommendations

1. Congress should adopt a forward-looking national policy to facilitate the transition of the "wireline," "wireless," and "cable television" industries to become part of a ubiquitous national open broadband network, regulated primarily at the federal and state levels.
2. The new policy should ensure that:
   a) Consumers can access all content and all applications of their choice online, without interference from any network provider; and
   b) Attach any device to any network, wired or wireless.

3. Congress and the Federal Communications Commission (FCC) should gather domestic and international information on broadband facts and policies to develop best practices.
4. In the mid-range, regarding all existing industries, and in order to avoid the creation of distorted market conditions, regulators should:
   a) Encourage new entrants by any means, anywhere; and
   b) Pay special regulatory attention to the rise of metered broadband services.

Part II: Infrastructures and Industries

The Existing "Wireline" Industry

With regard to the existing wireline industry, Congress and the FCC (each within its capacity as stated) will need to:

1. Adopt unbundling and wholesale access policies focused on broadband access, not on voice or other particular communications; Congress should define the unbundled elements narrowly and set the price formula in primary legislation rather than delegating more broadly to the FCC.
2. Modify forbearance procedures to protect pro-competitive policies from "deregulatory" commissions.
3. Enact structural or functional separation to better align carrier incentives and enforce pro-competitive policies.
4. Set up an operational "arbitrator" to ensure incumbents do not undermine competition through operational delay.
5. Ensure entrants have access to local rights of way.
6. Require divestiture of unused copper and cable lines, when fiber is deployed.
7. Provide financial assistance if necessary for deployment of open, unbundled fiber networks.
8. Enact network neutrality.
9. Include the public in any political debates or compromises that affect the future of our nation's broadband networks.

The Existing "Cable" Industry

All policies and rules adopted over the next several years with regard to the existing cable industry should be viewed as transitional, intended to facilitate the smooth conversion to a national, interconnected, nondiscriminatory broadband network, creating the virtual equivalent of line sharing with respect to the delivery of video services. That said, a number of current issues need to be addressed:

1. The *a la carte* issue should be separated from content regulation.
2. Multicast must carry should not be adopted.
3. Rules prohibiting arbitrary or anti-competitive discrimination in network management need to be enacted promptly. Serious discussion of the nuances of this issue should continue. Full disclosure of network management practices would be a useful first step.

4. The introduction of metered or capped broadband services should be closely monitored as they could lead to unanticipated harmful consequences. Usage-based pricing is potentially anti-competitive, arbitrary, slows growth, fails to recognize the current reality of the evolving video market, and creates perverse incentives.
5. The FCC should begin proceedings to:
    a) Require all televisions built following the earliest practicable date to accept direct Internet connections;
    b) Establish "open Internet TV" standards, just as it did with advanced television standards (these could be multiple standards), including standards for remote controls and integrated media browsers; and
    c) Set a "date certain" for the transition to an all IP network in which all screens connect to the Internet through an open standard that supports remote controls and media browsers.

For the longer term:

1. The challenges for protecting video over "open" broadband networks from undue dominance or predatory behavior are entirely different than with cable television. The bottlenecks may not be the local carriers but could be proprietary software, appliances, search engines, DRM, and advertising. The FCC should embark on studying these potential threats.
2. States should be encouraged to pass laws franchising wired video/broadband delivery systems, and replacing municipal cable franchises (to the extent permitted under federal law). A model law would be helpful in this regard, to encourage common standards.
3. State video franchises should be nonexclusive in fact as well as in form, and issued and supervised under an appropriate state agency
4. PEG access will need assistance to make the transition from analog to IP:
    a) states should determine and collect franchise fees or sales taxes on video programming (consistent with federal law) and return to communities an appropriate amount for access groups;
    b) state video franchises should include a mandatory definition of the technical quality of digital PEG access of at least equal to commercial video programs (channels) previously delivered as analog; and
    c) municipalities should be able to claim any residual authority not expressly preempted by federal or state law or regulation.

The Spectrum

While many might believe that the shortage of available spectrum, the "lifeblood" of wireless systems, is an inevitable result of the laws of physics, it is more rooted in the now-outdated laws and traditions of the federal government. Numerous measurement studies have shown that at any given time and location, much of the prized spectrum sits idle.

1. With regard to the management of spectrum, policies should be implemented that:
   a) alleviate today's shortage of available spectrum;
   b) decrease the cost of today's wireless services; and
   c) create opportunities for new wireless products and services.
2. These goals can be achieved through new spectrum policies that:
   a) encourage spectrum users to reduce their spectrum needs;
   b) allow and encourage more spectrum sharing; and
   c) decrease the cost of initial access to spectrum.
3. Near-term opportunities for achieving these long-term goals include reaping more spectrum dividends from the DTV transition in addition to the reallocation of many television channels in a 2008 auction:
   a) It should be possible to deploy wireless systems in the television "white spaces," and the debate over how best to use that spectrum should be expanded.
   b) This is an extraordinary opportunity to construct a nationwide broadband network that serves local first responders, eventually replacing the inefficient and ineffective systems of today, and that is financially sustainable. If it does, it will save spectrum, taxpayer dollars, and lives.
4. The next president should demand a detailed inventory of federal spectrum and an account of how this essential resource is used. Except for those bands that must be protected for reasons of national security, the results of this inventory should be made public. This would allow existing companies, entrepreneurs, and researchers to seek out opportunities to use the spectrum more efficiently. Those who find opportunities could make their case to the NTIA, the current license-holder, and Congress.
5. In addition to making more spectrum available, policy reform could make the spectrum that comes available via auction accessible to more potential license-holders. Under current policy, the auction winner makes a one-time payment to the U.S. Treasury equal to the winning bid. Instead, the auction winner should make an annual payment equal to the winning bid for as long as it retains the license. This would greatly reduce the funds that an auction winner needs initially, thereby allowing small entrepreneurial firms to compete with the giants. This arrangement would also encourage license-holders to surrender spectrum if their plans should fail, leaving the spectrum underutilized.

The Wireless Industry

Cutting-edge wireless services, such as true broadband access to the Internet, are not widely available in the United States, nor do national carriers regularly display global best practices in the nature, type, and pricing of services they offer. Wireless carriers appear able to delay investment in next generation networks, because the carriers have concentrated on leveraging money to acquire market share and buy out competitors.

1. The FCC must:
   a) begin to address the dangers of further concentration of the industry;
   b) recognize the need to subject wireless carriers to different degrees of regulatory oversight since the many types of services they offer trigger different degrees of regulatory oversight;
   c) retain streamlined common carrier regulation for conventional wireless telecommunications services and calibrate any further deregulation to an increase in sustainable, facilities-based competition;
   d) intervene with regard to information and video services only when necessary to ensure that wireless carriers operate accessible networks. This would not necessitate common carrier regulation, but it would require wireless carriers to establish clear service terms and conditions and to report instances where competitive necessity supports diversification in price and quality of service;
   e) adopt a wireless "Carterfone" policy, which would provide subscribers with the option of attaching an unsubsidized handset free of any carrier imposed attachment restrictions;
   f) prohibit carriers from favoring content supplied by corporate affiliates or ventures that seek to buy preferential treatment;
   g) not continue refraining from telecommunications service regulation of CMRS carriers until additional sustainable, facilities-based competition arises. In the absence of new players in the market, the FCC should not approve transactions that would lead to further market consolidation; and
   h) promote wireless technology alternatives to wireline networks when allocating funds that target universal service goals. Together with state public utility commissions, it should use reverse auctions to achieve lowest-cost bidding for service to high-cost areas subject to quality of service benchmarks. Before using reverse auctions the FCC should allow wireless carriers to qualify as eligible telecommunications carriers based on the wireless carrier's actual costs instead of the current practice of applying the incumbent wireline carrier's costs.

2. Congress should explicitly state that state public utility commissions and state courts can adjudicate disputes that pertain to quality of service and interpretation of service agreements. In the absence of legislation, the FCC should enforce existing truth in billing regulations and require CMRS operators to provide understandable service agreements that clearly specify all charges, fees, taxes, and surcharges. It should also void compulsory arbitration clauses.
3. The executive branch, Congress, and the FCC need to remain on guard against trends that would prevent wireless carriers from providing a competitive alternative to legacy technologies.

Media Ownership

Policymakers' goals should be focused on maximizing our contemporary potential for a democratic media system, on maximizing the contemporary technological tools at hand to craft a media system that is as diverse and competitive as it can be and that serves the informational needs and interests of local communities to the fullest extent that is technologically and economically possible. As a result:

1. In assessing and formulating media ownership policies, our current media system needs to be compared with its contemporary potential—not with its past.
2. Subjective value judgments about what level of ownership restrictions needs to be applied in order to best reflect fundamental First Amendment, and democratic principles cannot (and should not) be removed from the equation.
3. The primary goal of media ownership policies is not to preserve or promote the health of established industry sectors, particularly when it comes at the expense of the development of new industry sectors.
4. In assessing the contemporary media environment, the number of outlets or channels is far too superficial a unit of analysis. Instead, the distribution of resources for the production of content should be the focus. It is essential that policymakers and policy analysts see the forest through the trees and avoid confusing channel or outlet availability with content availability.
5. Recent iterations of the FCC's media ownership proceedings seem to have started from the position that, if harms associated with relaxing or eliminating particular ownership regulations could not be effectively demonstrated, then the regulations would be relaxed or eliminated. It would seem more than reasonable for policymakers to engage in an analytical

process that assesses not only the potential harms associated with relaxing media ownership regulations, but also the potential benefits.

6. In assessing and formulating media ownership policies, demands for rigorous data analysis must be accompanied and supported by rigorous data gathering.
7. In assessing and formulating media ownership policies, "putting the horse back in the barn" is not impossible. In fact, history tells us that, if the political will is there, such reversals in policy direction are indeed possible.

Part III: Access

Universal Service Policy

A future universal service policy can help prepare the United States for the competitive challenges that lay ahead, most prominently, the need to catch up with the rest of the developed world and assume a dominant role in the emerging broadband economy.

1. Short term universal service challenges include:
   a) The question of universal service funding: If the new administration does not address the question of universal service funding, it will not be able to find solutions for any of the other questions confronting the universal service programs. Policymakers' ability to expand the contribution base is limited; therefore, it is imperative in the short term that expenditures are capped at sustainable and effective levels for the various USF-supported programs. Specifically for the high-cost areas program, we recommend that a single service provider be identified in each territory to offer service using the most cost-efficient technology—this service provider may be identified through auctions or other appropriate mechanisms.
   b) The lack of accountability and monitoring in universal service programs. This challenge calls for their improvement as well as for the introduction of stronger institutional mechanisms to investigate allegations of fraud or misappropriation of funds.
   c) The inability of a growing percentage of households to have access to basic telephone service: federal incentives to states to actively promote Lifeline and Link-Up programs. Better enforcement of existing consumer protection laws or a new law specific to telecommunications is needed to protect consumers against aggressive marketing

of telecommunication services—a leading cause of disconnection because it causes unpredictable increases in monthly bills.

d) The proposals of the Federal-State Joint Board on Universal Service for reorganizing the high-cost areas program to create three new platform-specific funds—a broadband fund, a mobility fund, and a provider of last resort (POLR) fund should be replaced by encouraging the deployment of cost-efficient multiple services platforms such as WiMax, through funding support as well as other means, such as spectrum allocations and standard-setting. If implementation is devolved to the states, there has to be active federal standard-setting and monitoring.

For the long run, universal service policies need to move beyond the traditional focus on access.

2. Emphasis should shift from promoting network take-up through affordability ("low rates") to promoting it through increasing the value that consumers derive from network services.

3. Instead of providing a common service to all consumers uniformly (plain old telephone service—POTS), the new universal service programs should offer a multiplicity of services, with consumers able to choose the services that they value the most.

4. Policymakers should recognize that subscriptions in the new telecommunications environment will be driven by the quality and heterogeneity of services and by the ability of consumers to choose the services most valuable to them. As a result they need to pay attention to the middle of the value production chain, i.e., the place where new service innovations occur.

5. Unlike POTS, new telecommunications services require a degree of knowledge and skill on the part of consumers. Universal service policies in the new environment must incorporate efforts to promote digital literacy and training.

6. In taking the cue from universal service policies evolving around the globe, the "new universal service" should build on four dimensions:
   a) supporting network deployment;
   b) aiding network take-up by promoting digital literacy and consumer training;
   c) providing incentives for service/business innovation; and
   d) creating support infrastructures that enable the deployment of new services.

Of these, support for network deployment is the only one emphasized by traditional universal service policies.

Rural Access

A special challenge lies with regard to access in rural regions, in which roughly 17 percent of the U.S. population lives. Broadband subscription rates in rural regions are twenty-one percentage points lower than in urban and eighteen percentage points lower than in suburban regions, even though there is an equivalent level of interest in subscribing to broadband in both regions.

An alternative vision of universal service and its contribution to rural populations must focus on cultivating the ability of people to improve their lives—with the specific nature of those improvements to be determined by the people themselves. This, in turn, requires renewed focus on self-determination in the communications/telecommunications environment—a process made more viable with the onset of new media, networks, and new types of telecommunications services. Public policy that acknowledges not just parity with urban regions, but also self-determination, could make telecommunications more meaningful to life in rural regions.

The challenges that lie ahead in this field are several:

1. Recognizing the significance of this infrastructural element to all aspects of life in rural and nonrural regions of the country, and incorporating into economic, educational, and social policies the budgets and practices that will help exploit the potential of telecommunications.
2. Conceding that marketplace dynamics do not deliver timely services to more remote and less populous regions and developing improved mechanisms to improve services in those regions.
3. Crafting programs that systematically augment the range of services and available training and expertise around broadband services in rural regions.
4. The four factors that affect rural Internet subscription and use are:
   a) infrastructure availability;
   b) content applicability;
   c) pricing; and
   d) training.

Viable programs that influence these factors can take several forms. Since simple deployment alone, however, appears to be an insufficient driver, any programs that stimulate deployment must be linked to investments in training and use. The recommendations regarding rural connectivity are:

1. Adopt a national broadband policy that is capable of guaranteeing sustained investment in telecommunications infrastructure. The United States requires constantly updated capabilities that are affordable and available to all.

2. Establish grants for Internet training. These could be block grants and must be outcomes-oriented and outcomes-dependent. The target populations could be not only individual users but also small businesses. Increasing small business use of the Internet could have tremendous economic impact on rural regions. Grants within states themselves could go to various entities, including nonprofits, towns, counties, and local government units.

3. Universal service funds should be used to enhance projects undertaken by communities that are designed to extend their telecommunications capabilities. These funds could be used to match local investment in infrastructure, connectivity, public access, and similar access technologies. They could also be used to provide broadband infrastructure development and incentives to communities that can demonstrate their readiness to develop their own facilities/expertise as well as their abilities to use these facilities. Communities should match federal investment in some manner. They could purchase broadband services or develop their own infrastructures.

4. Invest in community college–based Internet applications capabilities classes for individuals and small businesses and create incentives for colleges that enroll small business owners, with some outcome-based measure being the trigger for an incentive "subsidy" or payment.

5. Create "rural leadership academies" that select aspiring or actual rural leaders for two to three weeks of leadership training that would include training not only in using the Internet but also in running computer education clinics or courses, in the "nuts and bolts" of broadband infrastructure, and in resource-sharing across institutions. These leaders would serve the purpose of catalyzing Internet availability and use in their respective communities, which would be left to decide what investments and services make most sense for them.

Municipal Broadband

Local governments have a role to encourage municipalities:

1. To own and manage wireless networks or at least to take an active role in creating them.
2. To design, build, and deploy wireless service that is as reliable as the other common utilities, such as water, power, and telephone, with clear performance standards established.
3. To design, build, and deploy wireless service coverage, which should include every household, business, organization, public space, and public transit corridor included in a municipality.

4. To charge for the wireless service prices that are affordable and nondiscriminatory, in order to ensure universal access for all.

In order to achieve the goals of this policy, it is essential to:

1. Identify a common standard for wireless broadband deployment, including Wi-Fi meshing.
2. Reallocate underutilized spectrum for unlicensed citizen access.
3. Expand the universal service fund (USF) to cover broadband service, including USF eligibility, distribution, and availability of funds for various types of broadband providers.
4. Encourage the federal government to offer grants to fund broadband deployment.

The E-Rate

The USF programs for schools, libraries, and rural health care should become a permanent component of universal service. The FCC should maintain responsibility for the USF programs for schools, libraries, and rural health care, but special advisory committees should be established, comprised of representatives from NTIA, DOE, and HHS, as well as from professional educational, library, and health care organizations. These advisory committees should also include experts on the utilization of ICTs and on the evaluation of ICT programs.

1. The following E-Rate policies should be continued:
   a) funding should be limited to connectivity and related facilities;
   b) discounts based on income and geographic region should be maintained; and
   c) a competitive bidding process for vendors should continue.
2. A triennial review of FCC and USAC administrative, application, and oversight procedures should be required to improve the efficiency, effectiveness, and transparency of the disbursement of funds.
3. Sources that support the factors critical to effective utilization of ICTs need to be identified: capacity-building for teachers and others who use ICTs, development and exchange of effective content for education, and other development and contextual applications (based on factors such as language, culture, ethnicity, and disabilities).
4. A small percentage of USF funds should be used for outreach to make more educators, librarians, and rural health care providers aware of the programs and for evaluation to update and analyze data on program utilization and to assess impacts of USF support.

Part IV: Content

Public Broadcasting

The need for public investment in media content and services has not abated, since the commercial market on its own is still unable to provide the media environment that makes for a thriving democracy. The task of redesigning federal public media subsidies provides an opportunity not only to take account of new technologies and modes of media production but also to rethink the purpose of noncommercial media in our society. For too long, the policy debates over public broadcasting have centered on "fairness and balance" in the programming that stations air and on whether or not the federal government should continue to subsidize entities in the existing structure. That debate today needs to turn to structural reform.

The objective of public broadcasting has always been to provide media content that the market will not. Broadly speaking, it is content that promotes citizenship, personal growth, and social cohesion. These goals remain important, but they need to be reinterpreted in the new media environment. Specifically, media policy needs to focus more on public media, not just public broadcasting.

What is needed is a system that focuses on supporting a wide range of noncommercial programs and services and that promotes universal access to, and opportunity to *engage with*, quality media content. This transition, though clearly needed, is politically difficult. It involves at least three components:

1. Restructuring the current system so that funds are diverted from the operation of broadcast facilities.
2. Redefining the entities that are entitled to public media funding.
3. Revamping the system of copyright exemptions and licenses so that public media entities have access to content on reasonable terms, can distribute public media content across all platforms, and can make content available for citizen engagement and reuse.

Digital Media and Young Audiences

The Internet and other new digital technologies hold great promise for youth, particularly for education, community-building, political involvement, and civic engagement. Therefore, marketing policies should only be a small part of a much broader media research and policy agenda. Among the issues that must be addressed are universal access to broadband, E-Rate policies, funding for noncommercial platforms, and support for education and training. If our goal is to have a generation that can help the country tackle its most pressing problems, then we need to provide it with a media environment that will help its members become effective contributors to our society and our democracy.

The next few years provide an important opportunity to develop commercial safeguards for children and teens, particularly in two key areas—public health and personal privacy. Several steps should be taken in the short term to enable the United States to move toward a fair and equitable media and marketing system for children and youth.

1. The appropriate congressional committees should hold hearings on contemporary digital marketing practices targeted at children and adolescents.
2. The FTC, the FCC, and Congress should work together, along with the industry and the public health and child advocacy communities, to develop a new set of rules governing digital marketing to children.
3. New regulations must take into account the full spectrum of advertising and marketing practices across all media, and apply to all children, including adolescents. Particular attention needs to be paid to how food and beverage products are promoted.
4. Among the areas of special focus should be the following:
    a) requirements for full disclosure of data collection practices, including so-called nonpersonally identifiable information, targeted at children and adolescents;
    b) restrictions on personal profiling and behavioral targeting aimed at individuals under the age of eighteen; and
    c) restrictions on certain practices that may be deceptive, such as "viral videos" and other forms of stealth marketing that do not disclose, at the outset, the companies behind the campaigns.
5. Clearly, government has a role to play in protecting adolescents' privacy. The proposals presented by the coalition of children and health groups, all of which would be within the agency's current statutory authority, would be an appropriate and necessary initial step for the FTC to take. These would include:
    a) adopting, as part of the industry's voluntary guidelines, a definition of "sensitive data" to include "the online activities of all persons under the age of eighteen"; and
    b) prohibiting "the collection of sensitive data for behavioral advertising purposes."

Digital Media and Broadcasting for Minorities

At this time and in the near future, the Internet and broadband technologies are not and will not serve as substitutes for broadcasting among minorities. Since minorities have less access to the Internet and broadband technologies, broadcast television, and radio, which reach 99 percent of the population and are consumed more frequently than Internet services by African Americans and Latinos/as, still represent for them a valid separate market.

The FCC's Report and Order and Third Further Notice of Rulemaking, which adopted nondiscrimination rules for market transactions and advertising, is insufficient to combat this problem, and with the shortage of spectrum to provide for new station licenses much of the effort to diversify media ownership has to focus on the sale of broadcast licenses in secondary markets. The following measures should be adopted:

1. Revive the FCC's Minority Tax Certificate Program—a program repealed in 1995 by Congress.
2. Reinstitute the distress sale policy and apply it to socially and economically disadvantaged businesses.

These programs should pass constitutional muster, both because after thirteen years of sharp decline in minority ownership, enough data is available to justify their reimplementation, and because they are narrowly tailored to meet the need for diversification of media ownership.

3. The United States should join the rest of the world and affirm its responsibility for protecting mutual respect within the diverse composition of its population. A statute should make diversity of media voices a core value and require that every action that the FCC takes is evaluated in the context of its effect on diversity of media ownership and media voices.
4. In order for people of color to have more access and content in the new world of ubiquitous broadband, two types of policies need to be implemented:
   a) policies that ensure universal access to broadband and network neutrality; and
   b) expansion of the tax certificate, distress sale, and SBA loan programs to providers of online content.

I
FRAMEWORKS

1

Broadband, Internet, and Universal Service

Challenges to the Social Contract of the Twenty-First Century

Jorge Reina Schement

Let it be remarked . . . that the intercourse throughout the Union will be facilitated by new improvements. Roads will everywhere be shortened, and kept in better order; accommodations for travelers will be multiplied and meliorated; an interior navigation on our eastern side will be opened throughout, or nearly throughout, the whole extent of the thirteen States. The communication between the Western and Atlantic districts, and between different parts of each, will be rendered more and more easy by those numerous canals with which the beneficence of nature has intersected our country, and which art finds it so little difficult to connect and complete.

James Madison[1]

MADISON'S VISION EMPHASIZES the importance of access to communications channels in the creation of a new nation. For those still unsure of the prospects of this new nation, his portrayal of an advanced eighteenth-century civilization provides hope for prosperity. Access to communications channels has always been taken for granted in the traditional American belief in the trinity of opportunity, participation, and prosperity—a belief so deep that it constitutes an enduring social contract.[2] And, as we will argue, it should also be taken for granted when revisiting that social contract in light of twenty-first-century exigencies.

This chapter sets out by proposing that this implied social contract, even as it continues to resonate, needs to be revised in a way that recognizes the growing influence of innovativeness and globalization. Second, it contends that the achievement of successful access requires the implementation of a policy framework that integrates connectivity, capability, content, and context—referred to here as the four Cs. Finally, it argues that broadband should constitute the universal service standard for a national information infrastructure with global aspirations.

A Social Contract for the Twenty-First Century

The men who convened the Constitutional Convention may have posited that colonial society evolved naturally, but, in reality, they imported and then reinvented British institutions along with their associated values. In so doing, they laid the foundation for an explicit system of governmental obligations culminating in the Constitution and Bill of Rights.[3] The people, meanwhile, evolved a mix of expectations loosely fastened to popular notions of liberty, democracy, and the American Dream. Together, elites and common folk established a kind of social contract, broadly understood as guaranteeing freedom and democratic participation, but also offering the opportunity for individuals to improve their quality of life.[4]

Throughout the nineteenth and twentieth centuries, commitment to the contract produced a succession of universally accessible infrastructures, beginning with the post road between New York and Philadelphia, then canals, turnpikes, railroads, telegraph, public libraries, mass transportation, public education, electrification, and telephone. In its time, each gave rise to a policy debate about the legitimacy of the commitment to a material "happiness," and the proper balance between public and private investment needed to reach it. Taken together, these debates reflect a longstanding tradition of universal service in American policy. The infrastructures that eventually emerged helped integrate a nation.

In the twenty-first century, the emergence of a society geared to the production, distribution and consumption of information reorients this democratic social contract by converging the requirements of democracy with the dynamics of a global information economy.[5] Whereas in the second half of the twentieth century, the universal service debate centered on the telephone, in the twenty-first century, it will focus on broadband.[6]

Five Reasons to Promote a Policy of Broadband Universal Service

In essence, universal service policy promises every person the opportunity to connect with and utilize the nation's information infrastructure. Yet, if it is to enable a world-class economy and quality of life, universal service must do even more: it must promise access to the most advanced information infrastructure in the world. Anything short of that undermines the competitive advantage of individuals, firms, and ultimately the nation. Hence, if universal service is to deliver on its promise, then it must offer each and every person the opportunity to exploit the network's economic, political, and personal resources.

Economic Participation—Opportunity

Americans built their economy through a succession of network infrastructures.[7] An early nineteenth-century web of canals and traces[8] opened new territories beyond the Appalachian Mountains, integrating the economies of new states with those of the original thirteen. Even so, the limitations of that web—narrow canals, waterlogged trails—throttled economic growth. Then came the railroads with a broadband solution and the first national information infrastructure. The new railroad network burst the constraints of the old infrastructure, overcame geography, bore enormous loads, and moved goods and information in such vast quantities that eastern manufacturers were able to assemble the first truly national markets. Its power did not stop there, for hundreds of millions of Americans also rode the rails of that network to their own economic futures.[9]

Like railroads, telecommunications networks distribute economic goods and services, while adding value to transactions, since information may itself be a distinct product or input to other products and services. If individuals and firms are to participate in the market fully, they must have the opportunity to avail themselves of information that will help them consume, produce, and innovate. The value of a network is determined by the number of members it has, for as the number of members increases, so too does the network's functionality and potential value to those already on it. Conversely, when people do not have effective access, they are less likely to contribute to the pool of positive effects generated from multiple interactions on the network.[10] For small businesses and individuals, access to the telecommunications network, therefore, offers the opportunity to participate more fully in an economy driven by the production and distribution of information. Broadband, with its capacity to multiply the traffic, intensifies that potential.

Public Participation—Civic Culture

Universal service also addresses the promise of democratic discourse. That is, democracy requires an informed and involved citizenry, yet this is possible only if the citizens have access to information about their government and the opportunity to participate in political discourse. There are, then, two dimensions to political participation—reception and distribution. On the reception side, citizens are better able to make informed contributions when they have heard a variety of opinions, especially when they have heard their favored opinions challenged in the marketplace of ideas. On the distribution side, citizens benefit when individuals are able to communicate and to engage in political dialogue beyond the confines of their immediate communities. Only then can democratic discourse transcend the walls of localness and the stifling of popular debate that occurs when only elites have access to the national communications channels. Indeed, the American concept of democracy comes embedded with a communications orientation; consequently, the pledge of equal access is not only logical, but also necessary to the conduct of a free and open society.[11] Emerson's classic explanation captures this tension:

> The crucial point, however, is not that freedom of expression is politically useful, but that it is indispensable to the operation of a democratic form of government. Once one accepts the premise of the Declaration of Independence—that governments derive "their just power from the consent of the governed"—it follows that the governed must, in order to exercise their right to consent, have full freedom of expression both in forming individual judgments and in forming the common judgment.[12]

In the twenty-first century, however, access and participation depend on the diffusion of an Internet infrastructure and meeting challenges faced by those institutions that stand to benefit from it most. Schools, where most Americans begin their civic education, must have high bandwidth access to the network. Public libraries, the people's portals, face enormous demands from patrons who lack Internet connectivity in the home and must connect to a broadband network. In theory, a democracy thrives when its citizenry is informed and involved. But if this is to happen, then telecommunications policies must guarantee full access to the nation's information infrastructure.

Social Participation—Community

Communication creates society. After all, humans define themselves not in isolation but through contact with others. Accordingly, a nation's telecommunications network is one of its most basic structures. Potentially, the range of information provided by any basic telecommunications infrastructure is infinite, ranging from the routine to the exceptional. To search for information on autism, to place a follow-up call for a job interview, to view a presidential debate, or to hear one's grandchild in California from New Jersey—all these activities generate value to the user, but they also strengthen society by rewarding participation, and, in return, encourage further participation. Essentially, participation in a network that saves lives, creates jobs, and gives every citizen the chance to pursue the full spectrum of life builds social capital with value far beyond the individual. The antithesis holds true as well: individuals who exist beyond the reach of the network have fewer opportunities, causing them to be isolated, alienated, and even downright hostile. Clearly, the network is an essential structure for overcoming social fragmentation, and, consequently, for creating community. It follows that if Americans want to encourage the sense of shared values and mutual interdependence that comes from social interaction, universal service policy must stress maximum access to the network, for in an information society, it is the network that holds us together.[13]

From Corrective to Catalyst

Political, economic, and social participation form the foundation processes of a vigorous democracy, while the promise of inclusion to all confers the stamp of democratic authenticity. The idea of universal service is rooted in a response to the challenge of the Constitution and the challenge of colonial geography. The post road mandated in the Constitution, the railroads, and rural free delivery—all these were solutions that helped overcome the obstacles of a narrow north-south geographical axis without natural pathways, and in this way, helped create a participatory democracy. In the twentieth century, similar challenges led to the Communications Act of 1934, which sought to finalize the diffusion of a telephone network already half a century old. Any policy with the goal of universal access finds itself tested at the margins, since it is easy enough to say that "all's right with the world" by pointing to the participation of society's favored members. [14] In the case of traditional universal service policy, the fact that seven million U.S. households (7 percent) are still without telephones indicates that even in this basic service success has its limits. Corrective measures designed to increase telephone penetration, therefore, also serve the principles of social justice.

This vision of universal service, rooted in the Depression era, now finds itself challenged by the new reality of a twenty-first-century global information economy—ironically, a made-in-the-U.S.A. product. Throughout the nineteenth and twentieth centuries, Americans sowed the seeds of a material culture based on the production and consumption of information by exploiting the exchange of information goods and services in the marketplace. They devised information applications to control the expansion of firms, and, in so doing, invented the multinational corporation and modern management. Swelling demand drew millions into the information workforce. Beginning with isolated tinkers, a vast R&D establishment introduced technologies that wove telecommunications networks with interconnections so dense they have yet to be fully mapped.[15]

In the twenty-first century, the success of that material culture can be measured in the number of countries that have embraced broadband telecommunications networks as a basis for their economic strategies.[16] Indeed, while a social contract emphasizing participation may be explicit or implied, new universal service policies advance at the same time a country's position as a global economic competitor. In those countries with the highest broadband penetration, universal service is not perceived as a corrective for an already established network; rather, it is seen as the driver of an information economy. From this perspective, universal service offers two additional advantages not considered in its twentieth-century manifestation.

Creative Participation—Innovation

The traditional justification for information infrastructure investments is that there are benefits deriving from network externalities. That is, the value of joining a telephone network goes up as more people subscribe to the network, which, in turn, encourages even more subscribers.[17] For about one hundred years, the idea has been that the larger the network the larger the dividend to subscribers. Recently, however, this "static" view of network externalities has come under reconsideration, in part, because of the success of Internet sites where subscribers also contribute content. On these sites, an increase in the number of members leads to an increase in the number of interactions, which, in turn, generates the creation of new content. New content attracts attention to the site, increasing the number of new members yet again, who go on to create more new content, thereby generating "dynamic" externalities. These "arenas of innovation" both depend on and stimulate "soft infrastructures" that enable participation. Services that facilitate payment, authentication, evaluation, encryption, privacy, and searching encourage individuals to participate and contribute their ideas.[18] This ferment in the crucible that is the Internet generates value above and beyond the value derived from the network's scale. Still, for it to do so, one basic condition must be present—broadband.

Global Participation—Competitiveness

An appreciation of the dynamism inherent in the Internet's arenas of innovation transcends the corrective frame for understanding universal service.

Without necessarily abandoning the social contract at its root, the catalyst of innovation reframes universal service from obligation to opportunity. It is in this reframing that universal service emerges as an instrument for promoting global competitiveness. Indeed, for those countries seeking a major role in the world's economy, broadband deployment has become the price of entry. This lesson has not been lost on the most competitive countries, those that hold the top five places in broadband penetration per household—Korea, Japan, Iceland, Finland, and the Netherlands. These countries have all pursued aggressive goal-directed, public policies to get them to this place. By contrast, the United States, ranked near the top in 2000—albeit with a weak universal service policy—now finds itself in twelfth place in penetration per household and in fifteenth place in penetration per capita.[19] Ironically, at a time when there is a new appreciation for the benefits of network externalities and universal service, Asian and European countries have achieved far greater successes in deploying their broadband infrastructures.

That said, to reduce an issue to a series of rankings seems more appropriate when covering the Olympics than when trying to assess the challenge confronting universal access. To get beneath the surface of this issue requires an understanding of connectedness as a social function.

The Four Cs of Access: Connectivity, Capability, Content, and Context

Madison's description of a unified nation dissected in a million ways continues to resonate in telecommunications policy discourse. At the macro level, the Telecommunications Act of 1996 projects a national intent: "To promote competition and reduce regulation in order to secure lower prices and higher quality services for American telecommunications consumers and encourage the rapid deployment of new telecommunications technologies." Yet, buried in the act, section 254 hints at complexities that lie beneath the surface: "Universal service is an evolving level of telecommunications services . . . taking into account advances in telecommunications and information technologies and services."[20] It is where the broad strokes of the Telecommunications Act break down into distinct town and communities that intent meets reality.

Mandating a connection to the national telecommunications network will not, by itself, guarantee successful implementation in communities. To move beyond simple notions of connectedness requires an understanding of the resources a community must marshal to make the most of the potential offered by access to national and global networks. After all, individuals must have access to information, if they are to participate, innovate, and communicate. Consequently, for communities to fully exploit the benefits of access, they will have to provide connectivity, capability, content, and context—the four Cs of access.[21]

Connectivity

The seemingly simple act of laying a cable to connect a household or community belies the complexity of attaining a level of connectivity sufficient to constitute a community asset. Though the FCC now defines basic broadband as connection speeds above 768 kbps, it is a bandwidth far below that required to effectively utilize many Internet applications in use today. Telemedicine applications call for a minimum of 1.5 mbps (T1.5) connections, and many Internet business applications necessitate bandwidths of at least T1.5 or multiple T1.5 connections. A fiber optic service, such as Verizon's FiOS, brings optical fibers directly into individual homes and offices; however, depending on the level of service purchased by the customer, FiOS Internet services range from five to fifty mbps downstream and two to five mbps upstream. To be sure, the level of a community's high-speed connectivity can be measured in different ways: a) points of access—availability at public sites such as schools, libraries or community centers, in the home, in businesses or institutions; b) the number of Internet service providers (ISPs) that offer high-speed Internet service in a given community; and/or c) the type and speeds of service offerings available from high-speed Internet providers—DSL, cable modem, wireless, T1.5, DS3, and so on. Yet, as governments, businesses, and content providers increasingly develop products and services that require high-speed Internet connections, underserved communities may experience a "broadband digital divide."

Capability

Because the utility of any technology is determined both by the skill of the user as well as the delivery capacity of local institutions, *capability* gauges the capacity to make the most of the service. For individuals, capability encompasses both formal and informal educational attainment and levels of technical sophistication and understanding, along with the willingness to adapt to new technologies and ways of thinking. Individuals with a high school diploma make up 52 percent of the U.S. population but only 64 percent of those in this group have home Internet access. 92 percent of college-educated individuals, a group that comprises 23 percent of the population,[22] have home Internet access. At the institutional level, capability refers to the resources a community makes available to stimulate workforce development and innovations by local entrepreneurs. For example, among public libraries surveyed in communities with medium to high poverty levels, 11 percent provide information about the community, 48 percent provide information services for job seekers, and 11 percent provide information for new citizens.[23] Clearly, the amount of resources available varies considerably from community to community. Nevertheless, investment pays off because capabilities are cumulative and recursive. Consequently, gaps in proficiency, knowledge, skills, and experience may lead to substantial differences in communities' abilities to leverage the potential of the network—especially the Internet.

Content

Once individuals and communities connect and develop the capabilities necessary to exploit the Internet, content becomes currency. Not only do Web sites appear spontaneously once Internet access takes root, but business models that depend on freely contributed content succeed as well. YouTube, for example, has achieved stupendous success using a business model whose premise is that users will freely contribute content, which, in turn, will attract more users who will contribute more content. This enabled YouTube to sell advertising based on about 175,000 submissions—per day.[24] By contrast, television networks spend millions to create content in order to achieve the same benefits from advertising. Furthermore, the benefits of content generated by those self-same users underscores the value of dynamic network externalities. Relevant content increases the value of the network by stimulating new content and providing a forum for interaction within local communities as well as a window to the outside world.

These benefits, however, do not accrue universally. Adults with low access, roughly 36 percent of the population, experience less success when searching for information about health matters and government benefits than do adults with high access. Not surprisingly, but worth noting, low-access adults are more likely to earn below the median household income, have a high school diploma or less, live in a rural community, have experienced unemployment recently, or are non-English-speaking Latinos.[25] In other words, the mere existence of content does not provide value to users. The many forms of marginalization translate into low levels of connectivity and limited capabilities, which, in turn, erect barriers within communities, that are compounded when they lag behind high access communities in the availability of neighborhood-level information on housing, childcare, health, and transportation. Consequently, when content of relevance to individuals and members of a community is unavailable, isolation is the result.

Context

The varieties of connectivity, capability, and content stem from an array of contextual forces and trends that must be considered in order to achieve access strategies that work. Environmental factors (e.g., air and water pollution, waste management), economic conditions (e.g., business incentives, tax structures, unemployment), and social indicators (e.g., crime, poverty, ethnicity, rurality) contribute to disparities in access, as well as different levels of success in implementing policies aimed at improving access. In other words, communications networks of all kinds operate within the multiple frames of society and culture. For example, Pennsylvania's Fifth Congressional District, the poorest, most rural area in the state, spans the ridges of the Appalachian Mountains, isolating towns in the valleys between the ridges. It has a population that is 97 percent white, has a median income of $33,254, and traditionally votes Republican. By contrast, Texas's Fifteenth Congressional District spreads out across the pampas-like plain of the rural Rio Grande Valley. It has a population that is 69 percent Latino, has a median income of $28,061, and traditionally votes Democrat.[26] Between Texas and Pennsylvania, the circumstances of connectivity, capability, and content vary considerably. And although context does not determine a community's developmental trajectory, it does suggest the importance of considering community attributes.

By conceptualizing the Internet as a pluralistic domain that includes the broader context in which the technical components are embedded, we explicitly connect social with technical to form the intimate interdependency of the Internet as a socio-technical network. A socio-technical perspective emphasizes the importance of context in determining community-level interventions and their evaluation, as well as the inherent difficulties involved in developing "best practices" that can be applied across diverse settings. Thus, the goal of connectivity, at the heart of most policies aimed at increasing access and/or bridging the digital divide, represents but a small first step toward functional access and empowerment. Capability, content, and context must be woven into any strategy seeking to achieve a better informational future for all.

From Legitimacy to Implementation

This chapter advocates an information age social contract that provides universal access to broadband. A social contract of this nature derives its legitimacy from the fundamental principles of democratic theory, from a new understanding of dynamic elements contributing to the theory of network externalities, and from the importance of competition in an emerging global information system. Yet legitimacy alone is not a prescription for access.

Consequently, successful access policies depend on implementation and recognition of practicalities on the ground—the four Cs—connectivity, capability, content, and context. This framework, first and foremost, acknowledges that local variability must be acknowledged and engaged if access policies are to make a positive difference in the lives of those at the margins.

The View on the Ground: Examples of Disparities in Access to, and Use of, Broadband

Theories and conceptual frameworks alone will not produce a population capable of exploiting the advantages of the new information infrastructure for the benefit of the economy and society. A country of more than one hundred million households challenges simple notions of access, as the following recent examples illustrate.

Trends in Internet and Home Broadband Adoption

Americans have a history of intense flirtations with household information technologies. In the 1920s, they jumped on the radiobox craze.[27] At the beginning of the 1950s, fewer than 10 percent of U.S. households owned a television set, but by the end of that decade, nearly 90 percent did.[28] Likewise, since the worldwide web (WWW) was launched, American households have been connecting to the Internet at an accelerated rate. Internet use among adults—irrespective of connection speed or point of access—rose from 14 percent in 1996 to just over 70 percent by the end of 2006. Although the trend line in figure 1.1 shows some leveling off in 2003 and 2004, on the whole Internet adoption has been on a steady upward path.

In June 2000, the Pew Internet Project first asked American adults (age eighteen and older) how they connect to the Internet from home (either dial-up or broadband). Since then, penetration of high-speed home Internet connections has increased by a factor of sixteen. While only five million American adults (less than 5 percent) had high-speed[29] connections at home in June 2000, by the end of 2006, 43 percent of adults reported high-speed connections at home—more than eighty million people, or about three-quarters of those who go online in the home[30] (see figure 1.2).

Home broadband adoption has proceeded at a rapid pace, especially when compared with the adoption of other consumer electronic technologies. If we date the beginning of widespread cable modem availability to 1995, digital subscriber line (DSL) service to 1997, and take 1996 as an interpolated starting point, then it took a bit more than five years for broadband to reach 10 percent

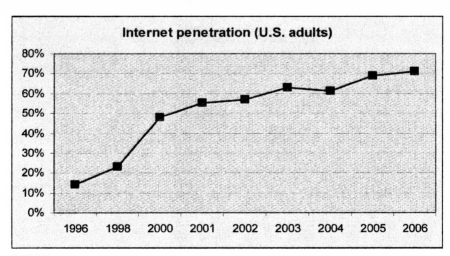

FIGURE 1.1
U.S. Internet Penetration

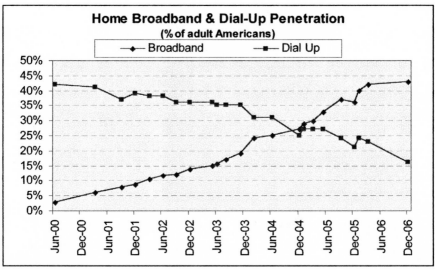

FIGURE 1.2
Broadband and Dial-up Penetration

of the population, a rate comparable to personal computers (four years), and compact disc players (four-and-a-half years), but faster than cell phones (eight years) and video cassette recorders (ten years). It took color television twelve years to reach 10 percent of the population[31] (see table 1.1).

TABLE 1.1:
Adoption Time for New Consumer Technologies

	Years to Reach *10% Adoption*	*Years to Reach* *50% Adoption*
Video Cassette Recorder	10	14
Compact Disc Player	4.5	10.5
Color TV	12	18
Cell Phones	8	15
Personal Computer	4	18

(*Source:* Federal Communications Commission, Presentation of Robert Pepper, "Policies for Broadband Migration," April 2002)

Rapidly reaching at 50 percent adoption rate, often thought of as the tipping point, is not a foregone conclusion. While it took relatively little time for 10 percent of the population to adopt personal computers, it took eighteen years until the 50 percent mark was passed. On the other hand, while it took a relatively long time for 10 percent of the population to adopt VCRs and color television, going from there to 50 percent happened quite rapidly, because these technologies enhanced an existing home technology, and thus built on an established base of users. Broadband Internet has similar characteristics in that it builds on a base of users with home Internet access and personal computers. In the early part of this decade, Pew Internet and American Life Project surveys showed that about 80 percent of Internet users had home access with the remaining 20 percent having access elsewhere. By 2006, about 90 percent of Americans who were classified as Internet users used the Internet from home, about 5 percent had access only at work and more than 5 percent had access at another place (e.g., a library).[32] Consequently, it is not unreasonable to project that half the population will have broadband at home by 2008.

New Media and Old Media Coexisting in a New Era

Does the Internet replace or displace older media? The conventional wisdom is that information acquired on the Internet replaces information acquired from traditional media, a phenomenon that threatens these older media. According to this view, democracy, as we know it, is endangered by the defection of citizens to the tumultuous world of unrestrained blogs. In reality, however, there is cause for optimism. The following tables (1.2, 1.3, and 1.4), which address news-gathering behaviors, illustrate the continued importance of traditional media alongside Internet news gathering.

Nevertheless, among home broadband users, the Internet plays a prominent role in news consumption—especially among people under the age of thirty-six. Among young people with a home high-speed connection, a

TABLE 1.2:
Getting News on the Typical Day (% of all in each group who say
they get news from specific source "yesterday")

	All Respondents	Non-Internet Users	Dial-Up at Home	Broadband at Home
Local TV	59%	57%	65%	57%
National TV	47%	43%	50%	49%
Radio	44%	34%	52%	49%
Local paper	38%	37%	41%	38%
Internet	23%	—	26%	43%
National paper	12%	8%	12%	17%
Average number of sources	2.22	1.80	2.45	2.52
Number of cases	3,011	1,080	633	1,014

(*Source:* Pew Internet Project December 2005 Survey)

TABLE 1.3:
Getting News on the Typical Day: Comparing Age Groups and Connection Speed
(% of all in each group who say they get news from specific source "yesterday")

	Under age 36		Between 36 and 50		Over age 50	
	Broadband	Dial-up	Broadband	Dial-up	Broadband	Dial-up
Local TV	51%	54%	60%	72%	61%	71%
National TV	40%	35%	49%	52%	62%	61%
Radio	41%	43%	53%	57%	57%	54%
Local paper	28%	27%	41%	40%	52%	55%
Internet	46%	21%	40%	30%	43%	26%
National paper	17%	2%	12%	10%	23%	21%
Number of cases	307	141	360	215	347	265

(*Source:* Pew Internet Project December 2005 Survey)

segment of the population considered generally uninterested in news, the Internet has contributed to increased news consumption, rivaling television as a source of news.

Although people who use the Internet for news tend to visit sites belonging to mainstream media, one-third of home broadband users also visit sites of international news organizations, news blogs (e.g., the Drudge Report), and alternative news sites (e.g., Slate or Salon). Therefore, in addition to the convenience of news from an "always on" broadband connection, a home high-speed connection exposes users to a diversity of news sources and perspectives.

For those concerned about how the Internet will affect democratic discourse, it is clear that it changes the old media equations; nevertheless, it also contributes to greater engagement in the political debates of our times, especially among those groups, like youth, that have historically been less reliant on traditional media.

TABLE 1.4:
Ownership of Consumer Goods

	Have Cable or Satellite TV	Watch Local TV News (typical day)	Watch National TV News (typical day)	Read a Local Daily Newspaper (typical day)	Get Any News Online (typical day)	Average Number of News Sources Consulted (typical day)
All	85%	59%	47%	38%	23%	1.8
Home broadband users	92%	57%	49%	38%	43%	3.2
Whites	86%	60%	49%	40%	24%	1.9
Blacks	83%	60%	42%	25%	16%	1.4
18-29	82%	48%	30%	23%	28%	2.3
30-49	87%	60%	46%	35%	27%	2.3
50-64	87%	68%	59%	46%	22%	1.7
65+	83%	60%	52%	48%	9%	0.6
under $30k	77%	53%	39%	33%	13%	1.1
$30-50K	84%	63%	48%	36%	24%	1.8
$50-75K	90%	64%	52%	41%	31%	2.5
> $75K	93%	63%	53%	45%	38%	2.9
LT HS	81%	47%	32%	25%	6%	0.6
HS Grad	84%	61%	45%	35%	14%	1.3
Some college	88%	62%	51%	38%	28%	2.2
College +	87%	61%	53%	46%	39%	2.8

Gaps in Broadband Adoption

Tables 1.5 and 1.6 below provide data on adoption over time among different demographic subgroups. For Internet and home broadband adoption, the clearest differences emerge along four dimensions:

- *Income*: Respondents who reported a household income of less than $30,000 per year are consistently below the average Internet penetration rate for all adults. Looking across the six years of data, the "under $30K" group generally has two-thirds the average Internet penetration rate and, starting in 2002, about half the home broadband penetration rate. Lower penetration rates compound the disadvantages of low income by putting beyond reach those dynamic externalities conferred on broadband users. In Pew Internet random digit dial telephone samples, about one-quarter of adult Americans report having household incomes below $30,000 annually.

- *Education*: Having attended at least some college establishes a clear dividing line. About half of the adult population has attended or graduated from college, while the other half has a high school diploma or less. At the end of 2006, just more than 50 percent of those with high school diplomas or less used the Internet, compared with nearly 90 percent among those who attended college or have a college degree. In tables 1.4, 1.5, 1.6, 1.7, and 1.8, the most striking contrasts in access and usage stem from differences in education.
- *Age*: Retirement-age Americans—namely, those over sixty-five—are least likely to go online and have less than half the Internet penetration rate of the general population, and one-third the broadband penetration rate. Online access falls off most sharply among Americans over seventy, who may not have been in the workforce when the Internet entered the mainstream. About half of those in the sixty-five to sixty-nine age group use the Internet, while only one-quarter of those aged seventy and older use it. Given the migration of essential government information to the Internet, this trend would appear to exacerbate the isolation of old age.
- *Ethnicity*: The American tendency to conflate major ethnic groups into the category "minorities" enables public discussion at the national level. Nevertheless, differences among ethnic groups in Internet adoption and use deserve attention.
- *African Americans*: One part of this story has to do with the narrowing gap between white Americans and African Americans. Although Internet adoption among whites is still nine percentage points over African Americans' according to the 2006 data, race is no longer a significant statistical predictor of online access. In other words, the lower adoption rate for African Americans is related to lower levels of educational attainment and income, not specifically race.
- *Hispanics*: Comprising 14 percent of the U.S. adult population, more than half (56 percent) of all Hispanics go online. By contrast, 71 percent of non-Hispanic whites and 60 percent of non-Hispanic blacks use the Internet. Among Latinos, language and national origin influence access. Just one in three Latinos who speak only Spanish goes online, compared with 78 percent of Latinos who speak predominantly English and 76 percent of bilingual Latinos. Mexicans represent the largest Latino group but are among the least likely to go online: only 52 percent of Latinos of Mexican descent use the Internet. Indeed, even when age, income, language, generation, or nativity is held constant, Mexicans are less likely to go online than other Latino groups. It is differences in levels of education and English proficiency that largely explain the gap in Internet use between Hispanics and non-Hispanics.[33]

TABLE 1.5:
Trends in Internet Adoption, 2000–2006

	2000	2001	2002	2003	2004	2005	2006
All	48%	55%	57%	63%	61%	69%	71%
Whites	50%	57%	59%	65%	63%	71%	72%
Blacks	36%	39%	45%	56%	54%	55%	63%
18–29	65%	75%	72%	83%	75%	82%	87%
30–49	58%	64%	67%	73%	69%	80%	82%
50–64	41%	50%	55%	59%	60%	68%	70%
65+	13%	16%	20%	26%	26%	28%	31%
under $30k	31%	34%	36%	43%	44%	50%	51%
$30–50K	52%	61%	62%	67%	66%	74%	77%
$50–75K	67%	78%	80%	81%	80%	86%	85%
> $75K	78%	87%	85%	89%	83%	91%	92%
LT HS	17%	19%	19%	28%	26%	37%	40%
HS Grad	35	42	46	52	52	60	64
Some college	63	72	74	78	76	80	83
College +	75	83	80	87	85	91	92

TABLE 1.6:
Trends in Home Broadband Adoption, 2000–2006

	2000	2001	2002	2003	2004	2005	2006
All	3%	9%	12%	19%	26%	36%	43%
Whites	3%	9%	13%	20%	27%	39%	44%
Blacks	1%	4%	5%	13%	16%	24%	33%
18–29	6%	12%	17%	28%	36%	46%	54%
30–49	4%	11%	14%	25%	32%	45%	52%
50–64	2%	5%	11%	14%	22%	34%	39%
65+	0%	2%	3%	4%	7%	11%	14%
under $30k	0%	3%	5%	9%	13%	20%	22%
$30–50K	1%	7%	12%	16%	25%	30%	42%
$50–75K	3%	10%	16%	25%	33%	50%	51%
> $75K	4%	23%	27%	41%	54%	64%	72%
LT HS	0%	3%	3%	9%	8%	14%	17
HS Grad	1	4	7	12	16	27	31
Some college	2	11	15	25	31	44	52
College +	3	17	23	31	42	55	66

The Significance of Gaps

In a medium that offers so much, gaps do matter. After all, in critical areas, Internet access delivers on the promise of the social contract. Still, as Horrigan documents in his work with the Pew Internet Project, it is what people do with their access that creates consequences for those who are connected as well as those who are not.

1. The Internet reduces uncertainty for users in important contexts. The availability of online health and medical information is perhaps the best example of how online information helps in the face of uncertainty. Many health or medical problems, in addition to being problems in themselves, can be exacerbated by the uncertainty they create. Online information can help in this regard in at least two ways. First, the availability of information on the Internet gives people the ability to learn more about a problem at their own pace and to ask more informed questions of health care providers during face-to-face appointments. Second, the Internet lets people connect with others facing similar medical problems, and, in this way, provides a source of comfort along with information on new treatment options.

2. The Internet as an information utility encourages civic engagement. People increasingly turn to the Internet for news about politics and to find out what is going on with their state, local, or federal governments. One-third of Americans obtained some news and information online about the 2006 midterm election and twice as many said they relied on the Internet as their main source of campaign news in 2006 as did in the 2002 midterm election. Connections to higher voting rates are hard to establish, but the mix of online political information and online contributions are undoubtedly affecting political discourse.

3. The Internet enables the creation of social capital and the utilization and maintenance of social networks. Boase, Horrigan, Wellman, and Rainie examined the size and composition of Americans' social networks, the technologies they use to stay in contact, and the role of social networks in decisions taken on matters of personal finance, job training, and job searches. The majority of Internet users reported that e-mail was their preferred tool for cultivating social capital—not just for sharing everyday goings-on among family and friends but also for getting advice or sharing important news.[34]

4. Internet users shape cyberspace through user-generated content. As an example of dynamic network externalities, many people with high speed Internet at home use the Internet as a platform for sharing something of themselves with the world. Whether it involves keeping an online diary with

TABLE 1.7:
Online Behaviors

	Download Video	Health Search	Get News/Info About Election Campaign	Visit State, Local, Federal Government Website	User-Generated Content	Take a Class for Credit	Take a Class for Enjoyment
All	14%	56%	31%	45%	27%	8%	8%
Home broadband users	26%	86%	53%	72%	44%	14%	15%
Whites	13%	57%	33%	47%	27%	8%	8%
Blacks	15%	46%	23%	36%	22%	8%	9%
18–29	30%	67%	39%	47%	45%	14%	11%
30–49	15%	67%	37%	59%	31%	12%	10%
50–64	8%	54%	28%	45%	21%	4%	9%
65+	3%	21%	13%	14%	6%	1%	2%
under $30k	12%	38%	16%	31%	18%	6%	7%
$30–50K	14%	57%	32%	50%	28%	8%	11%
$50–75K	17%	74%	35%	55%	29%	11%	8%
> $75K	19%	79%	54%	69%	41%	11%	15%
LT HS	11%	23%	11%	18%	11%	1%	4%
HS Grad	11%	42%	18%	31%	19%	3%	7%
Some college	17%	65%	34%	54%	34%	12%	11%
College +	17%	81%	57%	72%	39%	13%	10%

a blog, posting comments to other blogs or new sites, or posting photos or videos, 44 percent of Americans with high-speed connections at home upload user-generated content to the Internet.[35] In doing so, these users generate new ideas, thereby shaping the nature of online content available for everyone. They prove that users engage the Internet for considerably more than passive information consumption. People may come to this online commons as consumers, but once engaged, they begin to shape it.

American Competitiveness in an Emerging Global Information Order

The power of income and education is evident in the data presented here. So, too, is the potential of broadband Internet access to enable upward mobility. All this goes to underscore the importance of universal service policy. This realization began to take form in the early 1990s, when policymakers became concerned that despite 120 years of deployment and 60 years of universal service policy, 7 percent of U.S. households still did not have telephones.[36] As personal computers became more visible (22 percent of households possessing them in 1992), the debate quickly drew a line between those with and without them.[37] By the mid-1990s, Internet household penetration reached 15 percent (figure 1.1), and the debate shifted to Internet access. Halfway through this decade, the broadband policies and penetration rates in other countries drew attention to lagging penetration rates in the United States. Indeed, each turn in this cycle has expanded our understanding of the importance of access to information at every level of society, from the quotidian to the global.

However, as the gaps in broadband uptake and the social consequences of not having a home high-speed connection are viewed, the United States faces three challenges going forward.

- *Availability in rural America*: There is no publicly available data that maps the broadband infrastructure of the nation. But a Pew Internet survey from 2004 shows that rural Americans are twice as likely not to have access to broadband connections than nonrural Americans. This is one reason rural broadband adoption has lagged behind the rest of America by 25 to 45 percentage points in 2006 (table 1.8).
- *Network bandwidth*: There is also little reliable data on this issue, but it is widely thought that the bandwidth of (mostly) cable or digital subscriber line home high-speed networks is far slower in the United States than in some Asian and European countries.[38]
- *International standing*: Notwithstanding fast uptake, by many measures the United States trails other countries in home broadband adoption.

This chapter opened by arguing that the two-hundred-year-old social contract that promised an information infrastructure that would enable the processes of participatory democracy, is still relevant in the twenty-first century. It went on to contend that the value of the network increases dynamically in an Internet environment, where global competitiveness holds the key to economic success.

At the level of policy implementation, the chapter introduced the four Cs—connectivity, capability, content, and context—as factors in community-level interventions and, as such, standards for successful access policies when one size does not fit all. Taken together, data presented here offer a lesson in the complex contributions to patterns of access that challenge policymakers—further illustrating the importance of locally initiated policy.

The ultimate stakes are high, for an international order is emerging out of the diffusion of a global broadband Internet. The old industrial economy that rode the track of the railroads and the wires of the telegraph has been transformed into an economy that thrives on websites and high bandwidth Internet trunk lines. At the same time, the democracy of mass media and

TABLE 1.8:
Internet Usage Among Populations

	Home Broadband Users	Home Users Dial-Up	Internet Users	Population General (all respondents)
Gender				
Male	52%	47%	50%	48%
Female	48%	53%	50%	52%
Age				
18–29	26%	19%	24%	20%
30–49	47%	43%	45%	39%
50–64	22%	26%	24%	24%
65+	5%	11%	7%	17%
Ethnicity				
White (not Hispanic)	73%	74%	74%	73%
Black (not Hispanic)	8%	9%	9%	11%
Hispanic (English-speaking)	10%	11%	11%	10%
Education				
Less than HS	5%	9%	7%	13%
HS grad	28%	36%	32%	37%
Some college	26%	28%	26%	23%
College +	41%	27%	34%	27%
Household income				
under $30K	12%	21%	17%	24%
$30K–50K	21%	24%	22%	20%
$50K–$75K	16%	19%	16%	14%
over $75K	36%	18%	28%	22%
No answer	15%	19%	17%	20%
Community				
Urban	30%	27%	29%	28%
Suburban	58%	48%	54%	53%
Rural	11%	25%	16%	19%

(Source: Pew Internet & American Life Project April 2006 Survey)
N=4,001; margin of error is ±2% for the entire sample
For Internet users, n=2,822; margin of error is ±2% for this group
For home broadband users, n=1,562; margin of error is ±3% for this group
For home dial-up users, n=933; margin of error is ±3.5% for this group

one-way communications is in the process of absorbing the shock of blogs and Internet journalism. What role America will play in each of these arenas remains unclear. What is clear is that broadband Internet will be the great enterprise of the twenty-first century, and America's economic and political role in the world will depend on its success in providing broadband Internet access across the nation.

Notes

1. James Madison, "Federalist No. 14: Objections to the proposed Constitution from extent of territory answered," *New York Packet* (New York City, 30 November 1787). James Madison, fourth president of the United States, played a major part in the debates that led to the Constitution, helped frame the Bill of Rights, and contributed to the Federalist Papers. As president, he became a temporary refugee when British forces burned the capital during the War of 1812.

2. The idea of a social contract resonated strongly among the founders of the United States. In particular, they drew on the writings of Thomas Hobbes, John Locke, Jean-Jacques Rousseau, and Thomas Paine. See Thomas Hobbes, *Leviathan* (Oxford: Oxford University Press, 1651/1998); John Locke, *Two Treatises of Government: and a Letter Concerning Toleration* (New Haven, CT: Yale University Press, 1689/2003); Jean-Jacques Rousseau, *Social Contract and Discourse on the Origin of Inequality* (New York: Pocket Books, 1761/1989); Thomas Paine, *Common Sense* (New York: Viking Penguin, 1776/1982).

3. David H. Fischer, *Albion's Seed: Four British Folkways in America* (Oxford: Oxford University Press, 1989).

4. See, for example, Alexander Hamilton et al., *Federalist Papers* (New York: Bantam Books, 1788/1982), and Alexis de Tocqueville, *Democracy in America* (New York: Washington Square Press, 1835/1964). Also, Roland Marchand, *Advertising the American Dream: Making Way for Modernity* (Berkeley: University of California Press, 1985); Carlton Rochell and Christina Spellman, *Dreams Betrayed: Working in the Technological Age* (New York: Lexington Books, 1987); and Gary Cross, *An All-Consuming Century: Why Commercialism Won in Modern America* (New York: Columbia University Press, 2000).

5. In this chapter, we will follow the convention of referring to such a society as an information society.

6. As used here, broadband is a relative term referring to a signaling method for accommodating a range of frequencies, sometimes divided into channels—the wider the bandwidth, the greater the information-carrying capacity of the channel. In policy discourse, broadband sometimes refers to broadband networks or broadband Internet, but mostly to telecommunications technologies capable of delivering a greater volume of information. The common denominator in most references to broadband is use of the general term "broad," in contrast to "narrow," as in "narrow-band."

7. "A succession of navigable waters forms a kind of chain round its borders, as if to bind it together; while the most noble rivers in the world, running at convenient distances, present them with highways for the easy communication of friendly aids, and the mutual transportation and exchange of their various commodities." John Jay (31 October 1787), "Concerning Dangers from Foreign Force and Influence," FEDERALIST no. 2, in Hamilton et al., *Federalist Papers*.

8. *Trace* is an early nineteenth-century term for a path or track capable of supporting wagons. Most famously, the Natchez Trace stretched four hundred miles from Nashville, Tennessee, to Natchez, Mississippi, linking the Cumberland, Tennessee, and Mississippi rivers, in order to open the lower Mississippi Valley to American trade and

settlement. The word *trace* derives from the Latin *tractus* via Old French *trace* (noun). See C. T. Onions, ed., *The Oxford Dictionary of English Etymology* (Oxford: Clarendon Press, 1966).

9. See, for example, Denise Anderson and Jorge Reina Schement, "Information infrastructure and development in the USA: The role of government," *Industrial and Corporate Change* 4, no. 4 (1995): 727–35; Alfred D. J. Chandler, *The Visible Hand: The Managerial Revolution in American Business* (Cambridge, MA: Harvard University Press, 1977); and Richard B. Du Boff, "Business Demand and the development of the telegraph in the United States, 1844–1860," *The Business History Review* 54, no. 4 (1980): 459–79.

10. Roberta Capello, *Spatial Economic Analysis of Telecommunications Network Externalities* (New York: Ashgate Publishing, 1994); Patrick Cohendet, Gisele Umbhauer, et al., eds., *Economics of Networks: Interaction and Behaviors* (New York: Springer-Verlag, 1999); Michael L. Katz and Carl Shapiro, "Network Externalities, Competition and Compatibility," *American Economic Review* 75, no. 3 (1985): 424–40; Hal Varian, "Versioning Information Goods," in *Internet Publishing and Beyond: The Economics of Digital Information and Intellectual Property*, eds. Brian Kahin and Hal R. Varian (Cambridge, MA: MIT Press, 2000).

11. "Let it be remarked, in the third place, that the intercourse throughout the Union will be facilitated by new improvements. Roads will everywhere be shortened, and kept in better order; accommodations for travelers will be multiplied and meliorated; an interior navigation on our eastern side will be opened throughout, or nearly throughout, the whole extent of the thirteen States. The communication between the Western and Atlantic districts, and between different parts of each, will be rendered more and more easy by those numerous canals with which the beneficence of nature has intersected our country, and which art finds it so little difficult to connect and complete." James Madison (30 November 1787), "Objections to the Proposed Constitution From Extent of Territory Answered," FEDERALIST no. 14, in *Federalist Papers*.

12. Thomas I. Emerson, "Toward a General Theory of the First Amendment," *72 Yale Law Journal* 877, 883 (April 1963).

13. For a discourse on the relationship between community and democracy, see Robert D. Putnam, *Bowling Alone: The Collapse and Revival of American Community* (New York: Simon & Schuster, 2000). For an analysis of the failure of universal service policy for those at the margins of society, see Jorge Reina Schement, "Beyond Universal Service: Characteristics of Americans Without Telephones, 1980–1993," *Telecommunications Policy* 19, no. 6 (1995): 477–85; Jorge Reina Schement, "Telephone Penetration at the Margins: An Analysis of the Period Following the Breakup of AT&T, 1984–1994," in *Progress in Communication Sciences, Volume XV: Advances in Telecommunications*, Harmeet Sawhney and George A. Barnett. (Stamford, CT: Ablex, 1998), 187–215.

14. "God's in his Heaven/All's right with the world!" Pippa's song from Robert Browning's, *Pippa Passes*, published in 1841 as the first volume of his *Bells and Pomegranates* series. Pippa is a young innocent girl living at the crime-ridden margins of Victorian society.

15. James R. Beniger, *The Control Revolution* (Cambridge, MA: Harvard University Press, 1986); Michael K. Buckland, "Information as thing," *Journal of the American*

Society for Information Science 42, no. 5 (1991): 351–60; Manuel Castells, *The Rise of the Network Society* (Malden, MA: Blackwell, 2000); Chandler, *The Visible Hand*; and Jorge Reina Schement and Terry Curtis, *Tendencies and Tensions of the Information Age* (New Brunswick, NJ: Transaction, 1997).

16. Daniel K. Correa, "Assessing broadband in America: OECD and ITIF broadband rankings," *Washington DC, The Information Technology and Innovation Foundation* 10 (April 2007). OECD Directorate for Science, Technology, and Industry, "Broadband Statistics to December 2006," www.oecd.org/sti/ict/broadband (April 2006); OECD Directorate for Science, Technology, and Industry, "Multiple Play: Pricing and Policy Trends," www.oecd.org/dataoecd/47/32/36546318.pdf (April 2006); and OECD Directorate for Science, Technology, and Industry, "Multiple Play: Pricing and Policy Trends," www.oecd.org/dataoecd/47/32/36546318.pdf.

17. Capello, *Spatial Economic Analysis*; Cohendet, Umbhauer, et al., eds., *Economics of Networks*; and Varian, "Versioning Information Goods."

18. François Bar and Annemarie M. Riis, "Tapping User-Driven Innovation: A New Rationale for Universal Service," *The Information Society* 16 (2000): 99–108; Harmeet Sawhney and Seungwhan Lee, "Arenas of Innovation: Understanding New Configurational Potentialities of Communication Technologies," *Media, Culture & Society* 27, no. 3 (2005): 391–414; Krishna Jayakar and Harmeet Sawhney, "Universal Access in the Information Economy: Tracking Policy Innovations Abroad," *Benton Foundation Universal Service Project*, Jorge Reina Schement (Washington, DC: Benton Foundation, 2006): 12.

19. See note 16.

20. P.L. No. 104-104, 110 Stat. 56 (1996). Sec. 254 (c) (1).

21. Jorge Reina Schement and Marsha Ann Tate, *Rural America in the Digital Age* (Columbia, MO: Rural Policy Research Institute, 2003). Lynette Kvasny, Nancy Kranich, et al., "Communities, Learning and Democracy in the Digital Age," *The Journal of Community Informatics [online]* 2, no. 2 (2006).

22. Lee Raine, "Internet: The Mainstreaming of Online Life," *Internet 4* (Washington, DC: Pew Internet and American Life Project, 2005): 14.

23. Compiled from figure 24, "Public Library Funding & Technology Access Study 2006–2007," *ALA Research Series* (Chicago: American Library Association and Information Institute, College of Information, Florida State University, 2007): 215.

24. 78.3 million total as of 18 March 2008, suggesting 150,000 to over 200,000 videos published every day on YouTube: mediatedcultures.net/ksudigg/?p=163, accessed 5 May 2008.

25. Leigh Estabrook, Evans Witt, and Lee Rainie, "Information Searches That Solve Problems: How People Use the Internet, Libraries, and Government Agencies When They Need Help," *Pew Internet and American Life Project and Graduate School of Library and Information Science* (University of Illinois at Urbana–Champaign, 2007): 34.

26. *American Fact Finder: 110th Congress, Congressional Districts*, U.S. Census Bureau (2008).

27. Radio set ownership stood at 10 percent of households in 1925, and rose to 82 percent by 1940, on the eve of the U.S. entry into World War II when radio set production fell to a minimum. Series H 878-893, R 93-105, R 1-12 (1975). Historical statistics of the United States, colonial times to 1970 Washington, DC: GPO.

28. Cross, *An All-Consuming Century*; Jorge Reina Schement, "Three for Society: Households and Media in the Creation of 21st Century Communities," *Center: Architecture and Design in America* 11 (1999): 75–86; and Gary A. Steiner, *The People Look at Television: A Study of Audience Attitudes* (New York: Knopf, 1963).

29. The physics of electromagnetic energy preclude variations in speed; that is, all electromagnetic waves travel at the speed of light (286,000 miles per second). However, the term "high-speed" has entered common usage to differentiate "high-speed" broadband Internet access from "low-speed" dial-up Internet access. It is with that connotation that I use the term, "high-speed," in this chapter.

30. These figures are compiled from national random digit dial surveys conducted by the Pew Internet and American Life Project. More information about the project and data can be found at www.pewinternet.org.

31. John B. Horrigan and Jorge Reina Schement, "Consuming Information More or Less: An Examination of Information Consumption Behavior as a Strategy for Replacing, Displacing, or Supplementing the Consumption of Other Information Goods," Telecommunications Policy Research Conference, Washington, DC (2002).

32. A note on interpreting the data: general Internet adoption data captures use from anywhere, that is, a respondent is asked whether he or she is an Internet user, and respondents can (and do) answer "yes" to that question if they do not use the Internet at home.

33. Susannah Fox and Gretchen Livingston, *Latinos Online* (Washington, DC: Pew Hispanic Center and Pew Internet Project, 2007), 18.

34. Jeffrey Boase, John B. Horrigan, et al. *The Strength of Internet Ties* (Washington, DC: Pew Internet and American Life Project, 2006).

35. The 44 percent of home broadband users who have posted "user-generated content" to the internet have done at least one of the following things: created their own blog, participate, created, or worked on their own webpage; participated in group blogs or webpages; posted comments to a newsgroup; shared a personal creation (like artwork, stories, or videos); or taken online content and remixed it into an artistic creation of their own.

36. Total United States: 93.4 percent telephone household penetration; A. Belinfante, "Telephone Subscribership in the United States, Federal Communications Commission," Wireline Competititon Bureau, Industry Analysis and Technology Division (May 2007).

37. U.S. Census Bureau, Current Population Survey, October 1993.

38. M. J. Copps, "America's Internet Disconnect," *Washington Post*, 8 November 2006, Washington, DC, A27.

2

Digital Media, Modern Democracy, and Our Truncated National Debate

Ernest J. Wilson III

Introduction

W E ARE IN A MOMENT OF tremendous change and complexity in the
modern media space. Among the most dramatic is the rapid growth of
digital media like the Internet and the worldwide web. In this period of mul-
tiplying media platforms, new IT applications, fractioning attention spans,
and radically changing audiences, it is quite natural to focus on digital media,
and to be worried especially about business sustainability. New digital media
are expanding widely even as audiences for mainstream media platforms are
shrinking and the institutions that have traditionally supplied news and entertainment are shrinking along with them. Even media nonprofits like PBS are
worrying about how to pay their bills. Understandably, there is a great deal of
talk and worry about the most appropriate "business model" needed to sustain the core components of our modern media. Finding the most appropriate
business model is hugely important to media managers, workers, investors,
executives, and ultimately to many media consumers.

At the same time, there is another set of critical issues equally, if not more,
essential to our modern life, and that is the relationship between these new
digital media and democracy. This too is a central matter for policy makers
and public interest coalitions to consider. However, the current public discourse now devotes disproportionate attention to media business models and
insufficient attention to how the media affect the health of our democracy.
Phrased sharply—*are the changes in the contemporary media landscape good or
bad for American democracy?*

Where one comes out on such issues as an expert, advocate, or curious citizen depends largely on where one begins. If we begin with the challenges, imperatives, and opportunities of finding a sustainable media business model, we are led down one particular path with its own internal logic that leads to the bottom line. It is ultimately the bottom line that counts in a highly competitive commercial marketplace. By contrast, beginning with the challenges, imperatives, and opportunities for building sustainable democracy by strengthening media, we are led down a different path, also with its own logic.

Both are important, but the business model starting point is getting the lion's share of attention. Yet the relationship between the conditions of our modern media landscape and the current health of our democracy should also be a central concern to all, and it has not gotten its share of serious attention. There are important exceptions. Henry Jenkins' collection *Democracy and New Media* (2004),[1] and some more recent essays by Shane[2] and the work of McChesney[3] contribute greatly, but we need more such work in the policy and political debates. The state of contemporary democracy is an issue of great moment and importance around the world today, whether in Los Angeles, California, or Lhasa, Tibet, where it has recently become a matter of life or death. We have just experienced a remarkable period when democracy surged around the world. Scholars like Samuel Huntington[4] of Harvard have identified a third wave of democratization around the world, accelerating after the fall of the Berlin Wall in 1989, which, he and others argue, may now be on a secular downturn.

From Zimbabwe to Bosnia the state of democracy is fragile. In this light we should not forget the struggles for democracy in our own country, where for two hundred years the quality and depth of democracy has been a matter of life and death as well, from the beginning of the republic to the more recent struggles for equality of women, immigrants, and people of color.

The state of our contemporary democracy should be a matter of great concern to all attentive citizens. Despite the recent encouraging spike in citizen engagement during this particular presidential year, for the past quarter century the trends have been downward and worrying.

Democracy's Health Today

If we define democracy very simply as an ensemble of competition, participation, rights, responsibilities, and rule of law, and we add the creation and maintenance of durable public spaces free from government or corporate control, then in recent years on some of these core definitional dimensions the quality of democracy has stagnated, if not declined:

- The percentage of voter turnout in many if not most local, state, and congressional elections has been in the 30–40 percent range;
- Involvement in civic life—from bowling leagues to neighborhood organizations—is on the decline. Some observers like Robert Putnam[5] see this as a serious problem for democracy.
- Political rights are under pressure prompted by the war-related restrictions put in place by the Bush administration.

Not paying adequate attention to the health of our democracy is a luxury we cannot afford. So let me refine the opening question about democracy and media in order to answer it more directly. First, I want to underscore the need to review the contemporary media landscape, or media "ecosystem," as a whole. The media ecosystem has become a closely knit network, as digitalization has enabled the convergence of once-separate entities producing print, broadcast, and now online forms of communication, as it has empowered the entrepreneurs who would knit them together. This new ecosystem now comprises multiple institutions, large and small, public and private, analog and digital. It has multiple media platforms, infrastructures, applications, users, and the real-world institutions that house them. All of these elements interact with one another in new and multiple ways—digital media with analog, large established firms with small start-ups, and audiences with content producers. Indeed, not only has the distinction between media suppliers grown more complex, but also the once-ironclad distinction between supplier and audience has diminished.[6]

Not surprisingly, despite convergence, each medium retains its own stakeholders and enthusiasts with their own preferences for one platform over another, whether over the air broadcasting or terrestrial cable or newsprint. And, not surprisingly, each stakeholder group has a different experience with democracy and media, and differing interpretations of the challenges and opportunities presented by their intersections. Thus, while it is essential to understand the new digital media, it is equally important to grasp the relationship of traditional analog media and democracy as interpreted by the stakeholders. There is not one answer to the question of the relations between media and democracy. There are multiple answers, which depend instead on where you stand in the multiplatform media ecosystem.

Not having a single answer to a complicated question is not so terrible. That happens for lots of tough issues, from health care to national security, and the role of media in a democracy is no different. However, more problematic is that the talk about media and democracy is not yet a single mature integrated discourse. It is a fragmented, imperfect nondialogue, a nonexistent discourse. A genuine discourse requires a consistent conversation across multiple communities and stakeholders. Alas, we aren't there yet.

There are real costs to not having a national dialogue on media and democracy. As FCC commissioner Michael Copps[7] reminds us, in today's new media environment it is impossible to hold an informed and open debate on issues of consequence like health care or national security unless the citizens have adequate access to all the information they need to make wise judgments, and access to the public forums in which to speak their views. Getting adequate information requires adequate access to modern media, and articulating opinions increasingly requires getting access to virtual electronic, digital forums.

Of course, the relationships between our media ecosystem on the one hand and the health of contemporary democracy have already received serious attention from a number of scholars and other observers. Yochai Benkler, at Harvard's Berkman Center, addresses the issue head on in his magisterial book *The Wealth of Networks*,[8] as does Peter Shane in his excellent collection *Democracy Online*.[9] Some years ago Shanthi Kalathil and Taylor Boas looked at the democracy-Internet connections globally in their *Open Networks, Closed Regimes: The Impact of the Internet on Authoritarian Rule*.[10] All write compellingly and with nuance about the complex relationships between democracy and the new digital ecosystem, especially the influence of the Internet.

Despite their efforts, we are still too stingy by not giving enough close and thoughtful attention to the relationship between the media ecosystem on the one hand, and our democracy on the other. The topic is too important for us not to give it our skeptical best. In a nutshell, here is the skeptical question which I believe deserves much more investigation—*"If new digital media are indeed spreading so widely, and being adopted so rapidly, then at what point should we see some significant improvements of democratic practices, democratic values, democratic institutions and democratic outcomes?"* These are critical contextual issues that should inform and guide policymaking in the next administration.

Nonetheless, shouldn't we at least entertain the idea that some aspects of the new media ecosystem might actually undercut democratic practices, values, and institutions? The combination of "gotcha journalism" and cell phone diffusion may not contribute much to mature, modern democracy. The enthusiasms of political extremists of any stripe may create better visuals of sectarian violence on small hand-held screens than opportunities for thoughtful reflection.

Media and Democracy Relationships

Still, in their enthusiasm for the new digital media, many argue there is a one-to-one relationship between new digital media and democracy.

Enthusiasts proclaim that new digital media can resolve the distemper of modern democracy, and suggest the following formula: "One unit of new digital media will produce one unit of improved democracy." Digital media advances, and that makes democracy advance. Digital media rises, democracy rises. Said differently: "Take a cup of blog, add an hour of YouTube, and stir. And you've got democracy stew. Drop a laptop computer into a poor or economically backward community, and the opportunities for democracy expand exponentially." Real life is never that simple.

In the real world, the relationships between media and democracy are much more complicated. Furthermore, the ways that different communities discuss the media ecosphere and democracy are quite disparate. The different communities in the media ecosystem carry out the discourse differently. As one who operates at the borderlines and intersections of a variety of different media and political communities in the United States and abroad, I find that each community tends to have its own restricted views on media-democracy relations. This isn't surprising, since communities of practice also constitute epistemic communities with their own unique assumptions and norms based on their own unique experiences, and they spend most of their time talking to others like themselves about their own particular experiences with the media and much less time and attention listening and talking to others, and perhaps learning from them.[11]

Four Communities, Four Silos

Let me briefly describe four such communities of practice and provide a flavor of their treatment of this central issue. The main argument is that we will fail to leverage the manifold and powerful potentials of the digital media unless we do a much better job of advancing the discourses across the different stakeholders in the multimedia ecosystem. Currently, the conversations across these distinctive universes are stunted. Because they are stunted we have less robust conversations, imperfect research and analysis, very partial and one-sided conclusions, and therefore we miss opportunities to enhance democracy. I will suggest below that it should be the special responsibility of centers of learning and universities, including schools of communications and journalism, to enhance their convening function to bring these disparate stakeholders together in mutually respectful dialog.

Here then are four relevant, distinctive, and vocal communities that operate prominently in the media ecosphere (there are, of course, other communities, but these are especially salient). To sharpen (and shorten) the discussion, I offer representative syllogisms of how each tends to frame and articulate its own unique understanding of the relations between media and democracy.

The four communities of discourse are traditional newspapers, the digital media, public broadcasting, and commercial broadcast media.

The Traditional Media—Newspapers

The current difficult conditions of print media are well known. Here is how those in the newspaper community tend to frame their view of media and democracy.

- *Newspapers are a core bedrock of any democracy.*
- *Newspapers are dying.*
- *Ergo, democracy in America is at great risk.*

The Digital Media

Taken together, the community of digital media enthusiasts holds a contrasting view.

- *New media are opening new channels of communication for all, creating unprecedented opportunities for participation in traditional and new ways, and promoting the competition of ideas.*
- *Democracy is fundamentally about these matters.*
- *Ergo, democracy is being enhanced by digital media.*

Public Broadcasting

The traditionalists that enthusiastically uphold NPR, PBS, and other public broadcasting entities tend to phrase their syllogism as follows:

- *Noncommercial "space" is essential for democracy's survival.*
- *The main providers of noncommercial space—public broadcasting—are seeing declines in their audience shares, and are slow to move to digital media.*
- *Ergo, high quality democracy's survival is put at risk.*

Commercial Broadcast Media

By far, the largest and most influential player in the media ecosystem, the mainstream commercial broadcast media, has its own unique views on democracy.

- *Television is still where most people get their news, especially local news. Its popularity and universal accessibility make commercial broadcast television America's most inherently democratic medium.*

- *Broadcasters (and cable news channels) are giving their audiences what they want both over the air and online.*
- *Ergo, competition will drive commercial broadcast media to create convergent media properties that offer what people really want and democracy will be just fine.*

All of these perspectives are partial; none fully captures the complexity of the relationships they purport to describe. All share a cramped vision of society and a naiveté about politics that misinforms their arguments. Yet each position has something valuable to contribute. The traditional newspaper partisans are perhaps the most vociferous about the decline of democracy and the most ardent about defending it publicly. The digital media mavens are correct to point to the special features of these new media platforms—interactivity, participatory user-generated content, online communities, and openness—that offer such tremendous potentials for strengthening democracy. Public service media is exactly that—noncommercial specialty media designed to promote the commonwealth. And even the blunt self-interest of commercial media cannot hide their leading role in media innovations that can serve the public interest and advance democracy. Each perspective adds something valuable to the national debate—*if* we were having a fully realized national debate.

These media-based groups are uniquely engaged, and engaged in particular ways, in debates over democracy, but they certainly are not the only groups. Some like Free Press are deeply engaged in the politics of the interplay of democracy and media, and others like Common Cause or NOW are willing to tackle these issues in the political arena. But in too many instances, even reform-minded organizations continue to operate within their own silos, again undercutting the potentials that could prompt and sustain a genuine democratic dialogue.

Alas, most of us remain stuck within our separate silos. In today's heavily networked society where everything seems to be increasingly related to everything else, sticking within one's silo is not a good way to proceed. In a networked knowledge society, no one knows everything, and everyone knows something. Innovation is more likely to take place at the borders and intersections of things, not just at the old conservative core—think of the advances in biotechnology or nanotechnology.[12] The challenge is how to communicate more effectively in order to know what others know, in the form and application that you can access.

Ironically, perhaps, the very technologies that permit us to escape our silos are the same ones that encourage us to remain trapped within them. Here we have to confront the pathologies as well as the positives of digital media. Gregory Rodriguez, reporting on a study by Bill Bishop called "The Big Sort:

Why the Clustering of Like-Minded America is Tearing Us Apart," points out that "[g]iven all the media choices they have, Americans are increasingly segregating into 'gated' communities choosing to read and hear only the things that bolster their world view."[13] The risk is that the common middle shrinks as people move to the more extreme, and self-referential, edges. This is not a good thing for democracy.

When scholars are confronted with a phenomenon like multiple silos that block effective communication on essential topics, they seek to explain the underlying causes for the outcome. They postulate alternative and competing hypotheses about deep origins and dynamics. For example, the rise and persistence of silos could reflect:

- *individual and institutional inertia;*
- *institutional incentives and rewards;*
- *ideological factors;*
- *the weight of technologies; and/or*
- *political maneuvers and personal self-interest.*

It is beyond the scope of this chapter to explore the relative weight or accuracy of each factor. However, finding the answers to these questions is critical from both a scholarly and practical perspective. It is essential for all of us to know and explain root causes of conditions if we would change them for the better.

There is room for optimism for the future. It rests on the reality that the elements most central to the new digital media are also directly relevant to the core values and processes of democracy, notably *interactivity, participatory user-generated content, online communities, and openness.* Democracy consists of competition, rights and responsibilities, rule of law, and the maintenance of public spaces. It is easy to see how these two sets of attributes—those of digital media, those of modern liberal democracy—can be more tightly connected. Each media element could conceivably advance the core values of democracy, *if* there is a political coalition able to link them together and keep them linked.

And, of course, from Beijing to Harare and Boston, these links are being created by audiences and citizens anxious to enhance both democracy and media. So the stakes are high. According to McChesney and Nichols:

We need to establish rules and structures designed to create a cultural environment that will enlighten, empower and energize citizens so they can realize the full promise of an American experiment that has, since its founding, relied on freedom of the press to rest authority in the people.[14]

Yet the sustainability of these linkages between digital media and democracy, which may seem mutually supportive and perhaps even inevitable, are not inevitable. In the rough and tumble world of everyday political life, in the cutthroat context of hypercompetitive markets and growing media concentration, there is simply no guarantee that democracy and media will remain automatically joined at the hip. We simply cannot be sure of exactly how these disparate elements will be brought together, by whom, and for what purposes. As Larry Lessig regularly points out, there are monopolistic and corporate scenarios of the future of digital media and democracy, just as there are community ownership and local control scenarios.[15]

Some Possible Next Steps

Policy makers and regulators in the new administration, prodded by the new Congress and stakeholder groups, should root their deliberations about the potentials of the new media more explicitly in democratic theory. The country will benefit from more open and consistent democratic dialogues and citizen access to policymaking and media-making. Each of the stakeholders has unique resources and perspectives to be contributed to the broader national debate, but they need to reform their own behaviors.

- Advocacy groups interested in democracy and digital media must reach out to one another as they design their annual meetings and conferences, and take other serious actions to reduce these silos in order to enhance the design and conduct of more representative and progressive public policy.
- Government officials. The policy challenge for any administration, especially a new incoming administration, is to be more deliberately and aggressively consultative with these multiple groups, taking affirmative steps to seek out and listen to multiple voices. Many of the most critical issues today are so new that techno-geeks knowledgeable about digital media have not had time (or incentives) to move into senior government positions.
- Public intellectuals and policy intellectuals need to be more sophisticated and effective in creatively combining broad fundamentals like democracy and citizenship with the details and dynamics of the communications and information sectors.

One example of a common focus for all four groups is the need for much greater attention to extending the viability of noncommercial media, especially in this transition to a new environment that is both hypercommercial- and hypercitizen-controlled. The public service space needs to be greatly improved in this transition especially through strengthening the public spaces inside the new media ecosystems. The public broadcasting system has become so insular, complicated, and conservative that it needs the shakeup that can come from active engagement with the new media activists.

Politics is essential to create new policies. The immediate political challenge to these silo'ed distinct communities is to articulate new inclusive visions and to do the hard work of forging new political coalitions to provide the underlying political constituency necessary for a democratic transition to cyber-enhanced democracy. Such unified coalitions that want to unite digital media and modern democracy can then help design and promote new policies appropriate for the new digital age. This means breaking down the silos.

All who hold democracy dear, and who believe in the central empowering potential of media old or new, need to contribute what they can to break down the silos and open up the process of transformation more fully to the sunshine of debate. Some elements in each community must reach out to others to begin more robust dialogues. For this to happen, informed and visionary leadership is required to prompt sensible discussions within each silo, and to reach out and find partners in the other silos to gain the impacts that our country—and other countries—so badly need. I believe third party "connectors," think tanks (including philanthropies), and schools of communication can use their convening power to act innovatively and create opportunities and incentives for these conversations to take place.

We will all be poorer if the much-needed national debate on the media ecosystem and democracy does not occur. We can break down the silos and advance modern democracy. If we fail to do so, we will have no one to blame but ourselves.

Notes

1. Henry Jenkins and David Thorburn, *Democracy and New Media* (Cambridge, MA: MIT Press, 2004).

2. Peter Shane, *Democracy Online: The Prospects for Political Renewal Through the Internet* (New York: Routledge, 2004).

3. Robert W. McChensney and John Nichols, "Who'll Unplug Big Media? Stay Tuned," *The Nation*, 16 June 2008, www.thenation.com/doc/20080616/mcchesney.

4. Samuel P. Huntington, *The Third Wave: Democratization in the Late Twentieth Century* (Norman: University of Oklahoma Press, 1993).

5. Robert D. Putnam, *Bowling Alone: The Collapse and Revival of American Community* (New York: Simon & Schuster, 2000).

6. Jenkins and Thorburn, *Democracy*.

7. Michael Copps, *Remarks of FCC Commissioner Michael J. Copps to the National Conference on Media Reform*, Minneapolis, Minnesota, 7 June 2008, hraunfoss.fcc .gov/edocs_public/attachmatch/DOC-282821A1.doc.

8. Yochai Benkler, *The Wealth of Networks: How Social Production Transforms Markets and Freedom* (New Haven, CT: Yale University Press, 2007).

9. Peter Shane, *Democracy Online*.

10. Shanthi Kalathil and Taylor Boas, *Open Networks, Closed Regimes: The Impact of the Internet on Authoritarian Rule* (Washington, DC: Carnegie Endowment for International Peace, 2003).

11. I recognize the substantial expansion of participation in the 2008 presidential campaign. For the moment I assign most of the change to the substantive issues of the race and character of the candidates. But this interpretation is of course open to question.

12. John Hagel and John Seely Brown, *The Only Sustainable Edge: Why Business Strategy Depends on Productive Friction and Dynamic Specialization* (Boston: Harvard Business School Press, 2005).

13. Gregory Rodriguez, "The New American Segregation," *Los Angeles Times*, 26 May 2008, A23.

14. McChensney and Nichols, *The Nation*.

15. Lawrence Lessig, *Free Culture: How Big Media Uses Technology and the Law to Lock Down Culture and Control Creativity* (New York: Penguin, 2004).

3

Public Scholarship and the Communications Policy Agenda

Robert W. McChesney

W E ARE IN THE MIDST OF A COMMUNICATIONS and information revolution. Of that there is no doubt. What is uncertain is what type of revolution this will be, how sweeping, and with what effects. Precisely how this communications revolution will unfold and what it will mean for our journalism, our culture, our politics, and our economics are not at all clear. In a generation or two, we may speak of this era as a glorious new chapter in our history: democratizing our societies, revolutionizing our economies, lessening inequality and militarism, reversing environmental destruction, and generating an extraordinary outburst of culture and creativity. Or we may speak of it despondently, measuring what we have lost, or, for some, never had: our privacy, our humanity, our control over our own destiny, intellectual rigor, and our hope for the future. We may also end up somewhere in between.

Where we end up and how our communications revolution unfolds will be determined to a significant extent by a series of crucial policy decisions that will likely be made over the course of the coming decade or two. In my view, as much as any technological innovation, it is the democratization of media policymaking, and the democratization of politics in general, that will ultimately be seen as the truly remarkable aspect of this communications revolution.

Let me put this another way: If fifteen or twenty years from now, the outcome of the communications revolution turns out to be merely technological wizardry or a testament to enhanced market opportunities for the world's most privileged people, it will have been a failure. If it is about hooking up affluent consumers to more choices, investors to more opportunities, and making it easier for them to bypass the wretched of the earth, it may prove to be a dubious contribution to the development of our species. At the very least, it will be a missed opportunity, and I do not know how many more of those are coming down the turnpike. If within a generation social inequality has not begun to be dramatically reversed, democratic institutions are not considerably more vibrant, militarism and chauvinism have not been dealt a mighty blow, and the environment has not been significantly repaired, then we will have had an unfulfilled communications revolution.

Communications has been at the heart of our species from our very emergence some one hundred thousand years ago, and it is central to democratic theory and practice. New technologies are in the process of forming the central nervous system for our society in a manner unimaginable even in the media-drenched late twentieth century. No previous communications revolution has held the promise of allowing us to radically transcend the structural communications limitations for effective self-government and human happiness that have existed throughout human history. But such a revolution will not occur because of a magical technology; it will only occur because people have organized to make it happen.

This point is of acute importance to my fellow scholars across many disciplines. Because communications is interdisciplinary, vital contributions come from historians, economists, legal scholars, public policy scholars, education researchers, engineers, and social scientists from various disciplines. The field of media studies cannot undertake this alone, and all of these scholars need to begin the process of working with each other. In interdisciplinary work, the whole is vastly greater than the sum of the proverbial parts.

That being said, my argument is aimed directly at those who work in communications or media studies, and at our students, both graduate and undergraduate, past, present, and future. This is one constituency that has only begun to consider the nature of the historical moment we are entering and whose very existence depends upon coming to terms with it. Media studies must provide the substance that creates the gravitational pull to draw scholars from other disciplines together. I believe that scholars have a crucial and indispensable role to play in the coming period and that the best possible outcome for media policies depends upon their active involvement. We all have a stake in whether communications scholars and students grasp the potential of these times. Moreover, I believe that the future of the field of communications rides on how well the field adapts to what I consider a moment of truth. We need a revolution, of sorts, in the way scholars conceptualize, study, and teach communications.

In short, this should be the moment in the sun for the field of communications across American campuses. Regrettably, for reasons I elaborate upon elsewhere, such has not been the case.[1]

I believe that the gaping chasm between the role of media and communications in our society and the current direction and structure the field of communications is taking in the United States has reached a crisis point. This crisis affects not only the professors, students, and administrators associated with these departments, but our entire society. There are, as economists like to put it, considerable "externalities." Our nation desperately needs engaged communications scholarship from a broad range of traditions, which employs a diverse set of methodologies to address the issues before us. And assuming this scenario is not unique to the United States, other countries are facing crises as well. Why is this happening? Narrowly put, because what happens in communications departments and universities eventually affects everyone. In other words, ideas are important.

But the problem goes beyond this. The digital revolution raises fundamental questions about communications and how it affects economics, politics, culture, organizations, and interpersonal relationships. The most important questions, I suspect, have not yet been asked, let alone answered, in particular the following: How will the communications system of the coming era be organized, structured, and subsidized? How will decisions be made that determine these structures and policies? What values will be privileged? What will be the nature of accountability both for the communications system and for the policymaking process? If anything is certain, it is that the emerging communications system will go a long way toward shaping our economy, our politics, and, for lack of a better term, our way of life. It has become our central nervous system. Hence, if communications research tends to avoid these fundamental issues, then all the resources devoted to it will be of little use to the public when it looks to experts for assistance and context in addressing core policy decisions surrounding media, culture, and communications. Indeed, if communications scholars do not actively engage with this moment, this may well undermine the ability of the public to participate effectively and lead to undesirable and undemocratic outcomes.

I argue that the way out of the doldrums, the way forward, is for communications scholars to recognize what millions of Americans have come to understand: our communications system and, to an increasing extent, our political economic system are now entering a *critical juncture*, a period in which the old institutions and mores are collapsing.

The notion of critical junctures explains how social change works; there have been relatively rare and brief periods in which dramatic changes, drawing from a broad palette of options, were debated and enacted, followed by long periods in which structural or institutional change was slow and difficult.[2] During a critical juncture, which usually lasts no more than one or two decades, the range of options for society is much greater than it is otherwise.

The decisions made during such a period establish institutions and rules that likely put us on a course that will be difficult to change in any fundamental sense for decades or generations.

This notion of critical junctures is increasingly accepted in history and the social sciences. It has proven valuable for thinking broadly about society-wide fundamental social change and also as a way to understand fundamental change within a specific sector, like media and communications. The two types of critical junctures are distinct, yet, as I will demonstrate, very closely related. Most of our major institutions in media are the result of such critical junctures, periods when policies could have gone in other directions, and, had they done so, put media and society on a different path.

Based on my research, I have concluded that critical junctures in media and communications tend to occur when at least two, if not all three, of the following conditions hold:

- there is a revolutionary, new communications technology that undermines the existing system;
- the content of the media system, especially the journalism, is increasingly discredited or seen as illegitimate; and
- there is a major political crisis—severe social disequilibrium—in which the existing order no longer functions, and there are major movements for social reform.

In the past century, critical junctures in media and communications occurred three times: during the Progressive Era, when journalism was in deep crisis and the overall political system was in turmoil; during the 1930s, when the emergence of radio broadcasting combined with public antipathy to commercialism against the backdrop of the Depression; and during the 1960s and early 1970s, when popular social movements in the United States provoked radical critiques of the media as part of a broader social and political critique.

The result of the critical juncture in the Progressive Era was the emergence of professional journalism. The result of the critical juncture in the 1930s was loosely regulated commercial broadcasting, which provided the model for subsequent electronic media technologies like FM radio, terrestrial television, and cable and satellite television. The result of the 1960s and 1970s critical juncture, however, is less tangible for communications. In many respects, the issues raised then were never resolved but buried by the neoliberal epoch that followed.

Today, we are in the midst of a profound critical juncture for communications. Two of the three conditions for a critical juncture are already in place: the digital revolution is overturning all existing media industries and business models; and journalism is at its lowest ebb since the Progressive Era. The third condition—the overall stability of the political and social system—is the great unknown. There are certainly grounds for suspecting that a critical juncture is imminent. Our political system is awash in institutionalized corruption and growing inequality. The economy is in its deepest crisis in seventy-five years, and it appears likely that we are entering a period of structural transformation to points unknown. U.S. global military dominance is wobbling with the disaster of the Iraq war, and the combination of empire and republic is difficult to maintain.[3] In January 2007, the *Bulletin of the Atomic Scientists* moved its symbolic doomsday clock to five minutes to midnight. For the first time ever, the editors stressed the role of not just nuclear weapons but of global climate change in the impending catastrophes facing humankind. This is becoming a political and social crisis of major proportions.[4]

What remains to be seen is to what extent the people engage with the structural crises our society is facing, or leave matters to elites. In the critical juncture of the 1960s and early 1970s, for example, elites were concerned by a "crisis of democracy." This crisis was created by previously apathetic, passive and marginalized elements of the population—e.g., minorities, women, students— becoming politically engaged and making demands upon the system.[5]

All the longstanding presuppositions of communications scholars that were taken for granted in our society no longer hold. Both professional journalism and commercial broadcasting are in crisis and undergoing fundamental transformation. The communications system that emerges from this critical juncture will look little like the communications system of 2000 or 1990. Already, the media system of the 1960s seems about as relevant to the future as a discussion of the War of the Roses does to contemporary military strategists. Most important, it is clear that the structure of the emerging communications system will go a long way toward determining how our politics and economics, our way of life, will play out.

Although broader popular social movements are nascent, what is striking is that this critical juncture has spawned the birth of an extraordinary media reform movement in the past few years. Hundreds of thousands, perhaps millions, of Americans have engaged with media policy issues in a manner that had been previously unthinkable. Politicians and regulators are discovering, for the first time in their careers, that voters and citizens are watching what they do with regard to media closely, and they are beginning to respond. What remains to be seen is whether there will be a broader resurgence of popular politics in the coming period. If there is, it will shift the emerging "media reform movement" into much higher gear and the range of possible outcomes will increase dramatically. Such a boom in popular social movements would also combine with media reform to lead, at the least, to the sort of periodic reformation of institutions that happens every two or three generations in American history—one that is sadly overdue. Without such a popular political movement, there will still be a critical juncture in media and communications, only the outcomes will be more likely to serve the needs of dominant commercial and political interests, not the public.

Engaging with public policy issues from the vantage point of concerned citizens rather than from the perspective of owners and administrators opens new vistas for scholars, raising pressing new research questions and issues. In my mind, the evidence is clear that being connected to real-life social movements and political affairs can strengthen scholarship in the social sciences. In economics, for example, many of the great breakthroughs in theory were made by scholars directly engaged with the politics of their day, from Smith, Ricardo, J. S. Mill, and Marx to Marshall and Keynes. Even Milton Friedman is notable because pressing political concerns drove his work.[6] I think that this can be and should be true for communications as well.

My argument is not that communications scholars and students need to become full-time activists or dedicate a portion of their time to public engagement with media issues. That is fine for some of us but not for everyone. My point is simply that the notion of being in a critical juncture, of recognizing the political forces around us, should permeate all of our research agendas and our teaching. I am not arguing that scholars should shape their research to reach predetermined outcomes, or that they should place a political agenda ahead of the integrity of their scholarship. Rather, during a critical juncture, scholars simply need to broaden their horizons and engage with the crucial political and social issues of the moment. They should question presuppositions and abandon them or replace them, unless the weight of evidence justifies their maintenance. They should dive into their research headfirst, equipped only with curiosity, democratic values, and analytical skills, and see what happens.

For those of us who study communications, this is an opportunity that few other scholars can ever experience. With recognition of the historically unusual, if not uncharted, waters we are in, communications studies can leapfrog over the barriers that have constrained it heretofore and come to play a central role in social science research and education. It will not be an easy fight, for the barriers remain high, but it is the only way forward. Otherwise, our field loses much of its *raison d'etre*, and the legitimacy of its claim to society's scarce resources.

It is worth noting how the field of communications emerged and developed in the United States in response to the three great twentieth-century critical junctures already mentioned. The field was birthed in the first critical juncture, crystallized in the second critical juncture, and was rejuvenated by the third critical juncture. Without critical junctures, there might not have been much of a field at all.

The first critical juncture was during the late Gilded Age and Progressive Era, when U.S. journalism was increasingly the domain of large commercial interests operating in semi-competitive or monopolistic markets. Social critics ranging from Edward Bellamy to Henry Adams were highly critical of the corrupt and anti-democratic nature of U.S. journalism because of its private ownership and its reliance upon advertising.[7] Between 1900 and 1920, numerous muckrakers and social commentators wrote damning critiques of the anti-democratic nature of mainstream journalism. In many respects, this was the Golden Age of media criticism.[8] The depths of crisis for journalism came between 1910 and 1915. It was then that the newspaper magnate E. W. Scripps launched the ad-less pro-labor daily newspaper in Chicago, *Day Book*, and that Joseph Pulitzer considered leaving his newspapers as a public trust. Instead, Pulitzer left $2 million to Columbia University to endow its journalism school upon his death in 1911.[9] In 1920, Upton Sinclair's *The Brass Check: A Study of American Journalism* was published. This breathtaking 440-page account of the corruption of journalism by moneyed interests sold some 150,000 copies by the mid-1920s.[10] All but forgotten in the intervening years, it is a book that could well be the starting point for all assessments of journalism, if not contemporary media, in the United States. The topic of media control also became a part of progressive political organizing. The great progressive Robert La Follette devoted a chapter of his book on political philosophy to the crisis of the press. "Money power," he wrote, "controls the newspaper press . . . wherever news items bear in any way upon the control of government by business, the news is colored."[11]

It was as a response to the crisis in journalism that the revolutionary idea of professional journalism—the formal separation of the owner from the editorial function—emerged as the solution to the crisis. Citizens no longer needed to worry about private monopoly control over the news; trained professionals serving the public interest would take charge and have power. It was in this period that schools of journalism were formed. Although none existed before 1900, by 1920 the majority of major programs had been established, sometimes under strong pressure from leading newspaper publishers—desperate to reclaim legitimacy for their industry—on their state legislatures. At the University of Illinois, where I teach, the journalism department was formally authorized by the state legislature in 1927 and, by law, is one of only two departments that the university cannot close. Research as an aspect of these programs did not begin for another generation or two. Some prominent academics, like Robert Park and John Dewey, were affected by the turmoil surrounding journalism and dabbled in media issues during the Progressive Era, but for the most part, the field lay fallow into the 1930s. The tumult in society generated immense amounts of educated popular writing but did not establish much of a beachhead in the academy.

The first few decades of the twentieth century also saw the emergence of advertising, public relations, film, and radio broadcasting. The latter two would be instrumental in stimulating the rise of formal communications research in the 1930s, and during these years, there was also a nonacademic communications critique emerging in response to all the above. In the case of advertising, for example, a large and militant consumer movement that emerged by the 1920s and 1930s was highly critical of advertising and the consumer culture it spawned. This resulted in the formation of groups like Consumers Union.[12] Likewise, with the emergence of commercial radio broadcasting in the early 1930s, a feisty and heterogeneous broadcast reform movement emerged that was piercing in its criticism of the limitations of commercial radio for a democratic society.[13] Both of these movements were expressly dedicated to enacting political reform in Washington, DC, and both generated a sophisticated critique of advertising and media that anticipated some of the best academic criticism made five or six decades later.

But it was the overlay of the world crisis of the 1930s and 1940s, with the Depression and the global rise of fascism, that provoked the critical juncture in communications above all else. This was a period in which journalism was increasingly seen as a politically reactionary force, its credibility at the low ebb reached in the Progressive Era. William Allen White, the renowned editor of the *Emporia Gazette*, addressed the issue of crisis in his 1939 presidential address to the American Society of Newspaper Editors: "We must not ignore the bold fact that in the last decade a considerable section of the American press, and in particular the American daily newspaper press, has been the object of bitter criticism in a wide section of American public opinion. In certain social areas a definite minority, sometimes perhaps a majority of our readers, distrust us, discredit us."[14]

When communications did make its grand splash in the academy in the late 1930s, it did so by looking at the very big issues, in the context of social crisis. There was the matter of democracy and what it meant in the age of corporate capitalism and mass media. The master works of John Dewey and Walter Lippmann in the 1920s granted the topic sufficient gravitas and made matters of communications central to the debate in the leading intellectual circles in the nation.[15] There was the matter of propaganda, as it was employed not only by the Soviets and the fascist states, but also in Western democracies as a routine matter of course. The question was in whose interests and how would this propaganda be deployed. And there was the matter of media effects. How did the immersion of our society into a world of media affect us? All of these issues were linked, and they held the potential for a significantly critical approach to communications, with an eye to the reconstruction of society along more democratic lines.

The launching pad for communications research was not only at a few large Big Ten universities, but also at some prominent Ivy League universities like Princeton, Harvard, Yale, and Columbia. Dan Schiller has written brilliantly on this period, concentrating on the activities of Paul Lazarsfeld and Robert Merton. Schiller notes that all the elements for a powerful radical critique of propaganda were in place in communications, aided and abetted by a relatively sympathetic political climate, and elites concerned and confused by the world they were entering. But the critical approach was nonetheless unwelcome by commercial media sponsors, university administrations, and the key foundations, especially Rockefeller, which bankrolled much of communications research during these years.[16] In the hands of Harold Lasswell, propaganda research was turned on its head: It went from being a critique of propaganda as a threat to self-government to a theoretically informed treatise on how elites could use propaganda to manage people in their own interests.[17] After World War II, the practice became commonplace, only it was no longer called propaganda.

By the late 1940s, the critical impulse was effectively marginalized, if not purged, from U.S. communications studies. The opening created by the critical juncture disappeared, the progressive impulse of the New Deal replaced by the postwar American Century. Ironically, Lazarsfeld, who had framed communications research to be open to critical inquiry in the 1930s and early 1940s, became the icon of mainstream research.[18] The political climate was changing dramatically. The broad historical and intellectually informed sweep that informed the research of the 1930s and early 1940s was gradually replaced by an increasingly ahistorical approach that accepted the commercial basis of U.S. media and the capitalistic nature of U.S. society as proper and inviolable. Research became more closely tied to the needs of the dominant industry interests.[19] When the Hutchins Commission made its seminal study of the press and media in the immediate postwar years, it combined piercing criticism of commercial media with lame pleas for industry self-regulation as the solution.[20] Had the popular movements that opposed commercial broadcasting and advertising in the 1930s been more successful, the notion that commercial media were innately "American" might not have been regarded as a presupposition in the academy. Instead, the room for critical analysis and study was shrinking quickly.

The Cold War encouraged this anti-critical process; indeed, it made it almost mandatory. Christopher Simpson and Timothy Glander, among others, have documented the close relationship of the "founding fathers" of mass communications research to the emerging U.S. national security state in the 1940s and 1950s.[21] In this environment, notions that commercial interests might use their control of media to disseminate propaganda fell from grace; propaganda became something done only by "totalitarian" states and governments. This was a stunning change in both rhetoric and analysis. (In the early 1930s, for example, the U.S. advertising industry hailed Adolf Hitler and Josef Goebbels as brilliant fellow propagandists. "Whatever Hitler has done," the trade publication *Printers' Ink* wrote in 1933, "he has depended almost entirely upon slogans made effective by reiteration, made general by American advertising methods." That wasn't all: "Hitler and his advertising man Goebbels issued slogans which the masses could grasp with their limited intelligence. . . . Adolf has some good lines, of present-day application to American advertisers."[22] Such candid commentary on the use of propaganda by powerful interests in democratic nations was soon relegated to the lunatic fringe, where, in many respects, it remains.) Propaganda became psychological warfare and then became mass communications.[23]

By mid-century, the ideas that ownership and control over media were decisive and that media had large and important effects were applicable only to the study of the Soviet Union and other communist nations. In the United States, the conventional wisdom was that structure was irrelevant or benign, the system served the interests of the people, and media had limited effects. Had the U.S. political climate in the 1940s veered leftward—not as absurd a notion as some might think—rather than to the right, the critical juncture may have led to a different outcome and critical communications scholarship may have survived and even flourished as a viable entity in U.S. universities.[24]

By the 1950s, much of the enthusiasm among foundations for communications research had dried up, the critical juncture had passed, and the field had lost its toehold in the Ivy League. Thereafter, the balance of power shifted to the large public research universities of the Midwest. Critical work was not entirely dead. Kenneth Burke and, a bit later, George Gerbner, James Carey, and Hanno Hardt, among others, would keep the flame alive; Dallas Smythe and Herbert I. Schiller almost singlehandedly put the field of political economy of communications on the map in the United States in the 1950s and 1960s. But as influential as their work was, the times did not foster a legion of collaborators. Smythe returned to his native Canada in the early 1960s to find more fertile soil for critical scholarship. Much critical work on media returned to its traditional status and was done by people outside the discipline, like the educator Paul Goodman and C. Wright Mills, a sociologist at Columbia, or outside the academy. In many ways, Mills's work provided a superior framework for the critical evaluation of media. His *The Sociological Imagination* made a trenchant critique of the limitations of the sort of mainstream work that was ascending in the academy. Mills's untimely death at age forty-five in 1962 was a very dark moment in the history of critical communications.[25]

The explosion of popular politics—civil rights, black power, antiwar, student, feminist, environmental—in the 1960s and early 1970s brought the third great critical juncture to communications. This was the foundation of the critical juncture—the broader upheaval—because it brought all social institutions under closer examination. At that time, a communications technological revolution of sorts was under way, with the rise of satellite communications and cable television, which fomented visions of a decentralized and/or commercial-free television system.[26] In addition, the journalism of this era was under attack as inadequate, and consequently, there was a mushrooming of "underground" newspapers and journalism reviews.[27]

The consequences of this critical juncture for communications remain unclear. On the one hand, the sanctity of the commercial media system and the practice of professional journalism were never in question anywhere near the extent that they were during the earlier critical junctures. On the other hand, dramatic developments were taking place. Public broadcasting was established in 1967, and for a brief moment it held the potential to become a system far more independent and critical than what finally emerged.[28] In some respects, the 1960s also crystallized a majoritarian view of the First Amendment, a potentially much more radical and democratic interpretation than had been generally countenanced. Justice Byron White's majority opinion in the 1969 *Red Lion Broadcasting Co., Inc. v. Federal Communications Commission* ruling pertained to broadcasting alone, but the logic and spirit opened the door at least a crack for a very different way to envisage the role of media in a free society:

> But the people as a whole retain their interest in free speech by radio and their collective right to have the medium function consistently with the ends and purposes of the First Amendment. It is the right of the viewers and listeners, not the right of the broadcasters, which is paramount. . . . It is the purpose of the First Amendment to preserve an uninhibited market-place of ideas in which truth will ultimately prevail, rather than to countenance monopolization of that market, whether it be by the Government itself or a private licensee. . . . It is the right of the public to receive suitable access to social, political, esthetic, moral, and other ideas and experiences which is crucial here. That right may not constitutionally be abridged either by Congress or by the FCC.[29]

As was the case in the 1940s, had American politics gone in a different direction in the 1970s, this critical juncture may have paved the way for a dramatic reformulation of the communications system, along with other institutions in society. Instead, what can be said is that the late 1960s and early 1970s laid the foundation—in the form of unfinished business—for today's media reform movement, just as the Progressive Era critical juncture generated challenges that were taken up during the 1930s and early 1940s.

Critical junctures and communications are joined at the hip, in the way communications structures and institutions are established in our society

and in the way we study them in our colleges and universities. In our most
dynamic moments, critical junctures have given our field its identity and it
can and must be that way again. But it will not happen without concerted
and conscious effort to that end, as there are powerful forces committed to
maintaining the status quo.

❖

One particular feature of this current critical juncture is aiding and abet-
ting the transformation of communications study. The revolutionary nature
of digital communications technologies is eliminating traditional divisions
between media sectors, between media and telecommunications (e.g., telephony), and between mediated and interpersonal communications. The rise
of the Internet exemplifies and encourages this border collapse, as it encompasses both one-to-one and traditional mass communications simultaneously.
What does it matter if the origin is a newspaper or a cable TV station or a film
studio when audiences receive their content online? What does it matter if the
delivery system comes via a television network, a cable company, a telephone
company, or an electric utility? What is the difference between telephony and
media nowadays, when both deliver digital messages, some media, some interpersonal? Factoring in the radical proliferation of two-way communications
today, made possible by websites like MySpace, Facebook, and YouTube, it is
clear that this is a dramatically new world.

As extraordinary as the digital revolution is, as amazing and mind-boggling
as these technologies are, it is imperative that scholars maintain their focus
and their perspective. Even if the Internet is kept open and even if broadband
becomes inexpensive and ubiquitous—both huge policy battles for the coming generation—that will not resolve all of the core issues on the horizon. In
particular, there are three overriding concerns that only become more pro-
nounced in the digital era. First, there is the matter of the successful provision
of journalism, which is currently in a deep and prolonged crisis as corporate
cutbacks and erosion of standards are the order of the day. Corporate media
apologists argue that there is no reason to worry, since the new blogging craze
provides us with all the journalism we can handle and then some. Digital
technology will eventually solve the problem, the pundits tell us; in the mean-
time, just let the media conglomerates buy up all the media they can, lay off
reporters in the name of "efficiency," and rake in monopolistic profits so that
they can expand the economy and create jobs. You know the drill.

In fact, there is no endgame on the visible horizon that suggests the Internet
will magically provide the journalism a self-governing people require. What
society needs are multiple newsrooms of well-paid experienced journalists

with institutional support when they offend the powerful, which good journalism invariably does. The Internet offers great hopes for citizen involvement in journalism and can transform journalism for the better, but it does not solve this fundamental political economic issue of resource allocation and institution building. That is a policy matter, and generating effective policies for the establishment of viable news media is a central dilemma of our times. It has always been an issue, but with the twin blades of neoliberalism and the Internet, it is approaching crisis stage.

Second, even a digital nirvana with open, super high-speed networks and ubiquitous inexpensive access will not derail the hypercommercialism that permeates an increasing number of our institutions and, indeed, far too much of our social life. If anything, the Internet may prove to be the ultimate enabler of Madison Avenue and corporate America in its quest to enter our minds and empty our pocketbooks. If we learn nothing else from the political economy of media, it is that commercialism comes at a very high price and with massive "externalities." Derailing hypercommercialism, creating vibrant noncommercial zones, and protecting privacy is a mission critical in the coming era. It will not happen without organized citizens demanding explicit policies to that effect. There is a necessary role for media scholars in helping to craft them.

Third, as much as the Internet and the digital revolution empower people, they also ensnare them and make them susceptible to surveillance. We sacrifice something to get the gains. Only now are people recognizing the extent to which governments, often with sympathetic communications corporations assisting them, can intervene in digital communications systems to monitor our behavior, and the prospect is chilling. It is imperative that we devise policies to make governance accountable while preventing government intrusions into our privacy. We have to make the digital revolution serve our interests. Along these lines, we have to recognize that there may be grounds for concern about the unanticipated consequences of thorough immersion in digital technologies. Indeed, much of this frenzy is fed by self-interested commercial entities.

This leads directly to the ultimate and most important job of scholars: understanding and navigating the central relationship of communications to the broader economic, cultural, and political systems. In the United States, it seems to be a given, even within academic circles, that while a profit-driven economy may well have its flaws, it is the only possible option for a free people. That is to say, any prospective alternative entails invariably a decided turn for the worse. The Soviet example was such a nightmare that Americans are not even willing to consider the idea that humanity might benefit from an alternative to capitalism.

Regrettably, this close-mindedness is proving a significant barrier to obtaining a better understanding of how capitalism actually works and affects our institutions and us and to examining more humane and just alternatives. As much as pledging love for markets is standard practice in the United States, the system itself has significant flaws, some of which are already proving catastrophic and unavoidable unless it is dramatically reformed. I do not know exactly how reformable capitalism is, or what exactly the superior alternatives are. What I do know is that getting answers to both these questions requires research, experimentation, and an open mind. If we do not think along these lines, it will become ever more difficult to find humane and effective solutions for our deep social problems. Considering the centrality of communications to both the economy and politics, media scholars are at the heart of this process.

Notes

1. See Robert W. McChesney, *Communication Revolution* (New York: New Press, 2007).

2. See Ruth Berins Collier and David Collier, *Shaping the Political Arena: Critical Junctures, the Labor Movement, and Regime Dynamics in Latin America* (South Bend, Ind.: Notre Dame University Press, 2002; first published by Princeton University Press in 1991).

3. This was an obsession of James Madison, and likewise explains his obsession with having a viable independent press that would keep the government from becoming an empire. I return to this point later in the chapter. One scholar who has drawn the connection between the U.S. empire and domestic crisis that resonates well with a critical juncture analysis is Chalmers Johnson. See Chalmers Johnson, *Nemesis: The Last Days of the American Republic* (New York: Metropolitan Books, 2007).

4. Bulletin of the Atomic Scientists: It is Five Minutes to Midnight, www.thebulletin.org/.

5. Michel Crozier, Samuel P. Huntington, and Joji Watanuki, *The Crisis of Democracy: Report on the Governability of Democracies to the Trilateral Commission* (New York: New York University Press, 1975); an excellent discussion of this point can be found in Noam Chomsky, *Necessary Illusions: Thought Control in Democratic Societies* (Boston: South End Press, 1989), 2–5.

6. Friedman was a political theorist as much as an economist. His work is mandatory reading. See, in particular, Milton Friedman, *Capitalism and Freedom* (Chicago: University of Chicago Press, 1962). Chapters 1 and 2 lay out the premises of neoliberalism, and its implications for notions of democracy as well as anything I have read.

7. See, for example, Edward Bellamy, *Looking Backward: 2000–1887* (New York: Signet Classic, 2000).

8. See Robert W. McChesney and Ben Scott, eds., *Our Unfree Press: 100 Years of Radical Media Criticism* (New York, The New Press, 2004); see also Elliott Shore, *Talkin' Socialism: J.A. Wayland and the Radical Press* (Lawrence: University Press of Kansas, 1988).

9. Duane C. S. Stoltzfus, *Freedom from Advertising: E. W. Scripps's Chicago Experiment* (Urbana: University of Illinois Press, 2007); Pulitzer reference in Ben H. Badgikian, *The Media Monopoly* (Boston: Beacon Press, 1983), 46.

10. Upton Sinclair, *The Brass Check: A Study of American Journalism* (Pasadena, self-published, 1920). A new edition was issued by the University of Illinois Press in 2002, with an introduction by Robert W. McChesney and Ben Scott.

11. Robert M. La Follette, *The Political Philosophy of Robert M. La Follette*, compiled by Ellen Torelle (Madison, WI: Robert M. La Follete Co., 1920.)

12. Inger L. Stole, *Advertising on Trial: The Consumer Movement and Corporate Public Relations in the 1930s* (Urbana: University of Illinois Press, 2006).

13. See Robert W. McChesney, *Telecommunications, Mass Media, and Democracy: The Battle for the Control of U.S. Broadcasting, 1928–1935* (New York: Oxford University Press, 1993).

14. William Allen White, "Don't Indulge in Name-Calling With Press Critics," *Editor & Publisher*, 22 April 1939, 14.

15. John Dewey, *The Public and Its Problems* (New York: H. Holt and Company, 1927); Walter Lippmann, *Public Opinion* (New York: Macmillan, 1922).

16. Dan Schiller, *Theorizing Communication: A History* (New York: Oxford University Press, 1996), chapter 2; for a sense of the intellectual tenor of the times, see Robert S. Lynd, *Knowledge for What? The Place of Social Science in American Culture* (Princeton, NJ: Princeton University Press, 1939).

17. Harold D. Lasswell, *Propaganda, Encyclopedia of the Social Sciences*, 12 (1934): 521–27; Harold D. Lasswell, *Propaganda Technique in World War I* (Cambridge, MA: The MIT Press, 1971).

18. Paul F. Lazarsfeld, "Administrative and Critical Communications Research," in Paul F. Lazarsfeld, ed., *Qualitative Analysis: Historical and Critical Essays* (Boston: Allyn and Bacon. 1972), 155–67.

19. See Steven H. Chaffee, "George Gallup and Ralph Nafziger: Pioneers of Audience Research," *Mass Communication & Society* 3, nos. 2 and 3 (Spring and Summer 2000): 317–27.

20. Robert Leigh, ed., *A Free and Responsible Press* (Chicago: University of Chicago Press, 1947); William Ernest Hocking, *Freedom of the Press: A Framework of Principle* (Chicago: University of Chicago Press, 1947).

21. See Christopher Simpson, *The Science of Coercion* (New York: Oxford University Press, 1994); Timothy Glander, *Origins of Mass Communications Research During the American Cold War* (Mulwah, NJ: Lawrence Erlbaum Associates, 2000).

22. See Robert W. McChesney, "Springtime for Goebbels," *Z Magazine*, December 1997, 16–18.

23. This is the point Christopher Simpson makes in his book; Simpson, *The Science of Coercion.*

24. Considerable historical research has recast the 1940s as a pivotal decade in recent U.S. history, where progressive political forces were far stronger than much of the conventional thinking had presumed. See, for example, George Lipsitz, *Rainbow at Midnight* (Urbana: University of Illinois Press, 1994).

25. C. Wright Mills, *The Sociological Imagination* (New York: Oxford University Press, 1959).

26. See, for example, Michael E. Kinsley, *Outer Space and Inner Sanctums: Government, Business, and Satellite Communication* (New York: John Wiley & Sons, 1976); Dallas Smythe, *Counterclockwise: Perspectives on Communication*, ed. Thomas Guback (Boulder, CO: Westview, 1994), ch. 10; Charles Tate, ed., *Cable Television in the Cities* (Washington, DC: The Urban Institute, 1971); Ralph Lee Smith, *The Wired Nation: Cable TV: The Electronic Communications Highway* (New York: Harper & Row, 1972); Nancy Jeruale, with Richard M. Neustadt and Nicholas P. Miller, eds., *CTIC Cablebooks, Volume 2: A Guide for Local Policy* (Arlington, VA: The Cable Television Information Center, 1982); Brenda Maddox, *Beyond Babel: New Direction in Communications* (Boston: Beacon Press, 1972).

27. See, for example, David Armstrong, *A Trumpet to Arms: Alternative Media in America* (Los Angeles: J. P. Tarcher; Boston: distributed by Houghton Mifflin, 1981); Abe Peck, *Uncovering the Sixties: the Life and Times of the Underground Press* (New York: Pantheon, 1985); Robert J. Glessing, *The Underground Press in America* (Bloomington: Indiana University Press, 1970); Laura Kessler, *The Dissident Press: Alternative Journalism in American History* (Beverly Hills: Sage Publications, 1984); Margaret Blanchard, *Revolutionary Sparks: Freedom of Expression in Modern America* (New York: Oxford University Press, 1992), 351–54; Bob Ostertag, *People's Movements, People's Press: The Journalism of Social Justice Movements* (Boston: Beacon Press, 2006); and Robert J. Glessing, *The Underground Press in America* (Bloomington: Indiana University Press, 1970).

28. See, for example, Michael P. McCauley, *NPR: The Trials and Triumphs of National Public Radio* (New York: Columbia University Press, 2005); Jack W. Mitchell, *Listener Supported: The Culture and the History of Public Radio* (Westport, CT: Praeger Publishers, 2005); Glenda R. Balas, *Recovering a Public Vision for Public Television* (Lanham, MD: Rowman & Littlefield Publishers, 2003); Michael P. McCauley, Eric E. Peterson, B. Lee Artz, and Dee Dee Halleck, eds., *Public Broadcasting and the Public Interest* (Armonk, NY: M.E. Sharpe Inc., 2002); John Witherspoon and Roselle Kovitz, *A History of Public Broadcasting* (Washington, DC: Current, 2000); Tom McCourt, *Conflicting Communication Interests in America: The Case of National Public Radio* (Westport, CT: Praeger Publishers, 1999); Ralph Engelman, *Public Radio and Television in America: A Political History* (Thousand Oaks, CA: Sage Publications, 1996); James Day, *The Vanishing Vision: The Inside Story of Public Television* (Berkeley: University of California Press, 1995); Jim Robertson, *Televisionaries: In their Own Words, Public Television's Founders Tell How It All Began* (Charlotte Harbor, FL: Tabby House Books, 1993); Michael Tracey, *The Decline and Fall of Public Service Broadcasting* (Oxford: Oxford University Press, 1998); and John Macy Jr., *To Irrigate a Wasteland: The Struggle to Shape a Public Television System in the United States* (Berkeley: University of California Press, 1974).

29. Opinion located online at www.epic.org/free_speech/red_lion.html. The opinion also includes a reference to a related opinion from 1964: "Speech concerning public affairs is more than self-expression; it is the essence of self-government"; *Garrison v. Louisiana*, 379 U.S. 64, 74–75 (1964).

4

International Benchmarks

The Crisis in U.S. Communications Policy
through a Comparative Lens

Amit M. Schejter

[W]e in the United States believed in the importance of policies that promote "enabling environments" of pro-competitive, technologically neutral,
private sector-led, rule of law-based progressive regulatory policies and
authority. And we are seeing that these have increasingly become the policies and beliefs adopted by more and more of the world.

Ambassador David A. Gross, U.S. Coordinator for International
Communications and Information Policy, June 16, 2008

Introduction

THERE WAS A TIME WHEN THE United States was a world leader in broadcasting and telecommunications, a role model for other countries. Its
dominance across the globe served not only a source of national pride but
also as the basis for an economic boom. For many, it seemed this could go
on forever. Indeed, even when new obtrusive technologies threatened to
destabilize the global communications order, the assumption was that the
United States would continue to be the world trendsetter in regulation and
new technology adoption.

Fifteen years into the communications revolution that began at the tail end
of the twentieth century, many Americans are shocked to discover the following: not only are they no longer the world leader in broadband Internet
and mobile telephony penetration rates, but even in terms of the number of

citizens with access to these defining technologies, they have fallen behind. Today, there are proportionately more Europeans on the Internet and using advanced 3G mobile phones than there are Americans, and the number of Chinese connected to the world's most advanced information networks surpasses the number of Americans—all this in less than fifteen years.

How Did it Happen?

This chapter will briefly discuss and describe how the United States lost its edge. It will begin by describing past trends and how good sound policy-making helped bring the United States to the forefront. It will then describe the current diffusion of communications technologies across the globe and explain how countries in Asia and Europe have surged ahead of the United States by adopting more innovative policies. This will be followed by an analysis of why U.S. policy failed and, finally, recommendations for putting it back on track.

Some Historical Background

The United States has long been the world leader in accessibility to and penetration levels of information and communications technologies (ICTs). The acknowledgment of this leadership position often obscures the fact that this leadership was not attained through the unhindered supremacy of the market and market forces. In fact, between 1921 and 1984—during which time telephone penetration grew from less than 40 percent of households to more than 90 percent—local service was provided predominantly by the Bell system, which was also the exclusive provider of long-distance service.[1] It was the regulatory environment that ensured that monopoly power would be controlled in a manner that eventually benefited consumers.

In the United States, local exchange competition during the formative years of the technology, between 1894 and 1920, was a significant factor in telephone penetration even when alternative explanatory factors, such as diffusion theory or economic growth, were taken into account.[2] In Europe, telephone service was originally provided either through "free competition between private telephone systems; competition between a private system and a governmental system; governmental regulation of private monopolies; and municipal and national ownership of governmental monopolies."[3] In Japan, the government launched the telecommunications industry in the mid-nineteenth century by investing heavily in and nurturing a few key firms that provided all telecommunications services.[4] This diversity of designs worldwide, however, soon gave way to a world in which there was little that differentiated between telecommunications systems, aside the fact that in some, the telecommunications monopoly was privately owned, and in others, it was government-owned. One exception was the gradual erosion of the monopoly in the United States. Granted to AT&T under conditions first set in the Kingsbury commitment of 1913 and then in the Willis-Graham Act of 1921, the monopoly was first corroded when AT&T seemed to be abusing it, as it appeared to be doing in the 1950s, and with the help of new (albeit not very sophisticated) technologies. The United States adopted the "Hush-a-Phone," and then in the 1960s, the "Carterfone," policies, which gradually opened the customer premises equipment market to competition. In the late 1960s, when it appeared that AT&T was again abusing the system, the MCI decision and the "computer inquiries" triggered the functional separation between local and long-distance and between basic and enhanced services, respectively. By 1984, for lack of a better solution, the United States resorted to the structural separation of AT&T.

Nonetheless, by the mid-1980s, when technological, political, and business pressures mandated the introduction of competition into the telecommunications market, most world markets were still dominated by monopolies. The break-up of the telecommunications monopolies created the same three challenges in every market: how to ensure that all potential consumers[5] of telecommunications services enjoy the fruits of competition (and avoid "redlining," "cherry picking," and "cream skimming"); how to ensure that all consumers enjoy the positive network externalities resulting from the introduction of competitive operators and are able to connect to the growing network; and how to lower barriers to entry confronted by new operators and resulting from the entrenched market position of the existing monopolies and the advantages they enjoyed, having invested in their networks while benefiting from a captive market.

Sharing these same challenges, all those countries that introduced competition into their telecommunications markets adopted a three-legged approach, which consisted of some attempt at ensuring minimum service and connectivity to all at affordable prices ("universal service"), imposing a universal obligation on all telecommunication providers to interconnect ("interconnection") and providing a mechanism for removing the most flagrant barrier to entry—the duplication of infrastructure with no guaranteed customer base ("unbundling" obligations). It was the United States that served as the role model for other nations in this regard when it adopted the Telecommunications Act of 1996.

Universal service, while not explicitly mentioned in the law, was a "mythical" principle of the system for decades,[6] while the combination of an interconnection and an unbundling requirement was a feature of the system at least since the *MCI v. AT&T* decision of 1969.[7] When MCI started providing long distance point-to-point service in the 1960s, it needed to connect to AT&T's access network in order to reach consumers. The courts awarded MCI this right of access, using the term "interconnection," when, in fact, the right awarded was a form of unbundling,[8] as MCI was enabling its customers to connect to AT&T customers, but it was also using AT&T's network to access its own customers' premises. At the time, the court ruled that AT&T's access network was an "essential facility."

The second factor behind unbundling policy in the United States and worldwide were the "computer inquiries" held throughout the 1960s, 1970s, and 1980s in order to determine the boundaries between telecommunications and computer services. The conclusion was that the *sine qua non* for the development of competition in data services was the adoption of an "open network architecture," a policy that ensured data providers with access to the customers of the telephone monopoly.[9] In South Korea, the nineteenth-century government-owned and -operated monopoly[10] was replaced in the 1980s by five common carriers that were each designated to provide a properly defined subcategory of telecommunications services,[11] while the European Parliament's directive of 1997 incorporates all three terms into one title, namely, the "Directive on interconnection in telecommunications with regard to ensuring universal service and interoperability through application of the principles of Open Network Provision (ONP)."[12]

LLU and Universal Service in the European Union and Asian Markets

Unbundled local loops (LLUs), defined as "the physical twisted metallic pair circuit in the fixed public telephone network connecting the network termination point at the subscriber's premises to the main distribution frame or equivalent facility" is one of the main features of the new regulatory framework developed by European Union policymakers in the 1990s and early 2000s. LLU was adopted in a relatively short and unambiguous document—the regulation on unbundled access to the local loop[13]—and its logic is explained in one paragraph of the preamble:

- Local loops are necessary to gain access to consumers;
- They are controlled by incumbent operators that rolled them over a long period of time while enjoying monopoly status;
- Competitors cannot match the economies of scale and coverage of incumbents.

Based on this rationale, the conclusion was inevitable: if competitive access to consumers is desired, incumbents should be forced to share the local loop with competitors while the prices they charge for this usage need to be regulated. Adopting this policy serves the basic elements of network economics, as competitors are able to overcome the main barrier to entry into the market. In adopting the LLU directive, the European Union evoked the "essential facilities" doctrine and made it an integral part of telecommunications regulation.

Universal service was also not a central element of EU policy historically. As Garnham notes,[14] European policies were designed to guarantee continuity of service and not universality of supply, while protecting the monopoly telephone companies against legal action for damages incurred for failing to provide service. Universal service, as a pan-European goal, was first mentioned in the 1992 "review of the situation in the telecommunications sector." The 1997 directive[15] accepted that the concept of universal service must evolve in order to keep pace with technological and economic changes and defined it as "a defined minimum set of services of specified quality which is available to all users independent of their geographical location and, in the light of specific national conditions, at an affordable price." This, too, echoed the Telecommunications Act enacted in the United States a year earlier, which defined universal service as "an evolving level of telecommunications services that the Commission shall establish periodically under this section, taking into account advances in telecommunications and information technologies and services." Only two member states—France and Spain—had to establish funding mechanisms for universal service, since the narrow definition of the service allowed member states to fulfil the universal service obligation without the need for subsidies.[16]

One attempt to introduce competition in telephony without adopting the three-legged model took place in Japan in 1985, when the national telecommunications provider NTT was privatized.[17] The slow development of a competitive market, however, led to a rewriting of the rules as of the second half of the 1990s. In the new rules both interconnection and unbundling regimes were introduced.[18]

While the dynamic in South Korea was somewhat different, the basic elements were the same. After fifteen years of trial-and-error with issues of market liberalization and dominant operator privatization that began in the early 1980s, the South Korean government instituted a system based on interconnection and unbundling in the second half of the 1990s. The South Korean government also assigned the incumbent operator, Korea Telecom, with the task of providing universal service.[19]

When a policymaker adopts a policy, the process of implementation, as well as the results, provides information to policymakers in other industries and in other countries.[20] As Levi-Faur[21] notes, since the 1980s an international regulatory revolution has been gathering steam, accelerated by the diffusion of regulatory ideas among different countries on a broad range of issues. In some cases, the regulatory changes in one country require other countries to adapt to the changing environment; in other cases, regulatory solutions adopted in one country are learned and copied by others.[22] In the case of telecommunications, the United States has been the trendsetter. Its influence has gone beyond the ideological extending to outright pressure on other countries to liberalize their markets.[23] As the next section demonstrates, however, the result has been paradoxical. Countries influenced by the United States, which adopted the policies it created, have gone on to achieve far better results from them.

ICT Adoption Levels Worldwide

The two most revolutionary ICTs of the 1990s are the mobile phone and the Internet. While the former has rewritten the rules of personal communications and mobile access to information, the latter has made information itself more accessible than ever before, and the protocol governing its operation is rapidly becoming the means through which all traditional modes of communications— in particular, those modes which constitute communications as an industry, namely, voice and video—transport. Comparing trends in the adoption of the telephone and television in the first eighty years of the twentieth century with trends in the adoption of mobile phones and broadband Internet since the mid-1980s should yield some enlightening policy conclusions.

To begin with, the numbers are stunning. In 1960, there were 27.3 telephones per 100 inhabitants in the United States, compared with 4.8 in France, 5.8 in Germany, and 9.6 in the United Kingdom. This gap was maintained throughout the 1970s and 1980s, and only began to narrow when European PTTs became corporations in the 1980s and telephone penetration reached near saturation levels in the United States. In the beginning of the twenty-first century, South Korea had already surged ahead in broadband Internet penetration. By 2001, more than sixteen out of every one hundred inhabitants there subscribed to the service, compared with less than five in the United States and Japan and less than one in the United Kingdom and France. By 2007, the United States was lagging behind all these countries (see figure 4.1) and many more (see figure 4.2), ranking a dismal twenty-fourth in the world. These numbers are all based on data gathered by the International Telecommunications Union, as reported by the different countries, obsolescing the debate regarding undercounting and underreporting of certain levels of connectivity that have become a major means of confronting the bad news in the United States in recent years.[24]

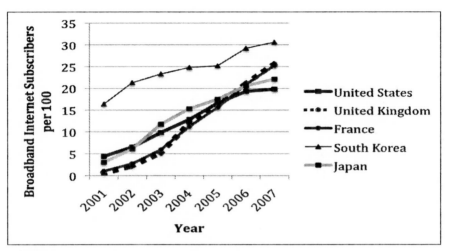

FIGURE 4.1
Broadband Penetration Trends, 2001–2007 (Source: ITU)

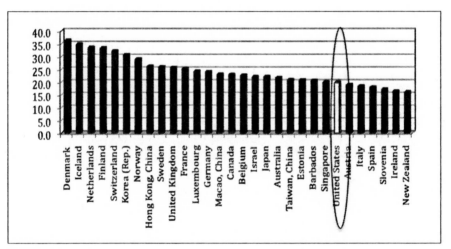

FIGURE 4.2
Broadband Penetration, Top Thirty Economies, 2007 (Source: ITU)

Although mobile phones were invented in the United States, by 2006, their penetration across the European Union had reached almost 93 percent, hitting 100 percent in eight member states, according to a EU report,[25] and more than thirty European countries by 2008.[26] A U.S. research firm estimates that 84 percent of Americans, including consumer, business, and double users, had mobile phones at the end of 2007 and that the rate would exceed 100 percent only in 2013.[27]

There is an ongoing debate in telecommunications policy circles over whether LLU promotes broadband access and can, therefore, explain the difference between the United States and other countries with regard to broadband penetration. A European study[28] maintains that while the U.S. broadband market is heading into a duopoly of incumbent telecommunications and cable network operators, "LLU and access obligations play important roles throughout Europe and have contributed to high deployment rates in countries lacking alternative infrastructure as well as in countries with competing platforms."[29] Line-sharing (a type of LLU) has also been identified as the engine behind the spectacular growth of DSL service in Japan, where its introduction at the end of 2000 brought the number of DSL subscribers up from 152,000 to 8 million in three years(!).[30] At the same time, LLU played a negligible role in the impressive Korean breakthrough,[31] which was fueled by fierce infrastructure competition that led to quality services at a low fixed price.[32] It should be noted, however, as will be discussed below, that this competition was achieved through active government intervention.

Clearly, managing LLU access and pricing is regulation-intensive.[33] Some maintain that LLU should be adopted as policy only temporarily[34] and that the introduction of "sunset clauses" provides new entrants with strong incentives to invest while allowing them to enter markets and compete in services alone while acquiring important knowledge about their new market.[35] Others believe that LLU may deter the development of the economically desired facility-based competition,[36] that sunset clauses do not improve social welfare,[37] and that LLU is a policy that has failed outright because it was poorly enforced.[38] The figures, however, appear to support the advocates, and quite impressively. Bauer, Berne, and Maitland[39] conclude that more aggressive policies in the European Union regarding LLU help explain the differences in Internet access in different parts of Europe. Marcus[40] observes that about one in four of the twelve million new Internet subscribers in Europe, during the twelve months preceding July 2004, can be explained by regulatory support for competitive access—fully unbundled lines, shared access, bitstream access, or simple resale—all made possible as a result of the LLU regime adopted by the European Union. Garcia-Murillo[41] asserts that unbundling has a significant positive impact on the availability of broadband services and that it contributes to a substantial improvement in broadband deployment in middle-income countries but not in their high-income counterparts. De Bijl and Peitz[42] conclude that while LLU may have failed to generate competition in voice telephony markets, due to their low levels of profitability, it has "large potential as a means to offer broadband access to end-users for entrants without local networks"[43] and Fransman[44] concludes that while unbundling by itself is not a definitive determinant of performance, it cannot be ruled out as having an effect.

Kim, Kim, and Kim[45] argue that incumbents may, in fact, benefit from enforced LLU, because when a competitor's request is denied, it may be forced to build its own facilities, thereby denying the incumbent of rental income. Gideon[46] contends that the incentive for investing in cost-reducing innovation did not diminish as a result of mandatory unbundling, as some operators often claim. Her assertion, supported by earlier studies like Kim, Kim, and Kim's,[47] is also backed by recent OECD data. As figure 4.3 demonstrates, the countries in which the percentages of fiber connections in total broadband subscriptions are the highest are Japan, Korea, and Sweden, all of which enforce LLU and boast higher penetration rates than the United States. Sweden is even considering, as will be discussed further on, enforcing the structural separation of its incumbent telephone company, an extreme version of LLU. The European Union reports that because of new regulatory measures, in particular those pertaining to pricing, and because of increased investment in infrastructure by new operators, the market for shared lines and unbundled local loops increased in 2003–2004 by 110 percent.[48] As for the Japanese, they apparently "think long term," as an October 2007 *New York Times* story reported, quoting a Japanese analyst.[49]

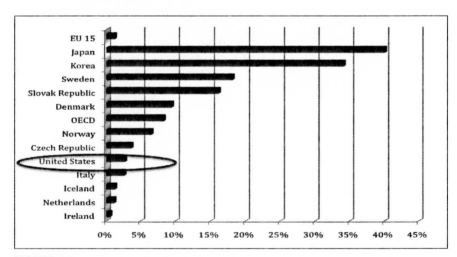

FIGURE 4.3
Percentage of Fiber Connections in Total Broadband Subscription (Source: OECD)

Government Role in Development

As experience in the field of telecommunications in general and broadband in particular has accumulated, new ideas on how to encourage broadband penetration through competition have been floated. Schechter,[50] for example, demonstrates that if customers owned the local loop themselves, "virtually all of the difficult problems involved in pricing interconnection disappear."[51] While local loop ownership has remained an academic idea running up the flagpole, another policy idea that has garnered scholarly and regulatory attention was furthering local loop unbundling and enforcing structural separation of the local loop from the parent incumbent's network. Indeed, the concept known internationally as "loopco" has its detractors, who believe it has limited benefits, is "potentially adverse," and a "high risk gamble,"[52] as its risks outweigh its benefits;[53] however, others argue that structural separation is more likely to increase innovation than is intrusive regulation.[54]

Some European countries, as well as the European Union, have launched policies promoting structural or functional separation of the local loop in order to further broadband penetration. This, despite already impressive levels of broadband penetration, which might have mandated a "wait and see" policy. In August 2007, the European Union's media commissioner announced that the structural separation approach, adopted by regulators in the United Kingdom to enhance competition, is a potential template for other European regulators and operators.[55] While the eventual path taken by the European Union was less extreme—namely, functional—separation,[56] other member states followed the United Kingdom's lead and introduced different levels of separation among network elements in order to promote further competition. Among those countries are Sweden,[57] which enjoys a lead in both penetration and deployment of fiber, as well as Italy,[58] which is a relative laggard in Europe when it comes to broadband.

This constant search for innovative ideas to achieve higher levels of broadband penetration is rooted in systems, though different in so many respects that share one common belief—that governments, by virtue of the fact that they are representatives of the public interest, have the right to set goals as well as take measures to achieve them. Indeed, it is more common than not worldwide that governments in the most developed of nations adopt sweeping information and communications strategies.

South Korea

A country that lends itself to study in this respect is South Korea. Government involvement was crucial in South Korea's recovery from the destruction of the Korean War and its transition into an industrialized economy, the first stage of which involved the launching of a wide literacy campaign.[59] The government was also actively involved in the development and liberalization of the country's telecommunications sector.[60] The introduction of partial liberalization was followed by a more intensive liberalization policy, incremental in nature, which was constantly being fine-tuned[61] in response to changing economic and international conditions.[62] Indeed, the government has been identified as the "key-driver" in South Korean efforts to adopt next-generation technologies and "[l]ong-term ICT strategy now stretches back over 20 years as a series of structured programs. Telecommunications is seen as a part of this, and also as a unifying policy for the nation."[63]

Broadband adoption is a key example of such a program. The South Korean government laid out the blueprint for an information structure in the early 1990s, and set as its goal the universal installation of high-speed networks. Government investment coupled with competitive policies drove the realization of these early goals, and while the plan to provide universal fiber to the home (FTTH) by 2015 was adjusted to the reality of technical progress in other technologies, South Korea continues to be a world leader in broadband adoption and continues to be ranked number one by the International Telecommunications Union in its Digital Opportunity Index, an index that measures ICT development across countries using conventional indicators of opportunity (affordability and accessibility), infrastructure (telephone, Internet, computer, and handheld device density), and utilization (usage and quality of service) (see figure 4.4).

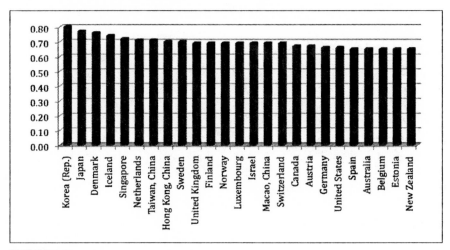

FIGURE 4.4
Digital Opportunity Index, 2007 (Source: ITU)

In 2006, while leading the world in ICT indicators, South Korea launched yet another innovative and ambitious initiative, the "u-Korea Master Plan" aimed at making it the world's first "ubiquitous society." The plan calls for a society based on four Us—a society in which everyone is "warmly accepted" (universal) and can use services easily (usable) while technologies interact harmoniously (unisonous) and new values are constantly created (upgrade).[64] Chairing the Informatization Promotion Committee formed by the government to lead the project was none other than the prime minister.

Japan

While it is common to lump Korea and Japan together under the category of Asian super powers, their paths to development have clearly diverged: Japan is a traditional and advanced industrial economy, while Korea belongs to the group of newly industrialized economies (NIEs) that includes Taiwan, Singapore, and Hong Kong.[65] In both cases, however, economic success can be attributed to state interventionist policies.[66]

Liberalization and privatization in Japan followed a similar path to that in other industrialized nations in the West, starting at around the same time in the 1980s.[67] The introduction of digital technologies that challenged telecommunications policymaking in Europe and the United States in the 1990s had a similar effect in Japan.[68] Although Japan initially lagged behind Europe and the United States, not yet having decided the proper policy path to take by the middle of the 2000s, it had become the country with the world's cheapest and fastest broadband service. It achieved this position of dominance thanks to the combination of a concentration of power in the hands of a government-controlled central PTT and a rigid open access policy.[69] As mentioned before, Japan also boasts the highest level of fiber to the home in the world.

Japanese policymakers, however, are not ones to rest on their laurels. In January 2001, the Ministry of Internal Affairs and Communication launched an ambitious new strategy that was to transform the goal of ICT policy so that by 2005 Japan would become the world's most advanced IT nation. The new policy, aptly named u-Japan, aims at "realizing a society where anytime, anywhere and by anyone benefits from IT," a "ubiquitous network society."[70]

Europe[71]

European policymaking is also characterized by constant adjustments to the realities at hand. The European Union reviews and adjusts its policies to changing technological and market conditions every two to three years. The first cross-European liberalization policy was only introduced in 1988, but by 1990, the European Union had identified the connection between growth in the information sector and economic competitiveness on a global scale and linked it to liberalization policies. By 1993, it had set a 1998 deadline for full liberalization of voice telephony, allowing member states and incumbent

PTTs a lengthy period of adjustment.[72] In January 1995, a "Green Paper on the liberalization of telecommunications infrastructure and cable television networks" was published, and as a result, in September of that year, the European Council urged the European Commission to create a regulatory framework that led to a series of directives enacted in 1997.

This initial European regulatory framework was reassessed over the next two years,[73] the outcome being a new regulatory framework that became law in 2003.[74] The issue deemed most urgent in this new regulatory framework was the adoption of a compulsory local loop unbundling regime. Hence, as early as December 31, 2000, the requirement that incumbent telephone operators unbundle their networks was passed into law. So while the focus of liberalization in 1998 had been voice telephony, by 2003, policy was aimed at enhancing Internet access.

The 2006 Review of the Regulatory Framework[75] was already designed to assess the efficacy of the 2003 regulatory framework and was the first step in the launch of i2010—another ambitious rewrite of telecommunication policies aimed at furthering access to and speed of ICTs that is being formulated and debated as this book goes to press in the summer of 2008.

This flurry of activity in the European Union has not left the member states indifferent. As mentioned before, both leading and laggard states started experimenting with different levels of functional and structural separation in order to further broadband penetration, speed and access. Other member states, in particular those enjoying high penetration rates, as figure 4.2 demonstrates, set ambitious goals for themselves. If the Asian theme is ubiquity, the European is "information society for all." Thus, the Swedish government, ranked ninth internationally in broadband penetration, decided in 2003 to appoint an IT Policy Strategy Group whose mandate, as stipulated in its report "Broadband for growth, innovation and competitiveness,"[76] was to advise the government and to be a driving force in achieving the IT policy goal of an "information society for all"[77] while working together with other groups to maintain Sweden's "vanguard position in the IT area." The strategy group set higher standards for its mission than those it perceived were envisioned by the Swedish parliament[78] and concluded that for the information society to realize its full potential, the goal of policy should be to close the digital gap, to implement an electronic democracy, and to design the policy in a manner that is both technologically neutral and future proof. The importance of the government in ensuring the digital gap is as small as possible was thus highlighted by the group's report.

France, which is ranked eleventh internationally and surpassed the United States in broadband penetration only in 2006, announced in May 2008 an ambitious goal of "broadband for all" by 2012.[79] This plan calls on the government to support the creation of digital content. These initiatives can be seen as paralleling the European Union's i2010 strategy—"a European Information Society for growth and employment"—to accelerate the roll-out of advanced broadband communications and create an open and competitive single market for information society and media services within the European Union. The European Commission has set as a target that high-speed broadband lines would be available everywhere in Europe by 2010. At the same time, it has encouraged member states to adopt and implement national broadband strategies. As demonstrated, the individual targets set vary from country to country.

European countries that are not members of the European Union have set similar goals. Norway's Ministry of Government Administration and Reform issued a report to the Storting titled "An Information Society for All,"[80] which acknowledges its leadership position in broadband penetration (ranked seventh worldwide) but states that "the present government holds that those countries that pursue a policy which taps into the potentials and reaps the rewards of ICT while successfully countering or mitigating unwanted effects also stand to achieve higher growth and better welfare than countries that fail to deal with the need for change."[81] Its declared objective is that all Norwegians be offered a connection to broadband Internet by the end of 2007, "to which end public funds will be used to assist in achieving broadband extension in areas where this is not commercially viable."[82]

How Did We Get Here?

It is probably axiomatic by now to say that it is a matter of national interest to promote access to broadband, no less so than it is a matter of public and individual interests. An examination of data on international broadband trends and rates makes it unequivocally clear that while Europe and Asia are soaring ahead, the United States, the original pioneer of regulation and Internet technology adoption, is falling behind. What is it that distinguishes Europe and Asia from the United States, and what can the United States learn from the experiences of others to revive broadband penetration?

While European and Asian regulators have been devising and restructuring policy with an eye toward promoting competition, benefiting consumers, and providing broadband access for all, regulators in the United States have spent nine years and countless hours in court only to reach a solution that effectively eliminated the unbundling regime[83] and caused the United States to lose its position of supremacy worldwide. While the United States has refrained from formulating goals and setting standards for deployment of broadband in rural and poor areas, Asian and European governments have not only devised explicit plans to do so but have set ambitious goals for achieving universal connectivity in the near future.

With regard to policies that promote competition, while in Europe and Asia, it is the local loop, and the local loop alone, that is required to be unbundled, U.S. law requires mandatory unbundling of all network elements that the FCC should deem necessary. While the Europeans have left it up to their regulatory authorities to determine whether "significant market power" lies with the incumbent while determining *a priori* the network element to be unbundled, American law defines *a priori* the incumbents who are required to unbundle and leaves it up to the regulators to determine which elements should be unbundled. As a result of this approach, the Europeans were able to mobilize a far weaker and decentralized governing body to adopt policies in conflict with the interests of incumbent operators for the purpose of promoting competition the central "government" perceived as serving the public interest and contributing to the more rapid penetration of advanced technologies. The outcome of the American approach has been stagnation.

Even though a hastened deployment of fiber to the home is to be expected by the elimination of an unbundling requirement, the U.S. performance has been dismal in face of a very vigorous regulatory activity. As of 2003, fiber providers were relieved of their unbundling obligations,[84] and as of 2004, this applied to multiple dwelling units as well.[85] But, as figure 4.3 demonstrates, the United States lags far behind other countries with more rigorous competition regimes when it comes to fiber deployment.

An indication of the extent of the crisis in U.S. telecommunications policy is provided by the most recent draft of a strategic plan published for public discussion by the FCC in June 2008.[86] While the Asian and European strategic plans set concrete goals and timetables, the FCC has very little to offer on these counts. The FCC's vision, as delineated in the plan, is that "all Americans should have affordable access to robust and reliable broadband products and services" and the objective derived from that is that the "Commission shall promote the availability of broadband to all Americans." Clearly, there is not much in the way of detail here.

Conclusion

The literature on deployment of broadband has identified two key issues in national policy debates: 1) Are market-led policies preferable to state-led policies, or are state-led policies preferable to market-led policies? 2) Is broadband a public good or a consumer good? Indeed, there is no answer that holds true for every type of political and cultural system or for every type of service offered over broadband. Simplifying the debate, however, along these lines may help the outside observer seeking to understand at least some of the reason for the decline of the American communications empire.

This chapter demonstrates that differences in broadband policy development in the United States and other countries can be attributed to the different views held on the two fundamental questions raised above. It would be an exaggeration to say that Japan, Korea, and the European Union do not appreciate the role of the market in the deployment of communications technologies or that they do not understand the driving force behind attractive consumer goods. At the same time, it would not be far from the truth to say that policymakers in the United States have forsaken the role of government in promoting the development of public goods on the nation's communications networks.

Asian and European policies take into account that there is a point where public and private interests intersect to promote the national interest. As such, these policies include technological neutrality on the one hand, and fierce enforcement of rules of competition and fairness on the other. They incorporate ambitious national goals and deadlines, and at the same time, foster creativity and ensure equality. Policy in the United States, by contrast, has tilted to one side: heavily influenced by corporate interests, it has all but forsaken the goal of providing equitable services to all its citizens and, most disturbingly, it has allowed government to dodge its responsibility of guaranteeing communications for all.

A balance must be struck—one that reflects a sensible equilibrium between public and private, consumer and citizen, market and government interests. As other countries have demonstrated, striking such a balance is critical to policy success. The following chapters will provide concrete recommendations for achieving this goal of pushing the United States back on the right track.

Notes

1. Claude S. Fischer, "The Revolution in Rural Telephony: 1900–1920," *Journal of Social History* 21, no. 1 (1987): 5–26.

2. Krishna P. Jayakar, "Local Exchange Competition in Early U.S. Network Development: Considerations for Developing Countries," *Telecommunications Policy* 23 (1999), 375–87.

3. A. N. Holcombe, *Public Ownership of Telephones on the Continent of Europe* (Cambridge, MA: Harvard University Press, 1911), ix.

4. Marie Anchordoguy, "Nippon Telegraph and Telephone Company (NTT) and the Building of a Telecommunications Industry in Japan," *The Business History Review* 75, no. 3 (2001): 507–41.

5. The term "consumers" rather than citizens is used here intentionally, as the process described is one in which competition is introduced in order to create markets.

Indeed, as I further clarify, this limited view of the affected public as "consumers first" contributes to the limitations of the policy.

6. Milton Mueller, *Universal Service* (Cambridge, MA: MIT Press, 1997).

7. *MCI Communications Corporation and MCI Telecommunications Corporation v. American Telephone and Telegraph Company*, 708 F.2d 1081 (Seventh Cir.) (Cert. denied).

8. Amit M. Schejter, "'From All My Teachers I Have Grown Wise, and From My Students More Than Anyone Else': What Lessons Can the U.S. Learn from Broadband Policies in Europe?" *International Communication Gazette* (forthcoming).

9. Robert Cannon, "The Legacy of the Federal Communications Commission's Computer Inquiries," *Federal Communications Law Journal* 55, no.2 (2005): 168–206.

10. Kenji Kushida and Seung-Youn Oh, "The Political Economies of Broadband Development in Korea and Japan," *Asian Survey* 47, no. 3 (2007): 481–504.

11. Shin Cho, Byung-il Choi, and Seon-Kyou Choi, "Restructuring the Korean Telecommunications Market: Evolution and Challenges Ahead," *Telecommunications Policy* 20, no. 5 (1996): 357–73.

12. Official Journal L 199, 26/07/1997, 32–52, europa.eu.int/ISPO/infosoc/telecompolicy/en/dir97-33en.htm.

13. Regulation (EC) No 2887/2000 of the European Parliament and of the Council of 18 December 2000 on unbundled access to the local loop, OJ L 336/4, 30.12.2000.

14. Nicholas Garnham, "Universal Service," in *Telecom Reform: Principles, Policies and Regulatory Practices*, ed. W. Melody (Lyngsbury: Technical University of Denmark, 2001), 199–204.

15. See note 12.

16. Maria Michalis, "The Debate over Universal Service in the European Union: Plus ca Change, Plus c'est la Meme Chose," *Convergence* 8, no. 2 (2002): 80–98.

17. Hidenori Fuke, "The Spectacular Growth of DSL in Japan and its Implications," *Communications and Strategies* 52, no. 4 (2003): 175–91.

18. See Kushida and Oh, "Political Economies."

19. Chang-Ho Yoon, "Liberalization Policy, Industry Structure and Productivity Changes in Korea's Telecommunications Industry," *Telecommunications Policy* 23 (1999): 289–306.

20. David Lazer, "Regulatory Capitalism as a Networked Order: The International System as an Informational Network," *Annals of the American Academy of Political and Social Science* 598 (2005): 52–66.

21. David Levi-Faur, "The Global Diffusion of Regulatory Capitalism," *Annals of the American Academy of Political and Social Science* 598 (2005): 12–32.

22. Zachary Elkins and Beth Simmons, "On Waves, Clusters, and Diffusion: A Conceptual Framework," *Annals of the American Academy of Political and Social Science* 598 (2005): 12–32.

23. See Yoon, "Liberalization Policy"; Kushida and Oh, "Political Economies."

24. As demonstrated, for example by an official letter from David Gross, the U.S. Coordinator for International Communications and Information Policy to the

Secretary General of the OECD in which Ambassador Gross disputes the OECD findings regarding broadband penetration, citing such "facts" as "[t]he United States has more Internet and broadband users and more Wi-Fi hot spots than any other country in the world" (www.state.gov/documents/organization/86519.pdf).

25. www.fabtech.org/content/view/1278.

26. Directorate-General for the Information Society and Media (2008). E-Communications Household Survey (can be accessed at ec.europa.eu/public_opinion /archives/ebs/ebs_293_full_en.pdf).

27. www.snl.com/press/20070823.asp.

28. Arnold Picot and Christian Wernick, "The Role of Government in Broadband Access," *Telecommunications Policy* 31 (2007): 660–74.

29. See Picot and Wernick, "Broadband Access," 672.

30. See Fuke "Spectacular Growth."

31. See Picot and Wernick "Broadband Access."

32. Heejin Lee, Robert M. O'Keefe, and Kyounglim Yun, "The Growth of Broadband and Electronic Commerce in South Korea: Contributing Factors," *The Information Society* 19 (2003): 81–93.

33. Maria Michalis, "Local Competition and the Role of Regulation: The EU Debate and Britain's Experience," *Telcommunications Policy* 25 (2001): 759–76.

34. Chris Doyle, "Local Loop Unbundling and Regulatory Risk," *Journal of Network Industries* 1 (2000): 33–54.

35. Kostis Christodoulou and Kiriakos Vlahos, "Implications of Regulation for Entry and Investment in the Local Loop," *Telecommunications Policy* 25 (2001): 743–57.

36. Marc Bourreau and Pinar Dogan, "Service-Based vs. Facility-Based Competition in Local Access Networks," *Information Economics and Policy* 16, no. 2 (2004): 287–306.

37. Marc Bourreau and Pinar Dogan, "Unbundling the Local Loop," *European Economic Review* 49 (2005): 173–99.

38. Pablo T. Spiller and Ulset, Svein, "Why Local Loop Unbundling Fails?" (paper presented at the Nordic Workshop on Transaction Cost Economics in Business Administration, Bergen, Norway, 20–21 June 2003), mora.rente.nhh.no/conferences /TCEWorkshop2003/papers/Ulset_Spiller.pdf (8 July 2008).

39. Johannes Bauer, Michel Berne, and Carlene Maitland, "Internet Access in the European Union and in the United States," *Telematics and Informatics* 19, no. 2 (2002): 117–37.

40. Scott J. Marcus, "Broadband Adoption in Europe," *IEEE Communications Magazine*, 2005, www.comsoc.org/ci1/Public/2005/apr/ (8 July 2007).

41. Martha Garcia-Murillo, "International Broadband Deployment: The Impact of Unbundling: Unbundling Facing New Challenges," *Communications and Strategies* 57 (2005): 83–105.

42. Paul W. J. De Bijl and Martin Peitz, "Local Loop Unbundling in Europe: Experience, Prospects, and Policy Challenges," *Communications and Strategies*, no. 57 (2005): 33–57.

43. De Bijl and Peitz "Local Loop Unbundling," 54.

44. Martin Fransman, *Global Broadband Battles: Why the U.S. and Europe Lag While Asia Leads* (Stanford, CA: Stanford Business Books, 2006).

45. Jeong-Yoo Kim, Sang Taek Kim, and Dong-Ju Kim, "Local Loop Unbundling and Antitrust Policy," *Information Economics and Policy* 12 (2000): 393–412.

46. Carolyn Gideon, "Technology Policy by Default: Shaping Communications Technology Through Regulatory Policy," in *Shaping Science and Technology Policy: The Next Generation of Research*, ed. D. Guston and D. Sarewitz (Madison: University of Wisconsin Press, 2006), 256–72.

47. See note 43.

48. Tenth Report on European Electronic Communications Regulation and Markets can be accessed at europa.eu/scadplus/leg/en/lvb/l24217e.htm, accessed on 22 August 2006.

49. NKen Belson, "Unlike U.S., Japanese Push Fiber Over Profit," *New York Times*, 3 October 2007.

50. P. B. Schechter, "Customer Ownership of the Local Loop: A Solution to the Problem of Interconnection," *Telecommunications Policy* 20, no. 8 (1996): 573–84.

51. Schechter, 584.

52. Martin Cave, "Is LoopCo the Answer," *Info: The Journal of Policy, Regulation, and Strategy for Telecommunications* 4, no. 4 (2002): 25–31.

53. Patrick Xavier and Dimitri Ypsilanti, "Is the Case for Structural Separation of the Local Loop Persuasive?," *Info: the Journal of Policy, Regulation, and Strategy for Telecommunications* 6, no. 2 (2004): 74–92.

54. Cadman, Richard and Helen Carrier, "Market Structure and Innovation in the Telecommunications Sector: A Framework for Assessing the Impact of Structural Separation of the Incumbent," *Info: The Journal of Policy, Regulation, and Strategy for Telecommunications* 4, no. 6 (2002): 9–15.

55. Laitner, Sarah and Philip Stafford, "EU Drops a Broadband Bombshell," *The Financial Times*, 30 August 2007.

56. Morgan, Kevin, "The European Debate About Structural Separation: Possible Implications for Australia," *Telecommunications Journal of Australional Encyclopedia of the Social and Behavioral Sciences*, eds. N. Smelser and P. Bates (Amsterdam: Elsevier, 2004), 3957–62.

57. www.telecompaper.com/news/printarticle.aspx?Id=199782&yr=2008.

58. www.marketwatch.com/news/story/regulator-wants-more-powe...73 -B0ED-7D6F88A29B0C%7d&siteid=aolRss&print=true&dist=printTop.

59. V. Chibber and D. Guthrie, "East Asian Studies: Economics," in *International Encyclopedia of the Social and Behavioral Sciences*, eds. N. Smelser and P. Bates (Amsterdam: Elsevier, 2004), 3957–62.

60. Eun-Ju Kim, "Telecommunications Development in the Republic of Korea: An Alternative Model," *Telecommunications Policy* 17, no. 2 (1993): 118–38.

61. See Yoon, "Liberalization Policy."

62. Dal Yong Jin, "Political and Economic Processes in the Privatization of the

Korea Telecommunications Industry: A Case Study of Korea Telecom, 1987–2003," *Telecommunications Policy* 30 (2006): 3–13.

63. Simon Forge and Erik Bohlin, "Managed Innovation in Korea in Telecommunications—Moving Towards 4G Mobile at a National Level," *Telematics and Informatics* 25 (2008): 292–308.

64. u-Korea policy: www.ipc.go.kr/ipceng/policy/enews_view.jsp?num=2146.

65. See Chibber and Guthrie, "East Asian Studies: Economics."

66. Dwight H. Perkins, "There Are At Least Three Models of East Asian Development," *World Development* 22, no. 4 (1994): 655–61.

67. Hajime Oniki, Tae Hoon Oum, Rodney Stevenson, and Yimin Zhang, "The Productivity Effect of the Liberalization of Japanese Telecommunication Policy," *The Journal of Productivity Analysis* 5 (1994): 63–79.

68. Mitsuo Igarashi, "Outlook on the Second Reform of Info-Communications in Japan," *Japan and the World Economy* 9 (1997): 431–39.

69. Takanori Ida, "The Broadband Market in Japan," in *Japanese Telecommunications: Market and policy in transition*, ed. R. Taplin and M. Wakui (London and New York: Routledge, 2006), 37–64.

70. u-Japan policy: www.soumu.go.jp/menu_02/ict/u-japan_en/new_outline01.html.

71. A major part of this analysis appears in A. Schejter (forthcoming), "'From All My Teachers.'"

72. Leonard Waverman and Esen Sirel, "European Telecommunications Markets on the Verge of Full Liberalization," *Journal of Economic Perspectives* 11, no. 4 (1997): 113–26.

73. See 1999 Communications Review (europa.eu.int/ISPO/infosoc/telecompolicy/review99/com2000-239en.pdf, accessed on 21 August 2006).

74. For a general introduction of the 2003 regulatory framework, see europa.eu.int/information_society/topics/telecoms/regulatory/new_rf/text_en.htm#Introduction, accessed on 21 August 2006. The five individual directives that comprise the new framework were Directive 2002/21/EC of the European Parliament and of the Council of 7 March 2002 on a common regulatory framework for electronic communications networks and services OJ L 108/33, 24.4.2002 (aka "the Framework Directive"); Directive 2002/19/EC of the European Parliament and of the Council of 7 March 2002 on access to, and interconnection of, electronic communications networks and associated facilities, OJ L 108/7, 24.4.2002 ("Access Directive"); Directive 2002/20/EC of the European Parliament and of the Council of 7 March 2002 on the authorization of electronic communications networks and services, OJ L 108/21 ("Authorization Directive"); Directive 2002/22/EC of the European Parliament and of the Council of 7 March 2002 on universal service and users' rights relating to electronic communications networks and services OJ L 108/51, 24.4.2002 ("Universal Service Directive"); Directive 2002/58/EC of the European Parliament and of the Council of 12 July 2002 concerning the processing of personal data and the protection of privacy in the electronic communications sector ("Data Privacy Directive").

75. COM(2006)68 final, Brussels, 20.2.2006.

76. www.sweden.gov.se/download/9a39e612.pdf?major=1&minor=76048&cn=

attachmentPublDuplicator_0_attachment.

77. See p. 7.

78. See p. 11.

79. www.telecompaper.com/news/printarticle.aspx?cid=621337.

80. www.regjeringen.no/upload/FAD/Vedlegg/IKT- politikk/stm17_2006-2007_eng.pdf.

81. See p. 3.

82. See p. 20.

83. See FCC decision, hraunfoss.fcc.gov/edocs_public/attachmatch/FCC-05-150A1. pdf, and accompanying news release, hraunfoss.fcc.gov/edocs_public/attachmatch /DOC-260433A1.pdf.

84. hraunfoss.fcc.gov/edocs_public/attachmatch/DOC-231344A1.pdf, and hraunfoss.fcc.gov/edocs_public/attachmatch/FCC-03-36A1.pdf.

85. hraunfoss.fcc.gov/edocs_public/attachmatch/FCC-04-191A1.pdf.

86. www.fcc.gov/omd/strategicplan/.

Part II

Infrastructures and Industries

5

Competition and Investment in Wireline Broadband

Marvin Ammori

Introduction

THIS CHAPTER SUGGESTS WAYS OF increasing private investment and competition in those U.S. wireline networks that provide open, high-speed Internet service or broadband. Policies that increase competition in wireline broadband services would increase investment, improve the network infrastructure, reduce prices, and increase innovation and broadband penetration.[1]

Today, the average American has access to one or two broadband options at speeds of around two to eight mbps. The policy recommendations included in this chapter would ensure that Americans have access, within four years, to multiple, competitive, scalable, and affordable connections that provide symmetrical speeds of at least one hundred mbps in our biggest cities and towns. Within ten years, this scalable infrastructure should be providing symmetrical, competitive, fiber-to-the-home connections providing speeds of one thousand mbps or more.

Over the last decade, the United States has abandoned pro-competition regulatory policies in favor of the "magic" of limited and ineffective competition between an incumbent local telephone monopoly and an incumbent local cable monopoly. Among those policies abandoned were "unbundling"—a policy that enabled new participants in the market to lease parts of an incumbent's wireline network to serve customers—and other "open access" or "wholesale access" policies, which allowed new entrants to buy capacity at wholesale rates and sell it to end-users at retail rates. These policies helped new competitors overcome the nearly impossible feat of building an entire local network from scratch to serve even one customer, while at the same time, competing with an entrenched incumbent that had been able to build its network without worrying about competition and had been able to enjoy a guaranteed return on investment. Although incumbents argued that unbundling and similar policies were doomed to fail, evidence from other countries suggests otherwise.

By abandoning pro-competition policies, the United States ceded its world leadership position in Internet penetration. Our global competitors, who today outrank us, have, on the other hand, been able to adopt these pro-competition policies successfully. Twenty-eight of the thirty OECD countries, for example, have adopted unbundling.[2] Carriers in these countries invest in and offer networks with higher speeds, greater capacity, greater availability, and lower consumer prices. Consequently, a person living in New York is required to pay around $100 more a month today for the same Internet speed connection as a person living in Paris and has fewer companies to choose from.[3]

This chapter puts forth several proposals for addressing this problem, including reimplementing unbundling and wholesale access policy to ensure robust broadband competition and improve implementation. While wireless policy, as well as competition and investment by local cities and cooperatives, is valuable, these issues are discussed in other chapters.[4] This chapter will focus on private competition.

Investment and Competition Problems

All Americans should have access to multiple, competitively priced offerings of high-speed, neutral, symmetrical connections.[5] Networks for providing Internet are basic infrastructure, like roads, canals, sanitation, and educational institutions, which have diverse uses and provide various benefits to our economy and democracy.[6] Unlike most basic infrastructure, which the government provides, private markets provide telecommunications services. Government can and must properly construct these private markets to ensure that they are efficient and meet defined social objectives. The proposals in this chapter seek to address two related problems in the private market: lack of investment and lack of competition.

Regarding investment, even in our biggest cities, when it comes to the capacity and speed of broadband, we lag far behind many of our global competitors, including Japan, Korea, France, and the United Kingdom. We have fallen behind in rural deployment (ten million households lack any wireline option), adoption (nearly half the population does not have broadband connections), price (we pay about twenty times more than Japan per megabit),[7] and the capacity and speed of our networks (half of our networks provide less than 2.5 mbps in either direction). Indeed, the fact that the United States has a large rural population[8] and relatively high poverty rate[9] plays a role in this. But even wealthy people in America's biggest cities do not have access to the type of broadband infrastructure that has been available for years in places like Tokyo, Seoul, and Paris.

To have such networks, we should be investing in connections constructed of fiber strands that reach the home. Rather than endorse a particular technology, we should be setting goals and working to ensure that many different technologies can help meet these goals. An interim goal could be technologically neutral: providing Americans with access, within four years, to competing, affordable connections that provide symmetrical speeds of at least one hundred mbps in our biggest cities and towns. With regard to telephone technologies, according to the Swedish telecommunications regulator, "fiber to the building" with copper wiring can provide one hundred mbps, and fiber to the curbside can provide forty mbps. Forty mbps is far faster than the average speed now available in the United States and should be available universally.[10] Cable technologies could reach such speeds if cable companies were to stop devoting almost all of their capacity (some estimates put it at up to 124/125 of capacity)[11] and monetary investments to television and started to devote more of their capacity and cash to the open broadband that consumers want.[12]

The long-term goal, however, should be to have a nearly infinitely scalable open network that provides symmetrical speeds far higher than one hundred mbps. Today, it appears the only technology up to this task is fiber to the home, which can provide up to one thousand mbps, if not more.[13] While expensive to deploy, partly because of the cost of laying lines, fiber is cheaper to maintain and upgrade once it is deployed than other technologies.[14] Practically speaking, fiber investments in any part of a network tend to increase that network's capacity and flexibility and, therefore, help attain this goal.[15] Because of the benefits of fiber, and its nearly infinite scalability, government policy should encourage deployment of fiber to the home, but, at the same time, it should be open to all technologies.[16]

Second, not only do we lack access to world-class networks, we lack competitive choice among broadband service providers. In the dial-up world, consumers had considerable choice among dial-up Internet service providers (ISPs). Drawing on the rules that applied to traditional telephone service, consumers would and could choose service from (or "dial-up") an ISP that was not the local telephone company—such as America Online, Earthlink, Juno, NetZero, or any of hundreds of smaller local ISPs. For broadband, however, consumers are generally stuck with the ISP owned by the local telephone or cable monopoly, because neither monopoly is required by law to permit access to competing ISPs.[17] Most businesses have access only to the telephone network. Other options, like satellite, wireless cell phones, wireless local loop, or broadband delivered over power lines, are inadequate because the connections are too slow, expensive, or simply unavailable.[18] For example, satellite and powerlines combined have less than a 1 percent market share. As a result, incumbent cable or telecommunications companies provide nearly 99 percent of all residential broadband connections.[19] Two companies (or one) is, at best, a highly concentrated market under almost any definition of competition, and even more so when the market is not open to new entrants, because of high barriers to entry.[20]

We also need to introduce competition on each of these platforms— telephone and cable—which unbundling and open access can do.[21] Competition should lead to greater consumer choice, lower prices, greater availability and variety of products, less deadweight loss, and increased investment.[22]

Historical Background

Over the past decade, the United States made the mistake of abandoning some important policies designed to promote competition. The most significant legislative event in recent modern telecommunications history was the 1996 Telecommunications Act, which amended the basic framework of the nation's communications law, the 1934 Communications Act. The 1996 act was meant to promote the development of the Internet and other two-way technologies. Section 706 of the 1996 act empowers the FCC and each state regulatory commission to "encourage the deployment on a reasonable and timely basis of advanced telecommunications capability," or broadband, "to all Americans." Another section of the act stipulates that it is the "policy of the United States . . . to promote the continued development of the Internet," "to preserve the vibrant and competitive free market that presently exists for the Internet," and "to encourage the development of technologies which maximize user control over what information is received by individuals, families, and schools who use the Internet and other interactive computer services."[23]

The act also sought to promote competition among local telephone networks in several ways, notably by mandating unbundling—or forced leasing of network elements—with wholesale access for data already required.[24]

Congress left almost all the particulars of unbundling to the FCC. The FCC had to determine which elements would be unbundled (in the event that the entrants' ability to offer service would be "impaired" without access to an element) and at what cost (the guideline being that the FCC price be "based on the cost (determined without reference to a rate-of-return or other rate-based proceeding) of providing the . . . network element").[25] Moreover, Congress did not specify whether the cable plant had to be unbundled when a cable company offered Internet service.

Unbundling can be considered necessary to competition because the cost of laying down lines for the first customer in a community is extremely high, whereas the cost of serving every subsequent customer is minimal.[26] For a new entrant to serve even one customer in a community, in which most people already have service, the entrant would have to undertake a massive investment to allow it to provide service to all people in that community. Though not unusual for networks, this cost structure is unusual for most goods. Imagine, for example, that a farmer could not sell produce to a single person until he or she have produced enough to supply all the people in a market, most of whom already have a contract with another farmer.

Unbundling changes this cost structure. It permits the entrant to build only part of a network and lease the rest of the network—generally those parts that are most expensive to build—and to provide service that way.[27] Like the farmer who would need to grow only as much produce as he or she anticipates selling, the entrant could in this way invest incrementally and expand production from week to week. The most expensive part of this investment is usually what is called the "local loop"—the "last mile" of the network that connects a network provider's local "central office" to every home. The economic logic behind the unbundling policy is that the entrant would build up a base of consumers through providing new and innovative services and as the number of customers grows it will lease fewer and fewer elements while investing in full-fledged facilities-based competition.[28]

Can Unbundling Work?

In the United States, unbundling failed—or, better put, was never really attempted.[29] Hence, more than a decade after the enactment of the 1996 act, there is still not much competition among local networks.

Opponents of unbundling argue that unbundling was destined to fail, because it involved managed competition through price-setting and other intrusive means, and promoting competition in this way is unfeasible.[30] Implementation was impossible, they say, because it required incumbents and new entrants to work together, but why would fierce competitors want to work together? Moreover, they argue, unbundling reduces investment and competition. Incumbents do not invest because they have to share the fruits of that investment at a fixed, cost-based rate with competitors, and entrants do not invest because they can always wait for incumbents to innovate and then lease the innovations. Regarding competition, the detractors argue that the only sustainable competition is facilities-based competition, and unbundling delays such competition because competitors can share incumbent facilities.[31]

More fundamentally, they argue that—even in principle—increased competition *decreases* investment and consumer welfare. Therefore, they need some sort of assured "return on investment" and anything that cuts into their profits—from network neutrality rules to competition—would reduce their incentive to invest.[32]

But market power and guaranteed returns do not encourage investment. According to basic economics, market power permits companies to reduce output and to increase prices by creating artificial shortages, thereby boosting their profits. Market power also reduces investment in innovation. Without fierce competition, companies lack the incentive to reinvest their profits to innovate or respond to consumer demand. Indeed, the U.S. broadband market has all the features of a concentrated market, with its high prices, low adoption rates, and lack of innovation. Moreover, the telephone and cable companies already have fat profits. Comcast, for example, makes 80 percent returns on its broadband offering—five to ten times the profit margins of the oil and pharmaceutical companies.[33] A *threat* to their profits would force incumbents to invest and cut prices, and new entrants would have to invest and innovate to overcome the established benefits of incumbency.

Today, the telephone and cable incumbents are not subject to an effective unbundling regime, and they invest little[34]— less than during the period they were subject to unbundling.[35] In the absence of competition, the telephone companies were slow to roll out DSL service and cable companies are slow to upgrade.[36] Capital spending was flat for fifteen years except for 1999–2000, when these companies faced competition.[37]

By contrast, competition policies have proven to work generally, and among them unbundling has been proven to work for many of our global competitors. After 1996, while incumbents were bent on eliminating unbundling in the United States, the Clinton administration's U.S. trade representative encouraged other nations to adopt unbundling, and many did. Several studies, including studies undertaken by consumer groups, academics, new entrants, and governmental authorities in Europe and elsewhere, have credited unbundling with increased broadband competition and investment worldwide.[38]

In Japan, for example, fiber deployment is nearly universal, there are competitive offerings of one hundred mbps, and prices per megabit are one-fourth of what they are in the United States.[39] France has seen broadband competition, with fifty to eighty mbps offerings, and competitors generating enough revenue to finance their own network-builds. In climbing the investment "ladder," one French entrant targets areas where its DSL product already enjoys 15 percent penetration, and attempts to convert DSL customers to fiber customers.[40]

If Unbundling has Worked Elsewhere, Why Did it Fail in the United States?

It wasn't that unbundling was destined to fail, but rather that incumbents worked very hard to kill it. Understanding why this happened can help shape the proposals that are made to promote robust competition, as well as help rebutting claims that unbundling failed because of its own internal economic logic.

The incumbents fought competition in Congress, the courts, the FCC, academia, and elsewhere. In retrospect, it is possible to learn from the mistakes made by both political parties, incumbents and entrants, judges and commissioners, in this process.

Congress: Failing to Define Details of Unbundling

The 1996 act failed to define many of the most important details of unbundling, paving the way for protracted battles in the FCC and courts without a clear congressional position. As Justice Antonin Scalia wrote: "It would be gross understatement to say that the Telecommunications Act of 1996 is not a model of clarity. It is in many important respects a model of ambiguity or indeed even self-contradiction."[41] As a result, industry groups continued fighting the details at the FCC,[42] and they were able to delay finalizing them, by challenging them in court—as administrative agencies are subject to an apparently more rigorous judicial standard than Congress.[43] Delays work to the benefit of incumbents, as entrants are not able to generate revenues as easily and would have more precarious sources of financing. In addition, delays prevent a shift in the public debate that might have been possible were there successes to point to among new entrants. Even though the FCC is an expert agency that should handle most technical details, Congress left too many issues unsettled, in the process, putting new entrants at a disadvantage, while benefiting incumbents.

Incumbent Litigation

When the FCC adopted rules for determining which elements would be unbundled, the incumbents appealed and won a ruling in their favor in the Eighth Circuit court, which was later overturned in the Supreme Court.[44] The FCC also set unbundling rates, which were likewise challenged by the incumbents in the Supreme Court.[45] The telephone industry would continue to challenge every FCC attempt to implement congressional directives pertaining to unbundling.[46] At the same time, the cable industry lobbied the FCC not to regulate cable broadband services as a telecommunications service subject to unbundling or open access, and brought suit against cities attempting to do so.[47] The courts, especially the "deregulatory" DC Circuit, succeeded in overturning many of the FCC's decisions. When the FCC attempted to set national wholesale prices for unbundling, it was struck down for overbroad regulation; when it delegated to the states the power to set these prices on a more local level, it was struck down for delegating to the states.[48] In the end, the DC Circuit effectively gutted the 1996 act's unbundling regime. Indeed, the FCC has been involved in thirty-seven court decisions pertaining to the implementation of the 1996 act.[49] Beyond that, many key FCC rules remained in legal limbo for years.[50]

Incumbent Operational Foot-Dragging

In terms of operations, the incumbents delayed and stonewalled in various ways, from servicing entrants slowly and poorly, inconveniencing their customers and employees, including pitching litigation over bathroom privileges, co-location matters, delaying payments, and other matters.[51] These delays hurt entrants, but as it turns out, they are not uncommon responses to the threat of losing market power.[52]

FCC's Michael Powell and Kevin Martin

Michael Powell, the first FCC chairman to serve under President George Bush, dismantled much of the unbundling regime. He even dissented (quite unusual for a chairman) from an order that did not eliminate unbundling as sweepingly as he wanted.[53] During his tenure, the FCC ignored a key element of the 1996 act, a compromise that allowed local incumbents to compete in the long-distance market when local competition was available in their territory by allowing them to enter the long-distance market before local competition took hold.[54] Powell also ruled that cable companies would not be subject to any unbundling or wholesale access requirements in the delivery of broadband services.[55]

His successor, Kevin Martin, completed Powell's work by eliminating unbundling and wholesale access on DSL lines, licensed-wireless broadband, and even the nascent broadband over powerlines.[56] Martin even eliminated some unbundling requirements in the business market through granting "forbearance" petitions (sometimes through regulatory loopholes), and thereby forbearing from imposing such requirements.[57]

FCC's Early Too-Expansive Unbundling

Beyond Powell's opposition to unbundling and open access, his predecessors Reed Hundt and Bill Kennard made their own mistakes. While Powell put an end to unbundling, earlier commissions may have extended it too broadly when they authorized unbundling of almost any element or combination of elements, going so far as to permit an unbundled platform that was effectively a resale of services.[58] Not only did this move alarm the Supreme Court, which had been quite deferential to the FCC compared with the appellate courts,[59] it also encouraged new entrants to lease the entire network rather than suffice with the most economically necessary elements.[60] Consequently, new entrants were tempted to engage in what was effectively a resale, rather than build their own networks.[61]

Congressmen Against Competition

Shortly after the 1996 act compromises were reached, and incumbent telephone and cable companies worked through their agents in Congress to undermine them. Several influential senators, who opposed the 1996 act's pro-competition provisions, provided political cover to those local telephone incumbents opposed to the act, as they repeatedly introduced legislation that would have eliminated all unbundling and other local regulation.[62]

FCC Including/Emphasizing Local Voice Service

While the United States has worked hard to promote competition in local voice telephone service, most other nations have focused their pro-competition policies on broadband. Since local voice service is merely one application on broadband—and a dying business otherwise—this focus has proven to be misguided.

FCC Refusing to Include Cable Broadband

The FCC refused to regulate cable companies as it regulated telephone companies, even when cable companies offered the equivalent high-speed Internet service. Under Kennard's rule, the FCC refused to classify cable broadband at all and continued to punt the issue despite litigation across the country and the resulting confusion in local governments and federal courts.[63] Indeed, the Kennard Commission issued a report to Congress that excluded the cable industry from certain universal service obligations and helped set the basis for exempting cable broadband from unbundling and open access requirements.[64] The absence of regulatory parity between the telephone and cable industries, when it came to nearly identical products, was untenable, and eventually both became unregulated.

Complex Arbitration and Jurisdictional Sharing

The 1996 act rested on the false assumptions that incumbents and new entrants had equal bargaining power and that jurisdictional sharing could work. The basic premise was that incumbents and entrants could negotiate terms and, if they failed to, an arbitrator could decide matters. But since incumbents had no incentive to negotiate, they would opt to delay, turning arbitration into a long, slow process. And, as previously noted, "delay is the death to innovation" in dynamic markets.[65]

Another problem was that the FCC had to share jurisdiction with state agencies. This meant it could only influence markets through the regulatory levers at its disposal, which were often less effective than state-controlled levers in opening up markets, among other things, because local telephone prices were regulated, while broadband prices were not.[66] In addition, the states were heavily involved in the selection of elements and their pricing, providing incumbents with the ability to thwart the entrance of new participants into the market. In addition, it forced the FCC to use policy levers divorced from particular outcomes, as it lacked the direct authority to implement some of those outcomes.[67]

Entrants: Mergers, Accounting Scandals, and Lack of Business Plans

The new entrants cannot lay the entire blame on the incumbents. The two best-known cases of new entrants in local telephone and broadband service were the then–long-distance companies of AT&T and MCI. AT&T purchased a cable company and became the nation's largest cable company.[68] Most analysts later agreed that AT&T had overpaid for it and that it required more maintenance and investment than had been anticipated.[69] MCI merged with WorldCom, which eventually filed for bankruptcy after it emerged that it had been involved in accounting fraud.[70]

Incumbents: Merging and Dividing Markets

Incumbents refused to compete in other geographical markets. SBC refused to use unbundling or any other competitive strategy to compete with Ameritech in Michigan or Illinois, nor did Ameritech attempt to compete with SBC in Texas. Indeed, before 1996, telephone companies could serve as ISPs in other markets through wholesale access, but they refused to assume this role. By contrast, the German incumbent has used unbundling to compete with the French incumbent, increasing competition in the French market.[71]

Rather than compete, U.S. incumbents merged.[72] They would argue that mergers provided them with the resources to compete other local markets. To obtain FCC approval, the merging companies would commit themselves to competing in other areas, but they would later ignore this commitment with impunity.[73]

War of Ideas

Though ideas alone are often not enough in "politics," they do matter in policy debates. The incumbent telephone and cable industries succeeded in winning the war of ideas, largely because they were able to fund an army of lobbyists, as well as scholars at universities and think tanks, many of whom published books and articles in the most cited law and economics journals supporting their cases.[74] These scholars argued that unbundling hurt investment, undermined intermodal competition, and that it was generally implemented unfairly and inefficiently.[75] Some argued that although other nations had adopted unbundling, they were sure to abandon it after it had failed so miserably in the United States. The United States, these scholars predicted, would cease to be a model of regulatory innovation,[76] and entrants using unbundling abroad, notably in Japan, would go bankrupt.[77] Whether or not these scholars truly believed what they were writing,[78] this storyline became the conventional wisdom in Washington, DC.

One reason they were so effective was the general lack of information about broadband networks domestically and internationally. Incumbents control information about where broadband is available, at what speeds, and at what prices. At the same time, there is no institution in this country that provides useful comparisons of international broadband policy issues to shed light on best practices.

Dot Com and Telecom Bubble

The Nasdaq and Internet bubble of the late 1990s and early 2000s coincided with the early years of the 1996 act. The irrational exuberance of investors, particularly when it came to technology stocks, led to wild swings in the share prices of new telecommunications companies. The shares of many new entrants were often overvalued, and the Nasdaq crash meant the end for many of them.[79]

Implementing Unbundling Should Be Different this Time

Ironically, unbundling, an American innovation, worked abroad but failed at home, largely because of the opposition of incumbents. But it is now time for the U.S. government to give unbundling a second chance, and this time, it should show conviction and be persistent. In order for unbundling to work in the United States, the government needs to overcome information asymmetries, regulatory capture, and operational delays. It should also allow the experiences of other countries to inform its policy.

Specific Policy Proposals

The United States should adopt the following principles to encourage investment and competition in local telecommunications networks.

Gather Domestic and International Information on Broadband Facts and Policies to Develop Best Practices

To better understand which policies are effective and ineffective at home and abroad, the FCC should compile, make available, and analyze granular data regarding broadband competition in the United States. It should also set up an office to analyze and report on international broadband policies and their effectiveness. Information exchanges have been critical abroad. The chief UK regulator, for example, reported that he "drew heavily on the successful policies of ARCEP [the French regulatory body] in local loop unbundling"[80] and set wholesale prices based on what was prevalent in the rest of Europe.[81] It should be noted that several nations now draw on the successful experience of the United Kingdom in functional separation.

Adopt Unbundling and Wholesale Access Focusing on Broadband, Including Cable and Fiber

The United States should focus policies on competitive, high-speed, general-purpose Internet networks, not local voice service or any other service. Voice is just one application, which can be provided by software like G-Chat or Skype, while Internet networks function as general-purpose infrastructure for all applications and users. The most successful unbundling was reported in nations that focused on broadband competition, not voice competition.[82] The United States enjoyed a predominant position worldwide in Internet penetration when the situation was one of the "FCC taking affirmative and aggressive regulation of communications networks, specifically for the benefit of the computer networks."[83] On the other hand, it started to lag behind when government policy eliminated competition in broadband access.

In focusing on broadband, the government should require unbundling of cable systems, which provide broadband access comparable to that provided by telephone companies.

Government should also require unbundling of fiber and dark fiber. While incumbents argue that unbundling rules would decrease their incentive to invest in local networks, this claim assumes that incumbents are not functionally separated. If an incumbent has been separated into retail and network divisions, the network division would have incentives to invest whether or not retail entrants can lease unbundled elements. Indeed, with functional separation, mandated unbundling would provide new entrants certainty in their business model, and provide the network division with ready retail customers, likely increasing the network division's incentive to invest. Several engineering forms of fiber to the home exist, and the highest capacity form is also the least difficult to unbundle, albeit the most expensive.[84] The government should ensure that companies lay the forms most easily unbundled with the highest capacity.

Unbundling fiber has worked abroad. In France, the entrant Iliad has built its own fiber to the home network and will voluntarily wholesale.[85] In Japan, the incumbent was required to unbundle fiber loops and interoffice fiber.[86] The European Union's telecommunications commissioner has agreed that any "regulatory holiday" for fiber would reduce competition and investment.[87]

In addition to unbundling at the local loop, the FCC should consider the necessity of unbundling in the backbone and dark fiber, as the market power of concentrated backbone providers increases and some fiber remains unlit, despite demand.

Congress Should Define the Elements Narrowly and Set a Low Price Formula

Rather than subject FCC decisions to extensive litigation and jockeying, Congress should determine which elements are subject to unbundling and the formula for unbundling. Congress need not establish every detail, however, since the FCC should make decisions regarding elements and cost formulas when implementing Congressional guidance. But Congress should at the least select the elements to unbundle, as the European Commission did, and a general price formula.

Congress should only select the elements that pose the largest barrier to entry, such as elements of the local loop. Those nations that have achieved the most success with unbundling have generally followed this model: a top-level definition of the element to be unbundled, which tends to include the local loop and related elements. Deciding which elements to unbundle is not easy. Some argue that nearly all elements should be subject to unbundling, so competitors can get a toehold on the ladder. Others counter that if entrants can lease everything, they may not build anything. And there are those who favor unbundling those elements that fit the "essential facilities doctrine." Under this doctrine, dominant companies must share facilities that cannot be economically replicated, and that entrants need in order to compete. The FCC should list elements that are most uneconomical to replicate, such as the local loop, but also include other elements that could be important barriers to entry.[88] And all incumbents should be subject to unbundling.[89]

Congress should require access to all network elements that allow full local loop unbundling. This usually requires the entrants' equipment at both ends of the connection to the consumer and the incumbent's local office, the high-frequency portion of the local loop used for DSL (known as line-sharing),[90] the high bandwidth architecture, including the equipment called the DSLAM in the incumbent's local office (known as bitstream access),[91] and wholesale transmission access.[92] Congress should also apply unbundling to both the cable plant and fiber loops (rather than exempting them).[93] Different products may spur competition. In Japan, for example, the low rate for line-sharing helped encourage competition and investment.[94]

Congress should also set the rate formula for unbundling elements near cost. It should set the cost as though it were setting a compulsory license fee, under the assumption that no market exists. Achieving precision is unnecessary in this case. Indeed, businesses do not always price things with precision, as peering in the backbone market demonstrates.[95] When prices are more attractive in some locations than in others, such as urban areas or, alternatively, rural areas, Congress could expedite procedures to revisit the pricing formula, or it could allow the FCC some leniency in changing rates. A low, cost-based rate should not unfairly advantage new entrants, as the entrant can only lease the most costly elements, like the local loop, rather than leasing every element and engaging in resale. Because incumbents may have economies of scale in the elements that entrants cannot lease, incumbents may still retain price advantages. In addition, incumbents have likely recouped their capital investment in the leased elements, so the entrants' rates should be calibrated more to ensure entry for entrants rather than to ensure capital recovery for the incumbents.

If Congress defines these elements, litigation is less likely to succeed, and political pressure on the FCC would likely be reduced. If Congress does not initially define these elements itself, it should direct the FCC to issue it a report on the matter.

Modify Forbearance Procedures to Exempt Unbundling and Wholesale

Congress should eliminate the FCC's authority, under section 10 of the Communications Act, to forbear from unbundling and wholesale, and it should forbid the FCC from defining broadband in a way that eliminates unbundling and wholesale requirements. Congress had permitted eventual forbearance in the past, but that practice should be eliminated.[96]

This would prevent incumbents from pressuring FCC regulators into eliminating competition, and, hopefully, it would encourage them to invest their dollars in competition and upgrading rather than in lobbying efforts.

Structural Separation, With Functional Separation as an Option

The government should set structural rules that give incumbents the institutional incentive to unbundle, weaken incentives for anti-competitive behavior, and provide government transparency to enable more effective regulation. Structural separation entails breaking up an incumbent into separate, unaffiliated companies, with one company typically controlling the network assets (with a wholesale business of selling capacity to ISPs) and another company controlling the ISP assets (with a retail business of selling service to business and residential consumers). In addition, wireline and wireless assets should be separated. A reason that wireless broadband offerings are complements, rather than substitutes for wireline access, is that the same companies often own the wireless and wired networks.

Functional separation, by contrast, requires the incumbent to create a division in the company (or a partly owned subsidiary) that controls the network assets or the "natural monopoly" parts of the business, including certain last mile and backhaul network assets.[97] If a subsidiary rather than a division owns them, a minority percentage of the subsidiary's stock could even trade separately on a stock exchange.[98] Functional separation requires the new division to provide wholesale capacity and network elements to all industry participants under the same terms and conditions as it provides them to the ISP division within the same company (sometimes called "equivalence of inputs").[99] In addition, governments could require the two companies to be housed in different buildings, to provide incentive pay to executives based on their division's performance, to have separate brand identities, to limit information-sharing, to have independent compliance and transparency committees, and so on.[100] Functional separation can help prevent price discrimination (including a margin squeeze) and non–price discrimination practices, such as those found in Sweden and other nations,[101] such as delaying processing orders, holding back relevant information, and planning network-builds with preferences for the affiliated ISP.[102]

Experts and policymakers have not reached a consensus about which form of separation is more effective[103] and in the United States, both have been tried.[104] With complete, structural separation, the network company has no reason to favor a particular ISP, and regulation costs are likely to be lower in the long run, because there would be less oversight of anti-competitive behavior than in the case of functional separation. The network company is no longer part of a larger company, so it would have no incentive, unlike a company division, to favor the affiliated ISP. In addition, the network company could be financed and traded as an infrastructure company, while the ISP company can respond to markets independently.[105] Functional separation has some advantages over structural separation. The initial costs of structural separation are very high and irreversible, as they include both the economic costs that fall on the divesting company and the political costs that fall on the government.[106] Moreover, with structural separation, the network company will want to immediately begin lobbying for entry into unregulated lines of business. After the AT&T divestiture, for example, the local Bell companies were restricted to local service, but they lobbied unrelentingly to enter long-distance and other markets.

Despite some theoretical drawbacks, functional separation has worked fairly well abroad.[107] Functional separation transformed unbundling in the United Kingdom, where it had previously failed.[108] Its implementation in the United Kingdom is considered "a huge success," among other reasons, because it did not inhibit investment.[109] It has been praised by the UK regulator[110] and by the chief executive of the country's lead incumbent, who said separation is "very good for the industry and very good for the customer."[111] In listing some of the benefits of functional separation in terms of financing, a BT executive noted that "investor confidence has not been dampened. . . . [functional separation of BT] provides a clearer picture of the financial performance of different parts of the business; is likely to lead to BT having greater analyst coverage and greater access to capital funding in the financial markets."[112] Even though functional separation "triggered a major price war in the broadband market" and "new wave of investment,"[113] BT's stock price rose immediately[114] and continued to go up, partly because the British regulator then deregulated retail prices.[115] Interestingly, a "culture" of nondiscrimination emerged at the network division, which is as important as compliance with particular rules.[116] Several nations, including Italy, New Zealand, and Sweden, are now considering following the UK model.[117]

The United States should adopt full structural separation, so that long-term regulation costs eventually drop, and network companies have no reason to favor particular retail ISPs. Certain exemptions could be provided to encourage competition. For example, government can permit a network provider to create an ISP subsidiary, but only if that subsidiary offers service on *other* incumbents' lines. This requirement could encourage competition, although incumbents have refused to take advantage of such exceptions in the past.

Regarding the cable industry, the government should require structural separation of the physical network from the cable channels and ISPs. In other words, Time Warner Cable should be functionally separated from HBO and from the Road Runner ISP. In addition, the cable set-top box industry should be separated. A major impediment to more innovative broadband services is control of devices,[118] which is as much the case for cable networks as it is for telephone networks.[119]

On the wireless side, companies like AT&T and Verizon, which have significant wired and wireless network assets, should be required to separate them, so that the two networks can compete in offerings, prices, and services.

Considering the political power of incumbents in the United States, they stand a good chance of fighting off structural separation and, even if not, they could lobby to eliminate any business restrictions. When the United Kingdom threatened its recalcitrant incumbent with structural separation, the incumbent, British Telecom, then agreed to functional separation, with separate subsidiaries rather than divestiture (and also cut prices by up to 70 percent).[120] So functional separation may be more likely an effective political negotiation endpoint, and a necessary minimum baseline.

Even if unbundling is not enacted, separation should be. With separation, the network company would have some incentives to deal with unaffiliated ISPs and other retail providers. The FCC would have to monitor the network company and enact light regulations to ensure that the network company does not favor the affiliated (or previously affiliated) ISP, but separation on its own should improve transparency and strengthen both competition and pro-competition regulation.

Operational "Arbitrator"

The United States should also take its cue from the United Kingdom in appointing a telecommunications arbitrator with deep operational expertise and wide-ranging authority to handle the day-to-day operational foot-dragging of incumbents. The United Kingdom appointed an arbitrator who had accumulated experience building successful and profitable networks around the world and who was able to get BT to end its operational foot-dragging. In the United States, such an operational office could also cut down on operational delays initiated by incumbents.

Access to Rights-of-Way

Entrants should have ready access to rights-of-way controlled by incumbents and by local governments to ensure that they are able to build and connect with networks. In France, an entrant was able to offer facilities-based competition, including fiber-to-the-home, with access to municipal sewer systems.[121] In Korea, entrants had access to the electric utility's infrastructure.[122] In the United States, entrants should have access to incumbents' ducts, conduits, poles, and rights of way at low terms, with operational oversight by the arbitrators.[123] Local governments should also work to ensure that entrants have ready access to rights-of-way. Congress should establish rapid federal review procedures to ensure incumbents do not exercise their lobbying power at the local level to thwart new entrants.

Requiring Divestiture of Copper or Cable Lines

The incumbent should divest its existing local network within four years of laying fiber. After building fiber to the home, the incumbent's old copper or cable network will remain unused. The incumbent will prefer to cut those old lines, because of the cost of maintaining two networks and because of the potential competition from owners or lessors of the old network undercutting the incumbent's fiber investment.[124] Government should require divestiture of such lines to increase competition and provide consumers with more options. But government need not require immediate divestiture, as the incumbent may need a few years to gain a toehold in the market, to educate consumers about the benefits of fiber, and to ensure software programmers will create products that can take advantage of fiber speeds. Four years later, most users should be used to fiber speeds, but the option of competition from older lines should also be available.[125] During those four years, the fiber lines would obviously be subject to unbundling.

Financing Support

Even though fiber investments are likely to pay off, stock markets often focus on short-term returns and punish companies for long-term investments in fiber. For example, when French provider Iliad announced plans to build fiber to the home, its stock price dropped 12 percent that day.[126] Verizon's stock price also dropped when it announced it would build fiber to the home. But the private sector can probably finance much of this investment. Completing a home fiber connection can cost a provider between $600 and $2,000 and falling, depending on certain factors.[127] With a monthly bill of $50–100, the investment can be paid off in just a few years.

If competition fails to encourage fiber to the home to the extent that is necessary, Congress could set tax credits or rapid tax depreciation schedules for open fiber networks.

Network Neutrality

Congress should enact a network neutrality law. For several years, the FCC and Congress have debated the issue of network neutrality. Network neutrality is meant to guarantee that broadband users can access all Internet content and applications. Without network neutrality, the Internet would be similar to cable television, and companies like Google or CNN.com would have to cut deals for "carriage" with network providers, while the network providers would be able to determine what content is available to Americans. Without network neutrality, the variety of available content and applications, as well as the rate of innovation in applications, would be limited. With less and less innovative content and applications, fewer people would subscribe, and those subscribers would get less value. For this reason, network neutrality must be preserved. Congress should adopt a network neutrality law that forbids a network provider from discriminating, speeding up or slowing down, Internet content, services, or applications based on source, ownership, or destination.

Congress should also apply network neutrality to all modes of delivering Internet, from wired to wireless delivery.

Political Compromises and Public Involvement

The government may have to make some political compromises, but the above principles should be preserved. If a compromise is necessary, unbundling should not be a chip traded away. Instead, it should be locked in.

One compromise may be to revise universal service funding so that it targets only broadband services that are subject to these unbundling and open access requirements.[128] Universal service could be the carrot for opening up networks, although this carrot would work best in rural locations, which receive much of the high-cost fund as detailed in part III of the book, which discusses access.

In addition, rather than simply handing out money to incumbents through the fund, the government could buy newly issued stock and, in that way, have a stake in ownership. Indeed, in many of those countries that have been most successful with broadband, there is *some* government ownership of the basic infrastructure companies.[129] Another compromise, which would protect worker rights and dampen union opposition, would be to require entrants to provide workers with similar benefits to those they receive from the network provider. In the United Kingdom, the incumbent received a commitment that the government would review the removal of retail regulation.[130] The FCC could also provide some minor regulatory relief (or not impose certain new regulations) as a carrot.

Fundamentally, any "compromise" should involve the American public. The FCC and Congress should help educate the public about its decisions by holding public hearings, being transparent about the industries' lobbying operations, and engaging nonprofit, civic, and academic organizations in decision making. Any future compromise or deal made about our communications infrastructure—in contrast to what happened in 1996—should be made in the sunlight, with full public participation.

Notes

1. The Organization for Economic Cooperation and Development (OECD) has found "significant price effects" for deployment and that (an admittedly oversimplistic measure) the number of years of a nation has required unbundled local loop competition is also significant. OECD Working Party on Communications Infrastructures and Services Policy, "Catching-Up in Broadband—What Will it Take?," 25 July 2007, 19. See also OECD, "Broadband Growth and Policies in OECD Countries," 17–18 June 2008, 41 (noting the connection between competition and lower prices and greater value). Other studies have similarly found a positive relationship between unbundling and both availability and access to broadband services. See, e.g., Martha Garcia-Murillo, "International Broadband Deployment: The Impact of Unbundling," *Communications & Strategies* 75:1, no. 83 (2005): 102–3; S. Derek Turner, "Broadband Reality Check II," Free Press, August 2006, 17. See also Sangwon Lee and Justin S. Brown, "Examining Broadband Adoption Factors: An Empirical Analysis Between Countries" (presented at the Thirty-fifth Research Conference on Communication, Information and Internet Policy, Arlington, VA, August 2007), 17 (concluding that "intra-modal competition through LLU [local loop unbundling] may be considered one of the main drivers of broadband diffusion"); Robert D. Atkinson et al., "Explaining International Broadband Leadership," Information Technology and Innovation Foundation, May 2008, 12, 14 (finding unbundling, and therefore intra-platform competition, and price to be among the most significant factors for penetration); and Robert W. Crandall, *Competition and Chaos: U.S. Telecommunications since the 1996 Telecom Act* (Washington, DC: Brookings Institution, 2005), 120.

2. OECD, "Broadband Growth," 53, 70–75.

3. "Open Up Those Highways," *The Economist* 17 January 2008; www22.verizon.com/content/ConsumerFiOS/packages+and+prices/packages+and+prices.htm; http://gigaom.com/2007/04/24/50-mbps-for-40-but-in-france/.

4. See contributions of Sharon L. Strover and Andrea H. Tapia in part III of this book.

5. Comments of Consumers Union, Consumer Federation of America and Free Press, in the Matter of Inquiry Concerning the Deployment of Advanced Telecommunications Capability to All Americans in a Reasonable and Timely Fashion, and Possible Steps to Accelerate Such Deployment Pursuant to Section 706 of the Telecommunications Act of 1996, GN Docket No. 07-45, 16 May 2007, 9–17; Free Press et al., In the Matter of the Petition of Free Press et al for Declaratory Ruling that Degrading an Internet Application Violates the FCC's Internet Policy Statement and Does Not Meet an Exception for "Reasonable Network Management," 1 November 2007, 2–7.

6. See Brett Frischmann, "An Economic Theory of Infrastructure and Commons Management," *Minnesota Law Review* 89 (April 2005), 4. Comments of Vint Cerf, Personal Democracy Forum, 24 June 2008; Comments of Consumers Union, Consumer Federation of America and Free Press, in the Matter of Universal Service Support, WC Docket No. 05-337, 2 June 2008.

7. See Atkinson et al., "Explaining," 6.

8. S. Derek Turner, "Shooting the Messenger," Free Press, July 2007, 12–14.

9. S. Derek Turner, "Universal Service and Convergence: USF Policy For the 21st Century" (presented at the Thirty-fourth Research Conference on Communication, Information and Internet Policy, Arlington, VA, September 2006).

10. Post and Telestyrelsen, "Improved Broadband Competition Through Functional Separation: Statutory Proposals for Non-Discrimination and Openness in the Local Loop," 14 June 2007, 40.

11. Crandall, *Competition and Chaos*, 122.

12. Alan Marks, "GPON vs. HFC: The next technology battle," *Lightwave Online*, lw.pennnet.com/display_article/298272/13/ARTCL/none/none/GPON-vs-HFC:-The-next-technology-battle/ (18 August 2008); Mike Robuck, "Comcast Eyes 100 Hours of HD VOD," *Communications Technology*, 15 June 2006, www.cable360.net /ct/news/ctreports/18508.html (18 August 2008).

13. Mark Halper, "Does High Tech Require High Fiber?," Time/CNN, 15 October 2006; Richard Thurston, "Finding a Funder for Fibre to the Home," ZDNet.co.uk, 6 May 2008 (noting that the European telecom commissioner said the need for fiber is "the most important topic in the telecoms world today").

14. "Verizon Announces Savings on Fiber to the Home," *Electrical Contractor Magazine*, December 2006; Verizon Communications, Inc, "FiOS Briefing Session," 27 September 2006, 42, investor.verizon.com/news/20060927/20060927.pdf (18 August 2008); Crandall, *Competition and Chaos*, 130.

15. "Video Takes Fiber Deep Using Technology from Aurora Networks," *ScreenPlays*, 3 July 2008; Jeff Baumgartner, "Videotron Plants 'Fiber Deep,'" *Light Reading*, 24. July 2008, www.lightreading.com/document.asp?doc_id=159499&site=cdn (18 August 2008). See also David Cleary, "Is GPON the access technology for the next decade?," *Lightwave Online*, lw.pennnet.com/display_article/328953/13/ARTCL/none /none/1/Is-GPON-the-access-technology-for-the-next-decade?/ (18 August 2008).

16. Vivian Reding, "The EU Telecoms Reform 2007," Eighth Annual ECTA Regulatory Conference, 28 November 2007, 4.

17. *NCTA v. Brand X Internet Services*, 545 U.S. 967 (2005); Appropriate Framework for Broadband Access to the Internet over Wireline Facilities, 20 FCC Rec. 14853 (2005).

18. Reply Comments of Consumers Union, Consumer Federation of America and Free Press, in the Matter of Inquiry Concerning the Deployment of Advanced Telecommunications Capability to All Americans in a Reasonable and Timely Fashion, and Possible Steps to Accelerate Such Deployment Pursuant to Section 706 of the Telecommunications Act of 1996, GN Docket No. 07-45, 31 May 2007, 3–8.

19. Analysis of Federal Communications Commission Form 477, collected 30 June 2007.

20. The nationwide HHI for the U.S. broadband market is above 1,400 (see www.leichtmanresearch.com/press/021908release.html). However, the nationwide HHI is misleading, as broadband DSL and cable providers are regionally based incumbents, and do not compete against each other. According to FCC Form 477 Data, non-incumbent broadband providers account for no more than 8 percent of all residential and business high-speed connections (assuming cable connections are provided by incumbent cable operators, except for those provided by RCN). This corresponds to an HHI well above 4,300. This level of market concentration is considered (by DOJ *Merger Guidelines*) a highly concentrated duopoly; see also "Broadband Deployment is Extensive throughout the United Sates, but it is Difficult to Assess the Extent of Deployment Gaps in Rural Areas," United States Government Accountability Office, Report to Congressional Committees, GAO-06-426, May 2006; James W. Friedman, *Game Theory with Applications to Economics* (New York: Oxford University Press, 1986); and Jean-Jacques Laffont and Jean Tirole, *Competition in Telecommunications* (Cambridge, MA: MIT Press, 2001).

21. See *Communications, Broadband and Competitiveness: How Does the U.S. Measure Up?*, Hearing before the United States Senate Committee on Commerce, Science and Transportation, 110th Congress, Testimony of Ben Scott, Free Press, 24 April 2007.

22. Aundreu Mas-Colell, Micahel D. Whinston, and Jerry R. Green, *Microeconomic Theory* (New York: Oxford University Press, 1995). See also the sources in note 1.

23. 47 USC. § 230(b).

24. Before the 1996 act, Ameritech Corp., the Midwestern incumbent, proposed unbundling in exchange for entering long-distance. See David Teece, "Telecommunications in Transition: Unbundling, Reintegration, and Competition," *Michigan Telecommunications & Technology Law Review* 1:47 (1995).

25. 47 USC. § 252(d)(1)(A)(i).

26. Also important is that these costs are not only fixed but also sunk, meaning a network provider that goes out of business must likely sell its network at a steep discount of the cost of building the network.

27. These may be the elements with the greatest "scale economies," with the highest upfront sunk costs and lowest marginal costs. See Crandall, *Competition and Chaos*, 10.

28. European Regulators Group, "ERG Opinion on Functional Separation," 2007, ERG (07)44,12.

29. "Mandated unbundling under the [1996] Act is widely viewed to have been a failure." Susan Crawford, "Network Rules," *Law and Contemporary Problems*, 70:51 (2007), n.165 (and citations therein).

30. Crandall, *Competition and Chaos*, 156–58.

31. Crandall, *Competition and Chaos*, 6.

32. See, e.g., Comments of National Cable and Telecommunications Association, In the Matter of Broadband Industry Practices, WC Docket No. 07-52, 15 June 2007, 37.

33. Vishesh Kumar, "Is it Time to Tune in to Cable?," *Wall Street Journal*, 3 April 2008; see, e.g., Exxon Mobile Corp., finance.yahoo.com/q/ks?s=XOM; Merck and Co. Inc., finance.yahoo.com/q/ks?s=MRK.

34. They are also decreasing expenditures in some cases. See Comcast, "Comcast Reports 2007 Results and Provides Outlook for 2008," 14 February 2008, available at library.corporate-ir.net/library/11/118/118591/items/279702/Q407_PR.pdf.

35. See, e.g., Crandall, *Competition and Chaos*, 18–19 (noting investment boom after 1996 act); Charles Ferguson, "The United States Broadband Problem: Analysis and Policy Recommendations," Brooking Working Paper, 31 May 2002, 5–6.

36. Ferguson, "Broadband Problem," 2–3.

37. Ferguson, "Broadband Problem," 6.

38. Turner, "Reality Check," 13.

39. Blaine Harden, "Japan's Warp-Speed Ride to Internet Future," *Washington Post*, 29 August 2007, A01.

40. See Wieland, "FTTH Battles." Jennifer L. Schenker, "Viva la High Speed Internet!," *Business Week*, 18 July 2007.

41. *AT&T Corp. v. Iowa Utilities Bd.*, 525 US 366, 397 (1999).

42. James K. Glassman, "Is Telecom's Future The Bells, The Bells, and Only The Bells?," *Reason Magazine*, 5 December 2000, www.reason.com/news/show/36079.html (19 August 2008); Alan Stewart, "RBOC slams new regs on competition—regional Bell operating company Ameritech unhappy with 1996 Telecommunications Act," *Communications News*, July 1996, findarticles.com/p/articles/mi_m0CMN/is_n7_v33 /ai_18456756/pg_1 (19 August 2008).

43. For example, a court can usually provide its own reasoned basis for a statute but can only uphold a regulation based on a reasoned basis actually provided by the agency.

44. *AT&T Corp. v. Iowa Utilities Bd.*, 525 US 366, 397 (1999).

45. *Verizon Communications v. FCC* (00-511) 535 U.S. 467 (2002).

46. See, e.g., *United States Telecom Association v. FCC*, 290 F.3d 415 (D.C. Cir. 2002); *United States Telecom Association v. FCC*, 359 F.3rd 554 (D.C. Cir. 2004); *Covad Commc'ns Co. v. FCC*, 450 F.3d 528 (D.C. Cir. 2006).

47. See, e.g., *AT&T Corp. v. City of Portland*, 216 F.3d 871 (Ninth Cir. 2000).

48. *United States Telecom Association v. FCC*, 359 F.3d 554, 564 (2004).

49. Harold W. Furchtgott-Roth, *A Tough Act to Follow? The Telecommunications Act of 1996 and the Separation of Powers* (Washington, DC: The AEI Press, 2006), 86–87.

50. Furchtgott-Roth, *A Tough Act*, 95.

51. Crandall, *Competition and Chaos*, 13.

52. See, e.g., Eric Bangeman, "AT&T Launches $10 DSL it Hopes No One Signs Up For," *Ars Technica*, 18 June 2007.

53. Separate statement of Michael K. Powell, in the matter of review of the Section 2512 Unbundling Obligations of Incumbent Local Exchange Carriers, CC Docket No. 01-338; Implementation of the Local Competition Provisions of the Telecommunications Act of 1996, CC Docket No. 96-98, Deployment of Wireline Services Offering Advanced Telecommunications Capability, CC Docket No. 98-147, 20 February 2003.

54. See, e.g., Crandall, *Competition and Chaos*, 14, 41, 51, 61.

55. Federal Communications Commission, Declaratory Ruling and Notice of Proposed Rulemaking, in the Matters of Inquiry Concerning High-Speed Access to the Internet Over Cable and Other Facilities, GN Docket No. 00-185; Internet Over Cable Declaratory Ruling; Appropriate Regulatory Treatment for Broadband Access to the Internet Over Cable Facilities, CS Docket No. 02-52, released 15 March 2002.

56. Federal Communications Commission, Declaratory Ruling, in the Matter Appropriate Regulatory Treatment for Broadband Access to the Internet Over Wireless Networks, WT Docket No. 07-53, released 23 March 2007; Federal Communications Commission, Memorandum Opinion and Order, in the Matter of United Power Line Council's Petition for Declaratory Ruling Regarding the Classification of Broadband over Power Line Internet Access Service as Information Service, WC Docket No. 06-10, released 7 November 2006; Federal Communications Commission, Report and Order, in the Matters of Appropriate Framework for Broadband Access to the Internet over Wireline Facilities, CC Docket No. 02-33; Universal Service Obligations of Broadband Providers; Review of Regulatory Requirements for Incumbent LEC Broadband Telecommunications Services, CC Docket No. 01-337; Computer III Further Remand Proceedings: Bell Operating Company Provision of Enhanced Services; 1998 Biennial Regulatory Review—Review of Computer II and ONA Safeguards and Requirements, CC Docket Nos. 95-20, 98-10; Conditional Petition of the Verizon Telephone Companies for Forbearance Under 47 U.S.C. § 160(c) with Regard to Broadband Services Provided Via Fiber to the Premises; Petition of the Verizon Telephone Companies for Declaratory Ruling or, Alternatively, for Interim Waiver with Regard to Broadband Services Provided Via Fiber to the Premises, WC Docket No. 04-242; Consumer Protection in the Broadband Era, WC Docket No. 05-271, released 23 September 2005.

57. See, e.g., Arshad Mohammed, "Verizon High-Speed Services Deregulated," *Washington Post*, 21 March 2006, D05.

58. See Crandall, *Competition and Chaos*, 10, 37.

59. See, e.g., *Verizon Communications, Inc. v. FCC*, 535 U.S. 467 (2002); *AT&T Corp. v. Iowa Utilities Bt.*, 525 U.S. 366 (1999).

60. See, e.g., Michael Glover and Donna Epps, "Is the Telecommunications Act of 1996 Working?," Administrative Law Review, 52:1013 (2000), 1022.

61. Something about UNE-P.

62. See Report of the Committee on Commerce, Science and Transportation on S. 652, 30 March 1995; Telecommunications Competition Act of 1998, S. 1766, 105th Congress, second session, sponsored by Senator McCain. See also Senate Report no. 367, 103rd Congress, second session, 112–19.

63. See, e.g., Comstock, *Access Denied*, 7n13 (citing William E. Kennard, "How to End the Worldwide Wait," *Wall St. Journal*, 24 August 1999, XI18).

64. Federal Communications Commission, Report to Congress, in the Matter of Federal-State Joint Board on Universal Service, CC Docket No. 96-45, released 10 April 1998.

65. See Internet Industry Association (Australia), "Submission on Request for Proposals for a National Broadband Network," 25 June 2008, 6. See id., 5–6.

66. Crandall, *Competition and Chaos*, 80.

67. Furchtgott-Roth, *A Tough Act*.

68. Mike Ricciuti, "AT&T, MediaOne Merger a Done Deal," CNET News.com, 15 June 2000.

69. See, e.g., William G. Shepherd, "Narrowing the Broadband," Economic Policy Institute, July 2002.

70. Other companies in the sector also engaged in accounting fraud. Om Malik, *Broadbandits: Inside the $750 Billion Telecom Heist* (Hoboken, NJ: Wiley, 2003); Crandall, *Competition and Chaos*, 4, 93.

71. Schenker, "Viva la High Speed Internet!."

72. See, e.g., Furchtgott-Roth, *A Tough Act*, 153–57.

73. Mark Cooper, "Broken Promises and Strangled Competition: The Record of Baby Bell Merger and Market Opening Behavior," Consumer Federation of America June 2005. See also Hearing on Internet Access and the Consumer, Senate Commerce Committee, 13 April 1999, 106th Congress, first session.

74. For a more recent discussion, see Bruce Kushnik, "Corporate-funded Research Designed to Influence Public Policy," *Nieman Watchdog*, 1 October 2007.

75. See, e.g., J. Gregory Sidak, *Is the Telecommunications Act of 1996 Broken? If So, How Can We Fix It?* (Washington, DC: AEI Press, 1999).

76. Crandall, *Competition and Chaos*, 3, 128–29.

77. Crandall, *Competition and Chaos*, 144, 154.

78. National Cable and Telecommunications Association, "Phone Companies and the Truth: A Bad Connection," 14 March 2006, www.ncta.com/DocumentBinary .aspx?id=299 (18 August 2008).

79. See, e.g., Crandall, *Competition and Chaos*, 4, 43–46, 151–52.

80. Richards, "Functional Separation," 8.

81. Graeme Wearden, "Ofcom Forces Action on Broadband Unbundling," ZDNet .co.uk, 13 May 2004.

82. Crandall, *Competition and Chaos*, 139, 144 (discussing Europe, Korea, and Japan).

83. See Robert Cannon, "The Legacy of the Federal Communications Commission's Computer Inquiries," *Federal Communications Law Journal*, 55:167 (2003), 180.

84. See, e.g., Anupam Banerjee and Marvin Sirbu, "Towards Technologically and Competitively Neutral Fiber to the Home (FTTH) Infrastructure" (paper presented at Telecommunications Policy Research Conference, Arlington, VA, 2003); Ken Wieland, "FTTH Battles Loom Large in Europe," *Telecom Magazine*, 24 January 2008 (discussing GPON, which is point to multipoint, and Ethernet point-to-point

architectures); and Richard Thurston, "Finding a Funder," noting that "Point-to-point does have virtually unlimited bandwidth, although it's 30 percent more expensive than PON").

85. Free (Press Release), "Free's Fibre-to-the-Home (FTTH) Service Will Be Opened Up to the Competition," 11 September 2006.

86. Douglas Galbi, "Ubiquitous Fiber Network in Japan," *Purple Motes*, 15 April 2007.

87. Reding, "The EU Telecoms," 4.

88. Unbundling is based on that notion but relies on legislation, not judge-made law; it also represents the legislative judgment that competition in communications networks is of signal importance and has remained elusive under existing policies.

89. Cf. Comstock, "Access Denied," 8n23 (noting that Congress required unbundling regardless of market power, despite Senate proposals).

90. Line-sharing was first introduced in the United States in 1999, but a court largely eliminated it in 2002. USTA, 290 F.3d 415 (2002).

91. Post and Telestyrelsen, "Improved Broadband Competition," 31–34.

92. See Earl W. Comstock and John W. Butler, "Access Denied: The FCC's Failure to Implement Open Access to Cable as Required by the Communications Act," *ComLaw Conspectus* 8:1, 4, 5n2 (2000).

93. The European proposed framework and the European Regulators Group both support unbundling of fiber loops, as do new entrants everywhere. ECTA, "Press Release: New Regulatory Framework is Best Package to Deliver Europe's Broadband Future," 13 November 2007, 2. Article Amit sent about advantage of unbundling fiber etc. maybe something on Japan, though Japan is not an example. GTE and CTC paper on unbundling cable, and the Netherlands

94. Galbi, "Ubiquitous"; Hidenori Fuke, "The Spectacular Growth of DSL in Japan and its Implications," *Communications & Strategies* 52:4, 175 (2003): 177–79. See also Atkinson et al., "Explaining," D2.

95. See Michael Kende, "The Digital Handshake: Connecting Internet Backbones," Federal Communications Commission, OPP Working Paper No. 32, September 2000. See also William W. Fisher, *Promises to Keep: Technology, Law, and the Future of Entertainment* (Palo Alto, CA: Stanford University Press, 2004).

96. As one commentator noted, the incumbent phone companies "made infrastructure investment contingent on securing massive regulatory liberalization," which would undermine competition. Rob Frieden, "Best Practices in Broadband: Lessons from Canada, Japan, Korea and the United States" (paper presented at the Telecommunications Policy Research Conference, Arlington, VA, July 2004), 9.

97. See Ed Richards (CEO, Ofcom), "Functional Separation in the UK," *La Lettre de l'Autorite (English Version)*, March/April 2007, 8.

98. British Telecom proposed to place 25 percent of the network company on the stock exchange. OECD Working Party on Telecommunications and Information Services Policies, "The Benefits and Costs of Structural Separation of the Local Loop," 3 November 2003, 17.

99. Post and Telestyrelsen, "Improved Broadband Competition," 67.

100. See, e.g., Alex Bowers (International Director, Office of Communications), "Functional Separation—The UK 'Openreach' Model," ANACOM Tenth Seminar, Lisbon, 9 November 2007, 13.

101. The incumbent serves its retail services with shorter lead times, rolls out exchanges with its own needs in mind, without regard to competitors', and denies other operators access. See Post and Telestyrelsen, "Improved Broadband Competition," 54–57.

102. See "Functional Separation: Pros and Cons," *La Lettre de l'Autorite (English Version)*, March/April 2007, 1–2, 4.

103. Ferguson, "Broadband Problem," 5–6; Brett Winterford, "Structural Separation is Cheaper Way Ahead for FTTN," ZDNet.com.au, 28 May 2008.

104. See Cannon, "The Legacy."

105. See Internet Industry Association, "Submission on Request," 2.

106. Functional separation also has costs, such as "the reorganization of the company, the duplication of technical staff and engineers and, in general, the splitting up of various activities had presented a certain degree of synergy," perhaps resulting in "increased network access costs for all operators," if not necessarily higher prices charged to those operators. See "Functional Separation: Pros and Cons."

107. Reding, "The EU Telecoms," 2–3.

108. See, e.g., European Regulators Group, "ERG Opinion on Functional Separation," 12–14.

109. Richard Thurston, "Finding a Funder."

110. Stan Beer, "Functional Separation Works for Broadband: UK Communications Regulator," *ITWire*, 6 July 2008 (discussing a report by Ofcom chief executive Ed Richards).

111. Michael Sainsbury, "BT Rebuffs Telstra on Anti-Separation," *The Australian*, 7 July 2008 (quoting the CEO of British Telecom, Ian Livingston, as nothing the United Kingdom surpasses the United States and Japan in broadband penetration, has "some of the lowest prices in the world," and enjoys competition among two hundred different broadband companies).

112. Forsyth, "Openreach," 7. See also Richard Lalande (Chairman of AFORST, French group of alternative providers), "So Why Are They So Against It?," *La Lettre de l'Autorite (English Version)*, March/April 2007, 7.

113. See Richards, "Functional Separation."

114. European Regulators Group, "ERG Opinion on Functional Separation," 9.

115. See Richards, "Functional Separation."

116. Winston Maxwell, "Functional Separation: What We Can Learn from the British Experience," *La Lettre de l'Autorite (English Version)*, March/April 2007, 9.

117. Internet Industry Association, "Submission on Request," 7; "Sweden: PTS Puts Forward New Broadband Strategy, Advocates Functional Separation and Fibre Access," *T-Regs*, 16 February 2007. See also Post and Telestyrelsen, "Improved Broadband Competition," 64–69; OECD, "Broadband Growth," 55–56.

118. Tim Wu, "Wireless Carterfone," *International Journal of Communications* 1:1, 389 (2007).

119. Comments of Free Press et al., in the Matter of Broadband Industry Practices, WC Docket No. 07-52, 13 February 2008, 55–59. See also Ferguson, "The United States Broadband Problem," 6.

120. See, e.g., Wearden, "Ofcom Forces Action."

121. Free, "Opened Up to the Competition."

122. Crandall, *Competition and Chaos*, 145.

123. This requirement already largely exists, but could work better. *See* Crandall, *Competition and Chaos*, 13. See also OECD, "Broadband Growth," 61–62.

124. See, e.g., Deborah Yao, "Verizon Copper Cutoff Worries Some Users, Small Rivals," Associated Press, 8 July 2007.

125. Google proposed something different in Australia, proposing the existing network remain during a transition period. See Mike Preston, "Competition Key To Australia's Broadband Future: Google," *Smart Company* (3 July 2008).

126. Halper, "Does High Tech."

127. Halper, "Does High Tech."

128. See, e.g., "Sweden: PTS." Other cities with fiber to the home projects are Cologne, Vienna, Milan, Stockholm, and Amsterdam. Wieland, "FTTH Battles." See also Turner, "Universal Service"; John Windhausen, "A Blueprint for Big Broadband," EDUCAUSE January 2008; Comments of National Telecommunications Cooperative Association, in the Matter of High-Cost Universal Service Support, WC Docket No. 05-337, 17 April 2008, 3n5; and "2007–2008 Request for Proposals," Universal Broadband Access Grant Program, State of New York, 7 December 2007.

129. See, e.g., Kenji Kushida and Seung-Youn Oh, "Understanding South Korea and Japan's Spectacular Broadband Development: Strategic Liberalization of the Telecommunications Sectors," BRIE Working Paper 175, 29 June 2006, 17–19. See also Atkinson et al., "Explaining," 23.

130. Grant Forsyth (Head of Global Interconnection at BT), "Openreach: BT's Vie," *La Lettre de l'Autorite (English Version)*, March/April 2007, 6.

6

U.S. Cable TV Policy

Managing the Transition to Broadband

Richard D. Taylor

The revolution now in sight may be nothing less than either of those [the book and the telephone]. It may conceivably be even more.

> *On the Cable: The Television of Abundance*, Report of the Sloan Commission on Cable Communications, 1971, on the high expectations for cable television

> Man came by to hook up my cable TV
> We settled in for the night, my baby and me
> We switched 'round and 'round 'till half-past dawn
> There was fifty-seven channels and nothin' on

> Bruce Springsteen,
> "57 Channels (and Nothin' On)," 1992, Album: *Human Touch*

Introduction

THE EARLY GROWTH OF CABLE TELEVISION created high hopes for both private and public uses. Whether these were fulfilled depends on what kind of balance between entertainment and other uses is viewed as optimal. In retrospect, cable television became a medium overwhelmingly—indeed, almost exclusively—dominated by entertainment. Once that happened, little could be done to rectify the situation. But the era of cable television, as we have known it, is ending, and the era of multi-use broadband networks is beginning. It is once again possible, then, for public policymakers to recalibrate the balance with respect to another new technology—the Internet—that is creating high hopes.

This chapter addresses select issues in cable television policy in the context of the evolving video market. It offers broad policy perspectives as well as specific recommendations. The main assumption here is that the "cable television" business is evolving away from a video delivery business and into a "broadband" business, and that this is a welcome development. A series of recommendations presented below about pending "cable" policy issues are designed to promote this transition.

Background

Cable television service[1] is regulated nationally under Title 6 of the Communications Act of 1934, which was passed in 1984 as the Cable Communications Policy Act (Cable Act),[2] as amended, particularly in 1992 and 1996. At the local level, some 6,635 cable systems operate under some 33,000 agreements[3] with local franchising authorities (LFAs). States have historically played a limited role in cable television regulation; however, before 2005, there were at least ten states with some level of control and/or oversight.[4]

Over the last several years, large incumbent telecommunications companies, such as AT&T and Verizon, have begun offering digital video services (IPTV). While it has yet to be established whether or not these services constitute "cable service" under the Cable Act, for the purposes of this chapter, they will not be considered part of the "cable television" industry, even though the companies may, in some cases, seek "cable television" franchises at the state or local level.[5] Spurred on by the companies making these offerings, more states have taken an interest in the creation of state-level video franchises (preempting LFAs), and today there are twenty-eight states in which this issue has been or is still being debated.[6]

At the national level, in 2006–2007, a number of proposals pertaining to federal and state franchising, network neutrality, and broadband universal service, which would have affected the cable industry either directly or indirectly, were presented to Congress. It is not within the scope of this chapter to cover all these topics, but a useful summary of many of the proposals and how they relate to the cable industry is available.[7]

Currently, most of these issues are pending further congressional, regulatory (FCC), or state action. Although there is no overall vision in the United

States today that might direct the final outcome, the evolution of cable television suggests some possibilities.

The Cable Television Industry Mid-2008

Broadly speaking, the term "cable industry"[8] refers to two related but different enterprises: one that manages networks and one that provides content (mostly video programming). This chapter focuses primarily on the former. One noteworthy development, discussed below, is that market forces appear to be creating pressure to separate programming content from distribution operations. The industry also offers voice products (e.g., VoIP), Internet broadband connectivity, and related services.

Scale

In 2007, the cable industry had total revenues of $75.2 billion. To put this figure in perspective, that same year Verizon had revenues of $93.5 billion, and AT&T had revenues of $118.9 billion. Comcast, the company with the largest number of cable television subscribers (about 24 million),[9] had revenues of $30.9 billion

With respect to residential video products,[10] as of December 2007:

- The number of U.S. households with television sets was 112,275,000.
- The number of households subscribing to "basic" cable television service was 64,800,000 (or 58 percent of the total). The four largest cable multisystem operators (MSOs) served 74.6 percent of all basic cable subscribers.
- The number of households subscribing to noncable multichannel video providers was thirty-two million (or twenty-nine of the total).
- The number of national video cable programming networks was 565.
- Cable television subscribership is at a seventeen-year low,[11] following a slow but steady decline. Since 2001, cable companies have lost two million subscribers.

With respect to residential high-speed Internet access, as of June 2007:

- The number of U.S. residential broadband subscribers was sixty-three million.
- The number of cable modem broadband subscribers was 32.9 million (52 percent of the total).[12]

- The number of DSL, fiber, and wireless broadband subscribers was 30.4 million (48 percent of the total). The top four telecommunications companies served 92 percent of all DSL subscribers.
- The top ten Internet service providers (ISPs) (includes cable and telecommunications operators) accounted for 75 percent of all Internet connections.[13]

Cable Industry Strengths and Weaknesses

Strengths

Virtually all cable systems have benefited for years from a *de facto* monopoly in their local markets. This provided them with all the benefits of incumbency and allowed them to build strong brand identification and customer relationships, develop attractive product offerings, sharpen their programming and marketing skills, and raise rates with little fear of competition. Coaxial cable is a proven, high-capacity technology with which they have extensive operational experience. National cable companies have established relationships with programmers, and their large subscriber base helps them attain significant discounts on program purchases. In some communities, they may share an interest with the LFA in discouraging competition.

Weaknesses

Increased competition from well-financed, aggressive telecommunications and satellite (and possibly wireless[14]) competitors has prevented further growth in basic subscribers—their key market. Other problems include:

- Increasing dependence on discretionary services, sales of which are declining in a soft economy, along with an increase in non-pay disconnects;[15]
- Growing reliance on service bundles, which are expensive and require extended commitments;
- Loss of younger viewers;[16]
- A nearly 50/50 split of the broadband market, with telecommunications operators, with DSL growing faster;
- Cost and time of converting networks to all digital (eventually all-IP) networks.
- Video content on the Internet is becoming a strategic threat to the cable business model (but is also driving penetration of, and shift to, broadband).

Overall, the stock market has taken a dim view of these developments, especially when it comes to companies with large cable holdings (such as Comcast, Time Warner, and Cablevision). Cable stocks were recently trading at ten-year lows on key metrics.[17] Time Warner's stock has lost one-third of its value since the beginning of 2007, prompting the well-received announcement that it was undertaking "a complete structural separation" from its cable division, a move designed to enable programming to reach its maximum potential.[18] Some cable stocks have recently seen a turnaround, but as of May 17, 2008, cable stocks overall were down 47 percent from their peak value in February 2007.[19]

Changes in the Video Market

The Current Evolution of TV: A New Model of Video Content Distribution

All existing video distribution models—broadcasting, cable, IPTV, satellite—are under pressure today for the following reasons: the multiplicity of channels and the segmentation of audiences, the movement of advertising to the Internet, time (TiVo) and place (Slingbox) shifting, the flight of younger audiences to alternatives (e.g., videogames, Web 2.0 sites), and the emergence of online video. But the biggest strategic challenge to the market is the emergence of the Internet as a potential competitor for the delivery of traditional video content, outflanking and making obsolete all "walled garden" models. Cable operators and broadcasters alike view the Internet as a truly disruptive technology.[20] As Time Warner Cable's CEO Glenn Britt noted at the May 2008 NCTA Cable Show: "[I]f you're talking about putting [a program] online for free on the same date [that it airs on television], that will erode your business model. The operators are the middlemen who guarantee [the cable networks'] revenue, so we have to intervene at some point."[21]

Some anticipate a shift in the balance between broadcast and cable television in the future. "In 15 years, broadcast TV will only be useful for high-profile live events like the Super Bowl, award shows, and programs like 'American Idol,'" says Ben Silverman, co-chairman of NBC Entertainment. "[O]ther shows will have to live on multiple platforms to survive. NBC plans to experiment with driving viewers to the web from TV."[22] "We will go wherever the viewers are" is the new programmers' credo.[23] For the new video model, content producers want as many forms of distribution as possible, a goal at times at cross-purposes with affiliation with particular distribution networks.

The new model is multiple platforms for content distribution. AT&T calls it the "three-screen strategy" (television, personal computer, and wireless), while the cable industry calls it "any stream to any screen," and Microsoft calls it the "unified entertainment marketplace." Already today, there is a wide array of broadcast and cable programming available online and on mobile devices, thanks to the following: the conversion from analog to digital, the higher speed provided to residential consumers over Internet connections, the migration of traditional television programming to the Internet, and the convergence of screens and emergence of TV 2.0.

Analog to Digital

AT&T's "U-Verse" video service is 100 percent IP-based,[24] and Verizon is migrating its FiOS video services to all-IP,[25] eliminating analog video channels. The cable industry is struggling with this transition and prefers to make it incrementally. Originally an all-analog network (for six MHz TV channels), cable has gradually been introducing digital (but not necessarily IP-based) technologies. This has left many operators with hybrid architectures (analog, digital, IP), but the industry as a whole is slowly moving to allocate more capacity to IP, using technologies related to its DOCSIS 3.0 initiative.[26] A move from analog to all digital, and ultimately IPTV, would significantly increase cable systems' capacity to carry additional or expanded services by freeing up spectrum currently used for analog video channels. Accordingly, Comcast has announced that it is moving to all-digital transmission.[27]

The cable industry's problem, as summed up in an article in the *Wall Street Journal*, is: "As online video becomes increasingly part of the daily lifestyle, consumers are going to expect to be able to download high-definition video straight from the Web to their TV sets. Once a great deal of content is available this way, viewers need an easy way to sort through it all, using their remote control to navigate an on-screen guide. For cable operators, the risk is that this process could leave them out of the equation altogether."[28] Indeed, the cannibalization of traditional cable revenues by their broadband offerings is perceived as a real threat to cable operators.

Steadily Increasing Transmission Speed

The trend among broadband providers has been to steadily increase the speed of the connection to consumers. Verizon has announced that it will be offering all its FiOS subscribers access to fifty mbps download speeds[29] and says it has equipment in the field that lets it boost speeds to more than one hundred mbps, with the capability to go up to four hundred mbps.[30] Comcast has started experimenting with fifty mbps service in Minneapolis. Comcast CEO Brian Roberts recently said the public could expect to see "speeds 10, 20 maybe 50 times higher than today."[31] While this would certainly represent an improvement on current (mid-2008) offerings, the United States still lags behind other developed countries in those services reported to be widely available to residential consumers. To cite one extreme case, it has been reported that a woman in Sweden has a forty gbps Internet connection to her home.[32]

Migration of "Television" Content to the Internet

Television has already begun its migration to the Internet, where major broadcast and network content is already accessible (e.g., Hulu, Joost, Fancast, Veoh).[33] NBC alone says it streamed fifty million shows from its site in October 2007.[34] Whole networks can be transferred into a web-based format, thus, for example, the Warner Bros. TV Group has announced it will resurrect its former broadcast network, The WB, as a new ad-supported web video–based interactive site, theWB.com, featuring the most popular shows from its library.[35] At present, most American broadcast and cable network channels are not being "simul-streamed" with their over-the-air transmission. However, this "simul-streaming" has already been started in Europe by Zattoo. com.[36] In principle, there is no reason every movie studio, network, television station and public access channel could not have a video-streaming website of its own, as radio (and online-only "radio") stations do. For example, www .chooseandwatch.com (by country) provides access to 6,500 TV/video channels from around the world. Video (both real-time streaming and downloaded) is also moving rapidly to mobile and "iPod" type devices.[37]

Convergence of Screens/TV 2.0

The race is on to turn television into an open content platform—making it yet one more screen upon which all available video content can be displayed.[38] This, of course, requires a broadband network connection. SONY is selling an Internet adapter for its Bravia line of televisions[39] and has announced it will stream movies directly to these sets.[40] A wired standard to connect computers/ television/home entertainment centers is expected to be on the market soon.[41] Cisco is producing Internet-enabled "converter" set-top boxes.[42] Set-top boxes for the Internet delivery of movies are currently available from Vudu[43] and Netflix.[44] Users of X-Box 360 can view programming from the Microsoft X-Box live service on their television sets.[45] The goal of consumer electronics manufacturers is to turn the home entertainment center into an Internet portal.

There is already a model hybrid "cable box" which operates with no "cable" content at all. Sezmi offers a service with a set-top box that integrates off-air signals (using a powerful HD antenna) and Internet-based video programming. It comes with one terabyte of storage and allows access to both pay-per-view and archived content.[46] While it may or may not succeed as a business model, the concept is to seamlessly integrate web video content and advertising.

The provision of all forms of video over the Internet has been referred to as TV 2.0[47] and can be broadly defined into four categories: aggregators, portals, desktop clients, and pay services. While these will be key business models in the future, they are outside the range of discussion of this chapter. Still, some information on this topic can be found in table 6.1 at the end of this chapter.

The Vision: Video Programming Circa 2020 or So . . .

In order to provide a longer-term vision that will help inform and shape regulatory policy, the following assumptions need to be made about how the market will look in 2020 if current trends continue and certain policy measures are taken.

Ubiquitous Broadband Networks Will be the Norm

- The former "cable" systems will have become all-purpose IP broadband networks. Since broadband access is an "information service," not a "cable service," there will no longer be any "cable systems" providing "cable services" under the Cable Act. Since they will be entirely IP-based, neither will there be any "channels."
- The primary product of the "transmission" part of the business will be broadband network access and related value-added services (e.g., VoIP) and bundled services and applications, not video programming
- There will be a ubiquitous national broadband network of around fifty mbps. Congress will have amended the Communications Act to supersede the 1984 Cable Act (as amended) and create a national broadband policy and a uniform, cross-platform set of broadband regulations. Wireline facilities-based carriers (formerly cable and telecommunications companies) will be primarily regulated at the federal and state level. All broadband carriers will have nondiscrimination and interconnection obligations. The NCTA and USTA will have merged into the National Broadband Telecommunications Association (NBTA) (NBA already having been taken).

Program Distribution Adopts an Internet Model

- Sources of video programming will be located anywhere and be accessible everywhere.
- Competition for video programming will flourish within the "pipe," not for the pipe.[48] Subscribers will have access to a vast selection of services.
- Cable program networks will be distributed over multiple platforms. Video products and packages will be provided mostly directly by originators or by aggregators. The former cable business will have separated into its two components: facilities-based transmission and program content.
- Traditional video content (broadcast and cable network program-type schedules) will be subsumed among a myriad of video resources available to viewers.
- Devices like the TiVo and Slingbox will separate viewers from their program sources by time and distance. Linear (scheduled) programming will decline in importance as the younger generation chooses to program itself; its value to advertisers dropping accordingly.

Broadband Policy

- All agreements with LFAs under the Cable Act will have been superseded or have expired and been replaced with federal broadband regulation and state video programming/broadband franchises.[49]
- State PUCs (or other designated agencies) will take over "franchising" role, which will include the following activities:
  - Collect "franchise fees" or comparable taxes on broadband revenues (not video programming), possibly making adjustments for multiple payers in the same area.
  - Assume greater responsibility for consumer protection.
  - Create state local access and programming funds and distribute resources to communities to support production and other costs of local access (formerly PEG) channels, now program sources connected to the Internet (see more, below).
- Regulation will be light where there is competition[50] and stronger where there is not. Forbearance is encouraged in the absence of demonstrable or highly likely abuses.

Policy Recommendations—Federal Government

All policies and rules adopted over the next several years should be viewed as temporary, intended to facilitate the smooth transition to a national, interconnected, nondiscriminatory broadband network. That said, a number of issues currently pending at the federal level need to be addressed.

Content Regulation and A La Carte Program Offerings

Regulation of indecency, violent programming, and other content, which cannot be directly regulated on cable television for constitutional reasons, has been tied by proxy to the idea of having cable operators offer their programs individually (*a la carte*). The benefits of *a la carte* channel sales are highly uncertain, and such a major disruption of a working business model should be based on unequivocal data. In addition to strictly economic data, regulation in the public interest might want to consider the consequences of *a la carte* for promoting diversity as well.[51]

The desire to regulate content—above and beyond filters, ratings, parental control devices, education, and parental involvement—has always been there. That doesn't make it less constitutionally suspect, especially when it comes to cable, and even more so, when it comes to the Internet, where video programming is migrating.[52] There are currently several legal cases pending, among them several before the Supreme Court,[53] which may help determine the extent of the FCC's and Congress's authority within the Constitution to regulate indecency, violence, and hate speech in electronic media. A novel approach to evading First Amendment issues of this sort was taken in the recent agreement between Time Warner Cable, Verizon, and Sprint with the New York attorney general to curtail access to child pornography.[54] This would seem to be a step in the direction of a model of liability for ISPs that is reportedly moving forward in Europe.[55] Another approach is evident in the FCC's June 27, 2008, "Further Notice of Proposed Rule Rulemaking," which would require the winner of an auction for broadband wireless spectrum to provide a so-called smut-free wireless broadband, blocking "obscenity" or "pornography" or any "images or text" that would be harmful to teens and adolescents five to seventeen years of age.[56] The goal here seems to be transferring responsibility for censorship to the carriers and ISPs.

Must Carry and the Digital Transition

It is the clear intent of Congress that no one be deprived of access to primary licensed local television broadcast signals either during or after the transition to digital broadcasting, regardless of the quality of broadcast. Apparently, some thirteen million households are at risk of losing their signals.[57] Historically, this has meant the broadcaster's single program channel; however, the transition to digital delivery has made it possible for local broadcasters to provide more than one-channel. It has been argued that a "multi-cast must-carry" requirement changes the rules and their original intent and, therefore, may be both beyond the FCC's jurisdiction as well as constitutionally questionable. Proposals that cable operators carry "every bit"[58] a licensed broadcaster may broadcast have gained even less support. "Must-carry" is about keeping the promise to viewers, not about creating a new business model for broadcasters. Eventually, when any user will be able to freely access any station's content, "must-carry" will become an historical artifact.

Traffic Management

Telecommunications network traffic management, hardly a new idea, is necessary to maintain network integrity and quality. In principle, it makes sense to ban discrimination among users, content, applications, services, and devices. But like with any rule, there are exceptions that should be considered. Comcast's alleged spoofing of BitTorrent users is well-known and was ruled as "discriminatory" by the FCC.[59] But was Comcast violating any rules when it blocked e-mails it decided were "spam"? (The court said no.)[60] It may be that blocking spam, viruses, trojans, and other kinds of malware is beneficial to users of the web.

It can also be argued that it is more important for some kinds of traffic to arrive in a timely stream than others. For that reason, it might be worth considering giving preference to certain kinds of traffic, such as emergency medical information, police and security information, and critical operational information (e.g., electric grid control, banking, air traffic control). One possibility is creating virtual private networks, which would not be subject to slowdowns, or, alternatively, moving them off the public Internet.

Some questions remain open. Will AT&T, for example, be in violation if it uses "deep packet inspection" to identify "illegal" content? Or if networks or ISPs employ DRM technology which intercepts purportedly illegal file transfers, would that be deemed "discriminatory"? What will happen if traffic on the network exceeds its capacity at a particular time? Neutrality is a complex issue. Some argue that all traffic should be slowed down to an equal pace and that more capacity is the only answer. Others argue that as more bandwidth becomes available, applications will assume the existence of broadband and increase the amount of bandwidth applications consume.[61] While rules prohibiting arbitrary or anti-competitive discrimination need to be enacted promptly, the same prompt, serious, and meaningful discussion of the nuances of this issue should continue. Full disclosure of network management practices would be a useful first step.

Metered Service

Jousting headlines tell the story: "Cisco Projects Growth to Swell for Online Video" (16 June 2008)[62] and "Top Cable Companies Try Reining in Heavy

Web Use (June 3, 2008)."[63] Based on the rapid growth in Internet traffic, some well-informed writers are predicting a "Broadband Train Wreck"[64] if steps are not taken to manage it, and have suggested two obvious solutions: 1) building more capacity, and 2) discouraging use by introducing usage-based pricing. Their argument is that "fairness" (to light users) and "necessity" (to finance network upgrades) need to be balanced. Seizing the opportunity, cable and telecommunications[65] broadband providers are now introducing programs to charge users by the number of bytes downloaded.[66] Because this proposal could lead to unintended harmful consequences, it is addressed here at a somewhat disproportional length as neither the "fairness" nor "necessity" argument hold it up. Here are some of the problems:

- Usage-based pricing is anti-competitive. It would have the effect of stifling incipient video competition to cable and IPTV "walled gardens." By comparison, one traditional DVD holds roughly 4.7 gigabytes. An HD DVD holds 30/50 gigabytes. Should users be required to pay $50 to view an HD movie online? Under this scheme Internet pricing could be geared to people who send only e-mail, discouraging dissemination of new and/or competitive applications to the broadband providers' core business, especially video.
- The pricing is arbitrary. There is no rational connection between the cost per gigabyte delivered and the proposed charges. Cisco predicts that the average household with two standard definition televisions, one HD television and two computers will be using 1.1 terabytes of data per month by 2010.[67] As an example, Time Warner is currently testing a forty-gigabyte-per-month cap with its $54.90 per month "fast" service[68] and charging $1 for each gigabyte over that. If Cisco's model were accurate, that would result in a monthly charge of $1,114.90 for the average household in 2010. For the carriers, bandwidth is a declining cost business; still, they want to charge customers more.
- Usage-based pricing slows growth. Even if many users have not yet reached their limit, they can get there very quickly; others will be discouraged or afraid of exceeding their caps. The slow initial growth of the Internet in Europe is widely attributed to usage-based pricing. The "all you can eat" model has been a great success globally in bringing online greater capacity and new and better applications, due in large parts to "network effects."
- It fails to recognize the current reality of the evolving video market. The viewing of video over the Internet is growing rapidly, especially among the under thirty demographic, and the quality is improving. Soon much online video will be HD, and as cable and fiber optic networks are

upgraded to speeds of fifty to one hundred mbps (already widely available in Korea, Japan, and Sweden), users will want to download more.

- It creates perverse incentives. For example, it encourages carriers not to increase bandwidth, and it encourages people to use the Internet less and develop fewer bandwidth-intensive applications. This is counterproductive and would give carriers a tollgate on the road to every other kind of service.
- While it is not unfair to low-volume users, they benefit indirectly from having a high-capacity network for those who want/need it and from having network capacity should they decide to use it. The low-volume user who sends only three e-mails a month may suddenly decide s/he wants to watch HD movies and television over the Internet. There is a significant benefit in having the network "standing by" to accommodate a change in usage patterns as more video becomes available online.
- It is not a necessary revenue stream. There are other means available for carriers to increase revenues, such as charging for speed of connection, quality of service, value-added services, bundled services, content provision, partnerships with websites, advertising, regulatory and fiscal accommodations, and public-private partnerships. And, as noted above, broadband is a declining cost business. To allow carriers to charge "by the drink" may stifle legitimate competition before it takes hold, burdening consumers with potentially vastly higher costs and slowing the growth of Internet usage and the development of new and beneficial applications that make use of higher bandwidths to deliver improved services.

Competition

To promote competition, policymakers need to undertake the following measures:

- Continue to encourage the trend toward platform-based broadband competition.
- Encourage existing providers to compete across their historic territories.[69]
- Reduce, not raise, regulatory barriers to entry and encourage anyone who wants to offer video/broadband service to do so, by any means, anywhere.
- Experiment with new ideas, especially public/private partnerships.
- Avoid subsidizing inefficient technologies.
- Provide economic incentives for introduction of video/broadband systems.

As broadband competition and universal service are further discussed in chapters 10 and 12, they will not be pursued further here.

Vertical Integration

Should the United States adopt a policy of "structural separation" with respect to conduit and content, this would present serious challenges, both politically and legally. Still, current market forces appear to be pushing in this direction. For the time being, an anti-trust based response with a private right of action seems to be the best available solution.[70] If this solution leads to rampant abuses, the issue can always be revisited. Today, only 14.9 percent of the 565 available program channels are vertically integrated or affiliated with at least one cable operator,[71] and they will be further diluted as they go online. A more subtle issue that needs to be addressed is the use by incumbents of their proprietary, managed IP networks for their own content, while relegating competitors' content and services to the "public" Internet.

Broadband Conversion

Just as Congress set a "date certain" for the switchover from analog to digital broadcasting, it should set a definite cut-off date for the adoption of all-IP based broadband networks. Congress and the FCC should adopt policies and rules to facilitate the transition to an all-broadband network, as well as the move from local to state regulation. The FCC should require all televisions built following the earliest practicable date to accept direct Internet connections. The FCC should work with appropriate professional groups to establish "open Internet TV" standards, just as it did with advanced television standards (these could be multiple standards), including standards for remote controls and built-in media browsers.[72]

Policy Regulations—State and Local Government/PEG

- State video services legislation: States should be encouraged to pass laws franchising wired, terrestrial video delivery systems, and replacing municipal cable franchises (to the extent permitted under federal law). A uniform model law would be helpful in this regard, to set common standards. To the extent possible, states should encourage competitive entry into video/broadband services by any technology, in any area. This includes, but is not limited to, facilitating and incentivizing existing carriers to overbuild each other, e.g., Verizon overbuild AT&T; Comcast overbuild Time Warner.

- State video franchises should be nonexclusive in fact as well as in form, and issued and supervised under an appropriate state agency, such as the PSC or PUC with experience in regulated industries. The state agency should monitor competition in its markets, and adopt a modified carrier regulatory model for oversight of unregulated markets.
- Build-out requirements: Build-out requirements are more a barrier to entry and a shield to incumbents than they are a public benefit. Open markets to the extent feasible and eliminate area-specific requirements except in cases intentional "redlining."[73]
- Consumer Protection/Customer Service Standards: Receipt of, and response to, customer questions and concerns that are not being addressed by the service providers can be handled at either the local or state level (or both) and must have enforceable consequences built into the state franchise.
- Collection/distribution of franchise fees/taxes (e.g., sales tax on video programming services) for PEG channels: States should determine and collect franchise fees or sales taxes on video programming (consistent with federal law) and return to communities an appropriate amount for access groups (either through the municipality or directly).
- Definition of "technically feasible": State video franchises should include a mandatory definition of the technical quality of digital PEG access of at least equal to commercial video programs (channels) previously delivered as analog. Language about "technical feasibility" should not be misused to diminish public access programming.
- State franchise renewal/revocation: State video franchises should be for a definite term of years, and should not be in perpetuity or provisioned with an "automatic" or "presumptive" renewal. They should include technical, commercial, customer, and public access performance standards, offering service of not less than commercial quality.

Local Franchising Authorities

- Revocation/Expiration: State video franchises should be revocable for cause after due notice and process for material failure to perform; a clear process and timeline should be established for revocation, and renewal proceedings on expiration. Right-of-way management and police power and local business regulation, consistent with federal and state law, stays with the municipality.
- Residual powers: State video franchises should not preempt the field. Municipalities should be able to claim any residual authority not specifically preempted by federal or state law or regulation.

- Franchise fees: State video franchises should contain franchise fee requirements consistent with federal law. Some states have chosen to use a sales tax approach. In either case, the states should work with the municipalities to share revenues on a basis equivalent to the previous value received (but not a windfall due to multiple overlapping franchises).
- Institutional networks (limited by FCC): Free Internet connections and service for public facilities can be requested. Municipalities and PEG access groups can negotiate with carriers and/or developers for the installation of a "dark" public fiber alongside commercial fibers in a condominium fiber with a separate "public" strands, when the fiber cable is installed. This is being implemented in places in Canada.[74]
- Other franchise related commitments may be implemented, within limits set by the FCC).[75]

PEG Access and Channels[76]

- If "franchise fees" or equivalent taxes are paid to the state instead of the municipality, the requirement and process to reimburse PEG access providers will have to be addressed in the state franchise law.
- PEG access is going to have to make the transition from analog to IP. However, it should not be reduced in accessibility, quality or features during or after that transition, relative to any other previously broadcast/ analog cable/IPTV channels. In addition, its needs for support may be increased relative to the expense of going digital. Mechanisms of partnerships with its local communities to assess needs and receive and distribute funds from the states need to be developed as part of the state franchising process and be clearly embedded in the rules.
- Studios, staff, and operating costs: New expenses related to digitization, Internet connection, and equipment—funded from state access contributions.

PEG-related issues that need to be addressed:[77]

- *Removal to digital tier*. PEG channels involuntarily moved from easy access on the analog "basic" tier to a digital tier, which may require special equipment (an extra fee), reach fewer viewers, and be more difficult to find.
- *PEG channel "slamming."* Arbitrary relocation of PEG channels away from the "basic" tier and/or aggregating PEG channels under a single channel (e.g., 99) as a separate application, requiring more "clicks" to get to the content, and making PEG inaccessible to "channel surfing."

- *Loss of closed captioning.* When PEG channels are moved from analog to digital tiers, the channel's closed captioning for the hearing impaired can be lost (e.g., on AT&T's U-verse).
- *Harder to find with remote.* Once PEG channels are removed from established channel locations and relocated to digital tiers or other forms of "cable Siberia," it takes them out of the main traffic pattern of the remote control, and makes it more difficult for users to find them.
- *Lower signal quality* (digital "PEG product"). The picture quality of digital PEG channels is inferior to the analog version, and often to that of commercial channels that have been moved (1.25 mbps MPEG-4 for PEG vs. 2 mbps for standard definition).
- *Channel latency.* In some cases, it can take up to over a minute for the PEG channel content to appear, once the correct channel has been selected.
- *Inability to record.* Digital PEG channels have been reported not to work with TIVOs and other DVR recording devices.
- *Cost of conversion of NTSC signal to digital.* Producers of PEG channels must incur additional production expenses for digital equipment and/or conversion of analog to digital signals.
- *Cost of interconnection with carriers.* PEG content providers are typically charged a fee to interconnect to deliver their signal to the carrier's network.
- *Public access.* Already with a limited audience, the public's only free cable "soapbox" will be harder to find and its funding will be more questionable at a time when its expenses will be going up.
- *Local access.* Local access groups will have to adapt the concept of going digital and the need to negotiate with new parties, in particular traditional telecommunications carriers ("phone companies") and the state PUC in place of, or in addition to, municipalities. This will involve a steep learning curve and extra effort in the transition. Perhaps first they might also want to webcast their content. In the best case, it could be a gateway to new partners and the expanded access and multiplicity of channels offered by the carriers and the Internet.
- Opportunities for growth in "hyperlocalism."[78] At a time when traditional local media of all kinds are declining, there may also be opportunities opening for PEG access organizations to partner with others, or to introduce new types of content and or programming of interest to various targeted groups.

Conclusion: Transition Policy Today for the Broadband
Network of Tomorrow

Looking Ahead to Future Challenges

In general, the ability to use the public Internet to deliver video programming undermines the status quo of the video market. Hence, it is reasonable to expect the incumbents, the "haves"—cable companies, IPTV providers, and the major networks and broadcasters—to coordinate to protect their interests. It is, therefore, not surprising to learn that the cable[79] and telecommunications[80] industries are holding discussions with the NAB to "work together in the digital age to find a win-win blueprint for delivering TV service." An open, nondiscriminatory, high-speed, broadband network inherently creates the virtual equivalent of line sharing, at least with respect to the delivery of video services.

The challenges for protecting video over "open" broadband networks from undue dominance or predatory behavior are entirely different than with cable television. The bottlenecks are not the local carriers but proprietary software, appliances, search engines, DRM, and advertising. Companies "of interest" may be those like Microsoft, Google, Cisco, and SONY, which can potentially leverage their control over key components of the network. Some possible control points these companies may have over the Internet include:

- Software/consumer electronics/home entertainment complex.[81]
- Search engines[82]/control of video search.
- Aggregators/dominance of product categories.
- Middleware/control of standards for key software.
- Advertising[83]/dominance of online advertising.
- DRM/a universal "digital rights management" scheme.
- Bundling/the ability to offer integrated services.
- Dominance of infrastructure through peering arrangements.
- Large companies' financial ability to serve more users at higher speeds.

The Challenge to Policymakers

This chapter has discussed some of the key issues and challenges facing the cable industry today, looking ahead to the future of the video market. It has presented a strategic vision for the video/broadband market of the future and has recommended policies and specific legislative and regulatory actions that would help the United States move toward an open, nondiscriminatory, ubiquitous broadband network in the shortest possible amount of time. Not all of these recommendations will be welcomed by interest groups, which benefit from the status quo. Indeed, the policies advocated in this chapter will probably not be to the liking of the powerful telecommunications, cable, broadcasting, and programming industries. But only if policymakers are able to take a broad view that will ultimately benefit society at large, and create new opportunities for broadband carriers and the creators and distributors of video program content, as well as local communities and the nation as a whole, will they be able to make the necessary decisions. It is unlikely they will have another chance.

An impressive new instrument of communication has been made available to society by the advance of technology. It remains for society to employ that instrument wisely and well (*On the Cable: The Television of Abundance*, Report of the Sloan Commission on Cable Communications, 1971, Conclusion).

TABLE 6.1:
SCHEDULE 1—TV 2.0

	Site	URL
Aggregators		
	YouTube	www.youtube.com
	Daily Motion	www.dailymotion.com
	Metacafe	www.metacafe.com
	Blip.TV	blip.tv
	Kyte	www.kyte.tv/home/index.html
Portals		
	MSN Video	video.msn.com
	AOL Video	video.aol.com
	Yahoo! Video	video.yahoo.com
	Myspace Video	vids.myspace.com
Desktop Clients		
	Joost	www.joost.com
	Vuze	www.vuze.com/app
	Babelgum	www.babelgum.com
	VeohTV	www.veoh.com/veohTV/getStarted.html
	Zattoo	zattoo.com
	Livestation	www.livestation.com
	Next.TV	next.tv/
	Jalipo	www.jalipo.com/epg
	Miro	www.getmiro.com
	RealPlayer 11	www.realplayer.com
	GubaTV	www.guba.com
	MobuzzTV	dailybuzz.mobuzz.tv

YouTV	www.youtvpc.com
AmericaFreeTV	www.americafree.tv/index.shtml
WebTVList	www.webtvlist.com
ManiaTV	www.maniatv.com
TV4All	wwitv.com/portal.htm
WorldTVRadio	www.worldtvradio.com
Ceedtv	www.ceedtv.com
Streamik	www.streamick.com

Multiple TV Feeds

Cozmo.TV	www.cozmo.tv/mainnew.html
TVexe.com	www.tvexe.com
TVoverinternet	www.tvover.net/TVStation.aspx

Paid Content

ITunes TV	www.apple.com/itunes/store/tvshows.html
Netflix	www.netflix.com
Amazon Unbox	www.amazon.com
Reeltime	www.reeltime.com
Movielink (movie rentals)	www.movielink.com
Akimbo (video on demand)	www.akimbo.com
Cinemanow (movies to rent or buy)	www.cinemanow.com
Vongo.com (movies on demand)	www.vongo.com

Notes

1. Complex definitional issues hide behind this phrase. What constitutes "cable service," although defined by law, is subject to considerable debate. Cable television operators offer a variety of ancillary services that arguably fall outside that definition, and the status of video offered by Internet Protocol (IPTV) is debated.

2. The Cable Communications Act of 1984, Pub. Law 98-549, 1984 98 Stat. 2779, codified at 47 U.S.C. sec. 521 *et seq.*

3. Jim DeMint and Dick Armey, "Perspective: An e-contract for the 21st Century," CNET News.com, 27 April 2006, news.cnet.com/An-e-contract-for-the-21st-century/2010-1028_3-6065530.html/ (19 June 2008); Federal Communications Commission, in the Matter of Implementation of Section 3 of the Cable Television Consumer Protection and Competition Act of 1992, MM Docket No. 92-266, adopted 31 December 1996, released 2 January 1997, IV.A.15.

4. Gerard Lederer, "The State of the States: A Report on Franchising Legislation at the State Level," Law Office of Miller and Van Eaton, presentation, 26 July 2007 to the Alliance for Community Media Conference, www.millervaneaton.com/ACM1.ppt/ (6 May 2008).

5. Verizon has applied for and been awarded numerous local and several state franchises for its FiOs video service. AT&T has argued that its U-Verse IPTV service is not a "cable service" and does not require a franchise (although a federal judge in Connecticut declared otherwise, see arstechnica.com/news.ars/post/20070727-federal-judge-att-u-verse-cable-tv.html/), preferring to enter into a "memorandum" with local communities.

6. Gerard Lederer, "The State of the States: A Report on Franchising Legislation at the State Level," Law Office of Miller and Van Eaton, presentation, 26 July 2007 to the Alliance for Community Media Conference, www.millervaneaton.com/ACM1.ppt/ (6 May 2008).

7. Linda Rushnak, "Cable Television Franchise Agreements: Is Local, State or Federal Regulation Preferable?," *33 Rutgers Computer and Technology Law Journal 41*, Fall 2006, accessed through Lexis-Nexis Academic (15 May 2008).

8. Originally offering only video programming, the "cable industry" has added voice services and Internet connectivity services to its portfolio. Acknowledging a process of evolution, the "National Cable Television Association" (NCTA) changed its name to the "National Cable and Telecommunications Association" in 2001, keeping the same acronym. Similarly, in 2008, the U.S. Telecom Association (USTA) became "U.S. Telecom: The Broadband Association."

9. National Cable Television Association, Industry Statistics, Top 25 MSOs as of December 2007, www.ncta.com/Statistic/Statistic/Top25MSOs.aspx/ (19 June 2008).

10. The statistics used here are from the National Cable and Telecommunications Association (NCTA). There is some dispute about them, particularly with respect to the calculation of the "penetration" of cable TV, i.e., the percent of TV households receiving their television programming from cable television companies. This dispute has serious regulatory implications, and the cable industry currently has an incentive to underreport its statistics. Warren Communications credits them with two million more.

11. Steve Donohue, "Cable Penetration Hits 17-Year Low," MultiChannel News on-line, 19 March 2007, www.multichannel.com/article/CA6425963.html/ (3 July 2008).

12. Updated statistics for all the categories are not available, but as of 31 December 2007, cable claims 37,100,000 broadband subscribers.

13. Alex Goldman, "Top 25 U.S. ISPs by Subscriber: Q4 2007," Internet.com, 10 April 2008, www.isp-planet.com/research/rankings/usa.html/ (1 July 2008).

14. A. Sharma, "AT&T is Set To Introduce TV Service for Cellphones," *The Wall Street Journal Online*, 1 May 2008, online.wsj.com/article_print/SB120961037199158513.html (3 May 2008).

15. Cynthia Brumfield, "Are Cable and Phone Companies Still Recession Proof?" Gigaom.com, 14 January 2008, gigaom.com/2008/01/14/are-cable-and-phone-companies-still-recession-proof/ (19 April 2008).

16. Teens in the twelve to seventeen demographic average 132 minutes of online video monthly, vs. 99 minutes averaged by users eighteen-plus. The twelve- to twenty-four age group watches about 42 percent of its video-based entertainment on TV, compared with the population average of 64 percent. That number is expected to

continue to increase. See Mike Shields, "Nielsen: Teens Biggest Users of Online Video," MediaWeek.com, 9 June 2008, www.mediaweek.com/mw/content_display/news /digital-downloads/metrics/e3i32a6c4ade2dd7b238403192b9ee8b8e0?imw=Y(10 June 2008); Daisy Whitney, "Video Use Seen Hitting Eight Hours a Day by 2013," TVWeek, 10 June 2008, www.tvweek.com/news/2008/06/web_video_consumption_seen_hit.php/ (11 June 2008); Brian Stelter, "In the Age of TiVo and Web Video, What is Prime Time?" *The New York Times Online*, www.nytimes.com/2008/05/12/business/media/12ratings .html?partner=rssnyt&emc=rss/ (12 May 2008).

17. Douglas McIntyre, "Can Cable Stocks Get Back in Vogue?," Bloggingstocks. com, 3 April 2008, www.bloggingstocks.com/2008/04/03/can-cable-stocks-get-back-in-vogue (19 April 2008).

18. Reuters, "Time Warner to Spin Off Cable Division," PCMag.com, 30 April 2008, www.pcmag.com/article2/0,1895,2289553,00.asp (3 May 2008).

19. Robert Marich, "Cable Show '08: Cable Stock Spurt—Can Mini-Rally Last?," *Broadcasting & Cable Online*, 17 May 2008, www.broadcastingcable.com/article/CA6561867 .html (1 July 2008).

20. Ryan Lawler, "At NAB: OTT vs. IPTV," *Lightreading*, 18 April 2008, www .lightreading.com/document.asp?doc_id=151467 (21 April 2008).

21. Kimberly Nordyke, "Cable Brass Debate Fee for Web Content," *The Hollywood Reporter Online*, 19 May 2008, www.hollywoodreporter.com/hr/content_display /news/e3i9189f73c48e7dd515d1d575b16d32c67 (5 May 2008).

22. Daisy Whitney, "NBC's Silverman: Broadcast to be Event-Driven," TVWeek.com, 1 May 2008, www.tvweek.com/news/2008/05/nbcs_silverman_broadcast_to_be.php (1 May 2008).

23. WorldTVPC.com, "Internet TV the future for satellite and cable TV on your PC," WorldTVPC.com Blog, posted 10 February 2008, www.worldtvpc.com/blog /Internet-tv-the-future-for-satellite-and-cable-tv-on-your-pc (5 May 2008).

24. AT&T, "AT&T U-Verse: Cooler than Cable," AT&T Media Kit, undated, www .att.com/gen/press-room?pid=5838 (19 May 2008).

25. Lightreading, "Verizon Phases out Analog," *Lightreading Cable Digital News*, 7 April 2008, www.lightreading.com/document.asp?doc_id=150330 (15 April 2008); Todd Spangler, "Verizon to Cut Off FiOS TV Analog in Massachusetts," *Multichannel News Online*, 29 April 2008, www.multichannel.com/article/CA6555758.html?nid=27 34&rid=1361613731 (3 May 2008).

26. Cable Television Laboratories (CABLELABS), "DOCSIS—Project Primer," *Revolutionizing Cable Technology*, www.cablemodem.com/primer (19 June 2008).

27. David Lieberman, "All-digital Cable Move May Spark Viewer Ire," *USA Today Online*, www.usatoday.com/money/media/2008-06-12-cable-digital_N.htm (13 June 2008).

28. David B. Wilkerson, "Cable Plan Faces Bumpy Road," *The Wall Street Journal Online*, 18 June 2008, online.wsj.com/article/SB121376250538583651.html (18 June 2008).

29. Brad Reed, "Verizon expands 50 mbps FiOS footprint," *Network World*, 19 June 2008, www.networkworld.com/news/2008/061908-verizon-fios.html?hpg1=bn (20 June 2008).

30. Residential one hundred mbps service is already widely available in Japan, Korea, and Sweden.

31. Bret Swanson, "The Need for Speed," *The Progress and Freedom Foundation*, released 10 April 2008, www.pff.org/issues-pubs/ps/2008/ps4.10needforspeed.html (22 April 2008); Vishesh Kumar, "Is Faster Access to the Internet Needed?" *The Wall Street Journal Online*, 10 April 2008, online.wsj.com/article/SB120779422456503907 .html?mod=todays_us_marketplace (6 May 2008); GigaOm, "As Broadband Growth Slows, Expect Speed Boosts," *GigaOM*, 29 April 2008, gigaom.com/2008/04/29 /as-broadband-growth-slows-expect-speed-boosts (5 May 2008).

32. Korea, Japan, and Sweden all report residential availability of one hundred mbps Internet connections. Looking ahead, the fastest reported line, although not widely available, is a demonstration forty gbps to a woman's home in Sweden. This suggests that there is still a lot of room for increasing speed. See *USA Today*, "Swedish Woman Gets World's Fastest Internet Connection," *Technology*, 19 July 2007, www .usatoday.com/tech/webguide/Internetlife/2007-07-19-swedish-woman-fast-Internet _N.htm?csp=34 (19 June 2008).

33. www.hulu.com, www.joost.com, www.veoh.com, www.fancast.com/home.

34. Nick Wingfield, "The Internet. The TV. Here's How to Finally Bring Them Together," *The Wall Street Journal Online*, 11 December 2007, online.wsj.com/article /SB119706406734417529.html (2 May 2008).

35. Sergio Ibarra, "The WB, Kids' WB Live Again Online," *TVWeek.com*, 28 April 2008, www.tvweek.com/news/2008/04/the_wb_kids_wb_live_again_onli.php (28 April 2008).

36. Zattoo, "Your Channel on Zattoo," Zattoo.com, zattoo.com/en/broadcasters (6 May 2008).

37. Reuters, "SONY to Show Films on MediaFlo Mobile TV," PCMag.com, 31 March 2008, www.accessmylibrary.com/coms2/summary_0286-34240851_ITM (15 April 2008).

38. Steve Rubel, "The Future of Cable TV in an Open World," *Micropersuasion Online*, 9 February 2007, www.micropersuasion.com/2007/02/the_future_of_c.html (5 May 2008).

39. Sony, "YouTube Content Now Available on Sony Bravia Internet Link," *Sony Electronics: News and Information*, news.sel.sony.com/en/press_room/consumer /television/release/35397.html (19 June 2008).

40. Leo Lewis, "Sony to Stream Movies to its Bravia LCD TV Sets," *Times Online*, 27 June 2008, business.timesonline.co.uk/tol/business/industry_sectors/media /article4221214.ece (1 July 2008).

41. Reuters, "Chip, CE Makers Launch New Wired Network Standard," PCMag.com, 29 April 2008, www.pcmag.com/article2/0,1895,2288936,00.asp (29 April 2008).

42. Cisco, "Cisco Reveals 8500 DHC Set-to-Box Series," 14 January 2008, www .engadgethd.com/2008/01/14/cisco-reveals-8500hdc-dvr-set-top-box-series (19 June 2008).

43. See www.vudu.com.

44. Danny Dumas, "Review: Roku Netflix Set-Top Box is Just Shy of Totally Amazing," *Gadget Lab*, 19 May 2008, blog.wired.com/gadgets/2008/05/review-roku-net.html (1 July 2008).

45. Nick Wingfield, "The Internet. The TV. Here's How to Finally Bring Them Together," *The Wall Street Journal Online*, 11 December 2007, online.wsj.com/article /SB119706406734417529.html (2 May 2008).

46. Harry A. Jessell, "Sezmi May be on to Something, Sez Me," *TVNewsday Online*, 2 May 2008, www.tvnewsday.com/login/error=access&url=aHR0cDovL3 d3dy50dm5ld3Nld3NkYXkuY29tL2FydGljbGVzLzIwMDgvMDUvMDIvZGFpbHkuN i8%3D (5 May 2008); Mark Hachman, "New Sezmi Set-top Blows Away the TV," *PCMag.com*, 1 May 2008, www.pcmag.com/article2/0,1895,2289653,00.asp (3 May 2008).

47. See, for example, Ed Horowitz, Jef Graham, and Blake Senftner, "Television 2.0," Forbes, 5 June 2007, www.forbes.com/opinions/2007/06/04/television-new-look-oped-cx_eh_0605tvnewlook.html (19 June 2008); Kevin Ohannessian, "Television 2.0: Coming to a (Computer) Screen Near You," *Fast Company.com*, August 2007, www.fastcompany.com/articles/2007/08/future-of-tv.html (19 June 2008).

48. Arguably, this will create a virtual functional equivalent of line-sharing or "unbundling," relieving some of the pressures around competition and vertical integration.

49. For this purpose, a state "video" franchise will serve as a satisfactory proxy for a "broadband" franchise. With respect to the scope of the powers of Congress and/or independent regulatory agencies to mandate or create carriage rules, the historical parallel with the natural gas pipeline industry may be instructive. See, for example, FERC Order 636, "The Restructuring Rule" (1992), discussed at www.eia.doe.gov/oil_gas /natural_gas/analysis_publications/ngmajorleg/ferc636.html.

50. Competition could be defined a number of ways. There could be a rebuttable presumption of competition based on one or more of: number of providers, percentage of market share, and traditional models for calculating market power/competition/concentration.

51. Matthew Lasar, "Civil Rights Groups Blast A La Carte Cable," Arstechnica.com, 30 May 2008, arstechnica.com/news.ars/post/20080530-civil-rights-groups-blast-a-la -carte-cable.html/ (2 June 2008).

52. International attempts to resolve this problem include the EU's 2007 Audiovisual Media Services Without Frontiers Directive (eur-lex.europa.eu/LexUriServ /LexUriServ.do?uri=OJ:L:2007:332:0027:0045:EN:PDF), which, in effect, abolishes the distinctions between broadcast, cable, and Internet content regulation.

53. John Eggerton, "ABC Stations Challenge FCC Fine, Not Authority," *Broadcasting and Cable Online*, 21 June 2008, www.broadcastingcable.com/article/CA6572207.html (23 June 2008).

54. Danny Hakim, "3 Net Providers Will Block Sites with Child Sex," *The New York Times Online*, 10 June 2008, www.nytimes.com/2008/06/10/nyregion/10Internet. html?_r=1&ref=todayspaper&oref=slogin (10 June 2008).

55. Ian Scales, "Swedes Protest Eavesdropping Law as the European Parliament Drifts Towards Ending 'Mere Conduit' Status for ISPs," *Telecom TV One*, 1 July 2008, web20.telecomtv.com/pages/?newsid=43428&id=e9381817-0593-417a-8639 -c4c53e2a2a10 (1 July 2008).

56. Matthew Lasar, "FCC Moves Ahead with Plan for Smut-free Wireless Broadband," *Ars Technica*, 22 June 2008, http://arstechnica.com/news.ars/post/20080622 -fcc-starts-proceeding-on-smut-free-wireless-broadband-plan.html (3 July 2008).

57. Paul J. Gough, "Digital TV Switch Will Hit 13 Million Households," Reuters, 18 February 2008, www.reuters.com/article/televisionNews/idUSN1448533020080220 (19 June 08).

58. Ted Hearn, "Martin Unveils New Must-Carry Plan," *Multi-Channel News*, 13 March 2007, www.multichannel.com/article/CA6424141.html?display=Breaking+Ne ws (19 June 2008).

59. hraunfoss.fcc.gov/edocs_public/attachmatch/FCC-08-183A1.pdf.

60. Todd Spangler, "Comcast Wins Ruling Against 'Spammer,'" *Multichannel News Online*, 14 April 2008, www.multichannel.com/index.asp?layout=article&articleid=C A6551411 (15 April 2008).

61. This is somewhat akin to the argument over traffic congestion. It would seem that the obvious answer to congestion is to build more highways, but experience shows that when you build more highways, what you get is more cars. See also Gary Kim, "Broadband Train Wreck," *IP Business News*, 15 June 2008, www.ipbusinessmag.com /departments.php?department_id=5&article_id=12 (15 June 2008).

62. Bobby White, "Cisco Projects Growth to Swell for Online Video," *The Wall Street Journal Online*, 16 June 2008, online.wsj.com/article/SB121358372172676391 .html?mod=dist_smartbrief&apl=y&r=690717.

63. Kenneth Li, "Top Cable Companies Try Reining in Heavy Web Use," Reuters, 3 June 2008, www.reuters.com/article/InternetNews/idUSN0335796120080603 (19 June 2008).

64. Gary Kim, "Broadband Train Wreck," *IP Business News*, 15 June 2008, www .ipbusinessmag.com/departments.php?department_id=5&article_id=12 (15 June 2008).

65. America's Network, "AT&T May Charge More for Heavy Internet Usage," 19 June 2008, www.americasnetwork.com/americasnetwork/article/articleDetail .jsp?id=524922#Top1 (20 June 2008).

66. Brian Stelter, "Charging by the Byte to Curb Internet Traffic," *The New York Times Online*, 15 June 2008, online.wsj.com/article/SB121358372172676391 .html?mod=dist_smartbrief&apl=y&r=690717 (16 June 2008). See also Peter Svensson, "Time Warner Cable Tries Metering Internet Use," *Yahoo! Finance*, 2 June 2008, biz.yahoo.com/ap/080602/tec_time_warner_cable_Internet.html (19 June 2008).

67. Chris Albrecht, "Cisco: Average Home to Use 1.1 Terabytes by 2010," *NewTeeVee*, 10 June 2008, newteevee.com/2008/06/10/cisco-avg-home-to-use-11-terabytes -by-2010/ (2 July 2008).

68. Peter Svensson, "Time Warner Cable Tries Metering Internet Use," *Yahoo! Finance*, 2 June 2008, biz.yahoo.com/ap/080602/tec_time_warner_cable_Internet.html (June 19, 2008).

69. See, for example, Matt Stump, "Verizon (FiOS) Begins Overbuilding AT&T (U-verse) in Texas," *Onetrak*, 9 June 2008, www.onetrak.com/ShowArticle.aspx?ID=3 487&AspxAutoDetectCookieSupport=1 (3 July 2008).

70. K. C. Jones, "Lawmakers Eye Net Neutrality As Anti-Trust Issue," *Information Week Online*, 9 May 2008, www.informationweek.com/news/Internet/policy/showArticle .jhtml?articleID=207601715 (10 May 2008).

71. Adam Thierer, "Where is the FCC's Annual Video Competition Report?" *The Progress and Freedom Foundation*, Release 4.11 May 2008, pff.org/issues-pubs/ps/2008 /ps4.11whereisFCCvidcompreport.pdf (15 May 2008).

72. Jeremy Allaire and Adam Berrey, "Open Internet Television: A Letter to the Consumer Electronic Industry," *Brightcove*, 2008, www.brightcove.com/about_brightcove /perspectives/open-Internet-television-letter-to-ce-industry.cfm (17 April 2008).

73. Unfortunately, "redlining," a term largely carried over from the banking industry, is "slippery" in that it can refer to economics, location, ethnicity, risk, or any kind of discrimination. It needs to be defined very carefully in the context of construction of broadband networks. It is also sometimes confused with "build out" requirements, which require some percentage of households, or of a geographic area, to be served within a particular time frame. There may be technical and/or financial reasons why it makes sense to address service areas in a particular order and timeframe. It is a public-interest concept, but needs to be articulated with precision to avoid future misunderstandings.

74. See, for example, www.mels.gouv.qc.ca/lancement/Villagesbranches /VillageBranche_a.pdf.

75. Cecilia Kang, "Court Upholds FCC Rule on Video Service," WashingtonPost. com, 28 June 2008, www.washingtonpost.com/wp-dyn/content/article/2008/06/27 /AR2008062703343.html?hpid=sec-tech (3 July 2008).

76. The various problems listed below with the digital delivery of PEG access channels are documented at reclaimthemedia.org/broadband_cable /comcast_and_at_ts_poor_showing%3D5764/, www.ourchannels.org/wp-content /uploads/2008/07/harm-survey-report-final.pdf/, and app-rising.com/2008/07 /reviewing_atts_peg_system.html.

77. For an example of the problems that emerge for access channels in connection with the conversion to digital, see Community Media Workshop, "AT&T Access Plan Challenged," Newstips, 5 June 2008, www.newstips.org/interior.php?section=Newstip s&main_id=882 (11 June 2008).

78. While it is not a direct topic of regulation, concern is often expressed about the future of local news. It is true that the economics of local media are changing, but the desire for local content is not. This is likely to lead to new partnerships for the collection and production of local news, information and events online, at lower cost, sharing expenses. This is an area of opportunity to explore. See, for example, Jeffrey Chester, "Progressive Internet Entrepreneurs," *The Nation Online*, 30 May 2008, www.thenation .com/doc/20080616/chester (3 July 2008).

79. John Eggerton, "V for Vendetta," Broadcastingcable.com, 10 December 2007, www.broadcastingcable.com/article/CA6510927.html (15 April 2008).

80. Carol Wilson, "NAB: Top Telcos Want Closer Ties with Broadcasters," *Telephony Online*, 14 April 2008, telephonyonline.com/iptv/news/telcos-content-broadcasters-0414 (15 May 2008).

81. The software which controls the connection points between the Internet and the home entertainment center, and which transmits and converts various digital stream within the house could potentially be dominated if it is not an open standard, providing a "chokepoint" for transit from which value could be extracted.

82. No "program guide" will be big enough to list all possible video sources. Heavy reliance will be placed on search engines. According to one report, "Traditional search engines like Google and Yahoo are poised to dominate the video search business because almost one-third of traffic to online video sites originates from search engines." "Twenty percent originates from Google alone." See Daisy Whitney, "Video: Search Giants to Rule Web Video," *TVWeekNews*, 1 July 2008, www.tvweek.com/news/2008/07/video_search_giants_to_rule_we.php (2 July 2008).

83. It is already apparent that advertising will be critical to the future business model of Internet video. If any one company has dominance of the sale and placement of advertising online, it will have important leverage with both advertisers and programmers.

7

A Spectrum Policy Agenda

Jon M. Peha

Introduction

For almost a century, wireless systems have played essential roles in the American democratic process, economy, and quality of life—from the radio addresses of Franklin Roosevelt to the wireless telephone lines that connected remote rural communities with the rest of the nation. Fueled by new technology and applications, wireless systems continue to grow in importance, but wireless can only reach its potential through significant changes in spectrum management policies.

The Internet is the most important and transformative communications media to emerge in many years. Initially, the Internet was a wired infrastructure offering service in fixed locations. Thanks to wireless technology, thirty-five million Americans accessed the Internet using mobile handheld devices as of June 2007. This marked an astonishing tenfold increase in penetration compared with just eighteen months earlier.[1] Perhaps even more important than mobility is the potential of other wireless technologies to bring broadband access to those communities and roughly ten million households where it is unavailable today.[2]

Even broadcasting is poised for change. Traditional broadcast television has steadily declined in importance as viewers switched to cable, but the future is less clear. Thanks to the upcoming transition to digital television (DTV), broadcasters can transmit up to six channels for every one they had before. This, combined with the ability to receive information from consumers more freely over the Internet, may lead to a communications medium that is unrecognizable to today's television viewers. Moreover, technology has already emerged that brings television to mobile handheld devices.

Clearly, short-range wireless technology can also change the way we live. Cordless telephones and Wi-Fi have already pushed aside their wired counterparts. Many more such innovations are probably on their way.

Unfortunately, development of new wireless products and services is substantially impeded by lack of available spectrum. Moreover, today's wireless services could be far less expensive if providers had easy access to more spectrum. While many might think this shortage of available spectrum is an inevitable result of the laws of physics, it is more rooted in the now-outdated laws and traditions of the federal government.[3] Numerous measurement studies have shown that at any given time and location, much of the prized spectrum sits idle.[4] New technology would enable much greater spectral efficiency, unleashing innovative new products and services, provided that we adopt appropriate spectrum policies.

The next section will discuss long-term issues for a spectrum policy that promotes efficiency. It will also introduce the issues that currently dominate the debate over fundamental change in spectrum policy: *property rights* and *spectrum commons*. The following discussion will focus on issues that deserve particular attention from the leaders of the next administration, because they warrant near-term action.

A Long-Term Policy for Spectrum Sharing

Advances in wireless technology have changed the way we can and should manage spectrum.[5] Some say that there are two roads forward, one based on "property rights" and another based on "spectrum commons." This is untrue. In reality, both concepts have value and a place in effective spectrum policy. Both concepts also become dangerously ineffective when taken to extremes. Focusing on these two approaches obscures a different set of reforms that hold great promise: reforms that advance spectrum sharing between primary license holders and secondary users. These will be discussed further on.

Spectrum Property

While a central regulator typically allocates spectrum resources, nations with market economies allocate other resources, such as land, by defining property rights and allowing the free trade of property. For almost fifty years, some economists have been arguing that spectrum should be treated more like other property with market-based mechanisms.[6] Many of the market-based concepts underlying a property system can be used to good effect in spectrum management, although, as we will discuss, rights granted to users of spectrum should not be quite as far-reaching as those granted to users of land.

There is no consensus on exactly what rights befall a property owner when the property in question is spectrum. The ambiguity over definitions causes confusion.[7] One definition of property is the right to hold, subdivide, transfer, use, and admit or exclude others from using a given item.[8] Some, but not all, of these rights are appropriate for spectrum.

In a market economy, land typically goes to those who value it most and are willing to pay for it. This occurs because owners can subdivide their land in any way that increases its value, and keep, sell, or rent every part. A similar phenomenon could occur with spectrum, when spectrum users assemble licenses that cover the geography, frequency range, and time period that they value most, and no more. In addition, property owners have an incentive to use their property efficiently, because they derive all the benefit from it. The same can apply when spectrum users have exclusive access. Thus, an argument can be made that license-holders should be able to subdivide, transfer, use, and admit or exclude others from using a block of spectrum.

Some believe that, by definition, property rights also include the flexibility to use spectrum in any way the license holder (or property owner) wishes, without interference from a regulator, and that property rights can never expire. Flexibility can certainly enhance the value derived from spectrum.[9] It allows a license holder to use spectrum for the most valued application, or, if other market mechanisms are in place, to transfer spectrum to someone who will. Nevertheless, there are dangers in taking property rights for all spectrum to that extreme. In some cases, there is value to regulator-imposed uniformity.[10] If all television stations use the same technical standard and operate in the same frequency band, then consumers can move anywhere and their televisions will still work. If television had emerged in an era when complete flexibility prevailed, incompatible standards or frequency ranges might have emerged in different regions. Moreover, increasing the license holder's flexibility also decreases the discretion of regulators to adapt to new needs and new technologies, which can sometimes undermine innovation. For example, the Federal Communications Commission (FCC) allowed a new kind of device based on ultra-wideband technology to operate in occupied spectrum, but at low power to avoid causing harmful interference.[11] This useful change in regulation would have been impossible if incumbent license holders in that spectrum had complete flexibility and property rights that never expired, and just one of the many thousands of license holders objected. A similar problem occurs when applications are only cost-effective across a large geographic region (such as a nation). If even one license holder in the region refuses to sell, progress may be impossible.[12] In such cases, licenses must expire, so that regulators have the opportunity to introduce change.

Spectrum Commons

There have been calls for extensive use of "spectrum commons," as a possible means of alleviating spectrum scarcity and encouraging innovation. In any commons model, spectrum is shared, and no one is given special priority. In that sense, one might view a commons as the opposite of property rights.

Sharing can come in different forms. Devices might *cooperate* or merely *coexist*. While both possibilities are sometimes lumped together under the ambiguous heading of "commons," they are entirely different.[13] The coexistence model exists in the United States today in the form of *unlicensed spectrum*, and it has spawned successful products such as Wi-Fi and cordless phones. When systems merely coexist, explicit communications is pointless; a cordless phone and a Wi-Fi card do not decode each other's transmissions (although one might try to sense when the other is transmitting for simple collision avoidance). By contrast, with cooperative sharing, devices must communicate with a common protocol and work together. For example, all devices could self-organize to form one network.

This model has unleashed innovations that would not have occurred otherwise. For example, in 1993, Carnegie Mellon University (CMU) began developing an experimental wireless system[14] designed to blanket the campus with broadband coverage indoors and out. CMU used a precursor of what later became the Wi-Fi standard. Without unlicensed spectrum, perhaps CMU could have obtained a license that provides exclusive access to spectrum throughout the neighborhood, but this would have been expensive, and deservedly so. Exclusive access would be incredibly inefficient. Computer communications are highly bursty, and some collisions are tolerable, so it makes sense for the universities, hospitals, businesses, and residences in this neighborhood to share spectrum. Alternatively, CMU could have tried to get highly localized site licenses for all transmitters and coordinated their locations with neighbors and/or with the FCC. However, this might have required the university to contact the regulator every time one of its eight hundred transmitters is deployed or moved. The transaction costs of explicit coordination could exceed the value of the system. Finally, CMU could have called a licensed wireless service provider, who might have offered a carrier-based third-generation cellular service that was more expensive, less flexible, less useful, and less spectrally efficient. This is just one example of a system, and ultimately a new technology, that flourished in unlicensed spectrum but would probably have failed if licenses were required, with or without market-based mechanisms.

Unlicensed spectrum has many advantages. It requires spectrum sharing, which can lead to greater spectral efficiency than exclusive access, since spectrum often sits idle because the license holder is not transmitting. Unlicensed spectrum is necessary to support mobile systems, such as a group of laptops that form an ad hoc wireless local-area network wherever they happen to be. It is useful for inexpensive low-power consumer products, such as cordless phones, in which the cost of coordination and licensing would unnecessarily dominate system cost and the interference impact on neighbors is small.

When releasing unlicensed spectrum, regulators must guard against two related sources of inefficiency. One is that unlicensed spectrum could attract applications that would operate more effectively and efficiently in licensed spectrum. The other is that engineers will design "greedy" devices (i.e., those that transmit with greater power, duration, or bandwidth than necessary, because they have little incentive to conserve spectrum that is shared). In extreme cases, when many devices are greedy all devices in the band may experience inadequate performance as a result.[15] Both dangers can be addressed by establishing appropriate technical rules to govern the unlicensed bands. This may include limits on power or transmission duration, deployment fees, wideband allocations, or mandated sharing mechanisms that implicitly reward spectrum conservation.[16]

As with market principles, there is much to be gained through a commons based on coexistence, but the approach should not be taken to its extreme. Unlicensed spectrum is not a replacement for licensed spectrum any more than public parks are a replacement for private homes. Licensed bands are more appropriate for some applications, such as broadcast television or public safety communications, for which quality of service should be guaranteed.

The characteristics of a commons based on cooperation are quite different.[17] In this type of commons, all devices cooperate, even though they serve different owners. Devices might autoconfigure into a mesh network and carry each other's traffic. Thus, if enough consumers purchase devices that cooperate and place these devices in their homes, the network may cover an entire region. This fundamentally changes the economics of wireless broadband, perhaps making it possible to bring broadband to places that cannot be served cost-effectively today.[18] It has also been shown theoretically that cooperation can lead to *cooperative gain*. In other words, the capacity in the system can actually increase with the number of active devices.[19] As more devices are added, the mean distance between devices decreases, allowing devices to transmit at lower power, thereby conserving spectrum. Thus, users of a commons based on cooperation may not fear oversubscription the way users of a commons based on coexistence do. These systems deserve serious consideration, as their potential advantages are great. However, this is a less mature technology than the commons based on coexistence. Challenges remain with respect to security[20] and network management that must be addressed. Moreover, effective procedures must be established for defining and continually updating the cooperative protocol.[21]

With either coexistence or cooperation, a "spectrum commons" could be created by a license holder instead of the regulator. This has not yet occurred, but should demand emerge, regulators should consider such requests seriously. Under this approach, rather than using unlicensed spectrum, a private entity might obtain a license, establish its own operating rules, and allow devices to operate in its spectrum.[22]

Primary-Secondary Sharing

Applications that need guaranteed quality of service are given exclusive access to spectrum through licensing. These exclusive allocations also ensure that spectrum will not be fully utilized, as there are generally times and/or locations where other devices could transmit without causing harmful interference. Thus, spectral efficiency can be greatly improved through primary-secondary sharing, in which one system has primary usage rights that make quality of service guarantees possible, and one or more secondary systems operate without causing harmful interference to the primary. Emerging technology offers many ways to do this, and spectrum policy could take advantage of this.

A secondary user can get permission to access spectrum that is licensed to a primary user either from the regulators or from the license holder. In the latter case, the license holder would probably demand payment. These two approaches lead to two different spectrum policies, each of which has important uses if the regulator constructs appropriate rules.

As with a commons, from a technical perspective, primary-secondary sharing can take one of two forms: cooperation and coexistence.[23] Cooperation means that there is explicit communications and coordination between primary and secondary systems, and coexistence means that there is none. When sharing is based on coexistence, secondary devices are essentially invisible to the primary. Thus, all the complexity of sharing is borne by the secondary, without changes to the primary system, which is especially good for legacy systems that are difficult to change. Thanks to a variety of emerging technologies, such as cognitive radio, global positioning systems (GPS), and sensor networks, opportunistic access to spectrum without cooperation is becoming more practical, although significant research challenges remain, and these challenges vary considerably depending on the types of systems involved.

On the other hand, cooperation may create more opportunities for the secondary to transmit. For example, a secondary device may ask the primary for permission to use spectrum before transmitting. This exchange provides an opportunity for the primary to guarantee quality of service for the secondary, which is an advantage of cooperation over coexistence for the secondary device. This is also an opportunity for the license holder to demand payment, which is an advantage of cooperation for the primary system. If payment is demanded, this is a form of secondary spectrum market, but one that can operate in real time.[24] The FCC has now laid the groundwork for this form of sharing,[25] although it may be necessary to adopt additional standards before usage becomes more common.[26]

In recent debates, such as those discussed further in the following sections, it has often been assumed that secondary spectrum users will be unlicensed. Actually, secondary users could be licensed or unlicensed. Both licensed and unlicensed secondaries are precluded from causing harmful interference to the primary. The difference is that a licensed secondary system need not worry about interference from other secondaries. Thus, quality of service can be guaranteed for the secondary when and only when activities of the primary do not get in the way. For example, a licensed secondary might cooperate with the primary system. A public safety communications system could also increase capacity by explicitly claiming the shared spectrum during a serious emergency but would otherwise leave the spectrum to secondary users.[27] The secondary might, in other circumstances, operate without cooperation with the primary, perhaps opportunistically using spectrum when the primary is idle.

Near-Term Opportunities

This section will present examples of areas in which significant progress can be made within the next four years.

Television Spectrum

The year 2009 will be remembered as a turning point in the use of spectrum in the United States, thanks to the transition from analog to digital television (DTV). When over-the-air broadcasters finally cease analog transmissions, they will release a large swath of prized spectrum. Because of the physical properties of spectrum at this frequency, it is particularly well-suited for serving large geographic areas from a single transmitter. This, of course, was useful for television, and it can also be useful for other services, from cellular telephony to broadband Internet. The first spectrum dividend from the DTV transition was the reallocation of many entire television channels, mostly in a 2008 auction. Additional opportunities remain.

Another benefit of the DTV transition is that digital television will be more immune to interference than today's analog television, which facilitates spectrum sharing. For this reason (and others), it should be possible to deploy wireless systems in the television "white spaces," i.e., within a band of spectrum that is used for a given television channel, but at a location where that television channel is unavailable. These white spaces serve as buffer zones to protect broadcasters in different cities from interfering with each other. Advances in technology make it possible to use parts of the white space while affecting only a small fraction of television viewers. The FCC[28] has recently been supportive of taking advantage of the white space after the DTV transition in 2009, although it has not committed itself to this course. Moreover, many specific issues remain undecided.

The debate so far has focused on whether it is technically possible for one form of unlicensed device to operate in the white space without excessive interference to television and other wireless devices. The next administration should continue discussing this issue but expand the debate. Leading high-tech companies have invested considerable efforts in creating relatively low-power devices that operate in this band, and the FCC has evaluated them.[29] Such devices would use cognitive radio to find a channel in which no nearby television broadcaster is active. These devices could even be mobile, as they will dynamically adjust when they find themselves to be too close to a television transmitter. These are worthy efforts, and this type of device deserves consideration. Another possible use of television white spaces, which also deserves attention, is to bring broadband service to unserved communities using fixed wireless technology.[30] If such systems were built, they would require (or at least greatly benefit from) a different set of spectrum regulations. For such systems, it would be more important to allow high-power transmissions in some (but not necessarily all) television channels so that large areas could be covered with less costly infrastructure. At the same time, it would be less important to support mobile devices, and the elimination of mobility would dramatically simplify some of the technical challenges associated with protecting television from harmful interference. Of course, the FCC should only make spectrum available for high-power devices if manufacturers and service providers demonstrate their intention to make use of such spectrum, and it remains to be seen how great this demand will be.

Public Safety Spectrum

Another enormous opportunity to free spectrum is in the area of public safety, e.g., systems used by police, firefighters, emergency medical services, the National Guard, and other emergency responders. Of course, freeing spectrum is not the only goal, or even the most important goal. The U.S. public safety communications infrastructure is prone to failures that have cost many lives. Some of these failures are due to inadequate interoperability, i.e., the ability to communicate and share information across organizational boundaries. Some failures are the result of designs that are not fault tolerant, so there are many components whose failure can bring down much of the system. Most emergency responders also lack capabilities that commercial and military users typically take for granted and that can help save lives, such as broadband service and the ability to determine the current location of mobile devices. Ironically, this limited system is even more costly than it needs to be,[31] which means U.S. taxpayers pay extra for this low-quality system.

There have been many calls from public safety agencies for more spectrum. This is understandable. Given the way public safety spectrum and public safety infrastructure have been managed, each agency needs plenty of spectrum. Depriving them of spectrum will lead to dangerous congestion when big emergencies occur. However, it is possible to meet public safety communications requirements with far less spectrum, while also addressing the above-mentioned problems through a new policy.[32] Indeed, using the most widely cited (although somewhat outdated) estimate of public safety spectrum needs, the spectrum requirements can be reduced by an order of magnitude if shared infrastructure were designed to serve much larger geographic regions and employed modern technology to reuse spectrum.[33]

The problems with public safety communications do not stem from mistakes by designers or operators, who are doing the best they can within current constraints. The problem is that U.S. policy views public safety communications as an issue for local government. This once made sense—but no longer. By building a nationwide system that serves local agencies, it would be possible to end interoperability problems, improve dependability and security, and introduce broadband capabilities. As long as the system is designed to meet all short-term and long-term needs of public safety, agencies can begin the (long) process of surrendering their existing systems and their existing spectrum, as they migrate to the new system. This will free up a significant amount of prime spectrum, and in the long run, should save a great deal of money.

Congress has required that some of the current television spectrum be allocated to public safety after the DTV transition. This is an extraordinary opportunity to construct the nationwide broadband network described above. At this point, it is unclear whether this will be possible. One problem is that, with the exception of the FCC, the current administration has shown no interest in a nationwide system, unless it exclusively serves the small fraction of emergency responders who work for the federal government.[34] Leadership from a federal agency in the next administration could make an enormous difference.

There are two viable approaches to constructing a nationwide network that would meet public safety needs. One is to build a system specifically for public safety. This would cost billions of dollars to build,[35] and this money must come from somewhere, although the Department of Homeland Security has spent a comparable amount in recent years propping up the old local systems rather than building a new nationwide system.[36] Moreover, had all of the money raised in the auction for television spectrum, beyond what the congressional budget office was expecting, been earmarked for a new nationwide system, as I have previously proposed,[37] it would have been enough to cover initial capital costs and some operating costs as well.

Another approach is to construct a system designed to meet the needs of both public safety and paying customers. This was the option chosen in 2007 by the FCC,[38] in part because this was the only option available to it without cooperation from other agencies, as stated by the FCC chairman.[39] The FCC's policy was to assign one nationwide spectrum band to a nonprofit organization that was to represent public safety and another band to a commercial company. The commercial company would then build out a system, in accordance with specifications that it and the nonprofit organization would define through negotiation. In a subsequent auction, no commercial company was willing to make the minimum bid. While the FCC deserves great credit for attempting to address the problem, the rules as defined could not work. So many requirements were left undetermined that the uncertainty would prevent any wise company from bidding. If a company did bid and was then unwilling to meet the still-unspecified requirements, it would be forced to pay a sizable financial penalty. At the same time, the requirements that were established were woefully inadequate to meet public safety needs. Wise leaders of public safety agencies would, therefore, have been unwilling to switch from their current systems to the new one even if it were built.[40] At this time, it is unclear what will happen.

The next administration will probably have a chance to make sure that a nationwide system is built that meets the long-term needs of public safety and that is financially sustainable. If it does, it will save spectrum, save taxpayer dollars, and save lives.

Federal Government Spectrum

There are many additional spectrum bands that could be made available for new uses, either exclusively or on a shared basis. While the greater pressure to make spectrum available typically falls on the FCC, the agency that manages spectrum for nongovernment users, by far the largest user of spectrum in the United States, is the federal government. The National Telecommunications and Information Administration (NTIA) manages federal spectrum, and its processes and procedures do not encourage efficiency. Federal agencies that reduce their use of valuable spectrum must often accept the burden of one-time transition costs, and there is no reward for these agencies when the process is over. Mechanisms could certainly be established through which those who gain access to spectrum cover the costs of those who relinquish the spectrum, as was the case with the personal communications services (PCS) band in the 1990s. However, government agencies lack incentive to seek out such arrangements, and those who want the spectrum lack the means of identifying opportunities.

The first step is to move the management of federal spectrum out of the closet. The next president should demand a detailed inventory of federal spectrum and an account of how this essential resource is used. Except for those bands that must be protected for reasons of national security, the results of this inventory should be made public. This would allow existing companies, entrepreneurs, and researchers to seek out opportunities to use the spectrum more efficiently. Those who find opportunities could make their case to the NTIA, to the current license holder and to Congress.

Reforming Spectrum Auctions

In addition to making more spectrum available, policy reform could make the spectrum that comes available via auction accessible to more potential license holders. Under current policy, the auction winner makes a one-time payment to the U.S. Treasury equal to the winning bid. Instead, the auction winner should make an annual payment equal to the winning bid for as long as it retains the license. This would greatly reduce the funds that an auction winner needs initially, thereby allowing small entrepreneurial firms to compete with the giants. This arrangement would also encourage license holders to surrender spectrum if their plans should fail, leaving the spectrum underutilized.

This policy also better aligns the objective of using spectrum effectively with the frequent congressional objective of balancing the federal budget. It creates an annual revenue stream, which can safely be used to cover annual expenses. One-time payments for spectrum have motivated Congress to manipulate the timing of spectrum auctions to the detriment of all. For example, some senators have pushed to delay the DTV transition so as to increase the revenues raised in the ensuing auction, even though the costs to society far outweighed the benefits for the budget.[41] On the other hand, in the 1990s, there was a push to move earlier toward the nominal beginning of the DTV transition, so the illusion of future auction revenues could be used sooner to offset federal spending. If one-time payments were replaced with annual payments, there would be greater incentive to set spectrum dates at the time that makes most sense for the users of spectrum.

Conclusions

Wireless systems play an increasingly important role in American society, and spectrum is the lifeblood of wireless systems. Alleviating today's shortage of available spectrum will decrease the cost of today's wireless services and create opportunities for new wireless products and services. This can be achieved through new spectrum policies that encourage spectrum users to reduce their spectrum needs, that allow and encourage more spectrum sharing, and that decrease the cost of initial access to spectrum.

The debate over long-term spectrum policy in the United States has sometimes devolved into a debate over property rights "versus" commons. Both perspectives have value. Advocates of "property" rights are correct in saying that market-based mechanisms can improve both technical and economic efficiency of spectrum. The United States has made significant advances in this area, but there is more that can be done to help make spectrum available to those who value it the most, in the amount they value the most, and for the purpose demanded most. Nevertheless, there are sound reasons not to take the property approach too far. We will need regulators who can change the way spectrum is used. For example, in response to new technology, a regulator might establish new rules for spectrum-sharing or make sure that spectrum is available in large contiguous blocks. Thus, spectrum licenses should retain expiration dates.

There is also merit in the arguments for shared spectrum commons. Because the FCC has cleared unlicensed spectrum bands based on coexistence, valuable products and services have emerged. There is reason to hope for more successes in the future. As demand for unlicensed spectrum grows, so may the need for more such bands. This approach to spectrum management can be effective for applications that were not well served under traditional licensing, including cases in which there are large numbers of low-powered devices, or in which entire wireless systems are portable, or in which best-effort service is adequate. But this commons approach should not be taken to extremes. There are applications that require guaranteed quality of service and are better served through licensing. Commons based on cooperation also appear promising, but significant challenges lie ahead before policymakers can take significant action, notably in the area of security.

Some of the most compelling new opportunities for improving spectral efficiency involve sharing between a primary license holder and one or more secondary systems that are not allowed to cause harmful interference to the primary user. Many such models are possible. Secondary systems may be licensed or unlicensed. They may get permission to operate from the regulator or from the license holder in exchange for payment. They may cooperate with the primary or coexist in a manner that is invisible to the primary. Once again, different spectrum-sharing models are more effective for different kinds of applications and circumstances, so all models have their uses.

Overall, a wide variety of models for spectrum use are becoming more practical. Different models are more appropriate for different applications. Rather than try to find the "best" approach, regulators should provide a variety of options to those who design and use wireless devices.

Given these general long-term objectives, we have identified four areas worthy of significant attention in the short term. Two are particularly timely because they exploit opportunities that come in part from the transition to digital television, which will occur in 2009. One such opportunity is to make better use of the "white spaces" within the television band. Any such action must be taken after serious thought has been given to how to avoid excessive interference to television signals and other systems. The bigger challenge will be to determine which kinds of applications are in great demand and to devise rules accordingly. For example, should the band be filled with short-range mobile consumer devices or long-range systems for broadband Internet access? While rules should in theory be technology-neutral, they will inevitably be more appropriate for some applications than others.

Another area that deserves immediate attention is public safety communications systems, particularly if we are to make effective use of the spectrum that becomes available in the DTV transition. The next administration could establish spectrum policies that would lead to a nationwide broadband network for public safety. This would save spectrum, and at the same time, it could give first responders broadband and other capabilities, as well as a system that does not fail when it is needed most. In the long run, this could also save money. On the other hand, if they do not act appropriately, policymakers could squander this opportunity and tie up a block of spectrum worth billions of dollars without meeting the needs of public safety or any other needs.

We must also find ways to make better use of the spectrum currently allocated to the federal government. There is no simple and fast way to achieve this broad goal, but an excellent first step would be to bring transparency to the process by collecting detailed information on federal spectrum and making that information publicly available.

Finally, we recommend a change in spectrum auction policy that would allow the auction winner to make more modest payments every year for the spectrum rather than a large one-time payment. This would allow smaller players to compete more fully in the auction, and it would also provide a reliable revenue stream for the Treasury.

Notes

1. Federal Communication Commission, Wireline Competition Bureau, Industry Analysis and Technology Division, *High-Speed Services for Internet Access: Status as of June 30, 2007*, March 2008, hraunfoss.fcc.gov/edocs_public/attachmatch/DOC-280906A1.pdf.

2. Jon M. Peha, "Bringing Broadband to Unserved Communities," Brookings Institute Report, July 2008.

3. Federal Communications Commission, *Spectrum Policy Task Force Report*, ET Docket No. 02-135, November 2002, www.fcc.gov/sptf/reports.html; Jon M. Peha, "Spectrum Management Policy Options," *IEEE Communications Surveys*, Fourth Quarter 1998, www.ece.cmu.edu/~peha/wireless.html; Jon M. Peha, "Emerging Technology and Spectrum Policy Reform," *Proceedings of United Nations International Telecommunication Union (ITU) Workshop on Market Mechanisms for Spectrum Management*, Geneva, January 2007; and Jon M. Peha, "Sharing Spectrum through Spectrum Policy Reform and Cognitive Radio," to appear in *Proceedings of the IEEE*. www.ece.cmu.edu/~peha/wireless.html.

4. U.S. Federal Communications Commission Spectrum Policy Task Force, *Report of the Spectrum Efficiency Working Group*, November 2002, www.fcc.gov/sptf/files/SEWGFinalReport_1.pdf.

5. Peha, "Sharing Spectrum through Spectrum Policy Reform and Cognitive Radio"; Peha, "Emerging Technology and Spectrum Policy Reform."

6. Ronald H. Coase, "Federal Communications Commission," *Journal of Law and Economics* 2 (October 1959): 1–40; Gregory L. Rosston, Thomas W Hazelett, et al., Comments of 37 Concerned Economists, in the Matter of Promoting Efficient use of Spectrum Through Elimination of Barriers to the Development of Secondary Markets, WT Docket No. 00-230, February 7, 2001, aeibrookings.org/admin/authorpdfs/redirect-safely.php?fname=../pdffiles/fcc1075290771.pdf.

7. Jon M. Peha, "Approaches to Spectrum Sharing," *IEEE Communications, February 2005*, www.ece.cmu.edu/~peha/wireless.html.

8. Howard A. Shelanski and Peter W. Huber, "Administrative Creation of Property Rights to Radio Spectrum," *Journal of Law and Economics* 41, no. 2 (October 1998): 581–607.

9. Peha, "Spectrum Management Policy Options."

10. Peha, "Spectrum Management Policy Options."

11. Federal Communications Commission, *First Report and Order*, Revision of Part 15 of the Commission's Rules Regarding Ultra-Wideband Transmission Systems, ET Docket 98-153, 14 February 2002, hraunfoss.fcc.gov/edocs_public/attachmatch/FCC-02-48A1.pdf.

12. Michael A. Heller, "The Tragedy of the Anticommons: Property in the Transition from Marx to Markets," *Harvard Law Review* 111, no. 3 (January 1998): 621–88.

13. Peha, "Approaches to Spectrum Sharing"; Peha, "Emerging Technology and Spectrum Policy Reform"; and Peha, "Sharing Spectrum through Spectrum Policy Reform and Cognitive Radio."

14. Alex Hills, "Wireless Andrew," *IEEE Spectrum* 36, no. 6 (June 1999): 49–53; Douglas Philips, "Wireless Andrew: Creating the World's First Wireless Campus," 2007, www.cmu.edu/corporate/news/2007/features/wireless_andrew.shtml.

15. Durga P. Satapathy and Jon M. Peha, "Spectrum Sharing Without Licensing: Opportunities and Dangers," in *Interconnection and the Internet: Selected Papers From the 1996 Telecommunications Policy Research Conference*, ed. Greg L. Rosston and David Waterman (Mahwah, NJ: Lawrence Erlbaum Associates, Inc., 1997), 49–75, www.ece.cmu.edu/~peha/wireless.html; Peha, "Sharing Spectrum through Spectrum Policy Reform and Cognitive Radio."

16. Satapathy and Peha, "Spectrum Sharing Without Licensing: Opportunities and Dangers," 49–75; Peha, "Sharing Spectrum through Spectrum Policy Reform and Cognitive Radio."

17. David Reed, "Comments for FCC Spectrum Task Force on Spectrum Policy," 10 July 2002, www.reed.com/OpenSpectrum/FCC02-135Reed.html; Yochai Benkler, "Overcoming Agoraphobia: Building the Commons of the Digitally Networked Environment," *Harvard J. Law & Tech* (Winter 1997–1998).

18. Jon M. Peha, Beth E. Gilden, Russell J. Savage, Steve Sheng, and Bradford L. Yankiver, "Finding an Effective Sustainable Model for a Wireless Metropolitan-Area Network: Analyzing the Case of Pittsburgh," Proceedings of Thirty-fifth Telecommunications Policy Research Conference (TPRC), September 2007, www.ece.cmu .edu/~peha/wiman.pdf.

19. Reed, "Comments for FCC Spectrum Task Force on Spectrum Policy"; Feng Xue and Panganamala R. Kumar, "Scaling Laws for Ad Hoc Wireless Networks: An Information Theoretic Approach," NOW Publishers, Delft, The Netherlands, 2006, black.csl.uiuc.edu/~prkumar/ps_files/06-07-18-scaling-laws.pdf.

20. Hyun-Jin Kim and J. M. Peha, "Detecting Selfish Behavior in a Cooperative Commons," proceedings of IEEE DySpan, October 2008, www.ece.cmu.edu/~peha/ wireless.html.

21. Peha, "Sharing Spectrum through Spectrum Policy Reform and Cognitive Radio."

22. Peha, "Spectrum Management Policy Options"; Peha, "Sharing Spectrum through Spectrum Policy Reform and Cognitive Radio"; and Peha, "Emerging Technology and Spectrum Policy Reform."

23. Peha, "Sharing Spectrum through Spectrum Policy Reform and Cognitive Radio"; Peha, "Emerging Technology and Spectrum Policy Reform."

24. Jon M. Peha, Sooksan Panichpapiboon, "Real-Time Secondary Markets for Spectrum," *Telecommunications Policy* 28, no. 7–8 (August 2004): 603–18, www.ece .cmu.edu/~peha/wireless.html.

25. Federal Communications Commission, Promoting Efficient Use of Spectrum Through Elimination of Barriers to the Development of Secondary Markets, Report and Order and Further Notice of Proposed Rulemaking, WT Docket No. 00-230, October 2003, hraunfoss.fcc.gov/edocs_public/attachmatch/FCC-03-113A1. pdf; Federal Communications Commission, Promoting Efficient Use of Spectrum Through Elimination of Barriers to the Development of Secondary Markets, Second Report and Order, WT Docket No. 00-230, September 2004, hraunfoss.fcc

.gov/edocs_public/attachmatch/FCC-04-167A1.PDF.

26. Jon M. Peha, "Business Implications of Dynamic Secondary Markets," *Wireless Technology* (August 2005).

27. Jon M. Peha, "Fundamental Reform in Public Safety Communications Policy," *Federal Communications Bar Journal* 59, no. 2 (March 2007): 517–46, www.ece.cmu .edu/~peha/safety.html.

28. Federal Communications Commission, FCC 06-156, First Report and Order, in the Matter of Unlicensed Operation in the TV Broadcast Bands, ET Docket No. 04-186, 18 October 2006, hraunfoss.fcc.gov/edocs_public/attachmatch/FCC-06-156A1.pdf.

29. Federal Communications Commission, Office of Engineering and Technology, *Initial Evaluation of the Performance of Prototype TV-Band White Space Devices*, Report FCC/OET 07-TR-1006, 31 July 2007, hraunfoss.fcc.gov/edocs_public/attachmatch /DOC-275666A1.pdf.

30. Peha, "Bringing Broadband to Unserved Communities."

31. Jon M. Peha, "How America's Fragmented Approach to Public Safety Wastes Spectrum and Funding," Proceedings of the Thirty-third Telecommunications Policy Research Conference (TPRC), September 2005, web.si.umich.edu/tprc /papers/2005/438/Peha_Public_Safety_Communications_TPRC_2005.pdf.

32. Peha, "How America's Fragmented Approach to Public Safety Wastes Spectrum and Funding."

33. Peha, "How America's Fragmented Approach to Public Safety Wastes Spectrum and Funding."

34. U.S. Department of Justice, Integrated Wireless Network, www.usdoj.gov /jmd/iwn.

35. Ryan Hallahan and Jon M. Peha, "Quantifying the Costs of a Nationwide Broadband Public Safety Wireless Network," *Proceedings of the Thirty-sixth Telecommunications Policy Research Conference (TPRC)*, September 2008.

36. Michael Chertoff, *Remarks by Homeland Security Secretary Michael Chertoff at the Tactical Interoperable Communications Conference*, 8 May 2006.

37. Jon M. Peha, "The Digital TV Transition: A Chance to Enhance Public Safety and Improve Spectrum Auctions," *IEEE Communications* 44, no. 6 (June 2006) (released in 2005), www.ece.cmu.edu/~peha/DTV.pdf.

38. Federal Communications Commission, Second Report and Order, in the Matter of Service Rules for the 698-746, 747-762, and 777-792 MHz Bands, WT Docket No. 06-150, 10 August 2007, hraunfoss.fcc.gov/edocs_public/attachmatch/FCC-07-132A1.pdf.

39. Kevin J. Martin, House Energy and Commerce Committee, Subcommittee on Telecommunications and the Internet, Hearing on Oversight of the Federal Communications Commission—the 700 MHz Auction, 15 April 2008.

40. Jon M. Peha, "A 'Successful' Policy for Public Safety Communications," Comments in the Matter of Implementing a Broadband Interoperable Public Safety Network in the 700 MHz Band, Federal Communications Commission PS Docket No. 06-229, 26 May 2008, www.ece.cmu.edu/~peha/safety.html.

41. Peha, "The Digital TV Transition: A Chance to Enhance Public Safety and Improve Spectrum Auctions."

8

The Way Forward for Wireless

Rob Frieden

Introduction

WIRELESS TELECOMMUNICATIONS PROVIDE opportunities for enhanced productivity and tetherless access to information, communications and entertainment (ICE) services. Increasingly, versatile handsets offer a third screen for accessing Internet-based content, serving as a supplement to, or potentially a partial substitute for, television sets and computer terminals.[1] More and more people rely on wireless telecommunications as their primary medium for telephone service, and next generation networks offer the promise of near ubiquitous access to both basic voice and enhanced information services.

As wireless telecommunications become a more essential part of the ICE marketplace, regulatory safeguards will remain necessary to ensure that competition remains robust and sustainable. Promoting competition requires intelligent regulatory policy that calibrates the scope of government oversight to that level needed to remedy shortcomings in the marketplace, such as insufficient options, discriminatory pricing, unreasonable restrictions on the use of wireless handsets, and other carrier practices that do not serve the public interest. Additionally, the executive branch and Congress need to reexamine how much radio spectrum the government requires with an eye toward achieving more efficient use so that it can share or reassign unused spectrum for private use.

For the last fifteen years, the Federal Communications Commission (FCC), with only limited congressional guidance and oversight, has embarked on a substantial deregulatory campaign based on the assumption that technological innovations can stimulate competition. The FCC has largely eliminated traditional common carrier regulatory requirements for cellular radiotelephone service providers, commonly referred to as commercial mobile radio service (CMRS) providers.[2] The commission has also started to rethink its spectrum management policies to promote more efficient use by opening up some spectrum assignments to competitive bidding, creating secondary markets for leasing spectrum that is not needed by current licensees, and permitting multiple noninterfering uses for the same spectrum allocation.

The FCC has justified reducing or eliminating regulatory safeguards on the grounds that market forces can ensure robust competition among wireless operators, thereby preventing any single carrier or group of carriers from engaging in practices that would not serve the public interest and could harm consumers. It has established policies that support premature deregulation based on an overly generous assessment of current and future competition. Additionally, it has supported concentration of ownership and control through mergers and acquisitions that have received its stamp of approval, and has abandoned or refused to establish rules that would stimulate facilities-based competition by making spectrum available to market entrants. The FCC even refrains from enforcing rules and regulations that it has not officially repealed.

Over the last several years, the FCC has abandoned rules that limited the amount of radio spectrum a single CMRS operator can control.[3] In addition, the commission has required carriers to make network time available for resale by unaffiliated ventures[4] and to specify in a tariff the terms and conditions under which their services are to be provided. At the same time, it has approved several multibillion dollar mergers[5] that have reduced the number of national CMRS operators to four, the top three controlling more than 77 percent of the market.[6] When it had the opportunity to craft rules that would encourage entry into the market of new ventures that had the capability of creating competing networks using newly available spectrum, the FCC allowed incumbent operators to acquire and possibly "warehouse" additional spectrum.[7] The FCC also concluded that it generally could assert preemptive jurisdiction over wireless policy decisionmaking by state regulatory agencies on such matters as wireless carrier rates and practices. The FCC's claim of primary jurisdiction would foreclose state courts from issuing binding decisions.[8]

The wireless telecommunications market in the United States juxtaposes marketplace success and global best practices in some categories with remarkably inferior results elsewhere. On the one hand, U.S. carriers offer subscribers access to cheap, subsidized handsets and large baskets of network minutes of use. The FCC has also begun to promote flexibility in spectrum use and leasing so that license holders can target and serve different types of users, with some spectrum available on an unlicensed basis for use by low-powered equipment, such as home Wi-Fi networking routers.

On the other hand, the FCC has allowed the wireless market to become dangerously concentrated through mergers and acquisitions,[9] jeopardizing the future of the commission's deregulatory campaign that relies on marketplace competition in lieu of government oversight. At the same time, it has done nothing to support the flexible use of wireless handsets by subscribers, or to ensure that wireless carriers operate in a nondiscriminatory manner when providing telecommunications, information, or video services.

Most CMRS subscribers agree to a bundled package that combines a subsidized handset with a two-year service agreement at rates that compensate carriers for the handset subsidy and create strong disincentives for consumers to change carriers. Subscribers are forced to pay substantial early termination financial penalties if they change carriers. Because they subsidize subscribers, CMRS carriers control the operational functions of handsets[10] and often disable features that would provide subscribers with greater freedom to access services offered by companies unaffiliated with the carrier.

The United States lags behind many other countries when it comes to mobile phone market penetration, particularly inexpensive prepaid services.[11] With less and less access to pay telephones, low-income Americans do not have many of the inexpensive, nonresidential wireless options available to their counterparts in most other developed and developing nations. U.S. wireless carriers may charge some of the lowest rates per minute of use, but they also manage to generate some of the highest average return per user (ARPU) by creating service tiers with large monthly minutes of use baskets and a commensurately high monthly rate.

They also do not offer most subscribers some of the cutting edge services available in Europe and Asia. While subscribers in the United States typically have handsets capable of just making telephone calls, sending text messages and storing ringtones, photos, and music, wireless subscribers in other countries already use their handsets for inexpensive, high-speed broadband access to the Internet and a variety of electronic commerce, location-based applications, including ones that allow subscribers to query databases that have the capability of mapping nearby commercial options.

Wireless carrier executives and trade associations representing the industry claim that extreme competition and enhanced consumer welfare justify further deregulation. For next-generation video and Internet services, they want carriers to operate as information service providers largely free of any FCC regulation, including still essential public interest, anti-trust, network neutrality,[12] and consumer protection safeguards. In light of market consolidation and considering that probably only a handful of national carriers will dominate the

CMRS marketplace, intelligent "light-handed" regulation will continue to be necessary. Moreover, the FCC should consider how wireless telecommunications networks could help achieve universal service goals with possibly cheaper and more widespread access than what wireline technologies offer.

Widespread Confusion Over the Nature and Type of Wireless Telecommunications Regulation

It may come as a surprise that CMRS ventures operate as common carriers subject to regulatory forbearance based on legislation enacted in 1993[13] that was designed to promote growth and competition. This means that while CMRS operators do not have to file tariffs and secure FCC authority to begin or stop providing a particular service, these carriers are still subject to numerous legal obligations, including the duty to operate without discrimination, to refrain from engaging in unreasonable practices that would violate their ongoing duty to serve the public interest, and to interconnect their networks with other carriers so that subscribers can use their handsets anywhere to access any wireline or wireless telephone number.

It appears that both the carriers and the FCC seek to downplay the fact that wireless carriers still must comply with most of the conventional telecommunications service regulations. Regardless of the rhetoric about how competitive the wireless market has become, the law requires the FCC to safeguard the public interest by applying traditional telecommunications, common carrier regulation.

The FCC has chosen to emphasize how competitive the CMRS market has become and how wireless carriers now also offer information services[14] when providing broadband Internet access. Because wireless carriers offer many services, a single, one-size-fits-all regulatory classification would not work in this case. Converging markets, the outcome of technological innovation, make it impossible for the FCC to treat wireless carriers solely as common carriers offering telecommunications services, or solely as private carriers offering information services. By concentrating on the new information services that wireless carriers can offer, the FCC appears disinclined to enforce consumer safeguards, or to reject mergers and acquisitions that further concentrate the industry.

The FCC must begin to address the dangers of further concentration of the industry as well as the need to subject wireless carriers to different degrees of regulatory oversight, because the many types of services they offer trigger different degrees of regulatory oversight. For conventional wireless telecommunications services, the FCC should retain streamlined common carrier regulation and calibrate any further deregulation to an increase in sustainable, facilities-based competition.

With regard to information and video services, the FCC should intervene only when necessary to ensure that wireless carriers operate accessible networks. This would not necessitate common carrier regulation, but it would require wireless carriers to establish clear service terms and conditions and to report instances where competitive necessity supports diversification in price and quality of service.

Wireless carriers appear to have exploited confusion about their current regulatory status. Not many of their subscribers understand much about the availability of regulatory safeguards. Instead, subscribers appear to conclude that they have no recourse beyond the limited safeguards available from nonnegotiable, "take it or leave it" service contracts. Indeed, CMRS service agreements—if read by a subscriber—offer little insight into what obligations the carrier has and what remedies subscribers can pursue. Worse yet, most such agreements force subscribers to abandon legal and regulatory agency options in lieu of compulsory and not necessarily unbiased or lawful arbitration.

Recently, the FCC needed to remind CMRS operators of their ongoing common carrier responsibilities. A CMRS operator must provide subscribers with access to any telephone number, including ones that would require the carrier to accept traffic from another carrier or to hand off traffic to another carrier, as is the case when a subscriber seeks to make or receive calls outside the home service territory.[15] Nonetheless, the FCC has expressed no interest in forcing wireless carriers to specify clearly their service commitments or to offer subscribers compensation and other remedies when the carriers fail to provide adequate service.

Locked Handsets and Locked Out Access to Content

The FCC has never stated explicitly that wireless carriers have to comply with the commission's "Carterfone"[16] policy requiring wireline carriers to separate the delivery of telephone service from the sale of handsets. As a result, most wireless consumers have not fully appreciated the consequences of such an arrangement, should it be enforced. The carriers have successfully touted the benefits to subscribers of using increasingly sophisticated handsets at subsidized sale prices to access a blend of ICE services. But in exchange for accepting a two-year service contract subject to a significant penalty for early termination, subscribers also accept significant limitations on their freedom to exploit the versatility and all the functions available from their handsets.

Even though wireless subscribers own the handsets they use to access network services, carriers control and limit handset freedoms through the following means:

- Locking handsets so that subscribers cannot access competitor networks (by frequency, transmission format, firmware, or software); in the United States, carriers even lock handsets designed to allow multiple carrier access by changing an easily inserted subscriber identity module (SIM);
- Using firmware "upgrades" to "brick," i.e., to render inoperative, the handset, or alternatively, to disable third party firmware and software;
- Disabling handset functions, e.g., bluetooth, Wi-Fi access, Internet browsers, GPS services, and e-mail clients;
- Specifying formats for accessing memory, e.g., music, ringtones, and photos;
- Creating "walled garden" access to favored video content of affiliates and partners; and
- Using proprietary, nonstandard interfaces that make it difficult for third parties to develop compatible applications and content.

Wireless service subscribers have begun to recognize how carrier-mandated limitations on handsets often have little to do with legitimate network management and customer service objectives. When handsets provided access primarily to voice telephone calls, text messaging, and ringtones, subscribers may have tolerated, or thought little about, limitations that blocked access to more sophisticated functions and to third-party software, applications, or content. Only recently have mobile phone subscribers started to comprehend the harmful ramifications of this decision. For example, a significant percentage of Apple iPhone purchasers have risked loss of warranty coverage and the possibility of "bricking" their handset—turning it into an expensive paperweight—to evade limitations imposed by their mobile operator (AT&T) regarding which wireless carrier, software, applications, and content iPhone subscribers can access.[17]

Almost forty years ago, the FCC established its Carterfone policy, which required all wireline telephone companies to allow subscribers to attach any technically compatible device. This simple policy has saved consumers money, promoted innovation and stimulated more diversified and expanded network use without any financial or operational harm to network operators. The Carterfone decision effectively separated telephone service from the sale or lease of the handset. The FCC initially refused to do this, but later enthusiastically embraced a court mandate to support the rights of consumers to attach any device to a network that is "privately beneficial without being publicly harmful."[18]

Wireless subscribers do contractually relinquish some freedom in exchange for a subsidized handset. But a wireless Carterfone policy would provide subscribers with the option of attaching an unsubsidized handset free of any carrier imposed attachment restrictions. Critics of applying Carterfone to

CMRS networks argue that device attachment freedom subverts the legitimate business practices of carriers. But as regulated telecommunications common carriers, CMRS operators have a duty to comply with lawful curbs on unnecessary subscriber restrictions that do not serve the public interest.

Wireless carriers remain regulated common carriers regardless of whether or not they also provide less regulated Internet access and other information services. In other words, the duties of common carriage do not evaporate simply because wireless carriers enjoy some regulatory forbearance when providing conventional telephone service. When wireless carriers also offer access to information and video services, the carriers do not operate as common carriers. Still, they should not be encouraged to favor content supplied by corporate affiliates or ventures that seek to buy preferential treatment.

Overstating the Scope of Competition

By law, the FCC is required to submit an annual report to Congress on the state of the CMRS market.[19] It uses this report and the statistics compiled as the primary source of evidence for supporting deregulation and dismissing concerns about industry ownership consolidation. Like most ICE industries, wireless has become increasingly concentrated as mergers and acquisitions reduce the number of facilities-based competitors. In addition, two of the four major national CMRS operators, AT&T and Verizon, also have dominant market shares in wireline local and long distance telephone service, as well as in broadband Internet access.

The ability to offer a bundled package of service exploits economies of scale and enables price reductions. But companies such as Verizon and AT&T have vast market power that the FCC blithely ignores. Rather than acknowledge statistics that confirm their growing market power, the FCC has opted to emphasize consumer benefits accruing from lower rates and access to large monthly baskets of network minutes of use. Here again, the commission seems unable to recognize the need for ongoing vigilance and instead chooses to emphasize the positive news supporting deregulation, all but ignoring emerging trends that are potentially harmful.

Spectrum Management Reform

Government management of radio spectrum has failed to take into account technological innovations that support greater flexibility in assigning licenses, particularly multiple non-interfering uses of the same frequencies. The traditional model for spectrum management involves a multilateral process, initiated by the International Telecommunication Union (ITU), a specialized agency of the United Nations, and followed up by national regulatory agencies such as the FCC. Both the ITU and the FCC have allocated spectrum in service-specific slivers, often specifying a single use for a particular frequency band. Technological innovations make it increasingly possible for multiple users to utilize the same frequency and for different types of services to share the same frequency band.

The FCC has cautiously supported flexible use and assignment of spectrum in two ways: 1) identifying more than one type of use for the same frequency band; and 2) encouraging the use of new technologies that promote greater efficiencies in the use of spectrum. The federal government has advocated ITU reallocation of wireless spectrum to allow shared use by operators on land, in air, and in international waters. Both the ITU and the FCC used to allocate mutually exclusive spectrum slivers for each category of usage.

A current dispute over such flexibility pits terrestrial commercial broadcasters against a satellite radio operator, Sirius, eager to install terrestrial signal repeaters to enhance reception.[20] Examples of FCC efforts to promote new spectrum conservation technology include allowing licensees to narrow channel bandwidth and to use compression techniques and new transmission formats that reduce the potential for interference.[21]

The executive branch can support the FCC's efforts and contribute to the successful commercial exploitation of spectrum by also embracing new spectrum conservation technologies. The federal government has reserved rights of access to vast amounts of spectrum that it does not use, uses sparingly, or can use more efficiently. When governments make do with less spectrum, it becomes possible to reallocate spectrum to private and commercial uses. CMRS and other wireless operators claim a shortage in available spectrum contributes to dropped calls and less than ideal quality of service. Making more spectrum available, through reallocation of reserved but unused government spectrum, would improve the quality of service available from private and commercial wireless operators. Better yet, more spectrum for next generation wireless services would promote more competition and greater diversity in the nature and type of services being offered to the public. Congress could help the FCC achieve this objective by requiring it to limit some new frequency bands to market entrants instead of incumbents keen on foreclosing additional competition.

Conclusions and Recommendations

Wireless technologies can provide users with extraordinarily versatile access to advanced ICE services in addition to telephone calls, short text messages, ringtones, and music storage. Unfortunately, the cutting edge services, such as true broadband access to the Internet, are not widely available in the United States, nor do national carriers regularly display global best practices in the nature, type, and pricing of services they offer. Wireless carriers appear able to delay investment in next generation networks, because the carriers have concentrated on leveraging money to acquire market share and buy out competitors. Nevertheless, the FCC continues moving along a glide patch toward total deregulation without any apparent worry that the CMRS market has become overly concentrated.

Market concentration appears to make it possible for the four major CMRS operators to avoid significant price competition while collectively applying almost identical service terms and conditions. For example, no wireless carrier offers discounted service to existing subscribers who opt not to acquire new, subsidized handsets, or to new subscribers seeking to activate used handsets. While Verizon has shown a willingness to offer a more open network, most wireless carriers continue to impose restrictions that violate the Carterfone policy. Even the much-touted Apple iPhone frustrates users with restrictions imposed by AT&T or Apple. An estimated 25 percent of all Apple iPhone purchasers engage in some sort of unauthorized modification to their handsets, despite the risk of voiding warranties and permanently ruining their handsets.

Wireless networks can provide a much-needed competitive alternative to legacy wireline networks and also help promote progress in achieving universal service objectives at a lower price. But such progress can be achieved only if the wireless market remains competitive, and not an adjunct or subordinate to the wireline business plans of major incumbent carriers. The executive branch, Congress, and the FCC need to remain on guard against trends that would prevent wireless carriers from providing a competitive alternative to legacy technologies.

The following specific recommendations should help promote robust facilities-based competition between wireless and wire-based technologies:

- The FCC should state that its Carterfone policy applies equally to wireline and wireless technologies. This policy would require wireless carriers to provide service to any compatible handset and to allow subscribers complete freedom to access any content, software, and applications that do not cause technical harm to the CMRS carrier's network as determined by the FCC or an independent laboratory;
- The FCC should recognize that technological and market convergence will result in wireless carriers offering a blend of telecommunications, information, and video services. It should apply different regulatory

requirements, based on the amount of competition the wireless carriers actually face. Even for lightly regulated information and video services, the FCC should require wireless carriers to disclose service terms and conditions, particularly when the carrier offers different qualities of service that might violate legitimate concerns about network neutrality;

- The FCC should not continue refraining from telecommunications service regulation of CMRS carriers until additional sustainable, facilities-based competition arises. In the absence of new players in the market, the FCC should not approve transactions that would lead to further market consolidation;
- The FCC should promote wireless technology alternatives to wireline networks when allocating funds that target universal service goals. Together with state public utility commissions, it should use reverse auctions to achieve lowest cost bidding for service to high cost areas subject to quality of service benchmarks. Before using reverse auctions, the FCC should allow wireless carriers to qualify as eligible telecommunications carriers based on the wireless carrier's actual costs instead of the current practice of applying the incumbent wireline carrier's costs;
- In light of the success of Wi-Fi and other wireless services, the FCC should allocate more spectrum for shared, unlicensed wireless services. It should also expedite efforts to identify and reallocate spectrum for wireless services including unused "white spaces" between two high-powered licensed spectrum uses. More broadly, the executive branch should reexamine the government spectrum needs with an eye toward more efficient use and the possible reassignment of unexploited spectrum for private use; and
- In light of lax FCC enforcement of consumer protection rules, Congress should explicitly state that state public utility commissions and state courts can adjudicate disputes that pertain to quality of service and interpretation of service agreements. In the absence of legislation, the FCC should enforce existing truth in billing regulations and require CMRS operators to provide understandable service agreements that clearly specify all charges, fees, taxes, and surcharges. It should also void compulsory arbitration clauses.

Notes

1. "Convergence in telecommunications gives many consumers access to multiple technologies or platforms that can be used to send and receive voice communications. Consumers are no longer limited to wireline platforms: they can choose from a range of platforms, including wireless and broadband. As wireless and broadband technologies have become more widely available to and used by consumers, they have increasingly

become part of the competitive continuum. As more consumers view and use wireless and broadband services as substitutes for wireline services, the extent to which wireline and broadband services are competitive with wireline services will increase." Ed Rosenberg, *Assessing Wireless and Broadband Substitution in Local Telephone Markets*, Publication No. 07-06 (Washington, DC: The National Regulatory Research Institute, 2007), 31; nrri.org/pubs/telecommunications/07-06.pdf (8 June 2008).

2. The Omnibus Budget Reconciliation Act of 1993, Pub. L. No. 103-66, 107 Stat. 312, amended section 332 of the Communications Act of 1934, to create the CMRS carrier category. The law defines CMRS as "any mobile service . . . that is provided for profit and makes interconnected service available (A) to the public or (B) to such classes of eligible users as to be effectively available to a substantial portion of the public." 47 U.S.C. § 332(d)(1).

3. Federal Communications Commission, 2000 Biennial Regulatory Report, Spectrum Aggregation Limits for Commercial Mobile Radio Services, Report and Order, WT Docket No. 01-14, 16 FCC Rcd 22668 (2001).

4. Petitions for Rule Making Concerning Proposed Changes to the Commission's Cellular Resale Policies, 6 FCC Rcd.1719 (1991) *aff'd sub nom.*, Cellnet Communication, 965 F.2d 1106 (DC Cir. 1992). See also *Cellnet Communications, Inc. v. Federal Communications Commission*, 149 F.3d 429 (Sixth Cir. 1998) (affirming the FCC's right to eliminate resale provisions, because elimination of such requirement does not upset customers' rights to use their telephones).

5. Applications of Nextel Communications, Inc. and Sprint Corporation For Consent to Transfer Control of Licenses and Authorizations, WT Docket No. 05-63, Memorandum Opinion and Order, 20 FCC Rcd 13967 (2005). Cingular Wireless had been a joint venture of AT&T and BellSouth Corporation ("BellSouth"). On December 29, 2006, AT&T merged with BellSouth. With the BellSouth acquisition, AT&T thereby acquired BellSouth's 40 percent economic interest in AT&T Mobility LLC ("AT&T Mobility"), formerly Cingular Wireless LLC, resulting in 100 percent ownership of AT&T Mobility. In 2007, AT&T began rebranding its wireless operations from Cingular to AT&T.

6. Leslie Cauley, "AT&T Eager to Wield Its iWeapon," *USA Today*, 21 May 2007 (displaying statistics compiled by Forrester Research); available at www.usatoday.com /tech/wireless/2007-05-21-at&t-iphone_N.htm (8 June 2008). While this chapter was being prepared Verizon sought to acquire regional wireless carrier Alltel leading to further industry concentration. See Andrew Ross Sorkin and Lauram M. Holson, "Verizon in Talks to Buy Alltel," *New York Times*, 5 June 2008, Technology; available at www.nytimes .com/2008/06/05/technology/05phone.html?_r=1&oref=slogin (1 July 2008).

7. Service Rules for the 698-746, 747-762, and 777-792 MHz Bands, Second Report and Order, FCC 07-132, 2007 WL 2301743 (released 10 August 2007). See also "*Ex Parte* Comments of the Public Interest Spectrum Coalition," *Service Rules for the 698-746, 747-762, and 777-792 Bands*, WT Docket 06-150 (5 April 2007), www.newamerica .net/files/700%20MHz%20NN%20Comments.pdf (8 June 2008).

8. Wireless Consumers Alliance, Inc. Petition for a Declaratory Ruling Concerning Whether the Provisions of the Communications Act of 1934, as Amended, or the

Jurisdiction of the Federal Communications Commission Thereunder, Serve to Preempt State Courts from Awarding Monetary Relief Against Commercial Mobile Radio Service (CMRS) Providers (a) for Violating State Consumer Protection Laws Prohibiting False Advertising and Other Fraudulent Business Practices, and/or (b) in the Context of Contractual Disputes and Tort Actions Adjudicated Under State Contract and Tort Laws, Memorandum Opinion and Order, 15 FCC Rcd. 17021 (2000).

9. "[The U.S.] is the last market in the world that people choose to bring a new wireless product to. Not second or third—the absolute last. Right now the policy of the FCC has been to encourage AT&T and Verizon to become the twin Bells that dominate the wireless business. They're allowed to buy all the spectrum they can find. The anti-trust laws are waived and ignored every time they appear to be a problem. The FCC is the only spectrum auction entity in the world that does not carve out spectrum for new entrants. They do it in Mexico, Canada, the UK, China, and Japan. Only here does the new entrant not get much of a chance. This is the only country in the world where the rule is the big guys can buy all of it. When you consolidate service providers, just like in the old days, when there was not two Bells like today but one, everybody knows what happens. It's very hard for innovators to get into the market, in terms of content or software or hardware." Reed Hundt, "Interview with Ed Gubbins," *Telephony Online*, 28 February 2008; telephonyonline.com/broadband/news/reed-hundt-auction-0228/ (8 June 2008).

10. "A shortsighted and often just plain stupid federal government has allowed it-self to be bullied and fooled by a handful of big wireless phone operators for decades now. And the result has been a mobile phone system that is the direct opposite of the PC model. It severely limits consumer choice, stifles innovation, crushes entrepreneur-ship, and has made the U.S. the laughingstock of the mobile-technology world, just as the cellphone is morphing into a powerful hand-held computer. . . . That's why I refer to the big cellphone carriers as the 'Soviet ministries.' Like the old bureaucracies of communism, they sit athwart the market, breaking the link between the producers of goods and services and the people who use them." Walt Mossberg, "Free My Phone," *All Things Digital Blog* (21 October 2007); mossblog.allthingsd.com/20071021/free-my-phone/ (8 June 2008).

11. The Organization for Economic Cooperation and Development ranks the United States 28 among OECD nations in terms of wireless market penetration at 72 per 100 inhabitants versus 152 in Luxembourg, ranked number one. OECD, *Key ICT Indicators, Mobile subscribers in total / per 100 inhabitants for OECD* (2007) www.oecd.org/dataoecd/19/40/34082594.xls (8 June 2008). The United States has one of the low-est rates of prepaid service penetration.

12. Network neutrality refers to the extent to which a network operators provides access on nondiscriminatory terms and conditions both to end users and sources of content delivered via the carrier's network. See Rob Frieden, "A Primer on Network Neutrality," *Intereconomics Review Of European Economic Policy* 43, no. 1 (January/February 2008): 4–15; "Internet 3.0: Identifying Problems and Solutions to the Net-work Neutrality Debate," *International Journal Of Communications* 1 (2007): 461–92 ijoc.org/ojs/index.php/ijoc/article/view/160/86 (8 June 2008); Rob Frieden, "Network

Neutrality or Bias?—Handicapping the Odds for a Tiered and Branded Internet," *Hastings Communications And Entertainment Law Journal* 29, no. 2 (2007): 171–216.

13. The Omnibus Budget Reconciliation Act of 1993, Pub. L. No. 103-66, 107 Stat. 312. "A person engaged in the provision of a service that is a commercial mobile service shall, insofar as such person is so engaged, be treated as a common carrier for purposes of this chapter, except for such provisions of subchapter II of this chapter as the Commission may specify by regulation as inapplicable to that service or person. In prescribing or amending any such regulation, the Commission may not specify any provision of section 201, 202, or 208 of this title, and may specify any other provision only if the Commission determines that—(i) enforcement of such provision is not necessary in order to ensure that the charges, practices, classifications, or regulations for or in connection with that service are just and reasonable and are not unjustly or unreasonably discriminatory; (ii) enforcement of such provision is not necessary for the protection of consumers; and (iii) specifying such provision is consistent with the public interest." 47 U.S.C. §332(c)(1)(A)i-iii. See also 47 U.S.C. §160(a) (establishing similar forbearance criteria for other telecommunications service providers).

14. See Appropriate Regulatory Treatment for Broadband Access to the Internet Over Wireless Networks, Declaratory Ruling, WT Docket No. 07-53, FCC 07-30 (released 23 March 2007); fjallfoss.fcc.gov/edocs_public/attachmatch/FCC-07-30A1.pdf (8 June 2008).

15. Reexamination of Roaming Obligations of Commercial Mobile Radio Service Providers, Report and Order and Further Notice of Proposed Rulemaking, WT Docket No. 05-265, FCC 07-143 (released 16 August 2007); www.fcc.gov/Daily_Releases/Daily_Business/2007/db0816/FCC-07-143A1.pdf (8 June 2008).

16. Use of the Carterfone Device in Message Toll Telephone Service, 13 FCC 2d 420 (1968), recon. denied, 14 FCC 2d 571 (1968).

17. "Of the 1.4 million iPhones sold so far (of which 1,119,000 were sold in the quarter ending Sept. 30), [Apple Chief Operating Officer Timothy] Cook estimated that 250,000 were sold to people who wanted to unlock them from the AT&T network and use them with another carrier." Saul Hansell, "Apple: $100 Million Spent on Potential iBricks," *New York Times*, 22 October 2007, Technology, Bits Blog Site, bits.blogs.nytimes.com/tag/iphone/ (8 June 2008). "You bought the iPhone, you paid for it, but now Apple is telling you how you have to use it, and if you don't do things the way they say, they're going to lock it. Turn it into a useless 'brick.' Is this any way to treat a customer? Apparently, it's the Steve Jobs way. But some iPhone users are mad as heck, and they're not going to take it anymore." Alexander Wolfe, "Apple Users Talking Class-Action Lawsuit Over iPhone Locking," *Wolfe's Den Blog*, www.informationweek.com/blog/main/archives/2007/09/iphone_users_ta.html (8 June 2008).

18. *Hush-a-Phone v. United States*, 238 F.2d 266, 269 (D.C. Cir. 1956) (reversing the FCC's prohibition on telephone subscriber use of an acoustic attachment not supplied by the telephone company).

19. Implementation of Section 6002(B) of the Omnibus Budget Reconciliation Act of 1993, Annual Report and Analysis of Competitive Market Conditions With Respect

to Commercial Mobile Services, WT 07-71, Twelfth Report, 2008 WL 312884 (released 4 February 2008).

20. Amendment of part 27 of the Commission's Rules to Govern the Operation of Wireless Communications Services in the 2.3 GHz Band, WT 07-293, Notice of Proposed Rulemaking and Second Further Notice of Proposed Rulemaking, 2007 WL 4440134 (released 18 December 2007); see also Digital Audio Broadcasting Systems and Their Impact on the Terrestrial Radio Broadcast Service, Second Report and Order First Order on Reconsideration and Second Further Notice of Proposed Rulemaking, 22 FCC Rcd. 10344 (2007).

21. Implementation of Sections 309(j) and 337 of the Communications Act of 1934 as Amended; Promotion of Spectrum Efficient Technologies on Certain Part 90 Frequencies, Third Memorandum Opinion and Order, Third Further Notice of Proposed Rule Making and Order, WT Docket No. 99-87, RM-9332, 19 FCC Rcd 25045 (2004); Replacement of Part 90 by Part 88 to Revise the Private Land Mobile Radio Services and Modify the Policies Governing Them, Report and Order and Further Notice of Proposed Rule Making, PR Docket No. 92-235, 10 FCC Rcd 10076, 10077 ¶ 1 (1995).

9

Rethinking the
Media Ownership Policy Agenda

Philip M. Napoli

History

MEDIA OWNERSHIP IS A POLICY ISSUE WITH a long and contentious history in the United States. It has become more contentious since Congress required, in the Telecommunications Act of 1996, that the Federal Communications Commission (FCC) revisit its media ownership regulations every two years (later modified to every four years) and repeal or modify any rules determined to no longer be in the public interest. This has meant that the issue of media ownership is almost always near the top of the U.S. communications policy agenda, since by the time one review of the ownership regulations ends (a process that typically drags on because of the inevitable court challenges) the next one is scheduled to begin.

Over the past forty years, the general trend has been a gradual and steady relaxation of ownership rules in some industry sectors and the complete elimination of ownership rules in others. For example, the number of television stations a single entity is permitted to own was expanded from seven to twelve. The numerical limit on the number of stations was then eliminated in favor of the current audience size-based limit, which prevents any single entity from owning television stations that reach more than 39 percent of the national television audience.[1] Restrictions governing how much prime time programming broadcast networks can own have been eliminated, a rule change that has facilitated extensive vertical integration among production studios, broadcast networks, and local stations. In cable television, rules limiting the national subscriber reach of multiple system operators, as well as rules limiting the holdings of cable systems in the channels they carry, have been struck down by the courts and have yet to officially reemerge from the FCC in any modified form.

In addition, the courts have rejected as unconstitutional a number of rules to encourage ownership of media outlets by women and minorities that were put in place in the 1970s.[2] Very recently, however, the FCC made efforts to introduce new policies designed to encourage investment in female and minority-owned media outlets, to encourage the sale of broadcast stations to female or minority owners, and to discourage discrimination in broadcast transactions.[3]

Today, the media ownership regulations in place put no limit on the number of radio stations that a single entity can own nationally, but they do limit radio station ownership within local markets to as many as eight stations, depending upon the size of the market. Similarly, there is no national television station ownership limit (only the audience reach limit noted above). Locally, a single entity can own up to two television stations in a market, depending upon the size of the market. Cross-ownership of radio and television stations in the same market is limited as well, with individual entities able to own up to two television stations and up to six radio stations in an individual market, depending upon the size of the market. A ban on cross-ownership of a daily newspaper and a broadcast station in the same market has been in place since 1975, but it was recently relaxed in the top twenty markets following the most recent iteration of the FCC's media ownership review.[4] The current rules also prohibit mergers among the "top four" broadcast networks.[5]

As important as the history of the rules themselves, and their evolution over time, are the underlying rationales that have historically motivated them. Specifically, media ownership regulations traditionally have been put into place to achieve both economic and noneconomic policy objectives. The FCC's overarching policy goals are competition, diversity, and localism.[6] What makes the case of media ownership regulation so difficult is that it involves all three of these policy goals—one of which (competition) is primarily economic in nature, and two of which (diversity and localism) are not. These economic and noneconomic policy goals can sometimes conflict.

From an economic standpoint, the key goal has been to maintain a sufficiently competitive media environment, particularly in the broadcast sector, where constraints on spectrum availability have limited the number of entities that can broadcast in any individual market. In the simpler media environment of years past, in which cable television, satellite radio/television, the Internet, and portable electronic devices did not exist as mechanisms for the delivery of content, the need for such regulations was perceived as much greater than it is in today's more competitive media environment.[7] Moreover, policymakers have responded to an increasingly "converged" media environment by considering competition not only within, but also across, media sectors. Consequently, policymakers often consider ownership regulations in terms of their potential impact on some industry sectors' ability to effectively compete against other industry sectors (hence, the frequency of the seemingly paradoxical tendency to allow greater concentration of ownership on behalf of competition).

Diversity and localism address different issues. Diversity, as conceptualized in the realm of communications policy, has focused on the diversity of information sources and content options available to the citizenry. In many instances, diversity of sources has been presumed to lead to diversity of content (hence, the traditional concerns about increasing female and minority ownership of media outlets), but this assumption has come under increased scrutiny.[8] Localism has traditionally referred to how media outlets address the distinctive needs and interests of their local communities, as well as how much media content originates from within the local communities. Local origination often has been presumed to be related to how content addresses the needs and interests of the local community; as a result, concerns about localism have often been raised in the face of policy decisions facilitating greater ownership of media outlets by out-of-market entities.[9] As should be clear, these concerns about diversity and localism have much less to do with the effective functioning of media markets and much more to do with how well the media system serves the informational needs of the citizenry, provides ample opportunities for expression, and facilitates the effective functioning of the democratic process.[10]

Current Challenges

In January 2008, the FCC released its most recent media ownership policy decision, which left most of the existing media ownership regulations unchanged but did relax the broadcast station/newspaper cross-ownership rule.[11] This decision is likely to be challenged in court by stakeholders on both sides of the issue. Those who feel that the FCC did not go far enough in relaxing ownership rules are likely to challenge its decision, as are those who oppose any relaxation of the rules.

The impending court consideration of the FCC's most recent media ownership decision is likely to illustrate what is perhaps the key challenge facing media ownership policymaking—establishing an analytical process that satisfies relevant stakeholders and an increasingly demanding judiciary. That is, the courts today seem to be far less deferential to a regulatory agency's "expert judgment" than they were in years past.[12] Rather, they increasingly demand that policy decisions be derived from, and supported by, rigorous empirical analysis. Decisions that are not derived from such evidence-based policymaking are declared arbitrary and capricious. The underlying assumptions and methods of decisions, however, have become subject to detailed scrutiny (not only by the courts, but by other interested stakeholders in the proceeding); and if they do not pass muster on these fronts, they are again declared arbitrary and capricious.

This conundrum played itself out over the FCC's 2002 media ownership proceeding, in which the commission created a diversity index to guide its decisionmaking on when/where it was appropriate to relax ownership regulations, only to see this index eviscerated by opponents of the resulting relaxation/elimination of ownership regulations and by the Court of Appeals for the Third Circuit (*Prometheus Radio Project v. Federal Communications Commission*, 2004).[13] The various assumptions and methods employed in the creation and implementation of the diversity index failed to pass critical muster.[14] The FCC's most recent ownership decision, which focused on the relaxation of the newspaper-broadcast cross-ownership rule, is likely to face similar scrutiny in the courts, where once again the focus likely will be on the adequacy of the analytical basis for the FCC's decision. Addressing this issue is the focal point of the next section.

Recommendations

The state of our media system is constantly changing, and, as a result, media ownership regulations are constantly up for reassessment (every four years, as mandated by Congress). The recommendations outlined here will, therefore, focus less on the question of what our media ownership regulations should look like today and more on the broader (and ultimately more important) question of how our media ownership regulations should be assessed, not only today, but also in future iterations of the FCC's media ownership proceedings. This section presents seven guiding principles for contemporary media ownership policymaking.

In Assessing and Formulating Media Ownership Policies, Our Current Media System Needs to be Compared With Its Contemporary Potential—Not With Its Past

Most assessments of media ownership policies begin with an assessment of the contemporary media environment, in terms of the technologies, content, and sources available to the citizenry. But more outlets or channels, or platforms for the delivery of media content do not represent *de facto* evidence that our media system is serving the needs of the citizenry better than it was in the past, and that, consequently, regulation of the ownership of our media outlets no longer serves the public interest. More importantly, even if a compelling case can be made that our media system is serving the citizenry and democracy better than it was in the past, the past should not represent the primary benchmark against which the contemporary media environment, and against which contemporary media ownership policies, should be measured. Rather, the key question is whether or not the contemporary media environment is reaching its full potential (as dictated, in large part, by the contemporary technological environment) in terms of its ability to serve the informational needs and interests of the citizenry and, more broadly, the needs of our democracy.

Just as it would not make sense to compare an individual's performance on a test at the age of thirty with his or her performance on the same test at the age of fifteen, neither does it make sense to compare the contemporary performance of our media system with its performance in decades past, when the technological environment was overwhelmingly different. Policymakers' goals should be focused on *maximizing our contemporary potential* for a democratic media system, on maximizing the contemporary technological tools at hand to craft a media system that is as diverse and competitive as it can be and that serves the informational needs and interests of local communities to the fullest extent that is technologically and economically possible. The past plays little meaningful role in such assessments.

Assessing and Formulating Media Ownership Policies Is As Much A Values-Driven Process As It Is An Empirical Process

Recent iterations of the assessment of U.S. media ownership policies seem to indicate that the answers to questions about how many radio or television stations one company should be permitted to own, or whether cross-ownership of broadcast stations and newspapers in the same market should be permitted, can be effectively provided through quantitative data analyses and econometric formulas.[15] As was noted above, this tendency has been fueled, in large part, by the analytical orientation of the courts. While social scientific research is a valuable tool in all areas of policymaking, it is naive to expect social science to be able to provide specific and definitive answers to questions like these. Alternatively, it may be the case that social scientific research pertaining to media ownership policy is used cynically, rather than naively, to justify adopting desired policies by showing that there are no conclusive findings that would suggest otherwise.

Subjective value judgments about what level of ownership restrictions needs to be applied in order to best reflect fundamental First Amendment and democratic principles cannot (and should not) be removed from the equation. The reasons for this are the limitations of contemporary methods of policy analysis, the nature of the objectives inherent in media ownership policies, and the underlying values associated with these objectives. Certainly, as is the case in many policymaking fields, social scientific analysis has been embraced in communications policymaking as a powerful tool.[16] But while it may be a very effective hammer, that does not mean it can perform the functions of a saw or a wrench. There are other tools that ultimately need to be brought to bear in media ownership policymaking. The hammer cannot do everything. And value-based judgments cannot be extracted from media ownership policymaking.[17]

The Primary Goal of Media Ownership Policies Is Not to Preserve Or Promote the Health of Established Industry Sectors, Particularly When It Comes at the Expense of the Development Of New Industry Sectors

The FCC's overarching policy goals are competition, diversity and localism.[18] If new technologies and new content delivery platforms are threatening the established business models and revenue streams of the traditional media, this would seem to be a welcome development for policymakers. Allowing increased concentration in a traditional media sector so that it can better withstand this competition from new media would, therefore, seem to be counterproductive. Policymakers of all stripes have praised the democratizing potential of the Internet. Because barriers to entry are low and the diversity of information sources is tremendous, they say, the Internet is in many ways an ideal medium for this day and age. Why, then, should their response to the model of competition and diversity that is the Internet be to allow other industry sectors—in which barriers to entry for individual proprietors have become virtually insurmountable and in which the diversity of available sources has been allowed to narrow considerably—to structure themselves *less* like the Internet? And why are such consolidation processes deemed necessary in an environment where traditional media outlets/firms are in the same position as the rest of us in terms of their ability to capitalize on the wide range of opportunities that the Internet and other new media technologies provide, and where they are able to leverage their formidable established brand identities as a key source of competitive advantage in the process?

Consider, for instance, the contemporary newspaper industry. Today, the per-reader revenues generated from an online newspaper reader do not yet match the per-reader revenues of a traditional newspaper reader. The ongoing migration of news readers from the print world to the online world explains, in large part, why traditional newspapers today are suffering financially. It is to alleviate this suffering that many policymakers and stakeholders are justifying the relaxation or elimination of the broadcast station—newspaper cross-ownership rule.[19] But is it the job of communications policymakers to help the traditional newspaper industry successfully navigate the rapidly changing media environment? And, if so, is relaxing or eliminating ownership regulations really an appropriate or effective means of doing so? It seems difficult to answer either of these questions in the affirmative.

The argument is often made that ownership regulations represent a handicap that unfairly burdens the traditional media, while not applying to the new media, thereby undermining the traditional media's ability to compete. This argument does not take into account that the traditional media already enjoy tremendous competitive advantages in the new media environment through their established brand identities, their tremendous content production resources, and their reservoirs of archived content. In this regard, any entity with a substantial toehold in the traditional media, no matter how heavily ownership in this sector is regulated, enjoys a significant advantage when seeking to compete in the new media environment. The substantial concentration of audience attention around websites owned and operated by traditional media outlets[20] suggests that the existing competitive environment already contains a healthy skew in favor of the traditional media. From this standpoint, it becomes difficult to accept the notion that ownership regulations represent a set of shackles that unfairly constrain the traditional media in the new media environment.

In Assessing the Contemporary Media Environment, the Number of Outlets Or Channels Is Far Too Superficial A Unit of Analysis. Instead, the Distribution of Resources for the Production of Content Should Be the Focus

Many assessments of the state of media ownership policy begin with detailed catalogs of all of the technologies, outlets, channels, and content options available to the contemporary media consumer.[21] This abundance of choice is then put forth as a key reason why ownership regulations are no longer necessary. Such catalogs, however, take a far too superficial view of the contemporary media environment—one that ignores fundamental characteristics of the economics of media content and the strategic dynamics within contemporary media industries. When we scratch the surface of this portrait of abundance, it turns out that it is a much more limited array of content that is circulating through this multichannel environment over and over and that it is feeding into, and supporting, many of the new content delivery platforms, outlets, and sources that are becoming available.

Citing the fact that the number of television channels available in the average household has more than doubled in the past decade does not, by any stretch of the imagination, mean that the amount of programming available in the average household has increased proportionately. Most new cable channels, for instance, exist primarily to repurpose programming originally produced by or for other channels. Consider, for instance, how many different HBO channels are available today and how often any one episode of *The Sopranos* has been viewable across all of these channels—not to mention any one episode's subsequent availability (multiple times) on the basic cable network A&E. The economics of media content production literally cannot support the incredible increase in available channels that has taken place. Recycling and repurposing are the rule, not the exception, in contemporary television programming. If the ratio of channel choices to hours of original programming were to be determined, the results would be startling.

Similar principles are at work online, where enthusiasm about the apparently unlimited array of information sources is finally beginning to be tempered by the recognition that much of the information flowing across the Internet originates from relatively few sources. Google primarily *aggregates* news produced by traditional news outlets. It is not, in and of itself, a *news source*. Online news production and consumption continues to be heavily weighted toward websites associated with traditional news outlets.[22] Bloggers bookend links to news stories produced by traditional news outlets with their own opinion and commentary. They are seldom, at this point, *producing* news.[23]

In these ways, substantial growth in the number of channels can dramatically obscure very modest growth, or even relative stagnation, in the growth of available content. In fact, the dramatic fragmentation of the contemporary media environment can actually provide disincentives for the production of additional content, as it has become more difficult, in some cases, to attract a sufficient audience to generate the necessary financial return. Recycling and repurposing have become the antidote to fragmentation.

In such an environment, it is essential that policymakers and policy analysts see the forest through the trees and avoid confusing channel or outlet availability with content availability. "Content," as Michael Eisner famously said, "is king." It is content that serves the informational needs of the citizenry. How much diverse and original content is being produced (particularly in relation to news/journalism) is what should matter most to policymakers, not how many different paths the same content can travel to reach the audience. This shift in analytical focus provides a very different perspective on the contemporary media environment and, by association, of the lens through which policymakers should assess the relevance of media ownership regulations.

In Assessing and Formulating Media Ownership Policies, the Burden of Proof Should Be Equally Distributed. Assessing the Potential Benefits of Any Policy Changes Is Just As Important As Assessing the Potential Harms

Recent iterations of the FCC's media ownership proceedings seem to have started from the position that, if harms associated with relaxing or eliminating particular ownership regulations could not be effectively demonstrated, then the regulations would be relaxed or eliminated. Such a stance represents a very uneven analytical playing field, in which those opposed to relaxing or eliminating ownership regulations face a much higher burden of proof (in what are, ultimately, adversarial proceedings conducted by the FCC) than those in favor of relaxing or eliminating ownership regulations. Given the magnitude of the issues at stake (First Amendment freedoms, the effective functioning of the democratic process), it would seem more than reasonable for policymakers to engage in an analytical process in which the burden of proof is more equally distributed, in which rules designed to enhance the democratic process and to promote a more equitable distribution of speech rights be considered not only in terms of the potential harms associated with their elimination, but also in terms of the potential benefits. How and why, for instance, would our media outlets function better in a more deregulated ownership environment? Such questions should receive equal attention as questions related to what harms might come from relaxing or eliminating existing ownership regulations. Only then can a balanced cost-benefit analysis take place.

In Assessing and Formulating Media Ownership Policies, Demands for Rigorous Data Analysis Must Be Accompanied and Supported By Rigorous Data Gathering

As noted previously, it is important for policymakers to set appropriate limits when relying on empirical analyses in their media ownership decisionmaking. At the same time, to the extent that such analyses do come into play, it is vital that the information environment be as conducive as possible to thorough and reliable analyses. Unfortunately, the last two media ownership proceedings demonstrated a troubling paradox—while the FCC tries to assess and formulate policy on the basis of rigorous empirical analysis related to questions such as the relationship between ownership structure and provision of various types of content, and on trends in ownership structure and characteristics across markets and over time, it does not gather, or have access to, the data necessary to effectively investigate these questions. Consequently, most of the analyses conducted or commissioned by the FCC have been subjected to withering criticisms by the courts or other stakeholders. The FCC's minority media ownership data are widely acknowledged to be inadequate to effectively guide policymaking.[24] The broadcast programming data deemed necessary for the FCC to conduct analyses of the relationship between owner-ship structure and the availability of various categories of programming are virtually nonexistent.[25] In addition, the different forms of media ownership data provided by a wide range of commercial data providers have various inadequacies when used for policy purposes, and, perhaps more importantly, often are only accessible to policymakers and other stakeholders at substantial cost, and with substantial access limitations.[26]

Conducting analyses under these constraints is equivalent to trying to build a house without wood or cement. If the policymakers are going to engage in, and rely upon, these kinds of rigorous research activities, they need to have at their disposal the necessary raw materials to do so effectively.[27] Otherwise, it is simply a case of garbage in, garbage out. And certainly the public interest deserves better than that.

In Assessing and Formulating Media Ownership Policies, "Putting The Horse Back In The Barn" Is Not Impossible

Many discussions of media ownership regulation inevitably contain the state-ment "We can't put the horse back in the barn," or "We can't put the genie back in the bottle." These statements are typically made to explain why, once relaxed or eliminated, media ownership regulations cannot later be strength-ened or reintroduced. The logistical, political, or legal roadblocks to such ac-tions are generally considered insurmountable.

But history tells us that, if the political will is there, such reversals in policy direction are indeed possible. We need only consider the government-mandated break-up of AT&T in the early 1980s[28] to remind ourselves that communications policies that have facilitated increased concentration of ownership can be, and have been, reversed. Thus, when assessing and for-mulating media ownership regulations, there is no logical reason that the institution of more stringent regulations is an option that needs to be taken completely off the table.

Conclusion

This chapter has attempted to provide historical background on the issue of media ownership policy in the United States and to outline a set of principles that can inform and guide future media ownership policymak-ing and policy analysis. These principles certainly cannot help answer all of the questions that inevitably will confront policymakers dealing with the issue of media ownership, but it is hoped that they can illuminate productive paths for future analysis and contribute to decision outcomes that can better fulfill the full range of objectives associated with media ownership regulation.

Notes

1. See Charles B. Goldfarb, *The FCC's Broadcast Media Ownership Rules.* CRS Report for Congress (March 2008). Retrieved 14 May 2008 from fpc.state.gov /documents/organization/103.

2. Christine Bachen, Allen S. Hammond IV, and Catherine Sandoval, "Serving the Public Interest: Broadcast News, Public Affairs Programming, and the Case for Minority Ownership," in *Media Diversity and Localism: Meaning and Metrics*, ed. Philip M. Napoli (Mahwah, NJ: Lawrence Erlbaum Associates, 2007), 269–308.

3. Federal Communications Commission, *Promoting Diversification of Ownership in the Broadcasting Services* (2008b).

4. Federal Communications Commission, *2006 Quadrennial Regulatory Review— Review of the Commission's Broadcast Ownership Rules and Other Rules Pursuant to Section 202 of the Telecommunications Act of 1996.* 23FCC Rcd 2010 (2008a).

5. For a more detailed summary of current ownership regulations, see Goldfarb, 2008.

6. Federal Communications Commission, 2008a.

7. For a detailed discussion of competition as a communications policy principle, see Philip M. Napoli, *Foundations of Communications Policy: Principles and Process in the Regulation of Electronic Media* (Cresskill, NJ: Hampton Press, 2001).

8. See Bachen, Hammond, and Sandoval, "Serving the Public Interest"; Adam Candeub, "The First Amendment and Measuring Media Diversity: Constitutional Principles and Regulatory Challenges," *Northern Kentucky Law Review* 33 (2006): 373–99.

9. For detailed discussions of diversity and localism as policy principles, see Napoli, 2001.

10. See C. Edwin Baker, *Media Concentration and Democracy: Why Ownership Matters* (New York: Cambridge University Press, 2007).

11. Federal Communications Commission, 2008a.

12. See Candeub, 2006.

13. *Prometheus Radio Project v. Federal Communications Commission*, 373 F.3d 372 (2004).

14. See Candeub, 2006; Philip M. Napoli and Nancy Gillis, "Media Ownership and Diversity Assessment: A Social Science Research Agenda," in *Media Ownership: Research and Regulation*, ed. Ronald E. Rice (Cresskill, NJ: Hampton Press, 2008), 303–22.

15. See, e.g., Federal Communications Commission, *202 Biennial Regulatory Review—Review of the Commission's Broadcast Ownership Rules and Other Rules Adopted Pursuant to Section 202 of the Telecommunications Act of 1996*, 18 FCC Rcd 13620 (2003).

16. See Michelle Connolly and Evan Kwerel, "Economics at the Federal Communications Commission: 2006–2007," *Review of Industrial Organization* 31 (2007): 107–20.

17. See Baker, 2007; Candeub, 2006.

18. Federal Communications Commission, 2008a.

19. See Federal Communications Commission, 2008a.

20. See, e.g., Lincoln Dahlberg, "The Corporate Colonization of Online Attention and the Marginalization of Critical Communication?," *Journal of Communication Inquiry* 29(2) (2005): 160–80.

21. See, e.g., Federal Communications Commission, 2003.

22. See James E. Katz and Ronald E. Rice, *Social Consequences of Internet Use: Access, Involvement and Interaction* (Cambridge, MA: MIT Press, 2002).

23. See Melissa Wall, "Blogs of War: Weblogs as News," *Journalism* 6, no. 2 (2005): 153–72.

24. Philip M. Napoli and Joe Karaganis, "Toward a Federal Data Agenda for Communications Policymaking," *CommLaw Conspectus: The Journal of Communications Law & Policy* 16, no. 1 (2007): 53–96.

25. Napoli and Karaganis, 2008.

26. Philip M. Napoli and Michelle Seaton, "Necessary Knowledge for Communications Policy: Information Asymmetries and Commercial Data Access and Usage in the Policymaking Process," *Federal Communications Law Journal* 59 (2007): 295–329.

27. For specific proposals, see Napoli and Karaganis, 2008.

28. Steve Coll, *The Deal of the Century: The Break-up of AT&T* (New York: Atheneum Books, 1986).

Part III
Access

10

Universal Service

Krishna Jayakar

THE 1996 TELECOMMUNICATIONS ACT INTRODUCED several reforms into the universal service system in the United States. It expanded the pool of beneficiaries through new programs, it instituted a new mechanism for funding and it promised that new services would be included in the universal service definition if certain criteria were met. In the years since, it has seen some successes and some failures. It has also been responsible for some rather significant, yet unintended, developments. A future universal service policy has to build on these successes and remedy the failures, while helping prepare America for the competitive challenges that lie ahead, most prominently the need to catch up with the rest of the developed world and assume a dominant role in the emerging broadband economy. In this chapter, we propose a vision for universal service policy as well and some proposed measures that may help realize it.

Background

The term "universal service" entered the U.S. policy lexicon not long after the telephone came into use. It was in 1907, at the height of the early competitive era, that Theodore Vail, the president of Bell Telephone Company, enunciated the goal of "one system, one policy, universal service." Though later scholarship[1] showed that Vail's idea of universal service did not correspond to the meaning it has taken on today, the term itself lived on. The 1934 U.S. Communications Act defined the contours of universal service, as we know it today, by announcing in its preamble the intention "to make available, so far as possible, to all the people of the United States a rapid, efficient, nationwide, and worldwide wire and radio communication service with adequate facilities at reasonable charges" (1934 Communications Act, Title 1, Section 2). Over the next fifty years, an elaborate system of geographical rate averaging and cross-subsidies emerged that supported low residential subscription prices and equalized monthly rates for rural and urban customers across the country. During this period, telephone penetration in the United States gradually rose to about 92 percent of all households. In the 1980s, as pressure began mounting to break up AT&T, the company tried—unsuccessfully, as it later emerged—to use this high household penetration, and the universal service system that made it possible, to argue for a continuation of its regulated monopoly. Even the opponents of monopoly agreed that universal service needed to be preserved. So after AT&T was finally broken up in 1984 and long-distance service became competitive, universal service was still supported by a system of above-cost access charges paid to the local exchange companies.

Today's system of universal service is based on the 1996 Telecommunications Act, the first major rewrite of communications policy in the United States since the 1934 Communications Act. The subject of universal service is dealt with primarily in section 254 of the act, which sets forth the following principles:

> (1) quality services should be available at just, reasonable, and affordable rates; (2) access to advanced telecommunications and information services should be provided in all regions of the nation; (3) consumers in all regions of the nation, including low-income consumers and those in rural, insular, and high cost areas, should have access to telecommunications and information services, including interexchange services and advanced telecommunications and information services, that are reasonably comparable to those services provided in urban areas and that are available at rates that are reasonably comparable to rates charged for similar services in urban areas; (4) all providers of telecommunications services should make an equitable and nondiscriminatory contribution to the preservation and advancement of universal service; (5) there should be specific, predictable and sufficient federal and state mechanisms to preserve and advance universal service; (6) elementary and secondary schools and classrooms, health care providers, and libraries should have access to advanced telecommunications services; and (7) such other principles as the [Federal-State] Joint Board and the [Federal Communications] Commission determine are necessary and appropriate for the protection of the public interest, convenience, and necessity and are consistent with this Act (Section 254(b)(1)-(7)).

These principles, while continuing the idea behind universal service, were also a radical departure in many respects. First, in pursuance of the principle to make universal service transparent, predictable, and competitively neutral, the 1996 act resulted in the creation of a universal service fund (USF) into which all telecommunications carriers would make contributions equal to a percentage (to be determined annually) of their interstate end-user telecommunications revenues. All universal service programs would be supported by disbursements from this fund. Second, the 1996 act dramatically expanded the list of entities eligible to receive universal service support. In the prior system, residential subscribers in general benefited from long-distance-to-local cross-subsidies, and geographical rate averaging helped subscribers in high-cost areas such as rural, remote, and mountainous regions. There were targeted programs such as Lifeline and Link-Up for low-income households as well (see below). But the 1996 act introduced new classes of beneficiaries, such as schools, libraries, and rural health care providers. Subsequent rule-making by regulatory agencies also created separate programs for the traditional categories of recipients. Currently, four separate programs are funded by the federal USF.[2]

- *Lifeline and Link-Up.* These are legacy programs that continue to be funded post–1996 act. Lifeline provides discounts to low income households for monthly service; Link-Up provides a one-time amount in support of and initial telephone installation or activation fees for low-income households
- *High-Cost Areas Program.*[3] This program supports local service providers that serve areas where the cost of providing service is high, such as rural, mountainous, or insular areas or Native American reservations.
- *Schools and Libraries.* Popularly called the E-Rate program, this provides discounts to schools and libraries for telecommunications or Internet access, or internal wiring to enable computer networks.
- *Rural Health Care Program.* This program supports health care providers located in rural areas to enable patients in rural America to have the same access to advanced medical services enjoyed by urban communities.

The third innovation of the 1996 act was a commitment to periodically review and, if necessary, update the set of services included in the universal service definition—a marked break from earlier practice, which confined universal service to plain old telephone service (POTS). To this end, section 254(c)(1) of the act said that the list of services included in the definition of universal service should be those that are essential to education, public health, or public safety; have, through the operation of market choices by customers, been subscribed to by a substantial majority of residential customers; are being deployed in public telecommunications networks by telecommunications carriers; and are consistent with the public interest, convenience, and necessity. To repeat, regulators were expected to wait until a "substantial majority of customers" had adopted a new service through normal operation of the market, leaving little room for anticipatory and proactive rulemaking. As a result, until recently, the Federal-State Joint Board meetings had not ended up adding new services to the universal service mix. In November 2007, the board made significant recommendations for reforming the high-cost areas program in this respect (see further discussion below).

Proposals for Reform

As the first major overhaul of communications policy in the United States in more than six decades, the Telecommunications Act has naturally attracted its share of kudos and criticism. It has chalked up a fair amount of success in fulfilling some of its objectives and some notable failures, but it is the unintended consequences of the act that have attracted the most criticism. In the following review of universal service, all of these aspects—successes, failures, and unintended consequences—will become evident.

Policymakers essentially have two choices with regard to universal service reform. The first one is to work within the contours of the existing universal service program and implement a series of reforms that build on its successes and remedy its failings. In the section below, these choices are discussed under the heading of short- and medium-term reforms. But in addition, policymakers may also want to consider some far-reaching reforms that would enable universal service programs to contribute to U.S. economic competitiveness in the twenty-first century. We label these the long-term policy choices.

Short and Medium Term

Foremost among the problems confronting the current universal service program in the short and medium term is the question of universal service funding. If the new administration does not address this issue, it will not be able to find solutions for any of the other questions confronting the universal service programs.

Funding

The 1996 act mandated the creation of a universal service fund (USF) into which all telecommunications providers are required to contribute a percentage of their interstate and international end-user telecommunications revenues. The fund is administered by the Universal Service Administration Company (USAC), which makes disbursements to all the universal service programs. Each quarter, a "contribution factor" is estimated, based on the USAC's projections of the financial needs for its various universal service programs for that quarter as well as projected end-user interstate and international revenues for the telecommunications industry.[4] Telecommunications service providers, in turn, are allowed to pass on their universal service contributions to their customers in the form of a line item on monthly bills. Data from the first-quarter of the year 2000 to the latest quarter (2Q 2008), for which the contribution factor has been estimated, are provided in table 10.1.

As the table indicates, projected quarterly USAC expenditures increased in this period from roughly $1.1 billion to $1.9 billion (for a cumulative growth of around 71 percent, or an average quarterly increase of 1.64 percent), whereas quarterly end-user interstate and international telecommunications revenues have stayed at almost the same level, $19.2 billion in 2000 to $19 billion in the latest quarter. The net result is that the contribution factor increased from 0.059 in early 2000 to 0.113 in the second quarter of 2008 (a cumulative increase of 92 percent and a quarterly rate of 2 percent). As a percentage of industry revenues, universal service support expenditures have increased from 5.8 percent to 10.3 percent—an increase of almost three-quarters. Much of the explanation for the rising contribution factors can be traced to the lack of growth in telecommunications industry revenues over the past few years. At the time the universal service programs in the 1996 act were legislated and implemented, telecommunications was widely regarded as a growth sector, along with other high technology industries. Since then, industry revenues have stagnated, but universal service expenditures, backed by the momentum of administrative machinery and the expectations of recipients, have not. After initial protests, the industry has apparently reconciled itself to this situation. It does, after all, pass on universal service contributions to customers in the form of long-distance surcharges. But the rising burden of universal service on consumers is still a matter of concern and raises questions about the continuing viability of the programs.

In light of the trends discussed above, policymakers have a limited number of options in terms of funding reform. Under the status quo, telecommunications companies will continue paying a share of their telecommunications revenues into the USF, and service providers in turn will pass on these contributions to their customers. But given the steady increase in the contribution factor over time, this may not be sustainable. The two options for reforming the status quo are: (a) increasing the contribution base from which universal service funds are collected, and (b) capping and reducing the expenditures in the various USF-supported programs. The contribution base may be increased

Table 10.1:
Cumulative Funding for Universal Service Programs and Contribution Factors

	Quarterly Projected USAC Expenses ($ billion)	Quarterly End-User Telecom Revenue ($ billion)	Projected USAC Expenses as a % of Telecom Revenue	Contribution Factor
1Q 2000*	1.114	19.176	5.81%	0.058770
2Q 2000	1.106	19.608	5.64%	0.057101
3Q 2000	1.118	20.403	5.48%	0.055360
4Q 2000	1.188	21.172	5.61%	0.056688
1Q 2001*	1.353	20.463	6.61%	0.066827
2Q 2001*	1.397	20.508	6.81%	0.068823
3Q 2001	1.374	20.141	6.82%	0.068941
4Q 2001	1.342	19.597	6.85%	0.069187
1Q 2002	1.379	20.450	6.74%	0.068086
2Q 2002	1.385	19.219	7.21%	0.072805
3Q 2002	1.505	17.158	8.77%	0.072805
4Q 2002	1.586	18.488	8.58%	0.072805
1Q 2003	1.501	18.705	8.02%	0.072805
2Q 2003	1.534	18.743	8.18%	0.091000
3Q 2003	1.606	18.844	8.52%	0.095000
4Q 2003	1.545	18.607	8.30%	0.091490
1Q 2004	1.495	18.894	7.91%	0.086823
2Q 2004	1.504	19.101	7.87%	0.086333
3Q 2004	1.515	18.707	8.10%	0.088980
4Q 2004	1.457	18.095	8.05%	0.088470
1Q 2005	1.758	18.352	9.58%	0.106981
2Q 2005	1.807	18.332	9.86%	0.110423
3Q 2005	1.679	18.370	9.14%	0.101585
4Q 2005	1.633	17.870	9.14%	0.101585
1Q 2006	1.689	18.451	9.15%	0.101796
2Q 2006	1.774	18.318	9.68%	0.108300
3Q 2006	1.763	18.774	9.39%	0.104657
4Q 2006	1.588	19.363	8.20%	0.090220
1Q 2007	1.622	18.549	8.74%	0.096776
2Q 2007	1.856	18.014	10.30%	0.116052
3Q 2007	1.867	18.566	10.06%	0.112959
4Q 2007	1.857	18.949	9.80%	0.109717
1Q 2008	1.746	19.194	9.10%	0.101052
2Q 2008	1.907	18.978	10.05%	0.112868
Geometric Mean (%)	1.64%	-0.03%	1.67%	2.0%
Cumulative Increase (%)	71.2%	-1.0%	73.0%	92.1%

(Source: FCC Public Notices on Universal Service Contribution Factors, Available at www.fcc.gov/omd
/contribution-factor.html)

by including revenues that are currently exempt from or have limited liability to make contributions to the USF. Currently, "interconnected VoIP services" (i.e., VoIP services that enable subscribers to receive calls from or make calls to the public service telecommunications network (PSTN)) are required to contribute to the USF.[5] In other words, pure VoIP calls that do not access the PSTN (for example, calls made computer-to-computer) do not contribute to universal service. But as more and more telecommunications traffic migrates to VoIP, policymakers may want to include VoIP calling as well in the contribution base, though this may create the technical difficulty of differentiating VoIP packets from other types of Internet traffic. Wireless services are another category of telecommunications that have limited liability to make universal service contributions. But given the rapid increase in mobile penetration, often at the expense of landline connections, the FCC in 1998 decided to impose a limited liability on wireless revenues, which it further increased in 2002 and again in 2006.[6] A more radical approach may be to require contributions from all types of telecommunications services, including those that are currently labeled as information services. However, some economists have pointed to the potential inefficiencies associated with a "tax" on broadband in the initial stages of its diffusion.[7] In sum, policymakers' ability to expand the contribution base is limited.

The second option is to cap and reduce the expenditures in the various USF-supported programs. The FCC has recently made attempts to cap expenditures on the universal service programs. The E-Rate program for schools and libraries has had a cap of $2.25 billion in annual disbursements right from its inception. The rural health care and the Lifeline/Link-Up programs too have had relatively stable expenditures year-to-year. However, the high-cost areas program has experienced explosive growth,[8] with annual program expenditures increasing from approximately $2.7 billion in 2001 to $4.3 billion in 2007, the last full year for which data is available. Much of this growth is driven by disbursements to competitive local exchange companies (CLECs), who get reimbursed on a per-line basis at the same level as the incumbent LEC, and not at the CLEC's own costs.[9] In May 2008, the FCC decided to cap the total annual support that competitive eligible telecommunications carriers (ETCs)[10] for each state receive at the level of support that competitive ETCs in that state were eligible to receive during March 2008 on an annualized basis.

Though this may temporarily resolve the issue of exploding high-cost area support, it leaves unresolved the fundamental question of eligibility to receive universal service support in each state. Under current rules, it is quite possible for multiple service providers to receive high-cost support for serving the same territory, sometimes even the same household if, for example, a consumer subscribes to both a wireline and a wireless phone. It is to avoid this wasteful duplicative use of resources that some have argued for an auction-based mechanism for the allocation of universal service obligations and funds to a single service provider in each territory that is allowed to offer service using the most cost-efficient technology.[11] We recommend that each territory should have a single carrier of last resort for universal service—this service provider may be identified using auctions or other mechanisms.

Accountability, Fraud, and Program Effectiveness

In addition to the problem of sustainable funding, and closely related to it, has been the lack of accountability and monitoring in universal service programs. This has in turn let to concerns about program effectiveness, and even accusations of fraud, especially in the E-Rate program. While E-Rate supporters argue that fraud has occurred only in isolated instances and is being brought under control, critics argue that the problem is widespread and inherent in the program's conceptualization itself. There are undoubtedly systemic factors that permit fraud to occur and prevent its timely detection. Many instances of fraud in the E-Rate program can be traced to the complexity of the application process and the lack of technical expertise on the part of school officials.[12] In the absence of such expertise, school officials come to rely on the guidance of the very contractors who bid for projects, raising obvious conflicts of interest. Certain policies implemented in 2003, such as a lifetime ban on vendors found misappropriating funds, have decreased the number of allegations of fraud.

A larger question about E-Rate concerns the effectiveness of computers and Internet access in the classroom. Though several observers have found the use of computers and the Internet in the classroom to have strong benefits,[13] others disagree; they argue that access alone does not create the same educational opportunities, unless there is also emphasis on teacher training, curriculum development, and integration into the overall educational process.[14] The more radical critics argue that the digital divide in computer and Internet access is not the most serious divide in education and that the enormous expenditure in wiring up schools and classrooms to the Internet may be a wasteful and unnecessary diversion of resources much needed elsewhere in the educational system.[15] Students in computer-enabled classrooms have been found to use computers mostly to complete assignments, play games, or search the Internet for information.[16] These cautionary reports serve as a necessary corrective to the widespread euphoria surrounding the use of information and communications technologies in education.

Questions of accountability and program oversight have also been raised in reference to the high-cost areas program. Since the high-cost areas support program was intended to ensure the comparability of intra-state rates, it was considered reasonable to let states oversee and certify that the high-costs area funding in their territories was being used appropriately.[17] But since not all states have the regulatory capability or resources needed to monitor implementation, associations of service providers, or even individual service providers, were allowed to certify the use of funding. Gabel expresses wonder at "how light the Commission's accountability regime is" (332) when compared with other federal programs, or even other universal service programs such as Lifeline. Possibly due to this lack of accountability, he found that receipt of "high-cost fund has no positive effect on the provision of advanced telecommunication services, and this is consistent with earlier research findings that money is handed out, but there is no mechanism for assessing performance" (344).[18] He argues for better monitoring and accountability, including making future funds available only if recipients of high-cost area funds show that the number of lines equipped to offer advanced services is higher at their wire centers that receive high-cost areas support.

To summarize, better monitoring and accountability of universal service programs may be needed to ensure efficiency and transparency. This is especially true of the E-Rate program that has been beset with allegations of fraud, as well as the high-cost areas program, in which funding support was not found to be correlated with the deployment of advanced services. Federal regulators may also need more resources and stronger institutional mechanisms to investigate allegations of fraud or misappropriation of funds. Currently, a number of agencies—the USAC, the FCC's Wireline Competition Bureau and the Office of the Inspector General (OIG), the Anti-trust Division of the Department of Justice, and even the Federal Bureau of Investigation (FBI)—investigate allegations of fraud in the E-Rate and other universal service programs. This divides responsibility and dilutes expertise resulting in ineffective monitoring.

Telephone Penetration

After almost seventy years of steady increases in household telephone penetration,[19] policymakers and analysts have considered universal service in POTS to be pretty much accomplished and have moved their attention to advanced services. But the most recent data suggest some reason for concern regarding basic service. The FCC's annual *Trends in Telephone Service, 2007* reported that from a peak of 97.6 percent of household units with telephone service in the year 2000, penetration dropped down to 94.8 percent in 2005, the latest year for which data is available.[20] This decline is not because of substitution to mobile, as might be assumed, since respondents were asked to list any type of telephone connection, including wireline, wireless, or fixed wireless.

Gabel and Gideon have investigated a number of hypotheses for this drop in penetration: increases in subscription prices due to rate rebalancing as companies responded to competition; changes in household income; unpredictable monthly bills due to the proliferation of advanced services, many of which are priced on usage; consumer churn between wireline and mobile; and so on.[21] According to them, prices may not be a big factor, since prior studies have found low price elasticity for monthly subscriptions. Neither is income likely to be a major factor, since the poverty level did not change much during this period. But month-to-month variations in charges have increased due to the proliferation of services, the increase in the number of services charging by usage (e.g., wireless beyond the free-call limit), and aggressive marketing of advanced services by telephone providers. Gabel and Gideon argue that low-income households may decide to switch to mobile when faced with an unexpectedly high wireline bill and then find wireless bills even more difficult to control. This may cause a household to lose telephone access altogether. They recommend that laws protecting consumers against unpredictable charges and aggressive marketing of advanced services may do much to alleviate this unintended consequence of wireline-mobile intermodal competition.

Associated with the problem of falling household penetration might be questions about the effectiveness of the Lifeline and Link-Up programs intended to benefit low-income households. An examination of data from 1997 and 2003 shows that only about one-third of eligible households were enrolled in the Lifeline and Link-Up programs.[22] There were also significant state-by-state variations, with state promotional efforts identified as an important factor explaining participation. For example, states that included Lifeline in a larger package of state programs intended for low-income families and cross-promoted it had greater success in encouraging participation. The federal government can offer states incentives to improve participation by requiring better monitoring and channeling more funds to states with better results in increasing participation rates.

The above analysis of the implementation of the universal service provisions of the 1996 act helps identify what possible reforms may be needed in the future. First, the inability of a growing percentage of households to have access to basic telephone service is worrisome, even as the rest of society moves toward an information economy. Research from a variety of sources has shown that subscription prices *per se* are not the reason why households do not subscribe to service. Indeed, every available study has found that telecommunications access demand is inelastic in the face of rising prices. Instead, it is unforeseen and exorbitant increases in monthly bills that force some low-income subscribers to disconnect. This, in turn, is caused by aggressive marketing of advanced services by telecommunications companies, the movement toward usage-based pricing for an increasing number of services, and lack of consumer protections against unlawful and exorbitant charges. Better enforcement of existing laws and/or a new telecommunications consumer protection law might enable more low-income families to stay connected to the network. Federal incentives to states to actively promote Lifeline and Link-Up programs might also be a positive step.

While there are solid reasons for advancing the reforms advocated above in the short-to-medium term, they are essentially remedial in nature and do not articulate a vision of universal service more suitable for the new information economy. Below, we attempt to define such a vision based on our prior work.[23]

Broadband Deployment

In recent years, a number of commentators have argued that universal service should be extended to broadband. Their concern is motivated by the low and declining ranking of the United States in international comparisons of broadband penetration, in some reports as low as sixteenth among major industrialized nations.[24] This lag is occurring at a time when digital technologies are mediating increasing shares of economic activity, raising questions about America's competitiveness. Many reasons have been advanced for differences in adoption rates across countries. One study found, for example, that inter-platform competition, local loop unbundling, broadband speed, information and communications technology use, and the availability of content were the significant predictors of broadband adoption across countries.[25]

In recognition of this growing demand, the Federal-State Joint Board on Universal Service announced a set of proposals to accommodate broadband in the universal service program.[26] The board advocated reorganizing the high-cost areas program to create three new funds—a broadband fund, a mobility fund, and a provider of last resort (POLR) fund. The broadband fund would primarily fund the construction of broadband infrastructure in unserved areas. Some funding would also go to enhancing coverage in areas where the existing service is substandard, as well as to support operational expenses of service providers in low population density areas. The mobility fund would offer support for construction of facilities in areas with no wireless service, including areas used by the traveling public, such as state and federal highways. As in the case of the broadband fund, the mobility fund would cover the operational expenses of carriers in areas where a business case cannot be made for service due to low population density. Finally, the POLR fund would continue the funding support for incumbent local exchange providers currently offered by the high-cost areas program.

The proposed reforms, if adopted, would address some of the current problems with the universal service system. First of all, it would include broadband in the universal service package in accordance with rising public demand—although the proposed level of funding for the broadband fund leaves much to be desired (see further discussion below). Second, the proposals acknowledge the financial problems with the USF. Accordingly, they call for an overall cap on funding under the high-cost areas program at $4.5 billion per year. In addition, the board would cap the mobility fund at $1 billion and allocate an initial corpus of $300 million to the broadband fund. The POLR fund would also probably be capped in line with the others. The board also proposes changes in the allocation of funds: the identical support rule by which competitive LECs are compensated at the same rate as the incumbents would be changed in favor of a system that would base each carrier's support on its actual costs. In addition, the board proposes that only one carrier in each area be eligible to receive support from a fund—in effect, only one broadband provider, one wireless provider, and one wireline provider would then receive funding in each area from the three proposed funds. It visualized that these proposed changes would be phased in over a period of time, tentatively identified as five years, in a way that would avoid radical or abrupt changes. For instance, competitive wireless providers would lose support under the POLR fund but would gain an equivalent amount of support under the mobility fund.

One of the more far-reaching changes proposed by the board has to do with the role of the states. Although states do have a role in the current universal service system, for instance, they identify eligible telecommunications carriers (ETCs) and manage the Lifeline/Link-Up programs—their role is much enhanced in the proposed system. The board proposes that states would effectively administer the broadband and mobility funds, defining the technical specifications of broadband, identifying unserved and underserved areas, approving construction projects for funding, and determining the eligible providers. The board also visualizes that states would provide part of the funding for these programs and be able to receive additional federal allocations, beyond a prescribed minimum, as they increase their own funding.

While these proposals are, on the whole, steps in the right direction, policymakers may be able to do better. First, if broadband is indeed considered to be a national priority, the proposed funding level of $300 million for universal broadband is ridiculously low. The board argues that as cost-control measures, such as the revocation of the identical support rule, are implemented, the resulting savings can be reallocated to broadband. However, it is not clear that this reallocation alone will solve the problem, given the continuing commitment to POLR funding. Others propose that the high-cost areas program should stop funding telephony altogether, except in the "very high cost" areas, and that corresponding savings would be transferred to the broadband fund.[27] A more serious issue relates to the role of the states: Under the proposed system, the states are expected to be primarily responsible for the implementation of the broadband and mobility funds. However, as the discussion of the Lifeline/ Link-Up program earlier showed, there are variations among states in the level of program enrollment partly because of their administrative and regulatory capabilities. More efficient states will be able to deploy broadband and wireless networks quicker, exacerbating rather than mitigating the digital divide. Letting states set technical, operational, and financial standards for broadband will also expose service providers to a patchwork quilt of requirements, unless there is a strong federal role in coordination and harmonization.

Finally, the proposals seem to be more interested in protecting the existing subsidy flows to different categories of service providers (broadband providers, wireless companies, local exchange providers), than in anticipating emerging technological trends. For instance, new technologies such as WiMax are able to provide broadband, wireless/mobility, and traditional telephony within the same platform, quickly, and in a more cost-effective manner.[28] A recent survey of industry professionals identified this as the breakthrough technology that would enable broadband service in wide swaths of unserved areas.[29] Instead of creating platform-specific funds, policymakers might want to encourage the deployment of cost-efficient multiple services platforms such as WiMax, through funding support as well as other means, such as spectrum allocations and standard-setting.

Long Term

So far, this discussion has focused on the short and medium term, which is where the current policy paradigm, defined within the prevailing industry structures and bounded by legislative/regulatory choices, is expected to operate. Our recommendations for universal services were, therefore, incremental and meant to secure the objective of equitable access given the constraints of the current system. Over the long term, however, emerging technological practices are likely to loosen or eliminate many of these constraints while introducing others. In this section, we discuss policy choices for the long term. This discussion is by definition speculative, but international comparisons with the major economic competitors of the United States are used as signposts to indicate how universal service policy in this country is likely to change.

Historically, universal service in most countries, including the United States, has been conceptualized as a homogeneous service—network access— that needed to be provided uniformly to all citizens at affordable rates. The historical emphasis on access was appropriate when local wired telephone networks had enormous sunk costs, creating barriers to entry especially in rural areas. But in the new telecommunications environment, emerging wireless broadband technologies promise to reduce these barriers to entry and effectively eliminate the last mile problem. With WiMax and related technologies, we may be entering a period of ubiquitous broadband access in the not too distant future. Universal service policies need to move beyond access in this new environment.

In historical universal service models, affordability was seen as the key to penetration. Indeed, it was believed that the price of telephone service had to be kept low enough to enable access by the vast majority of the population. But in the emerging environment, policymakers are beginning to recognize that subscription prices are only part of the equation—consumers will voluntarily subscribe to network services, if such services provide a genuine value. The emphasis thus shifts from promoting network take-up through affordability ("low rates") to promoting it through increasing the value that consumers derive from network services.

Policymakers are also recognizing that consumer tastes are not homogeneous. Different subscribers place different valuations on specific services. Hence, the value proposition also needs to incorporate consumer choice and flexibility. Instead of providing a common service to all consumers uniformly (plain old telephone service—POTS), the new universal service programs offer a multiplicity of services, with consumers able to choose the services that they value the most. This has close parallels with the "informed choice model."[30] Australia's national broadband strategy is a prime example of the new programs: "Different users in the economy have different needs from broadband. Some users need very high capacity and high speed, while for others, low latency or guaranteed redundancy may be more important. Achieving [the] full benefits from broadband requires matching specific needs with available solutions" (7).[31]

The new conceptual emphasis on heterogeneity and consumer choice necessitates a new tactical orientation as well. In the past, universal service programs have directed support at the two termini of the production chain: the service providers and the consumers. Subsidies were directed at service providers to keep network rollout costs low or to support operational expenditures (the high-cost areas program) or at consumers, to enable access (Lifeline/Link-Up, and the E-Rate program, since schools and libraries are also consumers of telecommunications services). But if we recognize that the subscription decision in the new telecommunications environment will be driven by the quality and heterogeneity of services and by the ability of consumers to choose the services most valuable to them, then policymakers may also need to pay attention to the middle of the value production chain, i.e., the place where new service innovations occur. For instance, Japan's U-Japan strategy—where the "U" represents "ubiquitous," "universal," "user-friendly," and "unique," according to policy documents—visualizes three simultaneous efforts: establishing a ubiquitous network environment, promoting the advanced use of ICTs, and upgrading the "enabling" environment for ICTs.[32] Similarly, the European Union's i2010 initiative has separate programs spanning three separate "pillars": the creation of a single European information space, investment and innovation in research, and inclusion, that is, better public services and quality of life. Of these, only the third "pillar," which stresses inclusion, may be considered part of the traditional universal access discourse. The other issue areas span a broad spectrum, including ICT standard setting, digital literacy, support for small business informatization, and deployment of government services online.[33]

While the new telecommunications environment provides definite business opportunities and consumer benefits with the proliferation of services, it also makes consumer skill a factor in the subscription decision. Unlike POTS, new telecommunications services require a degree of knowledge and skill on the part of consumers. Since consumers with these skills are likely to benefit from new services more and will value these services more, thereby influencing the subscription decision, universal service policies in the new environment must incorporate efforts to promote digital literacy and training.

A review of the "national broadband strategy" documents and other policy documents from other countries show efforts along four dimensions: supporting network deployment, aiding network take-up by promoting digital literacy and consumer training, providing incentives for service/business innovation, and creating support infrastructures that enable the deployment of new services. Of these, support for network deployment is the only one emphasized by traditional universal service policies. Below, we provide examples of initiatives in each of these areas drawn from the broadband leaders identified in OECD data compilations (OECD), among them Japan, the United Kingdom, Korea, Sweden, and Canada.

Supporting Network Deployment

Supporting network deployment continues to be an important element in the new universal service. A key difference is that the new universal service tends to favor local solutions, rather than systemwide solutions. In Canada, pilot programs such as Broadband for Rural and Northern Development (BRAND) (initiated in 2002) and the National Satellite Initiative support broadband access in remote, northwestern, and Aboriginal communities.[34] In Korea, the Cyber Korea 21 plan announced in 1999, partly in response to the Asian currency crisis, visualized public expenditure to increase connectivity speed from 155 mbps to 64 gbps in several of the country's regions. The Korean Ministry of Communications (MOC) announced its latest venture called e-Korea in 2002, with a projected spending of $53 billion on ICTs. In some cases, universal service programs in the United States also embraced this approach—for example, the high-cost areas program.

Promote Usage Through Digital Literacy

Korea's efforts at consumer training and digital literacy are perhaps the most comprehensive in this area. The National Basic Information System initiative laid the groundwork for this as far back as 1987–1996 by promoting the use of computer networks.[35] The Closing the Digital Divide Act, legislated in 2002, included a strong user-training component. It set up the Korea Agency for Digital Opportunity and Promotion (KADO), as well as a digital divide committee to administer a five-year master plan. As part of this project, half a million low-income students were given extracurricular training in computer use. Fifty thousand low-income students with good grades were provided with free personal computers and a five-year free Internet subscription. Post offices, community centers, and other public locations were provided with internet access (ITU). Korea has also invested heavily in educational technology to nurture the next generation of tech-savvy consumers. While focusing on these obvious target groups, the Korean government did not neglect the less visible segments of the population. Realizing that incremental usage could only come from the marginal consumer, the government devoted considerable attention to digital literacy training for groups such as the disabled, stay-at-home mothers, military personnel, and even prisoners.[36] The program's inclusion of stay-at-home mothers is especially significant, because this often-overlooked segment of the population controls a significant portion of household spending. It is estimated that as many as ten million Koreans (20 percent of the population) may fall into the disadvantaged categories targeted by the digital literacy programs.

Governments seem to have realized that programs that call for broad-based citizen participation require a strong element of local leadership and control. Canada's BRAND program and the National Satellite Initiative provide resources for local communities with a degree of autonomy. In Korea, government funding has been made available to set up neighborhood computer clusters called "PC bangs," around which a youth culture involving game playing, instant messaging, and web browsing has evolved. These clusters were the path that allowed many who could not have afforded ICT access to learn critical network skills.

Provide Incentives For Service/Business Innovation

Governmental efforts to encourage the deployment of content and services over broadband networks have multiple benefits. First, they directly encourage economic activity by providing businesses with a conduit to introduce innovative products and services and reach their customers. They also enhance the value of broadband subscriptions to customers and encourage penetration growth. This, in turn, creates a cycle in which new products and services attract customers, and a broader consumer base of end users, as well as other businesses, encourages even more business innovation. Korea has adopted this model successfully, with high broadband and mobile penetration acting as a catalyst for a variety of online products and services, such as mobile data, streaming video, video on demand, music on demand, in-car navigation systems, multimedia messaging services, information services for mobile platforms such as PDAs, and mobile commerce. Through its "e-Government Initiatives," the Korean government has aggressively invested in e-government and information technology (ITU). This has brought about two important outcomes: first, local information technology firms have found a ready market for their products and services, allowing them to reach critical mass quickly; second, the increased deployment of e-government services online has added value to broadband subscriptions and encouraged more users to join the network. In addition to providing content and services through e-government, Korea has also encouraged private businesses to go online. The government operates test beds in which private companies can experiment with new technologies with minimal financial risk to themselves (ITU).

Create Support Structures That Enable E-Commerce

A number of innovations are widely recognized to facilitate e-commerce and ICT use, among them micropayments, digital signatures, copyright clearing houses, and standards. An important role for government in the information society is the provision of these services to the information economy. The leaders in broadband deployment seem to have recognized this earlier than others. In Japan's U-Japan program, the promotion of an "enabling environment" is one of the three major policy concentrations. Under this heading, the Japanese government legislated a series of measures to prevent spam and fraudulent electronic communications, protect privacy and personal information, establish a National Information Security Center, and check the transmission of illegal content (Ministry of Internal Affairs and Communications). While these issues are not traditionally part of the universal service programs, governments are beginning to realize that creating an "enabling environment" for ICT use has a major impact on broadband deployment and use. In the European Union, the first annual report of the *i2010* program specifically recommended steps to protect digital copyright protected material through digital rights management (DRM) solutions and other means, as well as to update consumer and data protection rules. Efforts to create soft infrastructures have been made by other broadband leaders as well. In December 2002, Korea adopted a single standard for wireless Internet access called wireless Internet platform for interoperability (WIPI), becoming the first country in the world to do so (Korea Profile). In 1999, the Digital Signatures Act, which seeks to protect the authenticity and legitimacy of electronic documents, was passed.

While implementing these elements of a new broadband strategy, policymakers cannot forget the problem of digital exclusion in the new environment. While the increasing value of broadband subscriptions will drive penetration, the most underprivileged segments of society may still need to be supported to ensure that the benefits of a ubiquitous broadband network are available to all citizens. One option for ensuring access to the most needy would be to make broadband connectivity available through community institutions such as schools, libraries, and local governments. There is a limited but important role for programs such as Lifeline and Link-Up too in the new broadband environment.

Summary

Universal connectivity to the information infrastructure is one of the fundamental necessities of the emerging information economy, without which individuals, businesses, and communities would be disadvantaged economically, socially, and politically. Securing a ubiquitous information network should be one of the principal policy priorities for government. Such a network would provide multifaceted benefits for society and the economy.

Notes

1. Milton L. Mueller, "Universal Service in the 1990s," *Universal Service: Competition, Interconnection and Monopoly in the Making of the American Telephone System* (Cambridge, MA: MIT Press, 1997), 165–85.

2. These programs are not the only universal service programs existing in the United States. The Government Accountability Office (GAO) in a recent report includes as a universal service program the Telecommunications Relay Service (TRS) mandated by the Americans with Disabilities Act, and included in section 225 of the Communications Act (1934). This program is administered by the National Exchange

Carriers Association (NECA). NECA in turn collects contributions from telecom providers of interstate services, based on the carriers' interstate end-user telecom revenue. Annual funding is around $47 million. GAO, *Federal and State Universal Service Programs and Challenges to Funding* (Washington, DC: GAO, 2002). The report added that most states also have their own universal service support programs, with access services for deaf and disabled consumers and for low-income monthly support programs being the most frequently implemented.

3. Included under the single heading of the high-cost program, there are six separate mechanisms: "(1) High-cost loop support (HCLS), is provided to all ILECs based on their embedded costs, and 'provides assistance for non-traffic sensitive (NTS) local loop costs'; (2) Safety net additive support (SNAS), was created to encourage new investment in rural infrastructure, and is made available to those rural carriers who increase their per loop telephone plant in service by over 14 percent in one year; (3) High-cost model support (HCMS), is available to non-rural carriers based on forward-looking costs, and is targeted to wire centers with forward-looking costs above a national benchmark as determined by the Commission's cost model; (4) Interstate common line support (ICLS), for rate-of-return carriers converts implicit support in the access rate structure to explicit support. ICLS recovers any shortfall between allowed common line revenues of rate-of-return carriers and their subscriber line charge revenues and gradually replaces the carrier common line charge; (5) Interstate access support (IAS), for price-cap carriers replaces the implicit support previously collected through interstate access charges. It provides explicit support to ensure reasonably affordable interstate rates; (6) Local switching support (LSS), provides support for traffic sensitive local switching costs, and is recovered through the universal service support mechanisms instead of higher traffic-sensitive access charges. LSS provides support to ILECs with study areas of 50,000 or fewer access lines, to help defray the higher switching costs of small ILECs" (Gabel, 330n14).

4. FCC, *Proposed Fourth Quarter 1999 Universal Service Contribution Factor for November and December 1999* (Washington, DC: FCC, 1999). Until September 1999, the FCC made separate calculations of "contribution factors" for the schools and libraries and rural health care programs, and for the high-cost and low-income programs. The calculation of the contribution factor for the schools and libraries and rural health care programs included the intrastate, interstate, and international revenues of telecommunications providers in the contribution base. For the high-cost areas and low-income support programs, the contribution base included only interstate and international revenues. However, in July 1999, the United States Court of Appeals for the Fifth Circuit decided in Texas Office of Public Utility Counsel vs. FCC that the FCC cannot include intrastate revenues in its universal service support calculations (Texas Office of Public Utility Counsel et al. vs. FCC, 1999). The court also required the FCC to change how it calculated contributions from international revenues. Subsequently, the FCC began with the fourth quarter of 1999 to calculate a single contribution factor for all its universal service programs, based on interstate and international revenues alone. FCC, *Proposed Fourth Quarter 1999 Universal Service Contribution Factor for November and December 1999* (Washington, DC: FCC, 1999).

5. FCC, *Report and Order and Notice of Proposed Rulemaking in the Matter of Universal Service Contribution Methodology* (Washington, DC: FCC, 2006).

6. Since only interstate revenue is subject to USF contribution requirements, and given the difficulty in determining the percentage of wireless usage that is interstate vs. intrastate, the FCC in 1998 decided that a percentage of wireless revenues will be deemed to be from interstate revenues and therefore eligible to make USF contributions. This "safe harbor" percentage was determined to be 15 percent of total telecommunications revenues for cellular, broadband personal communications service (PCS), and digital specialized mobile radio (SMR) providers, 12 percent of for paging providers, and at 1 percent for analog SMR providers. In 2002, the safe harbor was raised to 28 percent, and to 37.1 percent in 2006. *FCC, Report and Order and Notice of Proposed Rulemaking in the Matter of Universal Service Contribution Methodology* (Washington, DC: FCC, 2006).

7. Austan Goolsbee, *The Value of Broadband and the Deadweight Loss of Taxing New Technology* (Cambridge, MA: NBER, 2006).

8. FCC, *High-Cost Universal Service Support Order* (Washington, DC: FCC, 2008).

9. In contrast, high-cost support to incumbent LECs has been relatively stable: $3.136 billion in 2003; $3.153 billion in 2004; $3.169 billion in 2005; $3.116 billion in 2006; and $3.108 billion in 2007 (FCC, *High-Cost*, 4).

10. An eligible telecommunications carrier (ETC) is a telecommunications service provider that has applied to the state public utility commission and has been designated to receive universal service support in that state.

11. Robert Frieden, "Killing with Kindness: Fatal Flaws in the Universal Service Funding Mission and What Should Be Done to Narrow the Digital Divide," *Telecommunications Policy Research Conference*, Ed.

12. Krishna Jayakar, "Reforming the E-Rate," *Info: The Journal of Policy, Regulation and Strategy for Telecommunications, Information and Media* 6.1 (2004): 37–51.

13. Harold Wenglinsky, *Does It Compute? The Relationship between Educational Technology and Student Achievement in Mathematics* (Princeton, NJ: Policy Information Center, Educational Testing Service, 1998); Norris Dickard, ed., *Great Expectations: Leveraging America's Investment in Educational Technology* (Washington, DC: Benton Foundation, 2002); Edwin Christmann, John Badgett, and Robert Lucking, "Progressive Comparison of the Effects of Computer-Assisted Instruction on the Academic Achievement of Secondary Students," *Journal of Research on Computing in Education* 29, no. 4 (1997): 325–36; Web-Based Education Commission, *The Power of the Internet for Learning: Report of the Web-Based Education Commission to the President and the Congress of the United States* (Washington, DC: Web-Based Education Commission, 2000).

14. John Carlo Bertot, "Universal Service in the Networked Environment: The Education Rate (E-Rate) Debate," *The Journal of Academic Librarianship* 26, no. 1 (2000): 45–48; Heather Hudson, "Universal Access: What We Have Learned from the E-Rate," ed., *Telecommunications Policy Research Conference*.

15. Larry Cuban, *Oversold and Underused: Computers in the Classroom* (Cambridge, MA: Harvard University Press, 2001).

16. Austan Goolsbee and Jonathan Guryan, *The Impact of Internet Subsidies in Public Schools* (Cambridge, MA: National Bureau of Economic Research, 2002); James Guthrie, "Computers Idle in Public Schools," *USA Today*, 18 March 2003, 15A.

17. David Gabel, "Broadband and Universal Service," *Telecommunications Policy* 31 (2007): 327–46.

18. Though advanced services are not supported directly by the 1996 Telecommunications Act, Gabel argues that this is a good criterion to use since one of the stated objectives of the act is to roll out advanced services to rural, insular, and high-cost areas; accordingly, the Telecommunications Act mandates that loops upgraded with the assistance of universal service funds should not impede the provision of advanced services. So the receipt of federal high-cost areas support should make a wire center more likely to have upgraded its local loop to offer DSL.

19. Though there have been fluctuations, the last time there was a sustained drop in household telephone penetration was during the Great Depression.

20. FCC, *Trends in Telephone Service* (Washington, DC: FCC, 2007).

21. David Gabel and Carolyn Gideon, "Disconnected: Universal Service on the Decline," ed., *Telecommunications Policy Research Conference*, 2006.

22. Mark Burton, Jeffrey Macher, and John Mayo. "Understanding Participation in Social Programs: Why Don't Households Pick up the Lifeline?" *The Berkeley Electronic Journal of Economic Analysis & Policy* 7.1 (2007): online.

23. Krishna Jayakar and Harmeet Sawhney, *Universal Access in the Information Economy: Tracking Policy Innovations Abroad* (Washington, DC: Benton Foundation, 2006).

24. OECD, "OECD Key ICT Indicators," Paris, 2007, 5 July 2008, www.oecd.org /document/23/0,2340,en_2825_495656_33987543_1_1_1_1,00.html.

25. Sangwon Lee and Justin Brown, "Examining Broadband Adoption Factors: An Empirical Analysis between Countries," *Info: The Journal of Policy, Regulation and Strategy for Telecommunications, Information and Media* 10, no. 1 (2008): 25–39.

26. FCC, *Recommended Decision in the Matter of High-Cost Universal Service Support; Federal-State Joint Board on Universal Service* (Washington, DC: FCC, 2007).

27. Gene Kimmelman et al., *Reply Comments of Consumers Union, Consumer Federation of America, Free Press and New America Foundation in the Matter of High-Cost Universal Service Support, Federal-State Joint Board on Universal Service* (Washington, DC: FCC, 2008).

28. Arunabha Ghosh et al., "Broadband Wireless Access with Wimax/802.16: Current Performance Benchmarks and Future Potential," *IEEE Communications Magazine* 43, no. 2 (2005): 129–36.

29. Eliamani Sedoyeka and Zaid Hunaiti, "Wimax in Tanzania: A Breakthrough for Underserved Areas," *Info: the Journal of Policy, Regulation and Strategy for Telecommunications, Information and Media* 10, no. 2 (2008): 34–46.

30. Jorge Reina Schement and Scott C. Forbes, "Offering a Menu of Options: An Informed Choice Model of Universal Service," *Telecommunications Policy Research Conference*, Ed.

31. Commonwealth of Australia, "Australia's National Broadband Strategy," Canberra, Australia, 2004, National Office for the Information Policy, 9 September 2006, www

.dcita.gov.au/ie/publications/2004/march/australian_national_broadband_strategy.

32. Ministry of Internal Affairs and Communications, "White Paper: Information and Communication in Japan: Stirrings of U-Japan," Ed., Information and Communications Policy Bureau. Tokyo, Japan: Ministry of Internal Affairs and Communications, 2005.

33. Commission of the European Communities, "I2010—First Annual Report on the European Information Society, Comm(2006) 215 Final," Brussels, 2006, European Commission, June 29 2008, eur-lex.europa.eu/LexUriServ/LexUriServ .do?uri=COM:2006:0215:FIN:EN:PDF.

34. Industry Canada, "The Programs," Ottawa, 2006, July 5 2008, www.broadband .gc.ca/pub/program/index.html.

35. ITU, "Broadband Korea: Internet Case Study," Geneva, Switzerland, 2003, www .itu.int/ITU-D/ict/cs/korea/material/CS_KOR.pdf. All subsequent parenthetical references to ITU in this chapter refer to this report.

36. John Borland and Michael Kanellos, "Digital Agenda: Broadband: South Korea Leads the Way," CNET News.com (2004), 19 April 2007.

11

America's Forgotten Challenge: Rural Access

Sharon L. Strover

Roughly 17 percent of the U.S. population lives in what is known as rural America. Numbering about fifty million, most of these people live near a larger town or even within an hour of a major city, but many also live in far more remote regions with limited road access and much less access to air transportation. Despite commonly held conceptions about the rural economy, only about one percent of Americans actually live on farms, and as of 2004, only 6.2 percent of nonmetropolitan jobs were in the agricultural sector. The rural population, spread over roughly 80 percent of the land area of the United States, is employed in diverse occupations, with about 12 percent working in manufacturing, and a growing percentage working in retirement-destination and recreation-related industries. Nevertheless, people in rural regions share certain challenges. There are some—such as those who live in colonias on the border with Mexico—who have no access to running water or sewage treatment facilities. While access to water, sewage, electricity, and telecommunications is taken for granted in most cities across the country, in rural areas these basic infrastructures and their attendant capabilities were established later (or not at all) and may still be inadequate.

The telecommunications topography of the United States has never been kind to rural regions.[1] While residents of major population centers are more often than not served by one of the dominant phone companies, such as AT&T or Verizon, in the more rural and remote regions of the country, people have long relied on local independent or cooperative phone companies for their basic service. The national map of telephone services is a checkerboard of different companies interspersed among the broad territorial swaths served by the legacy Bell companies.[2] In spite of the rhetoric of universal service, the AT&T monopoly of the twentieth century refrained from serving many of the most expensive, least populated, and remote regions of the country, leaving it to other vendors or the local populations themselves to fill the void. By the beginning of the twenty-first century, major carriers—AT&T (the product of several merged "Baby Bell" companies including SBC, Ameritech, Bell South, and Pacific Tel),[3] Qwest (including the former US West), and Verizon—provide about twenty-two million access lines in nonmetropolitan regions, while the independents and cooperatives provide another twenty-four million lines. These rural telephone companies are the "carriers of last resort" and sometimes represent a household's only communications link to the rest of the world.[4] For years, rural telephone companies have been relying on programs collected under the universal service label to help them maintain and upgrade their telephone networks. After all, universal service promised that telephone services in rural regions would be roughly equivalent in cost and capability to those available in metropolitan areas.

The 1996 Telecommunication Act opened the door to rethinking universal service. Section 706 requires the Federal Communications Commission (FCC) to continue to assess broadband capability, and section 254 provides programs of support to schools and libraries for Internet connectivity and mentions the possibility of embracing broadband connectivity as part of universal service. The 1996 act's hints at forward-looking provisions have encouraged critics and policymakers alike to speculate about alternative methods of achieving a "universal service" for broadband, or at least, about ways to enhance broadband connectivity, particularly in rural regions. Indeed, there have been numerous bills introduced in Congress to reform universal service, as well as a comprehensive report and set of recommendations presented by the Federal-State Joint Board on Universal Service in November 2007.[5] These, and in particular the broadband fund recommendation that will be addressed later, highlight the fundamental needs of rural regions.[6] A critical question is whether the goals of basic universal service with regard to telephone service have been met, and whether broadband availability needs to be the next threshold for basic universal service.

This chapter reviews the history of rural access and summarizes some of the economic factors that make improved telecommunications in rural regions necessary. Data regarding the contemporary status of broadband services and potential benefits in rural areas are addressed. Finally, the chapter concludes that reviving rural regions through improved telecommunications services means reconceptualizing and reprioritizing communities and their abilities to determine their communication environments—in short, it involves reformulating the idea of universal service in a way that goes beyond an implicit "social contract."

History of Rural Access

Rural populations historically received telecommunications services later than metropolitan areas.[7] The history of universal service in telephony, in fact, is one of a regulatory tradeoff that almost inadvertently benefited rural populations. The term *inadvertently* is used because at no time was either the government or AT&T proactively committed to ensuring that rural areas enjoy the same services common in towns and cities. Rather, the policy grew out of interconnection disputes between AT&T and other companies, and became enmeshed with practical problems involved in regulation of the rate of return, grants of monopoly service, and internal cross subsidies that the company supported for decades.[8] The upshot of this "universal service" policy (under the Kingsbury Commitment of 1913) meant that AT&T would interconnect with (or acquire) rival phone companies and sustain rates roughly comparable across its service locations. The company's arrangement with the government and state regulators kept local and residential phone call costs extremely low, while long distance and business calls were more expensive than actual costs would have required—an arrangement that continued throughout most of the twentieth century. These cross-subsidies funded the universal service practices that enabled many rural telephone customers to enjoy telephone service.

Under the pressures of AT&T's divestiture in the 1980s, however, universal service and these internal cross-subsidies became subject to closer economic scrutiny. As marketplace and deregulation rhetoric swept across U.S. government agencies, and as the word "subsidy" became synonymous with inefficiency and government-mandated bloat, those universal service programs that transferred funds to higher cost networks in rural areas and that supported lower local calling became the target of reform. The rhetoric of competition, however, was rarely used to address the market dynamics of more remote, low population regions. Consequently, neither AT&T's divestiture in the early 1980s nor the competition policies gradually instituted between 1982 and 1996 adequately addressed the fundamental issue of ensuring telecommunications service in rural areas. Section 254 of the 1996 Telecommunications Act affirms the basic principles of universal service and even states that "access to advanced telecommunications and information services should be provided in all regions of the Nation." The definition of "advanced services," however, has become the subject of much controversy ever since.

That said, most U.S. households enjoyed basic telephone services by the time the act was passed, and into the early 1990s, national telephone penetration rates stood at about 94 percent (despite poor or nonexistent service in tribal regions).[9] With the development of the Internet, and the growing dependence of households and businesses on wireline infrastructure in order to access it, new infrastructure pressures materialized. First dial-up access and later broadband access required a wireline system more robust than the one designed to support voice calls; the overall phone network had been optimized for voice calls of short duration, but Internet use required much longer connections, and with more bandwidth-intensive actions enabling work with music and video files, more network capacity as well. The basic telephone infrastructure in many rural areas had older switches and longer loops, translating into slower connections, when there were suitable connections at all. Some studies have shown that many rural areas had no Internet service providers in the local calling area so that accessing the Internet required a long distance or toll call.[10]

As noted above, the 1996 act recognized the growing importance of Internet connectivity by authorizing the FCC to ensure that broadband services (with broadband defined as merely two hundred kbps)[11] develop equitably and quickly and by creating universal service programs to improve institutional (schools, libraries, rural medical facilities) Internet access. In the late 1990s, the National Telecommunications and Information Administration began to support modest innovation projects under its telecommunications opportunities program (TOPS, the successor to a program called TIIAP, or the telecommunications and information infrastructure assistance program, dedicated to the same goal), and worked with the Census Bureau to gather information on computer and Internet use. At about the same time, several states also began initiating programs to investigate, map, or augment telecommunications infrastructures with a view to improving access for rural regions and economically disadvantaged populations. These activities were encouraged through national pronouncements—rather than official policy or funding—about a national information infrastructure, promoted and espoused by then–Vice President Al Gore.[12]

As Internet connectivity assumed growing importance on the national stage, study after study documented a gap between metropolitan and rural areas in terms of access to broadband—that is, the availability of broadband services. (Actual subscription to broadband is another question that will be discussed later.) The FCC's monitoring of broadband deployment, under the requirements of the 1996 act, consistently showed that broadband was being deployed at a healthy pace across the nation, but these statistics were never independently verified and were (and continue to be) entirely reliant on vendor reporting using FCC Form 477.[13] As many critics have noted, the FCC broadband data illustrate the existence of subscribers where vendors already serve but do not begin to take stock of areas where broadband is not available. Moreover, the zip-code unit reporting used for FCC inquiries is meaningless in rural regions where zip codes can cover large geographic areas. The way

FCC statistics are collected does not allow differentiation between areas being served by one provider and areas being served by two or three providers—in other words, they do not differentiate between monopolistic and competitive markets. Neither do the data provide insight as to whether there is but a single instance of a broadband connection in a given zip code or whether it is intensively used in a region. (The FCC addressed some of these shortcomings in March 2008, when it adopted a new system that measures broadband availability in terms of the geographically smaller unit of "census tracts" that are composed of several census block groups, which in turn are composed of several census blocks. It also will begin noting five categories of speed in its assessments.)[14]

The FCC's March 2008 report *High-Speed Services for Internet Access: Status as of June 30, 2007*[15] presents information about deployment and subscribership to broadband, including advanced services from wireline telephone companies, cable operators, terrestrial wireless service providers, satellite service providers, and any other facilities-based providers.[16] Among other things, it found that more than 99 percent of the country's population lives in the 99 percent of the zip codes where a provider reported having at least one high-speed service subscriber. It also found that high population density is positively associated with subscribership to high-speed Internet. By contrast, low population density was associated with lower subscribership.

While this data would seem to indicate the widespread availability of broadband access, anecdotal and other findings suggest otherwise.[17] For example, the General Accountability Office[18] issued a report to Congress critical of the FCC's assessment of broadband deployment in the United States. It recommends improvements, and notes:

> For its zipcode level data, the FCC collects data based on where subscribers are served, not where providers have deployed broadband infrastructure. Although it is clear that the deployment of broadband networks is extensive, the data may not provide a highly accurate depiction of local broadband infrastructures for residential service, especially in rural areas.[19]

> It is more costly to serve areas with low population density and rugged terrain with terrestrial facilities than it is to serve areas that are densely populated and have flat terrain. It also may be more costly to serve locations that are a significant distance from a major city. As such, these important factors have caused deployment to be less extensive in more rural parts of the country.[20]

> Households residing in rural areas were less likely to subscribe to broadband service than were households residing in suburban and urban areas. Seventeen percent of rural households subscribe to broadband service, while 28 percent of

suburban and 29 percent of urban households subscribe to broadband service. We also found that rural households were slightly less likely to connect to the Internet, compared with their counterparts in suburban areas.[21]

In two other studies examining deployment, Grubesic and Murray[22] examined broadband competition in the United States across a year-and-a-half period. They concluded that the lack of competition in rural areas contributes to a clear urban-rural hierarchy in broadband Internet access, and that although competition continues to grow at the national level, it does not benefit rural and smaller metropolitan areas as much. Prieger[23] analyzed comprehensive telecommunications services data that covered technologies, demographics, language, market size, location, and telecommunication companies. He found that while services were less likely to be available in rural locations, market size, education, Spanish-language use, commuting distance, and a Bell operating company presence increases availability. In contrast to other studies, he found little evidence of inequality based on income or on black or Hispanic population concentration, and mixed evidence concerning availability to Native-American and Asian concentrations.

Naturally, many studies of the digital divide take into consideration Internet access along with basic access to computers and computer training. Focusing on access alone, however, neglects the broader problem of computer literacy that plagues rural regions. Indeed, several studies have documented the systematic lags that rural regions experience in computer ownership and use, Internet use, and broadband availability.[24] The issue of broadband availability is certainly important, but it is not the only factor that needs to be considered when analyzing the problems rural areas face as they grapple with the dynamics of the information economy in the twenty-first century.

State Programs

Over the past several years, many states have initiated their own universal service programs, generally in response to the changing competitive environment in their regions and the prospect of reduced federal support to carriers. For the most part, they obtain funds directly from telecommunications customers or from telecommunications companies that in turn impose a fee on customers. A study by the Government Accountability Office found that state universal service programs, generally aimed at telephone service, have favored services for the deaf and disabled as well as lower income households, typically concentrated in central city and rural regions.[25]

As noted earlier, several states have initiated programs or projects to explore or expand broadband access, among them Texas' telecommunications infrastructure fund[26] and Michigan's well-publicized state technology plan (dating back to 1998) as well as the LinkMichigan initiative (launched in 2001). Telecommunications companies and private sector advocates have spearheaded a more recent crop of initiatives, with ConnectKentucky in the vanguard of efforts to cooperatively develop telecommunications capabilities through coordinated and locally based efforts. California took a somewhat different approach when it passed Executive Order S-23-06, Expanding Broadband Access and Usage in California,[27] in 2006, and, more recently, assembled a comprehensive broadband task force report that systematically analyzes existing broadband infrastructure throughout the state and identifies policy actions to enhance connectivity and Internet use throughout the state.[28]

Finally, the Federal-State Joint Board report of 2007 urged the federal government to work closely with states to direct universal service funding to specific unserved or underserved regions that need support. If this recommendation is implemented, it can be expected that much more effort will be focused on broadband access in rural areas within states.[29]

While the overall picture is encouraging, a great deal of variation exists among states in how they approach the issue of access to telecommunications—both telephone and broadband—in rural regions. Some profoundly rural states appear to ignore the problem entirely, while others have taken a more proactive approach. A more integrated federal-state approach would probably be quite beneficial.

Federal Universal Service Program

The primary federal response to the problem of broadband access in rural regions has taken the form of universal service programs. Most of the $6.5 billion budget for the federal universal service programs goes to the high-cost program (roughly 70 percent of outlays) and the schools and libraries program (roughly 25 percent of outlays), according to the Congressional Budget Office figures for 2004.[30] Rural regions benefit significantly from these two programs. Nevertheless, as the universal service fund faces shortfalls (even though not all of the program receipts are always allocated) and as new technologies, such as Voice over IP, promise improved services to rural areas[31] even as they displace some of the services that traditionally contributed to the universal service program, a major overhaul of the universal service program becomes necessary if rural areas are to keep pace with the rest of the country.

While the E-Rate program favors less economically well-off areas—which generally include rural regions—it does not directly or solely tackle access problems of rural residents. Indeed, even though E-Rate programs are highly valued, many rural, and especially minority, populations do not feel capable of or comfortable using computers and the Internet in public institutions such as libraries or schools. Even if that were not the case, the problem would still exist, since there is growing evidence that regular use of computers and Internet access—the sort of use that implies ready access either at home and/ or at work—contributes to productivity gains.

The high-cost program has undoubtedly been helpful in maintaining telephony in rural regions that face greater than average expenses because of low population density and greater distances. Funding through this program has been used to upgrade lines so that Internet access may be feasible. However, the relatively new crop of wireless carriers who receive a growing portion of the fund (as eligible telecommunications carriers) and add little to the broadband capabilities of rural regions has contributed to the ballooning demands on the universal service fund.

The Joint Federal-State Board, which monitors broadband services under the 1996 act, came up with trenchant recommendations for reforming universal service in its report *In the Matter of High-Cost Universal Service Support Federal-State Joint Board on Universal Service*,[32] adopted by the FCC in November 2007. In particular, it advocated adopting what it called a comprehensive policy to address the problems of broadband in rural regions on the grounds that the historically piecemeal problem-solving tactics used in the past were insufficient to solve contemporary problems of access.

Whether universal service funds will directly support rural broadband deployment remains to be seen. Several bills introduced in 2007 would make broadband services an integral part of universal service. The Universal Service for Americans Act[33] proposes to create a fund specifically for broadband in unserved areas and the Universal Service Reform Act of 2007[34] explicitly proposes funding broadband and creating a broadband mandate. The picture is considerably complicated by the demands of wireless carriers on the existing fund, which deflect attention from the broader issue of broadband connectivity.

Access and Use

Just as rural regions lag behind in network infrastructure development, so too they have lagged behind in computer ownership and use. The National Telecommunications and Information Administration studies of the late 1990s and early 2000s, which analyzed computer ownership and Internet access by race, household income, location, education, and other demographic indicators, became a short-lived benchmark for documenting a "digital divide" in the United States.[35] These studies, however, never went much beyond illustrating "lags" across ethnic and racial groups, and age, income, education, and location categories. While gaps between men and women in computer and Internet use, for example, have declined over time, gaps between urban and rural regions—though smaller than they once were—have endured.[36] More current data from the Pew Internet and American Life Project[37] are summarized in the following tables. What emerges from this data is that rural households have less access to broadband at home and at work, and they use the Internet less frequently than do urban and suburban households (table 11.1).[38]

Indeed, Pew data from 2008 shows that broadband subscription rates in rural regions are nineteen percentage points lower than in urban and twenty-two percentage points lower than in suburban regions, even though there is an equivalent level of interest in subscribing to broadband in both regions.[39] Some rural telephone companies have reported lower subscription rates for broadband than those reported in urban areas, but that may be explained by the fact that the price of the service is also higher in rural areas. Finally, some studies suggest that differences in Internet use—the geography-based digital divide as well as other differences related to age, education, and race/ethnicity—may be linked to opportunities available for computer training as well as to the ability to understand the importance of Internet-based resources in daily life.

The lower penetration rate of broadband Internet and the slower speeds that typify rural Internet networks may be key factors in understanding the differences in Internet use (as opposed to access) between rural and urban people. As table 11.2 based on Pew data indicates, among broadband users in rural and urban areas, there are only small differences in Internet use. In other words, rural and nonrural Americans are nearly equally likely to use the Internet when it is available.

Table 11.1:
Internet Access and Use by Community Type—All Internet Users

	Urban	Suburban	Rural
Access to Home Broadband	38%	40%	24%
Access to High-Speed Internet at Home or Work	49%	49%	35%
Frequency of Internet Use 1: "online yesterday"	64%	67%	57%
Frequency of Internet Use 2: "online several times a day"	44%	43%	35%
Number of Online Activities	2.2	2.2	1.9

Table 11.2:
Internet Use by Community Type—Home Broadband Users

	Urban	Suburban	Rural
Frequency of Internet Use 1: "online yesterday"	79%	75%	73%
Frequency of Internet Use 2: "online several times a day"	54%	55%	49%
Number of Online Activities	2.8	2.8	2.7

Table 11.3:
Online Activities by Community Type—All Internet Users

	Urban/Suburban	Rural
Buy or Make a Reservation for Travel Service	65%	51%
Online Banking	43%	34%
Online Classified	37%	30%
Read a Blog	28%	21%
Download Screensavers	22%	28%
Download Computer Games	20%	25%
Class for Credit	11%	15%
Fantasy Sports	7%	9%

There are, however, "lifestyle" differences in rural and nonrural regions that may be carried over to online activities, as table 11.3 illustrates.

Some possible explanations for differences in Internet use that are related to lifestyle include:

- The greater distance from airports and train stations increases the cost of travel for rural Americans, making the Internet more attractive for them.
- Less access to online banking combined with greater reliance on traditional banking services in rural areas makes rural Americans less likely to use online banking.
- Online classified services tend to be organized around specific cities, which would make rural Americans have less interest in them.
- The absence of large electronics stores that sell computer game software in rural areas encourages rural Americans to download such software online.
- The greater distances from colleges and other educational institutions provide an incentive for rural Americans to take classes online.

Other research on the business uses of broadband has also found key differences between rural and nonurban regions. Pociask's[40] "Broadband Use by Rural Small Businesses" found that small businesses in rural areas subscribe to broadband less frequently and are less likely to benefit from the range of new technologies that broadband facilitates (such as VoIP). Oden and Strover[41] note major differences in how rural businesses that had broadband access performed, compared with rural businesses that did not.

The broader ramifications of increased computer and Internet access are not sufficiently explored in much of the existing literature. Assumptions regarding the need for certain skills and their implicit benefits abound, but little research has been done on the actual life-changing force of such "improvements." In general, there is a lack of strong empirical data that would provide compelling evidence that economic and community development goals could be realized through programs that promote computer and Internet access.[42] A major goal of policymakers over the past ten years has been facilitating access. But the more important goal of ensuring meaningful access for communities and individuals has gone by the wayside. Put another way, there is scant evidence that telecommunications can transform lives in the absence of change in other structural features, such as household income and education levels.

In this regard, rural communities have frequently found themselves in the vanguard, as they actively attempt to improve their communications environments through locally based efforts like municipal Wi-Fi, public computer and Internet access, and cable television services. Universal service programs, specifically the E-Rate program that targets schools and libraries, have been helpful to public institutions, which in rural areas often lack funding for such technology. Still, they cannot entirely compensate for the absence of funding required for investments in computers, computer education, and subscriptions to broadband services. As of 2004, the average annual income of non–farm workers in rural areas was $31,582, compared with $47,162 in metropolitan areas.[43] Considering that demand for and interest in Internet services is similar in both areas, the absence of suitable network infrastructure combined with the lack disposable income available to pay for broadband services means that rural Americans will remain at a disadvantage in terms of their ability to fully exploit the capabilities of contemporary communications networks.

Challenges: Why Rural Regions Need Broadband

If national and state policies have not sufficiently improved the environment for affordable and ubiquitous broadband access in rural areas, should this be a cause for concern? After all, populations continue to migrate from rural areas, and many of the economic activities associated with rural regions, such as farming and manufacturing, now require very little human labor because they have been mechanized. Daniel Bell's vision of an information society[44] nourished critics who warned that the uneven pattern of development associated with the contemporary economic drivers of telecommunications technology could lead to profound inequities in certain regions and for certain populations.[45] Others argued that the "trickle-down" effects of telecommunications-based capabilities would bring important benefits to even the most remote areas.[46] Optimistic foresight in the 1970s and 1980s, predicting a so-called death of distance were particularly popular (later publicized by Frances Cairncross[47]); however, they have been replaced by more recent, spatially based views of society and the economy that focus on the lag in telecommunications capabilities in rural America (and, indeed, in rural regions throughout the world).[48]

The distribution of telecommunications capabilities tracks that of other human resources: Where there is more wealth and more education, resources tend to be more plentiful; where there is knowledgeable leadership, capabilities increase; where multifaceted coalitions of groups or organizations join together to plan and share assets, they multiply. In other words, the spatial distribution of telecommunications resources is in part a function of hardware and software, but it also is a function of the human resources that are available to exploit the infrastructure's potential.

The economic trend of incorporating information technology into all productive activities is evident in rural areas as well as urban areas. While companies such as Google, AOL, Cisco, and Dell may epitomize contemporary information companies, virtually all consumption and production centers in the United States—from Wal-Mart to the local paper mill, from the grocery store to the concert theater—incorporate computer-based information systems and technologies. The traditionally resource-dependent industries that once characterized rural regions are no exception, and some of the newer industries basing themselves in these areas—recreation and retirement centers, for example—will also depend on information infrastructures. Indeed, as retirement communities begin to flourish in rural America, the information-intensive health industry is likely to follow suit. Studies of some of the most distressed regions of Appalachia have found that in communities where local businesses and services—whether health, education, banking, manufacturing, or services—incorporated telecommunications capabilities, productivity improved.[49] Telecommunications-intensive industries have a special role in bringing more infrastructure and knowledge to a community, and while many such industries are not located in rural areas, their impact is particularly striking when they are.

Information industries and technologies penetrate virtually all sectors of life as they dynamically interact with local strengths to create new capabilities. This renders pointless any policy-based separation of information and telecommunications technologies from activities in the normal domains of education, culture, and work. Since technologies create access to opportunities on all fronts, rural regions must be able to use them and harness their power; otherwise, the United States will be heading toward a two-tiered society, in which rural areas will become a true backwater.

The challenges that lie ahead are several: (1) recognizing the significance of this infrastructural element to all aspects of life in rural and nonrural regions of the country, and incorporating into economic, educational, and social policies the budgets and practices that will help exploit the potential of telecommunications; (2) conceding that marketplace dynamics do not deliver timely services to more remote and less populous regions and developing improved mechanisms to improve services in those regions; and (3) crafting programs that systematically augment the range of services and available training and expertise around broadband services in rural regions.

Recommendations

The following are some of the main points discussed in this chapter:

- The demand for "advanced" services seems less certain in rural regions than in metropolitan areas, but studies show that when access exists, demand appears to track the usage rates in metropolitan areas.
- The FCC's broadband deployment data are problematic, and connectivity in rural areas is still questionable, and even inadequate, according to various demographic surveys.
- While improving connectivity is a necessary first step, in order to exploit the powers of new technologies in rural regions, knowledge and expertise are required as well as improved network capabilities.
- Access and usage data suggest rural populations do not have access to broadband at home or at work as the same levels as nonurban populations.
- Small businesses in rural areas do not incorporate the Internet into their operations as widely as small businesses in metropolitan regions.
- The E-Rate program has undoubtedly benefited rural areas. It remains unclear whether, in the absence of E-Rate funds, rural schools, and libraries would be able to maintain their educational technology infrastructure.

Drawing on economist Amartya Sen's capabilities approach, an alternative vision of universal service and its contribution to rural populations must focus on cultivating the ability of people to improve their lives—with the specific nature of those improvements to be determined by the people themselves.[50] This, in turn, requires renewed focus on self-determination in the communications/telecommunications environment—a process made more viable with the onset of new media, networks, and new types of tele-communications services. Public policy that acknowledges not just parity with urban regions, but self-determination as well could make telecommunications more meaningful to life in rural regions. While reformulating the principles of universal service is no small feat, there is no better time for this undertaking: The legacy models of regulation, technology definitions (information services, telecommunication services), regulatory ability, and accountability are splitting apart and becoming unmanageable. A new valuation methodology that is technology-neutral but outcomes sensitive is what can help telecommunications services cater to the varied needs, strengths, and opportunities existing in rural areas—indeed, in all areas of the country.

A capabilities approach to universal service would alter the way we approach this constellation of priorities. It implies at minimum: (1) a process of ascertaining needs and localized constructions of priorities; and (2) broadening the range of activities that could be supported under this program. Some of these principles are embedded in the recommendations of the Federal-State Joint Board report from 2007.

Infrastructure availability, content applicability, pricing, and training are the four factors that affect rural Internet subscription and use. Viable programs that influence these factors can take several forms. Since simple deployment alone, however, appears to be an insufficient driver, any programs that stimulate deployment must be linked to investments in training and use. Continuous formative and summative evaluations are essential in order to monitor the utilities of these programs for individuals and communities. The following options focus on building community capabilities and are premised on the notion that cultivating them will ultimately draw additional vendor interest. In other words, a capabilities approach to public policy enhances social goods and can work with a market-based approach to telecommunications.[51]

Recommendation 1

Adopt a national broadband policy that is capable of guaranteeing sustained investment in telecommunications infrastructure. The United States requires constantly updated capabilities that are affordable and available to all.

Recommendation 2

Establish grants for Internet training. These could be block grants and must be outcomes-oriented and outcomes-dependent. The target populations could be not only individual users but also small businesses. Increasing small business use of the Internet could have tremendous economic impact on rural regions. Grants within states themselves could go to various entities, including nonprofits, towns, counties, and local government units.

Recommendation 3

Universal service funds should be used to enhance projects undertaken by communities that are designed to extend their telecommunications capabilities. These funds could be used to match local investment in infrastructure, connectivity, public access, and similar access technologies. They could also be used to provide broadband infrastructure development and incentives to communities that can demonstrate their readiness to develop their own facilities/expertise as well as their abilities to use these facilities. Communities should match federal investment in some manner. They could purchase broadband services or develop their own infrastructures.

Recommendation 4

Invest in community college-based Internet applications capabilities classes for individuals and small businesses and create incentives for colleges that enroll small business owners, with some outcome-based measure being the trigger for an incentive "subsidy" or payment.

Recommendation 5

Create "rural leadership academies" that select aspiring or actual rural leaders for two to three weeks of leadership training that would include training not only in using the Internet but also in running computer education clinics or courses, in the "nuts and bolts" of broadband infrastructure, and in resource-sharing across institutions. These leaders would serve the purpose of catalyzing Internet availability and use in their respective communities, which would be left to decide what investments and services make most sense for them.

Notes

1. Sharon Strover, "Rural Internet Connectivity," *Telecommunications Policy* 25, no. 5 (1999): 331–47.

2. GTE was the largest independent telephone company, rivaling some of the Bell companies in terms of size. It merged with Bell Atlantic to become Verizon in 2000. AT&T has remerged with most of the companies it originally spun off after its divestiture in the early 1980s.

3. AT&T's merger with Bell South was approved at the end of 2006.

4. Cell phone service is absent in many rural areas even if a carrier has the authorization to provide service in the region. A typical practice is to establish service in only the most populous town of a rural area licensed for mobile services.

5. Federal-State Joint Board on Universal Service, *In the Matter of High-Cost Universal Service Support* (CC Docket No. 96-45) (2007).

6. In section 12, the report notes: "The Broadband Fund would be tasked primarily with disseminating broadband Internet services to unserved areas, with the support being expended as grants for the construction of new facilities in those unserved areas. A secondary purpose would be to provide grants for new construction to enhance broadband service in areas with substandard service. Another secondary purpose would be to provide continuing operating subsidies to broadband Internet providers serving areas where low customer density would suggest that a plausible economic case cannot be made to operate broadband facilities, even after receiving a substantial construction subsidy." (Federal-State Joint Board on Universal Service (cc Docket No. 96-45) (2007).)

7. Cable television is the sole exception to this pattern, but even it was originally motivated by rural communities' desire to receive the television signals that populations in more metropolitan regions already enjoyed.

8. Robert Horwitz, *The Irony of Regulatory Reform* (New York: Oxford University Press, 1989).

9. FCC, *Trends in Telephone Service. Industry Analysis and Technology Division*, Wireline Competition Bureau (2005).

10. Strover, "Rural Internet Connectivity," 331–47.

11. It was increased to a standard of 768 kbps in March 2008.

12. The National Information Infrastructure pronouncement grew out of the High Performance Computing and Communication Act of 1991.

13. Statistical data and summaries are available at Local Telephone Competition and Broadband Deployment pages within the FCC's website(www.fcc.gov/wcb/iatd /comp.html).

14. See www.washingtonpost.com/wp-dyn/content/article/2008/03/19/AR20080 31903356.html.

15. FCC, *High-Speed Services for Internet Access: Status as of June 30, 2007* (2008).

16. Previous releases of additional broadband statistics are available at www.fcc .gov/wcb.stats. This report can be seen at hraunfoss.fcc.gov/edocs_public/attachmatch /DOC-280906A1.pdf.

17. See, for example, Robert Atkinson, "The Case for a National Broadband Policy," *Information Technology and Innovation Foundation*, June 2007, www.itif.org/files /CaseForNationalBroadbandPolicy.pdf.

18. General Accountability Office, "Broadband Deployment Is Extensive throughout the United States, but It Is Difficult to Assess the Extent of Deployment Gaps in Rural

Areas," 2006, www.gao.gov/new.items/d06426.pdf.

19. General Accountability Office, "Broadband Deployment Is Extensive throughout the United States," 3. For example, under the present data collection scheme, FCC counts a zip code as covered by broadband service if it contains at least one broadband subscriber. Also, a zip code is counted as broadband service area even if carriers only serve businesses. As a result, the number of zip codes serving broadband services is likely overstated in terms of the availability of residential broadband services. Additionally, there is no consideration given to the price, speed, or availability of connections across the zip code.

20. General Accountability Office, "Broadband Deployment Is Extensive throughout the United States," 4.

21. General Accountability Office, "Broadband Deployment Is Extensive throughout the United States," 12–13.

22. Tony H. Grubesic and Alan T. Murray, "Waiting for Broadband: Local Competition and the Spatial Distribution of Advanced Telecommunication Services in the United States," *Growth & Change* 35, no. 2 (2004): 139–65.

23. James E. Prieger, "The Supply Side of the Digital Divide: Is There Equal Availability in the Broadband Internet Access Market?," *Economic Inquiry* 41, no. 2 (2003): 346–63.

24. Sharon Strover and Michael Oden, *Links to the Future: The Role of Information and Telecommunications Technology in Appalachian Economic Development* (Washington, DC: Appalachian Regional Commission, 2002); Pew Internet and American Life Project, *Rural Broadband and Internet Use*, February 2006, www.pewinternet.org /pdfs/PIP_Rural_Broadband.pdf (29 April 2006); Edwin Parker, Heather Hudson, Don Dillman, Sharon Strover, and Frederick Williams, *Electronic Byways: State Policies for Rural Development through Telecommunications* (Boulder, CO: Westview Press, 1992).

25. Government Accountability Office, *Federal and State Universal Service Programs and Challenges*, Report to the Ranking Minority Member, Subcommittee on Telecommunications and the Internet, Committee on Energy and Commerce, House of Representatives (2002), 13.

26. Gary Chapman, "Missing Links: Lessons on the Digital Divide Form Texas' Telecommunications Infrastructure Fund," 2005, telecom.cide.edu/include/internet _conference_2005/Gchapman_paper.pdf.

27. State of California, Executive Order S-23-06 *Expanding Broadband Access and Usage in California* (2006).

28. California Broadband Task Force, *California Broadband Task Force Report* January 2008, www.calink.ca.gov/pdf/CBTF_FINAL_Report.pdf (15 April 2008).

29. The Federal-State Joint Board Report, 2007, section 13, states: "Effective use of federal funds for broadband will require a detailed knowledge of the areas in which effective terrestrial broadband service is unavailable. Collecting information on areas without broadband or where broadband is substandard is a complex task. Broadband availability can vary on a street-by-street basis, sometimes on a house-by-house basis. Moreover, the facts can change quickly, for example when a wireless Internet

service provider opens or closes its doors. To effectively apply federal funds to expand broadband deployment, primarily through new construction grants, it is essential that the agency responsible for dispensing the funds have access to detailed, current geographic information. The Joint Board believes that the Commission has engaged in some broadband mapping activities, but not at the scale necessary to administer broadband construction grants. States are generally more capable of performing this task, in large part because they have smaller areas and have more sources of information about local needs. Moreover, several states have already assembled data approaching or exceeding the required level of accuracy."

30. Congressional Budget Office, *Financing Universal Service* 2005, www.cbo.gov /showdoc.cfm?index=6191&sequence=0 (12 September 2006).

31. Voice over Internet Protocol (VoIP), for example, would substitute an "Internet" connection for a landline connection, and one type of service had contributed to the universal service fund while the other did not. In June 2006, the FCC added VoIP to the list of universal service contributors; however, the same issue will be faced with other new technologies in the future. The drain on universal service funds posed by multiple wireless service providers was recognized as a growing problem by 2006.

32. Federal-State Joint Board on Universal Service, *In the Matter of High-Cost Universal Service Support* (CC Docket No. 96-45) (2007).

33. U.S. Congress, January 2007, S.101.IS Universal Service for Americans Act.

34. U.S. Congress, February 2007, H.R. 2054.IS Universal Service Reform Act of 2007.

35. U.S. Department of Commerce, National Telecommunications, and Information Administration, *Falling Through the Net: A Survey of the "Have Nots" in Rural and Urban America* (Washington, DC: NTIA, 1995). www.ntia.doc.gov/ntiahome/fallingthru .html (July 2003); U.S. Department of Commerce, National Telecommunications, and Information Administration, *Falling Through the Net II: New Data on the Digital Divide* (Washington, DC: NTIA, 1998), www.ntia.doc.gov/ntiahome/net2 (July 2003); U.S. Department of Commerce, National Telecommunications, and Information Administration, *Falling Through the Net: Toward Digital Inclusion. A Report on Americans' Access to Technology Tools* (Washington, DC: NTIA, 2000), www.ntia.doc .gov/ntiahome/fttn99.contents.html (July 2003).

36. Todd M. Gabe and Jaison R. Abel, "Deployment of Advanced Telecommunications Infrastructure in Rural America: Measuring the Digital Divide," *American Journal of Agricultural Economics* 84, no. 5 (2002): 1246–52; Edwin Parker, "Closing the Digital Divide in Rural America," *Telecommunications Policy* 24 (2001): 281–90.

37. Pew Internet and American Life Project, *Rural Broadband and Internet Use* (February 2006). www.pewinternet.org/pdfs/PIP_Rural_Broadband.pdf.

38. Pew Internet and American Life Project.

39. www.pewinternet.org/pdfs/PIP_Broadband_2008.pdf

40. Stephen Pociask, "Broadband Use by Rural Small Business," *Small Business Administration* 2005, last accessed 20 July 2008, www.sba.gov/advo/research/rs269tot.pdf (20 July 2008).

41. Strover and Oden, *Links to the Future.*

42. Some research attempts to quantify the contribution of broadband to the economy, but too often the assumptions in the analyses do not match the actual conditions of rural America. Sharon Gillett, *Measuring Broadband's Economic Impact,* report prepared for the Economic Development Administration (U.S. Department of Commerce, 28 February 2006); Robert Crandall, Charles Jackson, and Hal Singer, "The Effect of Ubiquitous Broadband Adoption on Investment, Jobs, and the U.S. economy," report for the New Millennium Research Council, 2003, www.newmillenniumresearch .org/archive/bbstudyreport_091703.pdf.

43. Lorin Kusmin, "Rural Employment at a Glance," *Economic Information Bulletin Number 21,* Economic Research Service, U.S. Department of Agriculture, December 2006, www.ers.usda.gov/publications/eib21/eib21.htm (20 July 2008).

44. Daniel Bells, *The Post Industrial Society* (New York: Basic Books, 1973).

45. Manuel.Castells, *The Rise of the Network Society* (Oxford: Blackwell, 1996); Jorge Schement and Leah Lievrouw, *Competing Visions, Complex Realities* (Norwood, NJ: Ablex, 1987); Mark Hepworth and Kevin Robins," Whose Information Society? A View From the Periphery," *Media Culture and Society* 10 (1988): 323–43; Robin Mansell, "New Media Competition and Access," *New Media & Society* 1, no. 3 (2000): 155–82.

46. Jurgen Schmandt, Frederick Williams, Robert Wilson, and Sharon Strover, eds., *Telecommunications and Rural Development* (New York: Praeger, 1991), 262.

47. Francis Cairncross, *The Death of Distance: How the Communication Revolution Will Change Our Lives* (Boston: Harvard Business School Press, 1997).

48. Sharon Strover, Michael Oden, and Nobuya Ingaki, "Telecommunications and Rural Economies: Findings from the Appalachian Region," in *Communication Policy and Information Technology: Promises, Problems and Prospects,* ed. Lorrie F. Cranor and Shane Greenstein (Cambridge, MA: MIT Press, 2002), 317–46; Castells, *The Rise of the Network Society.*

49. Strover and Oden, *Links to the Future.*

50. Amartya Sen, *Development as Freedom* (New York: Random House, 1999).

51. Daniel Bell, "The Information Society: The Social Framework of the Information Society," in *The Microelectronics Revolution,* ed. Forester (Cambridge, MA: MIT Press, 1983), 500–549.

12

Municipal Broadband

Andrea H. Tapia

Introduction

IN THIS CHAPTER, WE WILL SET OUT BY DEMONSTRATING that broadband Internet services offered by private telecommunications providers and services offered by municipalities and public entities serve very different purposes. We will then show that existing state-level policies and the absence of federal policy have combined to produce a patchwork of municipal responses, most of which are not effective. Finally, we will advocate adopting a strong federal level policy, which would encourage municipalities to participate in providing broadband Internet services when private telecommunications providers are not meeting the needs of their constituents.

Context: Municipal Broadband in the United States

Approximately four hundred municipalities in the United States have entered the telecommunications arena with the intent to develop and deploy some form of municipal broadband Internet. Local governments have become increasingly frustrated by the comparatively slow pace of broadband Internet build-out, and a considerable number have recently begun providing the new technologies that supply Internet access themselves. Recent initiatives demonstrate that many municipalities view wireless broadband as a way to strengthen economic development, promote digital inclusion, and improve the efficiency of government services. In addition, some municipalities have assumed the role of providing Internet service in order to decrease telecommunications expenses by lowering the cost of broadband Internet access for government institutions and citizen users.

The central goal of most supporters of municipal entry into the telecommunications arena is to deliver high-quality broadband service to all citizens and government employees at an affordable price. The gist of this argument is that incumbent providers do not offer ubiquitous service, because it is not cost effective in some areas. Those who oppose municipal entry argue that municipalities possess unfair advantages and incumbents are not able to compete on a level playing field with them. They also say that municipalities may not possess the organizational competencies to deploy and manage the network without jeopardizing taxpayer dollars and assets.

Policy that deals with telecommunications services provided by local municipalities is in a state of flux at both the state and federal levels. Approximately one-third of the fifty states have initiated some form of broadband-related policy that regulates the role of municipalities in offering broadband services, although these differ widely. In addition, there are several federal bills pending that address municipal involvement, yet as of June 2008, none have passed.

Interestingly, the number of new municipalities that have assumed the role of telecommunications providers is dropping, and many more municipal projects have been abandoned or failed. This continues a trajectory of the past four years. In 2004, municipalities entered the broadband market as a technological imperative. They were creative, hopeful, and idealistic. The year 2005 saw intense incumbent lobbying, a policy backlash against these first municipal entrants, the result of which was a torrent of proposed state legislative restrictions. In 2006, a year of compromise and accommodation, municipalities developed creative business plans to accommodate the needs of incumbents as well as gain higher quality broadband service for more of their constituents. Telecommunications incumbents backed off from their intense lobbying efforts and many legislative proposals in the states were passed in a less stringent form, or failed altogether. This trend continued in 2007 with more municipalities forming complex partnerships with local incumbents, further reducing the need for lobbying and future legislation.[1]

Most importantly, in 2007, the trajectory took a downward turn, with many small municipalities abandoning their projects and several large-scale projects (in Philadelphia, San Francisco, and Chicago) ending their development efforts very publicly. In late August 2007, Earthlink was retreating from the municipal wireless market,[2] Chicago was delaying its network development,[3] and the proposed development of a municipal Wi-Fi network for San Francisco stalled.[4] As of June 2008 the Philadelphia Wireless project suspended its network.

This chapter argues that the failures of the municipal projects do not stem from the municipal actions or the technologies involved. Rather, it is the state-level policies that have forced municipalities into complex, undesirable business plans and partnerships with private providers and undermined the potential success of these projects. The disconnect between the goals of the municipalities and those of their private partners is responsible for the failed projects.

Broadband Internet Services as a Utility, Not a Luxury

Broadband is not a luxury. Broadband is an essential component of the national infrastructure of the United States. Citizens who have access to and the skills to use the Internet are: (1) more successful economically, with respect to education, jobs, and earnings; (2) participate more in the political and civic discourse; and (3) receive more government services and other public goods than those who do not.[5] "Immediate and asynchronous connectivity, together with the diversity of information accessible via the computer can, furthermore, increase social inclusion and social position."[6] Increased access to the Internet also provides greater access to education, income, and other resources.[7] Computerization and use of the Internet are also associated with higher wages.[8] Internet users tend to consume more information offline than nonusers and to be more active in other ways as well.[9] Shah et al. found that informational use of the Internet had a significant positive impact on community participation.[10]

Broadband Internet access should be considered essential, just like water, gas, and electricity, and the patchwork of private companies now offering broadband access are exacerbating problems in rural and urban pockets of poverty in the same way other private utilities did in the recent past.[11] Treating broadband Internet as a public utility may, therefore, help alleviate some of the causes and symptoms of poverty and social exclusion.

The United States has recognized the importance of broadband Internet services and has adopted a variety of measures to promote broadband. In some ways, the federal government is already acting as if broadband Internet service is a necessity rather than a luxury, but the policies it has adopted based on this assumption have largely failed.

Most of the actions taken by the federal government have relied on the marketplace to address the nation's need for broadband connectivity. Unfortunately, the microeconomic motivations of the private industry do not take into account macroeconomic and social welfare needs.[12] The private sector is primarily motivated by short-term profits and cannot take into account the positive externalities of widely available broadband networks.

The real issue is not whether broadband is good and more is better, but whether the market alone will provide the proper amount in the desired time frame. For most market-oriented conservatives, the correct amount is the amount that the market provides. Yet, because of significant positive externalities from broadband, the right amount—the amount that maximizes social welfare—is in fact greater than the amount the market alone provides. This means that active public policies to spur broadband, in addition to policies to remove barriers to deployment, are critical to ensure the best possible broadband future for the United States.[13]

Broadband is not just a consumer technology product, but rather a gateway to full civic participation in American life. Government intervention is, therefore, required to assure equal and fair distribution of it as a national resource. In addition, broadband access produces more than simple household access to the Internet.[14] It has strong positive externalities that will produce powerful social, economic, and network effects outside the Internet itself, once the majority of Americans are connected and using the Internet.

Historic Public Ownership and Regulation of Telecommunication Providers

Historically, the United States has depended on the private sector, to a large extent, for its delivery of telecommunications services.[15] The government has dealt with the problem of monopolies, in some cases, through direct ownership of what were considered "natural monopolies," such as the postal service.[16] However, in other cases, regulation rather than ownership was favored (for example, in the airline, railroad, and telecommunications industries). This was typically undertaken through industry-specific regulatory commissions at the federal and/or state level.[17]

The U.S. government has played an active role in the telecommunications market, both as a regulator and as a provider of subsidies. It has not, however, chosen to compete directly in the marketplace, on the grounds that when private companies enter the telecommunications market they contribute to the development of competition and ultimately reduce the need for government regulation.[18] Indeed, this is the vision of the Telecommunications Act of 1996 and the intent of policies pursued by the Federal Communications Commission (FCC) under this act.[19]

The twelve years that have passed since, however, have made it clear that the 1996 act failed to anticipate the development of wireless technologies and the role that municipalities might take in the less regulated environment.[20] Existing laws do not apply to broadband services because of their designation as advanced services by the 1996 act. In addition, a growing number of local governments have become convinced that they should find ways to participate in the marketplace creatively and ways to raise capital through innovative techniques. These newly formed government-initiated utilities see the appearance of competition in telecommunications markets as opportunities for growth and expansion. The pace of government entry into telecommunications and Internet services markets is rapid and increasing.[21]

The primary reasons for municipal entry into the market for broadband service provision is simply that the technology now makes it possible. FCC regulation of wireless broadband technology has been extremely limited, as the technology has matured. Through the creation of the Wireless Broadband Access Task Force, the FCC has proactively worked to remove obstacles to widespread deployment. The only substantive regulation on wireless broadband devices comes from FCC Rule Part 15, which governs wireless devices that operate in the unlicensed spectrums. The FCC has also reserved the 4.9 GHz band for wireless networks dedicated to public safety at the local level. As a result, municipalities are able to leverage both the unlicensed spectrum and the spectrum reserved for public safety to support a metro-scale wireless network. This low barrier to entry has motivated many urban and rural municipalities to explore deploying wireless broadband technology.

State Law and Policy Regarding Municipal Broadband

Telecommunications regulations have been largely initiated at the federal level and have restricted state and municipal involvement in telecommunications provision. However, in the context of municipal broadband deployments, this "top-down" model of policymaking has been flipped on its head, with the power shifting away from the FCC to city halls and state legislatures.

In 2004, the Supreme Court sided with the FCC and various incumbent local exchange carrier (ILEC) lobbyists in its *Nixon v. Missouri Municipal League* ruling, which allowed states to bar their subdivisions from providing telecommunications services. This opinion gave states the authority to determine when and where municipalities can deploy telecommunications services. This meant that all cities within a state were considered subdivisions of the state, not separate entities. This pro–states' rights decision gave states wide latitude to pass legislation pertaining to the provision of telecommunications services by municipalities. The outcome of this decision has been that the states have begun to develop their own policies for municipal broadband, leaving the nation with a patchwork of policies that lack uniformity.

Fueled by strong objections from incumbent telecommunication providers, state legislatures have been the locus of policy regarding municipal
broadband. The central argument of those lobbying state legislatures is that
the public funding and support of municipal broadband networks unfairly
impacts competition in municipal markets between traditional private telecommunications providers and new ventures funded in part with public tax
funds.[22] These private providers have expressed concern that cities providing
wireless broadband service have several advantages. These include an unlimited base from which to raise capital, the ability to regulate local rights of way
and tower permits, existing public infrastructure that is necessary for network
deployments (including streetlights), and tax-exempt status. Many companies
have sought legislative relief at the state level to regulate or restrict a municipality's ability to provide wireless broadband services to the public. These
legislative initiatives have aimed to ensure that a majority of local residents are
behind the initiative, the broadband project will not negatively affect a city's
finances, and the broadband deployment does not compete, or competes on a
level playing field, with private carriers.

To ensure that a majority of their constituents supported the initiative,
several states included a requirement that municipalities hold hearings and/or
referenda about the broadband deployment. These activities also help address
the second concern—that the project did not negatively affect finances. In addition to reporting to the public, some states have also required that plans be
submitted for approval to a state entity or agency. Tools used to achieve this
objective included a variety of stipulations ranging from providing the local
exchange carrier (LEC) the right of first refusal to an outright ban on competing with LECs. In some cases, municipalities were prohibited from charging
for services altogether.[23]

Effects of State Level Policy: More Partnerships and
Less Municipal Ownership

Currently, most states have legislation proposed, pending, or passed that prohibits municipalities from providing telecommunications services directly or
indirectly. In some cases, state legislatures have prevented municipalities from
expanding existing networks. In other cases, state legislatures have not out-
rightly prohibited the development and deployment of municipal broadband
networks but have created organizational and bureaucratic barriers which
cause these networks to be curtailed, reconfigured, or resized.

This patchwork of policies has had both intended and unintended effects
on municipal efforts to develop and deploy municipal broadband Internet

networks. For example, while some municipalities may speed up network deployment to "beat" the deadline of enacting restrictions, others may either roll back their plans or abandon the proposed project altogether. Still others may create new business plans in which ownership of the network is transferred to private partners, while some may sell off municipal rights-of-way in exchange for discounted/wholesale services. According to Tapia and Ortiz,[24] municipalities have had a variety of responses to the legislation, the most overriding response being the development of public-private partnerships between municipalities and private service providers. Another striking outcome has been a change in business plans designed to ensure that the municipality would not be the sole owner of the network.

There are many reasons why a municipality might choose to build, deploy, and manage its network via a third party in the form of some public-private partnership. Generally speaking, a public-private partnership offers considerable advantages, such as improved service quality, lower project costs, less risk, framework, incentives for innovation, more rapid project execution, easier budget management, and a potential source of additional revenue. It has been argued that a private company brings in a level of specialization that often is too expensive for a municipality to develop on its own as well as years of experience gained from working with other municipalities with similar and unique challenges.

While on the surface these partnerships seem to offer significant benefits to municipalities, they are not without major costs. Tropos Networks, in their white paper, *Build vs. Rent Build Versus Rent: Why Municipal and Industrial Organizations Should Own Their Outdoor Broadband Infrastructure*,[25] argue that municipalities gain in five key areas if they own their network: (1) flexibility, (2) resiliency, (3) capacity, (4) cost, and (5) the capacity for a truly multi-use network. The authors note that "[c]ontrol, flexibility and cost savings associated with ownership versus rental are the overriding considerations and more than offset the additional planning and skill required to build, own and operate these systems. The increased performance and feature set of broadband wireless, coupled with lower cost and reduced complexity is now driving the strong case for city and enterprise ownership of these systems."

It may also be the case that these partnerships are behind the failure of many of the very large-scale, prominent initiatives, such as those undertaken in Philadelphia, San Francisco, and Chicago. Many of these initiatives ceded ownership of the network to a single for-profit entity. When that entity and the free-market failed, so did the project. According to Meinrath: "The Philadelphia model is a corporate franchise granted to EarthLink—much of the problem stems from the fact that the municipality has no control or ownership over the network and EarthLink has demonstrated no accountability to the local community . . . where Earthlink's wireless networks have been taken over by municipalities, they've continued to operate, while those that haven't (e.g., Philly and New Orleans) they're being shut down."[26] In addition, municipal networks may have strongly different goals than for-profit entities in providing broadband Internet.

Federal Level Law and Policy Regarding Municipal Broadband

There is no federal-level broadband policy today that addresses the future rights of municipalities to participate in the telecommunications market. In the last three sessions of Congress, more than a dozen bills related to broadband adoption were proposed. All of them are now in the initial stages of the legislative process, under committee consideration, and may undergo significant changes in markup sessions. Most of them have been referred to the Senate Commerce, Science, and Transportation Committee.

H.R. 2726, "Preservation Innovation in Telecom Act of 2005,"[27] was introduced by Representative Peter Sessions (R-TX) and proposes instituting state and federal barriers to municipal broadband. In essence, it prohibits municipal officials from providing telecommunications, cable or information public services except to rectify market failures by ILECs to provide such service infrastructures. This legislation is viewed as the most prohibitive of the federal bills.

S. 1294, introduced by Senators Frank Lautenberg (D-NJ) and John McCain (R-AZ), is called the "Community Broadband Act of 2005."[28] The bill would amend the Telecommunications Act of 1996. It preserves and protects the ability of local governments to provide broadband capability and services. This bill would prohibit the creation of any state policy or regulation that restricts or prohibits a public provider from providing, to any person or public or private entity, advanced telecommunications capability, or any service that utilizes such capability. It protects incumbent providers by prohibiting the municipality from discriminating against a telephone company project when it acts as both a competitor and the franchising authority.

S. 1504, introduced by Senator John Ensign (R-NV), is titled "The Broadband Investment and Consumer Choice Act of 2005."[29] This legislation would require cities to inform private providers of plans to build municipal broadband networks; would allow bids from private sector companies to deploy, own, and operate the infrastructure; and would give preference to nongovernmental organizations in the required bid process. It would create a market-driven marketplace and eliminate government-driven competition.

HR 5252, introduced by Representatives Joe Barton (R-TX) and Bobby Rush (D-IL), is titled the "Communications, Opportunity, Promotion, and Enhancement (COPE) Act of 2006."[30] This bill is designed to update U.S. laws to address changes in voice, video, and data services. It would allow phone companies to enter the broadband market nationally without getting permission or approval from local sectors. In addition, it would authorize the FCC to enforce rules that require broadband Internet providers to provide consumers with unfettered Internet access and that allow them to run any Internet-based applications.

S. 2686, introduced by Senator Ted Stevens (R-AK), is titled "Communications, Consumer's Choice and Broadband Deployment Act of 2006."[31] This bill attempts to address such issues as the war on terrorism, interoperability, and universal service. It is an important bill for municipal broadband issues because it permits telecommunications companies to charge competitors higher rates for service. This effectively prevents municipalities from providing advanced telecommunications services. Within this proposed bill, both Title V and Title VI address municipal broadband directly and contain provisions that would "preempt any State or local law, regulation, rule or practice that is inconsistent with the requirements" of the bill. If passed, municipalities would have to allow access to "public rights of way" without favoring themselves or any other advanced communications carriers they might be affiliated with. Municipalities would be required to publish public notices of their intent to provide advanced telecommunications services and "provide opportunity for commercial enterprises to bid for the rights to provide such capability during a thirty-day period following publication of notice." Section 2.D. stipulates that the public provider must also publish information if it intends to serve advanced communications capabilities to low-to-moderate income areas or other similar areas. Senator Stevens's bill provides private companies a right-of-first-refusal and the public provider may only proceed to provide services if no private company submits a bid within a thirty-day period. It would also exempt any network whose sole objective is to serve public safety and does not serve the public in any other way beyond the municipal.

There are two bills that may affect municipal broadband because they address the digital divide and universal access of broadband. The goal of the proposed Internet and Universal Service Act of 2006 (S. 2256)[32] is "to ensure the availability to all Americans of high-quality, advanced telecommunications and broadband services, technologies, and networks at just, reasonable, and affordable rates, and to establish a permanent mechanism to guarantee specific, sufficient, and predictable support for the preservation and advancement of universal service, and for other purposes." The Universal Service Reform Act of 2006 (H.R. 5072)[33] that Representatives Lee Terry (R-NE) and

Rick Boucher (D-VA) introduced in late March 2006 would allow USF funds to pay for broadband services from contributions of service providers that use telephone numbers, IP addresses, or offer network connections to the public.

Three additional bills would allocate unused spectrum for broadband, again impacting municipal broadband, but indirectly. A "white space" bill (H.R. 5085)[34] introduced by Representatives Marsha Blackburn (R-TN) and Jay Inslee (D-WA) would allow use of broadcast television spectrum in the band between 54 and 698 MHz (other than 608–618 MHz) by unlicensed devices, including broadband services. The Wireless Innovation Act of 2006 (S. 2327 or the "Winn Act")[35] would facilitate the development of wireless broadband Internet access by allocating the so-called white spaces between television channels for other uses. Similarly, the American Broadband for Communities Act (S. 2332)[36] would allocate unused broadcast spectrum for unlicensed wireless devices and potentially provide communities with wireless broadband and home networking.

Future Law and Policy Related to Municipal Broadband

The United States has taken a deregulatory approach under the assumption that the market can build enough capacity to meet the demand. The market may do a good job of providing reliable infrastructure with reasonable quality of service, but it has no incentive to provide universal, ubiquitous coverage if it cannot generate sufficient profits in the process.[37] The business pressures of providing connectivity do not ensure that networks will be built with the standards deemed important by communities. It is essential that alternative approaches to infrastructure development remain a priority for municipal governments and national policymakers.[38]

Currently, broadband policy pertaining to local government exists only at the state level, the result being a mish-mash of policies. It is essential for the United States to consider a federal level national broadband policy that would incorporate the regulation of municipal wireless. It is especially important for the federal government to take a stronger regulatory stance on broadband, framing it as a national utility, and begin plans for a nationwide broadband network.[39] The current patchwork of broadband entry and service provision policies complicates any hope for large-scale, nationwide broadband deployment plans.

The 2004 Supreme Court *Nixon* ruling increased the power of the states to regulate municipal entry into telecommunications markets and led to a patchwork of divergent policies. The states may have hoped in this way to increase the number of telecommunications providers in a given market and thereby increase competition, coverage, quality, and service, while at the same time lowering prices. But this was not what happened, and often, the reverse was the case. For this reason, it is essential that the government create streamlined rules and regulations that promote broadband deployment.

Indeed, a national broadband policy that promotes social inclusion and ubiquitous, high-quality service and allows local governments to be involved in providing it is of the essence. The goals of this national policy should be to encourage municipalities:

(1) To own and manage wireless networks or at least take an active role in creating them;
(2) To design, build, and deploy a wireless service that is as reliable as other common utilities like water, power, and the telephone, with clear performance standards established;
(3) To design, build, and deploy wireless service coverage, which should include every household, business, organization, public space, and public transit corridor located in the municipality;
(4) To charge for the wireless service prices that are affordable and nondiscriminatory in order to ensure universal access for all.

In order to achieve the goals of this policy it is essential to begin taking stock of what broadband services are available, of what quality, and at what cost. This challenge, it should be noted, is already being addressed. The FCC published a "Report and Order" that makes significant changes in the way it collects data concerning broadband in the United States. At present, Internet service providers (ISPs) report the number of broadband subscribers based on zip codes; under the new system, however, they must report these numbers based on census tracks. In addition, ISPs are now required to break down the number of subscribers according to broadband speeds. These changes may improve the ability of the FCC to understand the extent of broadband deployment and enable it to continue to develop and maintain appropriate broadband policies, and in particular, to carry out its obligation under section 706 of the Telecommunications Act of 1996 to "determine whether advanced telecommunications capability is being deployed to all Americans in a reasonable and timely fashion."[40]

In addition, it is essential to identify a common standard for wireless broadband deployment, including Wi-Fi meshing. It is also imperative that underutilized spectrum be reallocated for unlicensed citizen access. This would encourage an "open spectrum" policy that could speed the deployment of ubiquitous and affordable wireless broadband networks. In addition, the USF should be expanded to cover broadband service, including USF eligibility, distribution, and availability of funds for various types of broadband providers. It is also recommended that the federal government offer grants to fund broadband deployment.

Conclusion

Municipalities have fundamentally different goals in providing broadband Internet access than does private industry. Municipalities are interested in promoting civic engagement, social inclusion, and economic development across all neighborhoods and communities through the deployment of their wireless network. Private industry, on the other hand, must be concerned with the bottom line and, therefore, provides service with a mind toward profit rather than social welfare. Traditionally, the United States has relied on private industry and competition to achieve greater quality and efficiency in the provision of Internet services. This approach, however, appears to have failed, since the United States has been falling behind the rest of the world in terms of broadband rollout and the average speed and quality of the service. To make matters worse, significant portions of inner cities and rural areas remain without service, and the price of the service continues to rise.

The United States must take a stronger regulatory approach to broadband, beginning with the adoption of a national broadband policy, as state-level policy is not working, and the various state-level regulations vary widely. In the most extreme cases, municipalities have been prevented from offering any form of Internet service. In other cases, restrictions have created uncomfortable partnerships between municipalities and private providers, often leading to conflicting goals and failed projects.

The goals of a national policy would be to encourage the deployment of municipal networks that are inclusive, ubiquitous, and affordable. The path to enacting this future national municipal broadband policy would include conducting a broadband census, creating new standards, allocating more spectrum, further developing the universal service fund, and promoting grants.

It is essential that municipalities and communities remain engaged in providing Internet services. Their voice is the voice of the people. It is possible that public involvement in the provision of Internet service will diminish as the private sector provides higher quality, more reliable services than those provided through most municipal projects. With municipalities playing the role of entrepreneur, they may spur private sector innovation, or at least wider broadband deployment. Citizens may then become convinced that the networks offered by private industry serve their interests. Regardless of who provides the service, municipalities should assume the role of encouraging private industry to adopt the practices and policies needed to ensure that their networks provide broadband connectivity that is in the public interest and meets the various needs of the municipality, not just access.

Notes

1. Andrea Tapia, Carleen Maitland, and Matt Stone, "Making It Work for Municipalities: Building Municipal Wireless Networks," *Government Information Quarterly* 23, no. 3–4 (2006): 359–80; Andrea Tapia and Julio Ortiz, "Municipal Reponses to State-Level Broadband Internet Policy" (paper presented at the Thirty-Fourth Research Conference on Communication, Information, and Internet Policy, Alexandria, VA, 2006); "Policy and Plan Convergence for Municipal Broadband Networks" (paper presented at the Thirty-Fifth Conference on Communication, Information, and Internet Policy, Alexandria, VA, 2007); and Andrea Tapia, Matt Stone, and Carleen Maitland, "Public-Private Partnerships and the Role of State Legislation in Wireless Municipal Networks" (paper presented at the Thirty-Third Research Conference on Communication, Information, and Internet Policy, Alexandria, VA, 2005).

2. Joe Panettieri, "2007 Muni Wireless State of the Market Report," Muniwireless .com, 2007, www.muniwireless.com/2008/01/04/2007-muniwireless-state-of-the -market-report (26 February 2007).

3. Carol Ellison, "Wimax Previews in Chicago to an Approving Audience," Muni-Wireless.com, 2007, www.muniwireless.com/2007/09/26/wimax-previews-in-chicago -to-an-approving-audience (14 January 2007).

4. John Letzing, "Google-Earthlink San Francisco Wi-Fi on Hold," in *Market-Watch*, 2007.

5. James E. Katz and Ronald E. Rice, *Social Consequences of Internet Use: Access, Involvement, and Interaction* (Cambridge, MA: MIT Press, 2002); William E. Kennard, "Equality in the Information Age," in *The Digital Divide: Facing a Crisis or Creating a Myth?*, ed. Benjamin M. Compaine (Cambridge, MA: MIT Press, 2001), 195–222; Michael Oden, *Beyond the Digital Access Divide, Developing Meaningful Measures of Information and Communications Technology Gaps* (Austin: The University of Texas Press, 2004); Michael Oden and Strover Sharon, "Links to the Future: The Role of Information, and Telecommunications Technology in Appalachian Economic Development" (Washington, DC: Applachian Regional Commision, 2002); and Zeytep Tufekcioglu, "In Search of Lost Jobs: The Rhetoric and Practice of Computer Skills Training" (Austin: University of Texas Press, 2003).

6. Oden, *Beyond the Digital Access Divide*.

7. Benton Foundation, "Losing Ground Bit by Bit: Low-Income Communities in the Information Age," 1998; Erik P. Bucy, "Social Access to the Internet," *The Harvard International Journal of Press/Politics* 5, no. 1 (2000): 50–56; Paul DiMaggio, Eszter Hargittai, Coral Celeste, and Steven Shafer, "Digital Inequality: From Unequal Access to Differentiated Use," in *Social Inequality*, ed. Kathryn Neckerman (New York: Russell Sage Foundation, 2004), 355–400; Donna L. Hoffman and Thomas Novak, "Bridging the Racial Divide on the Internet," *Science*, 17 April 1998, 390–91; and Sharon Strover, "Rural Internet Connectivity" (paper presented at the Twenty-eighth Research Conference on Communication, Information, and Internet Policy, Alexandria, VA, 1999.)

8. Richard B. Freeman, "The Labour Market in the New Information Economy," *Oxford Review of Economic Policy* 18, no. 3 (2002): 288–305; Ernest P. Goss and Joseph

M. Phillips, "How Information Technology Affects Wages: Evidence Using Internet Usage as a Proxy for It Skills," *Journal of Labor Research* 23, no. 2 (2002): 463–74.

9. John P. Robinson, Meyer Kestnbaum, Alan Neustadtl, and Anthony Alvarez, "Mass Media Use and Social Life among Internet Users," *Social Science Computer Review* 18 (2000): 490–501.

10. Dhavan V. Shah, Jack M. McLeod, and So-Hyang Yoon, "Communication, Context, and Community," *Communication Research* 28, no. 4 (2001): 464–506.

11. Wayne Sanderson, "Broadband Communications over a Rural Power Distribution Circuit" (paper presented at the Southestcon 2000, Cambridge, MA, 2000.)

12. John Windhausen, "A Blueprint for Big Broadband," *EDUCAUSE* 2008, net .educause.edu/ir/library/pdf/EPO0801.pdf (14 February 2008).

13. Robert Atkinson, "Broadband Blues," 2007, www.huffingtonpost.com/robert-d -atkinson-phd/broadband-blues_b_49358.html (17 January 2007).

14. Atkinson, "Broadband Blues."

15. Michael A. Crew and Paul R. Kleindorfer, "Incentive Regulation in the United Kingdom and the United States: Some Lessons," *Journal of Regulatory Economics* 9, no. 3 (1996): 211–25; Jeffrey A. Eisenach, "Does Government Belong in the Telecom Business?" in *Progress On Point* (Washington, DC: The Progress and Freedom Foundation, 2001).

16. Christopher D. Foster, *Privatization, Public Ownership and the Regulation of Natural Monopoly* (Oxford: Blackwell Publishers, 1992).

17. Elizabeth E. Bailey and John C. Panzar, "The Contestability of Airline Markets During the Transition to Deregulation," *Law and Contemporary Problems* 44, no. 1 (1981): 125–45; Martha Derthick and Paul J. Quirk, *The Politics of Deregulation* (Washington, DC: Brookings Institution Press, 1985).

18. William Lehr and Lee W. McKnight, "Wireless Internet Access: 3g Vs. Wifi?," *Telecommunications Policy* 27, no. 5–6 (2003): 351–70; Thomas M. Lenard, "Government Entry into the Telecom Business: Are the Benefits Commensurate with the Costs?" in *Progress on Point* (Washington, DC: Progress and Freedom Foundation, 2004).

19. Senate, Telecommunications Act of 1996 (S. 56), 1996.

20. Thomas Bleha, "Down to the Wire," *Foreign Affairs*, May/June 2005; Lehr and McKnight, "Wireless Internet Access," 351–70.

21. Lenard, "Government Entry into the Telecom Business."

22. Tapia, Maitland, and Stone, "Making It Work for Municipalities," 359–80; Tapia, Stone, and Maitland, "Public-Private Partnerships and the Role of State Legislation in Wireless Municipal Networks."

23. Tapia, Maitland, and Stone, "Making It Work for Municipalities," 359–80; Tapia, Stone, and Maitland, "Public-Private Partnerships and the Role of State Legislation in Wireless Municipal Networks."

24. Tapia and Ortiz, "Municipal Reponses to State-Level Broadband Internet Policy."

25. Tropos Networks, "Build Versus Rent: Why Municipal and Industrial Organizations Should Consider Owning an Outdoor Broadband Infrastructure," 2008, www .tropos.com/tropos_downloads/BuildvsBuy/BuildvsBuy.html (12 June 2008).

26. Sascha Maeinrath, "Philadelphia Network Flop Points to Failure of Corporate Franchise Model," *New America Foundation*, 2008, www.newamerica.net/publications /articles/2008/philadelphia_network_floppoints_failure_corporate_franchise _model_7205 (10 June 2008).

27. House of Representatives, Preservation Innovation in Telecom Act of 2005, 2005.

28. Senate, Community Broadband Act of 2005, 2005.

29. Senate, The Broadband Investment and Consumer Choice Act of 2005, 2005.

30. House of Representatives, Communications, Opportunity, Promotion, and Enhancement (Cope) Act of 2006, 2006.

31. Senate, Communications, Consumer's Choice, and Broadband Deployment Act of 2006, 2006.

32. Senate, Internet and Universal Service Act of 2006 (Netusa) (S. 2256), 2006.

33. House of Representatives, Universal Service Reform Act of 2006 (H.R. 5072), 2006.

34. House of Representatives, H.R. 5085, 2006.

35. Senate, The Wireless Innovation Act of 2006, 2006.

36. House of Representatives, American Broadband for Communities Act of 2006, 2006.

37. Catherine A. Middleton and Christine Sorensen, "How Connected Are Canadians? Inequities in Canadian Households' Internet Access," *Canadian Journal of Communication* 30, no. 4 (2005); Amelia B. Potter and Andrew Clement, "A Desiderata for Wireless Broadband Networks in the Public Interest," (paper presented at the Research Conference on Communication Information, and Internet Policy, Arlington, VA, 2007.)

38. Catherine A. Middleton, Graham Longford, Andrew Clement, and Amelia B. Potter, "ICT Infrastructure as Public Infrastructure: Exploring the Benefits of Public Wireless Networks" (paper presented at the Thirty-fourth Research Conference on Communication, Information, and Internet Policy, Arlington, VA, 2006); Potter and Clement, "A Desiderata for Wireless Broadband Networks in the Public Interest."

39. Windhausen, "A Blueprint for Big Broadband."

40. Senate, Telecommunications Act of 1996 (S. 56), 1996.

13

The Future of the E-Rate

U.S. Universal Service Fund Support for Public Access and Social Services

Heather E. Hudson

The telecommunications companies wanted more competition and the ability to expand. In exchange, we insisted on a strong, continued commitment by the telecommunications companies to "preserve and advance" universal service including access to advanced telecommunication services for schools, rural health care providers and libraries.

Senator Jay Rockefeller (D-West Virginia)[1]

The Context: Internet and Broadband Access in the United States

AFFORDABLE ACCESS TO SERVICES AVAILABLE over broadband is recognized as an important contributor to social and economic development. A 2001 Brookings study by Robert Crandall and Charles Jackson estimated that widespread adoption of basic broadband in the United States could add $500 billion to the economy and produce 1.2 million new jobs.[2] In 2004, Charles Ferguson argued that as much as $1 trillion could be lost over the next decade because of present constraints on broadband development.[3]

Yet despite U.S. global leadership in communications technologies and Internet services, according to the OECD, it ranks as low as fifteenth among industrialized countries in broadband access per one hundred inhabitants.[4] Broadband costs in the United States also remain high. American consumers pay ten to twenty-five times more per megabit than do users in Japan. To make matters worse, the average speed of broadband in the United States has not increased in the past five years; consequently, consumers in France and South Korea have residential broadband connections that are ten to twenty times faster than in the United States.

American broadband adoption is also highly dependent on socioeconomic status: almost 60 percent of households with annual incomes above $150,000 have broadband, compared with fewer than 10 percent of households with incomes below $25,000.[5] The gap between rural and urban areas persists: broadband penetration in urban areas is almost double that in rural.[6] Rural subscribers with dial-up are much more likely than their urban counterparts to list lack of availability as the reason they do not have higher speed Internet connections.[7]

Access is especially limited in the poorest regions of the country. Seven of the ten states with the fewest high speed lines per capita are also among the ten poorest states in the country: Alabama, Arkansas, Idaho, Kentucky, Mississippi, Montana, and West Virginia.[8] Six of these same states are among the ten with the fewest Internet users per one hundred residents.[9]

Broadband access is important for schools because it allows multiple users to be online, while enabling data-rich applications, such as multimedia web access and video-conferencing. An Alaskan analysis of school bandwidth requirements stipulates that "[d]ial-up connectivity does not allow for efficient data flow and usually will not allow such services as e-mail for group use. Normally, a school with dial-up will only transmit information, not being able to rely on downloading or browsing."[10] It notes that "[l]ess than T-1 [1.544 mbps] connectivity allows Internet use for data transfer, Web searches, e-mail and Web posting. Under normal circumstances, information flows at speeds allowing for group use, but may be overwhelmed. Video services can be used with some loss of picture and sound quality, but usually will require that other traffic, such as Internet use, be shut down." Also, as applications become more demanding of bandwidth, many K–12 schools have expressed an interest in an Internet 2 connection. A study by the Pennsylvania Department of Education found that full use of the applications provided by Internet 2 requires nearly ten megabits per second.[11]

Expansion of Universal Service

The original programs of the universal service fund (USF) were designed to subsidize voice telephony access for low-income residents and to extend reasonably priced telephone services to rural and other underserved areas. The Telecommunications Act of 1996 expanded the definition of universal service to include schools, libraries, and rural health care facilities, as well as access to "advanced services." The goal was to provide opportunities for students and community residents to take advantage of these "advanced services" even if they were not yet available in their homes. In order to help to bridge what became known as the "digital divide," access to the Internet was seen as a high priority:

> Elementary and secondary schools and classrooms, health care providers, and libraries should have access to advanced telecommunications services. . . . All telecommunications carriers serving a geographic area shall . . . provide such services to elementary schools, secondary schools, and libraries for educational purposes at rates less than the amounts charged for similar services to other parties.[12]

The FCC sets the overall policy for the program, which is administered by a nonprofit entity, the Universal Service Administrative Company (USAC). Funds come from telecommunications carriers, which are required to contribute a set portion of their revenues to the universal service fund. Carriers generally pass these costs down to customers through itemized charges on their telephone bills. USAC makes payments from this central fund to support the schools and libraries program, the rural health care program and other universal service programs (low-income and high-cost).

The E-Rate (short for "education rate") was created by Section 254 (h) of the 1996 act[13] to provide discounts on a wide variety of telecommunications, Internet, and internal connection products and services. All public and private nonprofit elementary and secondary schools are eligible (except those with an endowment of more than $50 million). Libraries are also eligible, as long as they meet the definition in the Library Services and Technology Act and have a budget completely separate from a K–12 school.

The Funding Process

Up to $2.25 billion in discounts can be made available each year through this program. First priority is given to requests for support for telecommunications services (services to communicate electronically between sites) and Internet access, with requests for internal connections (e.g., wiring, routers, wireless local area networks to connect classrooms) and maintenance of internal connections deemed second priority. Priority 1 services are funded first, and the remaining funds for priority 2 are allocated first to the most economically disadvantaged schools and libraries.[14]

Schools may apply for all "commercially available telecommunications services," ranging from basic telephone services to T-1 and wireless connections,

Internet access including e-mail services, and internal networking equipment. Discounts are not available for computers (except network servers), teacher training, and most software.[15] Approved costs are billed directly to USAC, up to the limit of the subsidy. Schools and libraries are responsible for the remainder and must demonstrate that they can cover their portion of the costs.

The applicable discount rate is based on a school's economic needs and location, as outlined in table 13.1. The proxy for economic need is the percentage of students who are eligible for free or reduced-priced lunches under the National School Lunch Program. The library's discount rate is based on the school district or districts in which they are located. Support for telecommunications services and Internet access is provided to all eligible applicants regardless of their level of need.

Decisions to seek E-Rate support may be made at the school, library, school district, or state level. In some instances, states submit applications on behalf of all the districts in their jurisdiction. Schools are required to prepare a technology plan, which must be approved by the state before they are eligible to apply for E-Rate funds. The purpose of this requirement is to ensure that school staffs consider issues such as sources of funding for other equipment and maintenance, training for teachers and students, and strategies for integrating use of computers and the Internet into the curriculum. The application process is rather complex, with a series of forms that must be completed and submitted, according to set guidelines and deadlines concerning eligibility, discount categories, service and equipment requirements, allowable equipment and services, and so on. Once the application is approved, the school or library's requirements are posted on USAC's website (www.usac.org) for twenty-eight days, following which it may select from competitive bids or negotiate with the carrier serving the area, according to E-Rate procurement rules and guidelines.

TABLE 13.1:
Discounts Available for Schools

% of Students Who Qualify for the National School Lunch Program	Discount for Schools Located in an Urban Area	Discount for Schools Located in a Rural Area
Less then 1%	20%	25%
1% to 19%	40%	50%
20% to 34%	50%	60%
35% to 49%	60%	70%
50% to 74%	80%	80%
75% to 100%	90%	90%

E-Rate Allocations: Following the Money

Funds Allocations for Schools and Libraries

About $21.1 billion have been allocated through this program since funds were first disbursed in 1998. Of the total funds, more than 86 percent (probably more than 90 percent, because of additional funding to school/library consortia) went to schools. Libraries received 2.9 percent, and consortia of schools and libraries received 11.4 percent, as detailed in table 13.2.

TABLE 13.2:
Amount Allocated for Schools and Libraries

Applicant Type	$ Amount 1998–2007	% of $ Total
Schools/School Districts	18,146,404,271	85.73%
Libraries	610,140,020	2.88%
School/Library Consortium	2,410,533,002	11.39%
Total	$21,167,077,293	100.00%

Allocations by Discount Levels

From 1998 to 2006, 34.5 percent of the funds went to schools and libraries eligible for a 90 percent discount, while about 77 percent went to those eligible for discounts of 70 percent or more and 87 percent to those eligible for discounts of 70 percent or more,[16] as detailed in table 13.3. Thus, it appears that funds were disbursed primarily to schools in disadvantaged regions—in rural/remote or low-income urban areas. (USAC does not break down most

TABLE 13.3:
Amount Allocated by Discount Bands, 1998–2006

Discount Band	Percent of Funds by Discount Band 1998–2006	Percent of Funds by Discount Band 2007
20–29%	0.13%	0.13%
30–39%	0.38%	0.44%
40–49%	5.99%	6.52%
50–59%	6.53%	7.23%
60–69%	9.86%	12.09%
70–79%	14.22%	18.56%
80–89%	28.42%	26.63%
>90%	34.48%	28.40%
Total 60% – >90%	86.98%	85.68%

allocations by rural versus urban location, apparently because funds are often granted to large jurisdictions, although the jurisdictions must provide that data in order to qualify for a discount rate.)

Allocations for Services

From 1998 to 2007, $10.3 billion or 47.8 percent of total funding was allocated for internal connections (within schools and libraries). About $8.6 billion or 39.6 percent was allocated for telecommunications services. About $2.3 billion or 10.6 percent was allocated for Internet services, as detailed in table 13.4.

The allocations have changed in recent years, with 49.2 percent funding telecommunications services and 12.9 percent funding Internet access in 2007. The funding for basic maintenance of internal connections has been available only since 2005. Most funding for internal connections has gone to schools eligible for discounts of 70 percent or more, as detailed in table 13.5.

TABLE 13.4:
Allocations by Service, 1998–2007

	$ Total	*Percentage*
Internal Connections	$10,329,922,194	47.77%
Internet Access	$2,299,930,050	10.63%
Telecom Services	$8,598,028,474	39.63%
Basic Maintenance of Internet Connections	$398,270,253	1.84%
TOTAL:	$21,626,150,971	100.00%

TABLE 13.5:
Allocation by Service, 2007

	$ Total	*Percentage*
Internal Connections	$726,471,209	31.69%
Internet Access	$295,381,178	12.89%
Telecom Services	$1,127,614,659	49.20%
Basic Maintenance of Internal Connections	$142,635,505	6.22%
Total	$2,292,102,551	100.0%

Allocations by State

Between 1998 and 2006, the amount of funding provided per capita through the program varied widely from state to state. Four of the ten poorest states

TABLE 13.6:
Top Ten States in Funding per Capita, 1998–2006

State	E-Rate Funds/Capita
Alaska	$201
District of Columbia	$200
New Mexico	$176
New York	$138
Mississippi	$109
Oklahoma	$100
South Carolina	$95
Louisiana	$87
Texas	$86
Arizona	$76
Kentucky	$76

Note: Bold indicates states among poorest ten states in GSP/capita.

TABLE 13.7:
Top Ten States: E-Rate Funds/Capita, 2006

State	E-Rate Funds/Capita
Alaska	$27.60
District of Columbia	$19.21
Louisiana	$16.94
New Mexico	$15.27
Mississippi	$13.15
Oklahoma	$10.53
Alabama	$10.10
New York	$9.85
South Dakota	$9.81
Arizona	$9.37

Note: Bold indicates states among poorest ten states in GSP/capita.

(measured in gross state product per capita terms)—Mississippi, Oklahoma, South Carolina, and Kentucky—were among the biggest E-Rate recipients per capita. The allocations are detailed in table 13.6.

In 2006, the ten states that received the biggest E-Rate fund commitments in funding per capita included only three of the poorest states, measured in gross state product per capita. Three states that have significant Native American populations and isolated areas (Alaska, New Mexico, South Dakota) were included in the list as well, as detailed in table 13.7.

The bottom ten states in terms of funding received only $12 to $32 per capita between 1998 and 2006, as detailed in table 13.8. Among them were

TABLE 13.8:
Bottom Ten States in Funding per Capita, 1998–2006

State	E-Rate Funds/Capita
New Hampshire	$12
Delaware	$13
Nevada	$17
Vermont	$25
Idaho	$26
Hawaii	$27
Maryland	$29
Iowa	$30
Washington	$31
Virginia	$32

Note: Bold indicates state among poorest ten states in GSP/capita.

several states with significant rural areas, such as New Hampshire, Nevada, Vermont, Idaho (also one of the poorest states), Hawaii, and Iowa.

Is it an intentional rejection of federal funding or the availability of significant alternative sources of support from the state and local governments that explains this phenomenon? New Hampshire, Nevada, Maryland, Washington, and Virginia rank among the top fifteen states in high-speed lines per capita, according to FCC data. Are organizational problems, such as small school size or lack of mentorship, hindering some of these states that could benefit from more funding support? Quite possibly so, at least according to field interviews conducted in Vermont.[17]

Benefits of the E-Rate

Following a decade during which the E-Rate allocated more than $21 billion in funds, there has been little rigorous evaluation of the utilization or impact of this program. Reports that have addressed the issue have generally been based on case studies or anecdotal evidence.

In 1996, about two-thirds of public schools in the United States had Internet access. By 2003, virtually every public school could go online. *Education Week* notes: "Perhaps even more striking, high-poverty schools, as well as their low-poverty counterparts, could boast near-universal access to the Internet by that point."[18] A report sponsored by the Education and Library Networks Coalition (EdLiNC) credits the E-Rate with increasing the percentage of public classrooms with Internet access from 14 percent in 1996 to 95 percent in 2005.[19] Internet access for libraries has also increased dramatically during this period; more than 95 percent of U.S. libraries had

Internet access in 2006, compared with 28 percent in 1996.[20] As shown above, more than one-third of E-Rate funds went to the poorest schools (those eligible for discounts of 90 percent or more), and a total of more than $18.4 billion went to schools eligible for a discount of 60 percent or more.[21] But would most schools and libraries have gained Internet access without the E-Rate program through state or local initiatives? Perhaps not, although the causality link is missing.

An EdLiNC report published in 2003 concluded that:

- The E-Rate is an important tool for economic empowerment in under-served communities;
- The E-Rate is beginning to bring new learning opportunities to special education students;
- The E-Rate is transforming education in rural America;
- E-Rate-supported technical infrastructure in schools is vital to reaching student achievement goals in No Child Left Behind legislation;
- Schools and libraries are devoting significant resources to completing E-Rate applications.[22]

Case studies of Chicago, Cleveland, Detroit, and Milwaukee, carried out on behalf of the Benton Foundation, identified several benefits, but also new challenges resulting from E-Rate support:

- Network infrastructure deployment has been accelerated, and Internet access has improved dramatically;
- E-Rate funding has enabled school districts to leverage existing financial resources;
- Professional development needs are increasing geometrically;
- School districts are highly dependent on E-Rate funding;
- The E-Rate has led to changes in school district planning practices, re-quiring new knowledge and new collaboration;
- The current E-Rate process taxes relationships with vendors;
- The need for building upgrades (in wiring and other hardware, for example) can delay deployment of information technology.[23]

Beyond Access

Effective utilization of the Internet for education requires not only connectivity, but also capability, content and appropriate context. *Education Week*'s "Technology Counts 2008" study uses several criteria to evaluate states on their technology leadership in three core areas of technology policy and practice: access to technology, use of technology, and capacity to use technology.

Concerning Internet access, a teacher commented in Benton's 2002 study: "It's a great leash, but there's no dog."[24] Since 2002, the average level of computer access has hardly changed, remaining close to four students per instructional computer. In 2007, there were 3.7 students for every high-speed Internet-connected computer in U.S. public schools. However, the number of students sharing a high-speed Internet-connected computer ranged from less than two (1.9 in South Dakota) to five or more (in Mississippi and California).[25]

Education Week found that study respondents listed professional development and connectivity/networking as their two highest priorities for technology spending this school year. Nationwide, 15 percent of public schools reported that the majority of their teachers were at a "beginner" skill level in their use of technology. However, like computer access, teacher skill levels vary from state to state. In 2006, at least one-third of schools in Mississippi and West Virginia reported a majority of teachers were beginners, compared with only 3 percent of schools in South Dakota.[26] Yet technology skills alone are not sufficient. A budget for technical support and maintenance is needed; otherwise, tech-savvy teachers may end up becoming "electronic janitors," who merely keep the equipment running.[27]

Effective use of the technology also requires applications that can enrich curricula and extend learning. *Education Week* notes: "[S]tates are taking steps to help expand the use of educational technology both through standards for students and via efforts to push the boundaries of conventional schooling."[28] Twenty-three states have established a state virtual school, and sixteen states have at least one cyber charter school.[29] About 19 percent of public schools now offer their own distance-learning programs for students. These initiatives raise the question: Are state and local initiatives building on the foundation of E-Rate support, or substituting for it?

Rural Health Care

In section 254 of the Telecommunications Act of 1996, Congress sought to provide rural health care providers "an affordable rate for the services necessary for telemedicine and the instruction relating to such services." Specifically, Congress directed telecommunications carriers "to provide telecommunications services which are necessary to health care provision in a State, including instruction relating to such services, to any public or nonprofit health care provider that serves persons who reside in rural areas of that State, at rates that are reasonably comparable to rates charged for similar services in urban areas of that State."[30]

The Rural Health Care Division of USAC administers a program that provides up to $400 million annually so that rural health care providers pay no more than their urban counterparts do for the same or similar telecommunication services. To qualify for universal service support, a health care provider (HCP) must be a public or not-for-profit organization located in a rural area. In addition, not-for-profit HCPs, in both rural and urban areas, may qualify for Internet access assistance if they are unable to access the Internet via a toll-free or local call and must, therefore, dial into the Internet via a toll (long-distance) call.

The HCP may seek support for eligible services, which include mileage-related charges, various types of connectivity from leased telephone lines to frame relay, integrated services digital network (ISDN) or T1 circuits, mileage charges, and one-time installation charges. End-user equipment, such as computers, telephones, and fax machines, as well as maintenance charges, are not eligible for support.[31] All telecommunications common carriers may participate, including interexchange carriers (IXCs), wireless carriers, and competitive local exchange carriers.

Each eligible HCP requests bids for telecommunications services to be used for providing health care through postings on the USAC website. Requests for bids must be posted on the USAC website for twenty-eight days before the HCP can enter into an agreement to purchase services from a carrier. The HCP must consider all bids received and select the most cost-effective method to meets its health care communications needs.[32]

By 2003, only 1,194 of 8,300 potential applicants had received support, and the fund disbursed only $30.25 million in its first five years out of a potential pool of $200 million. The FCC, therefore, implemented several changes to eligibility requirements and comparative pricing guidelines designed to make the USF discount more widely available and simpler to implement.[33] For example, eligible health care providers could receive 25 percent discounts on the cost of monthly Internet access,[34] and rural health care providers in states considered to be entirely rural could receive support equal to 50 percent of the monthly cost of advanced telecommunications and information services.[35]

Despite these modifications, the program continued to be underutilized. As the FCC noted: "[I]n each of the past 10 years, the program generally has disbursed less than 10 percent of the authorized funds."[36] According to USAC data, a total of $168.5 million was disbursed for rural health care from 1998 to 2005 inclusive.[37] Some $97.4 million or 58 percent of the funds during that period went to Alaska, primarily to link village clinics to regional hospitals, and to link the hospitals to medical centers in Anchorage, under the Alaska Federal Health Care Access Network (AFHCAN) initiative.[38]

The FCC subsequently introduced a two-year pilot program in September 2006 that could allocate up to $100 million in RHC funds for construction of dedicated broadband networks to connect health providers in a state or region and to support the cost of connecting these networks to Internet 2. Another purpose of the pilot program is to provide information that could guide revision of the current RHC rules so that the increasing broadband connectivity serves additional purposes: "If successful, increasing broadband connectivity among health care providers at the national, state and local levels would also provide vital links for disaster preparedness and emergency response and would likely facilitate the President's goal of implementing electronic medical records nationwide."[39]

In November 2007, the FCC announced allocation of more than $417 million for construction of sixty-nine statewide or regional broadband telehealth networks in forty-two states and three U.S. territories under the health care pilot program.[40] This initiative merits careful evaluation to determine whether it contributes to both health care and infrastructure access goals.

Key Issues

Universal service policy is now under review by Congress and the FCC. Following a decade of operation, it should be possible to assess the effectiveness of the E-Rate and other USF programs. However, policy decisions do not usually wait for conclusive research. The recommendations below are based on what we do know.

Should the E-Rate Program be Continued?

Yes. Despite the lack of hard data, there is significant evidence that the funds have contributed to providing access to the Internet for school students and for community residents through public libraries. However, the program needs some revision and greater oversight as detailed below.

Should the E-Rate Program Remain Under the FCC?

Some federal officials have proposed that the E-Rate should be merged with other Department of Education technology programs. However, because of its direct role as a key component of universal service policy, the E-Rate should remain independent of other government departments and under the administration of the FCC.

But should a community access program be run by an agency comprised primarily of lawyers, economists, and engineers? Not without other input. The Federal-State Joint Board includes some state commissioners and consumer advocates, but other types of expertise are needed. Oversight should include representatives from other federal agencies, including NTIA (National Telecommunications and Information Administration) concerning national communications infrastructure policy, as well as the Department of Education (DOE), and Health and Human Services (HHS), which is already involved in the rural health care initiatives. Advisors on the research and evaluation of E-Rate applications should also include experts and possibly representatives of federal research bodies, such as the National Academy of Sciences and National Science Foundation. The latter agencies could be made responsible for guiding evaluation research on the utilization and impact of E-Rate funding.

What Key Elements of the E-Rate Process Should be Retained?

The E-Rate funds allocation process has several unique features that should be retained.

Awards to the User

The E-Rate funds are awarded to the user (school or library) rather than directly to the carrier or vendor. This approach can empower the schools and libraries as customers of the carriers, rather than supplicants. In some cases, schools and libraries have become "anchor tenants" for these carriers, encouraging them to bring broadband into previously unserved communities.

Competitive Bids

The E-Rate process requires competitive bids for approved services through the USAC website. This approach not only creates incentives to minimize costs but also encourages new entrants, in addition to incumbents and large vendors, to provide equipment and services for schools.

These approaches differ from the models used in most other countries, where subsidies go directly to carriers, and incumbents may be required to provide discounted or free service to schools. In these other models, carriers have no incentive to provide high quality of service to schools if they see no revenue potential. Furthermore, if they receive direct government subsidies to provide the service, they may have no incentive to minimize costs. The incentive-based E-Rate model, while not perfect, is far superior.

Should the Funding Formula be Changed?

Graduated discounts are greatest for schools and libraries in rural/remote and low-income urban areas. This general formula should be maintained.

However, given the limited support for schools and libraries that are not eligible for significant discounts, it can be argued that funding should be available only to those that are clearly disadvantaged, e.g., eligible for discounts of 60 percent (or possibly 70 percent) or more. Allocations to other applicants could be gradually phased out. Alternatively, the discount percentages could be reviewed and possibly lowered. An important consideration is whether discounts of 80 or 90 percent provide sufficient incentives to schools and libraries to find additional sources of funding, and/or to be prudent and efficient in their utilization of ICT facilities and services.

Some of the remaining funds might then be made available for capability and content, as well as for research on the E-Rate program (see below). A small amount of funds should also be allocated for outreach, to ensure that all eligible recipients are aware of the program and to provide training and support to help them with the funding process.

Should E-Rate Funds Support Capability and Content?

Some educators advocate expanding E-Rate funding beyond connectivity to support training, technical support, and content. In general, given the pressures on the funding base and ongoing requirements for connectivity subsidies, E-Rate funds should be limited to supporting connectivity, while alternative sources should be tapped for these other important needs.

However, as noted above, if funding formulas were changed, some E-Rate support could be allocated for these purposes. For example, a small percentage of funds (e.g., up to 10 percent) could be used for competitive grants for training and content development, for example, the $650 million that was unused and carried forward from funding years 2001–2004 could be used for capability and content.

Several alternatives have been proposed to fund additional activities involving technical training and support and content development. One approach is to provide support from other government agencies, such as the federal Department of Education. The Enhancing Education Through Technology (EETT) program, for example, which was authorized as Title II-D of the No Child Left Behind Act (NCLB), enables schools to address core teaching and learning needs through technology, including access to courses online, professional development programs for teachers, and technology skills and tools for students.[41]

Under the EETT, states distribute funds to school districts, with 50 percent allocated by a poverty-weighted formula and 50 percent by competition. EETT gives schools broad discretion in using program resources for technology-related acquisition, enrichment, professional development, and integration purposes aimed at improving student achievement and student technology access.[42]

Although the EETT was provided with $1 billion per year through the NCLB legislation, in actuality, it only received about $690 million for its first three fiscal years, 2002–2004, and then only $496 million in fiscal year 2005 and to $272 million in fiscal year 2006.[43] Clearly, additional funds are needed to enable this program to achieve educational technology goals and to complement the support for connectivity through the E-Rate.

Another source of federal funds could be the proceeds from FCC spectrum auctions. Digital Promise proposes establishing a nonprofit nongovernmental digital opportunity investment trust (DO IT) "designed to meet the urgent need to transform learning in the twenty-first century." The trust would use FCC spectrum auction funds for learning software and tools to make use of the Internet and for information and communications technologies for education. The proponents draw parallels to the historic use of revenues from the sale of public lands "which helped finance public education in every new state and created the great system of land-grant colleges voted by Congress and signed by President Lincoln during the darkest days of the Civil War."[44] Digital Promise was passed by both the House and Senate in July 2008, as part of the reauthorization of the Higher Education Act, and signed into law by President Bush in August 2008. However, its mandated National Center for Research in Advanced Information and Digital Technologies remains unfunded.[45]

How Can the E-Rate Process be Improved?

Better Management

The slow and cumbersome process of allocating funds has continued to plague the Universal Services Administrative Company (USAC), the organization established to manage the distribution of USF funds, formed by the amalgamation of two separate entities (for schools/libraries and rural health care), which was initially set up to implement the programs. In May 2007, USAC projected that $650 million allocated for schools and libraries from funding years 2001–2004 had not been spent. The FCC authorized these funds to be carried over to the next funding year to increase disbursements for schools and libraries.[46] This amount represents nearly 29 percent of the funds available ($2.25 billion annually) during the four-year period.

The E-Rate program has been accused of insufficient oversight. Some school districts have purchased equipment that was unnecessary, too costly or beyond their capability to manage. Equipment vendors have been accused of fraud and price-rigging.[47] In 2003, USAC, with support from the FCC, created a task force to recommend steps to strengthen and improve E-Rate compliance procedures and prevent waste, fraud and abuse.[48] In December 2003, the House Committee on Energy and Commerce asked the Government Accountability Office (GAO) to prepare a report on the FCC's management and oversight of the E-Rate program. The GAO found evidence of some mis-management of E-Rate funds, bureaucratic delays in disbursing funds and some waste of E-Rate resources. Its report called for the FCC to strengthen its management and oversight by determining comprehensively which federal accountability requirements apply to the E-Rate, establishing E-Rate perfor-mance goals and measures, and taking steps to reduce beneficiary appeals.[49] In March 2005, the House Committee held hearings on the GAO report.[50]

USAC and the FCC have taken significant steps to rectify these problems. They are also being addressed through the FCC in its Notice of Proposed Rulemaking (NPRM) on USF management, administration, and over-sight.[51]

A triennial review of FCC and USAC administrative, application, and over-sight procedures should be required to improve efficiency, effectiveness, and transparency of funds disbursement and to examine changing needs for ICT access.

At the Federal Level

Although there are strengths in the E-Rate allocation process, the program has proved difficult to implement and administer. Some educators and librar-ians have found that it places a heavy burden on them in terms of time, effort, and expertise. The application process is demanding and requires careful monitoring and attention to detailed specifications and submissions. The un-spent $650 million from funding years 2001 to 2004 (representing nearly 29 percent of available funds) indicates that something is seriously wrong with the disbursement process.

The required technology plan was meant to force schools to think about how they would address issues such as teacher competency and relevant con-tent, as well as how they would fund ongoing technical support and mainte-nance. Some schools, however, have simply outsourced the preparation of the technology plan or used a "cookie cutter" model that satisfies the requirement but does provided the intended benefit of thinking through the plan.

At the State and Local Level

States and school districts could work to improve the process and the funding available to their schools. While most E-Rate funds go to poor and disadvantaged states and school districts, there are still eligible schools that remain unfunded. Some have secured funding from their state or from local sources. But others that could benefit from the funds have not applied. One strategy that the school districts and state coordinators could use more effectively is mentoring. A resource person who is able to provide advice, critique draft submissions, and troubleshoot the process can make a major difference. Alaska's significant success in obtaining E-Rate funds has been attributed to the appointment of a state librarian to the position of state E-Rate coordinator responsible for helping the schools and libraries prepare applications and navigate the E-Rate labyrinth. This coordinator provides advice, explains the requirements, and assists in completing the forms and tracking their progress.[52]

Some educators and librarians are already organized to take advantage of state technology initiatives, such as the Texas Infrastructure Fund (TIF). State officials in Vermont, on the other hand, have noted that their school districts are very small and may not have the staff time or expertise necessary to complete the process.[53]

Many school districts say that they would have difficulty finding funds to pay for connectivity if E-Rate funds and discounts were discontinued. While this observation demonstrates the value of the E-Rate subsidy to the schools, it also shows that school districts need to examine how they allocate their available technology dollars, and whether they can diversify their funding sources or include connectivity costs in their annual budgets.

Should the Rural Health Care (RHC) Program be Continued?

Should a program that has disbursed less than 10 percent of its allotted funds since 1998 be continued? The answer is not as simple as it would appear. First, the sum of $400 million per year, which it received, was based on a very rough estimate without much foundation. Second, the program has received very limited publicity. Third, its application procedures are very complex, and until recently, only a minimal discount was offered for high-speed connectivity in many rural areas.

The FCC has now changed the formulas for calculating the discounts and has included discounts for Internet access. It has also announced a two-year pilot program to support investment in broadband infrastructure in order to link HCPs and provide guidance for the future of the program.

The evidence for rural health care is limited primarily to Alaska, where the funds have proven instrumental in upgrading communications between hospitals and village clinics. However, the revised health care initiative should be given a chance to deliver. The RHC should be allowed to continue at least through the next two years, subject to findings from the pilot program, which should include an independent evaluation.

Should the USF Fund Infrastructure?

The RHC pilot program includes funding for broadband infrastructure. In addition to linking health facilities, these networks, as the FCC points out, could also provide vital links for disaster preparedness and emergency response and facilitate the goal of implementing electronic medical records nationwide. There is some evidence (for example, in rural Alaska) that the extension of broadband networks to connect schools and libraries has also brought broadband to neighborhoods and rural communities that previously lacked access. The FCC should commission studies to determine to what extent E-Rate funding has contributed to extending infrastructure and should build funds for such research into the new RHC pilot program.

Conclusions and Recommendations

While not flawless, the Universal Service programs for schools, libraries, and rural health care have helped many students use the Internet and other electronic resources for educational purposes; they have helped community residents gain access to the Internet in their libraries, and they have helped patients who are dependent on rural health care services.

Based on the above analysis, the following policies are recommended in the future:

1. The Universal Service Fund programs for schools, libraries, and rural health care should become a permanent component of universal service.
2. The FCC should maintain responsibility for the USF programs for schools, libraries, and rural health care, but special advisory committees should be established, comprised of representatives from NTIA, DOE, and HHS, as well as from professional educational, library, and health care organizations. These advisory committees should also include experts on the utilization of ICTs and on the evaluation of ICT programs.
3. The following E-Rate policies should be continued:
    a. Funding should be limited to connectivity and related facilities;
    b. Discounts based on income and geographic region should be maintained; and
    c. A competitive bidding process for vendors should continue.
4. A triennial review of FCC and USAC administrative, application, and oversight procedures should be required to improve the efficiency, effectiveness, and transparency of the disbursement of funds.
5. Sources that support the factors critical to effective utilization of ICTs need to be identified: capacity-building for teachers and others who use

ICTs, development and exchange of effective content for education and other development and contextual applications (such as language, culture, ethnicity, and disabilities).

6. A small percentage of USF funds should be used for *outreach* to make more educators, librarians, and rural health care providers aware of the programs and for *evaluation* to update and analyze data on program utilization and to assess impacts of USF support.

Notes

1. Senator Jay Rockefeller (D-WVA) quoted in Norris Dickard, ed., "Great Expectations: Leveraging America's Investment in Educational Technology," Benton Foundation and Education Development Center, 2002.

2. Robert Crandall and Charles Jackson, "The $500 Billion Opportunity: The Potential Economic Benefit of Widespread Diffusion of Broadband Internet Access," in *Down to the Wire: Studies in the Diffusion and Regulation of Telecommunications Technologies*, ed. Allan L. Shampine (Hauppauge, NY: Nva Publishers, 2003), 155–94.

3. Cited in Thomas Bleha, "Down to the Wire," *Foreign Affairs*, May/June 2005.

4. www.oecd.org/sti/ict/broadband, December 2006.

5. S. Derek Turner, "Broadband Reality Check," Free Press, August 2005.

6. S. Derek Turner, "Broadband Reality Check," Free Press, August 2005.

7. "A Nation Online: Entering the Broadband Age," National Telecommunications and Information Administration, September 2004.

8. Measured in gross state product per capita. (New Mexico, also in the bottom ten in high-speed lines per capita, is the eleventh poorest state measured by GSP per capita.) Source: FCC, as of 30 June 2005, and U.S. Census Bureau, October 2005.

9. Alabama, Arkansas, Mississippi, Oklahoma, South Carolina, and West Virginia. Source: "Computer and Internet Use in the United States: 2003," U.S. Census Bureau, October 2005.

10. Della Matthis, "E-Rate in Alaska: Telecommunications—Expanding Education and Library Service," June 2006, library.state.ak.us/usf/Bandwidthreport5-06.doc.

11. Matthis, "E-Rate in Alaska."

12. Telecommunications Act of 1996, Public Law No. 104-104, 110 Stat. 56 (1996).

13. Also known as the Snowe-Rockefeller-Exon-Kerrey amendment.

14. See www.universalservice.org/sl/tools/reference/eligserv_framework.asp. Starting in 2005, eligible entities are able to receive support for Internal Connections in two of every five funding years.

15. For details, see www.sl.universalservice.org/Reference/eligible.asp.

16. Derived from cumulative annual commitment data available at www.universalservice.org.

17. Personal interviews with Vermont officials, April 2004.

18. Christopher B. Swanson, "Tracking U.S. Trends," *Education Week*, 4 May 2006.

19. EdLiNC, "E-Rate: Ten Years of Connecting Kids and Community," Education and Library Networks Coalition, February 2007.

20. Source: American Library Association website, www.alawash.org.

21. Derived from cumulative annual commitment data available at www .universalservice.org.

22. EdLiNC, "E-Rate: A Vision of Opportunity and Innovation," Education and Library Networks Coalition, 2003.

23. Andy Carvin, ed., "The E-Rate in America: A Tale of Four Cities," Washington, DC, Benton Foundation (2000): 16–17.

24. Quoted in Norris Dickard, ed., "Great Expectations: Leveraging America's Investment in Educational Technology," Benton Foundation and Education Development Center, 2002, 20.

25. "Technology Counts 2008," *Education Week*, March 2008, www.edweek.org.

26. Swanson, "Tracking U.S. Trends."

27. Dickard, "Great Expectations," 23.

28. Swanson, "Tracking U.S. Trends."

29. "Technology Counts 2008," *Education Week*.

30. Public Law 104-104, the Telecommunications Act of 1996. See 47 U.S.C. (h)(2)(A).

31. For details, see www.rhc.universalservice.org/eligibility/services.asp.

32. The FCC defines "most cost effective method" as "the method of least cost after consideration of the features, quality of transmission, reliability, and other factors relevant to choosing a method of providing the required services." See www.rhc.universalservice.org.

33. Federal Communications Commission, "Report and Order, Order on Reconsideration, and Notice of Proposed Rulemaking in the Matter of Rural Health Care Support Mechanism," 13 November 2003.

34. Federal Communications Commission, "2003 Rural Health Care Report and Order and FNPRM."

35. Federal Communications Commission, "2004 Rural Health Care Report and Order and FNPRM."

36. Federal Communications Commission, "In the Matter of Rural Health Care Support Mechanism," WC Docket No. 02-60, adopted 26 September 2006, 3.

37. Analysis by the author of annual commitment data provided at www.rhc .universalservice.org/funding/asc.

38. See www.afhcan.org, and Heather Hudson, "Rural Telemedicine: Lessons from Alaska for Developing Regions," Proceedings of Med-e-Tel 2006, Luxembourg, April 2006.

39. Federal Communications Commission, "Rural Health Care Support Mechanism," 1–2.

40. "FCC Launches Initiative To Increase Access To Health Care In Rural America Through Broadband Telehealth Services," 19 November 2007. See www.fcc.gov/cgb /rural/rhcp.html.

41. Other uses include computer-based testing, and disaggregating and reporting of student data.

42. Coalition on School Networking: www.cosn.org/about/press/071906.cfm.

43. Coalition on School Networking: www.cosn.org/about/press/071906.cfm.

44. Source: www.digitalpromise.org.

45. See www.digitalpromise.org/newsite.

46. FCC Public Notice DA07-2470, released 11 June 2007.

47. See, for example, Randy Dotinga, "Fraud Charges Cloud Plan For 'Wired' Classrooms," *The Christian Science Monitor*, 17 June 2004.

48. Recommendations of the Task Force on Prevention of Waste, Fraud, and Abuse, September 2003.

49. Government Accountability Office, "Telecommunications: Greater Involvement Needed by FCC in the Management and Oversight of the E-Rate Program," Report to the Chairman, Committee on Energy and Commerce, House of Representatives, February 2005.

50. "Problems with The E-Rate Program: GAO Review Of FCC Management And Oversight," Hearing Before the Subcommittee on Oversight and Investigations of the Committee on Energy and Commerce, House of Representatives, 16 March 2005.

51. Federal Communications Commission, Notice of Proposed Rulemaking, "Comprehensive Review of Universal Service Fund Management, Administration, and Oversight," WC Docket No. 05-195, released 20 July 2005.

52. Personal interviews with Della Matthis, Alaska E-Rate coordinator.

53. Personal interviews with Vermont officials, April 2004.

Part IV
Content

14

Public Service Media 2.0

Ellen P. Goodman

Introduction

THIS CHAPTER WILL PRESENT IDEAS FOR transitioning the system of public broadcasting to a system of digital public media, focusing on television. This transition, though clearly needed, is politically difficult. It involves at least three components: (1) restructuring the current system so that funds are diverted from the operation of broadcast facilities; (2) redefining the entities that are entitled to public media funding; and (3) revamping the system of copyright exemptions and licenses so that public media entities have access to content on reasonable terms, can distribute public media content across all platforms, and can make content available for citizen engagement and reuse.[1]

History and Factual Background

Origins

The U.S. public television broadcasting system was assembled in the 1960s from scattered local stations, which provided instructional and other educational programming.[2] In 1965, the independent Carnegie Commission issued *Public Television, A Program for Action*, in which it called for a new system of "public television."[3] This system would retain its local character and its connections with local and regional institutions like universities.[4] It would also develop and distribute distinctive national programming.[5] Finally, as E. B.

White put it in a letter to Carnegie Commission personnel, public television would "address itself to the ideal of excellence" through programs that "arouse our dreams [and] satisfy our hunger for beauty," delivered by a system capable of becoming "our Lyceum, our Chautauqua . . . and our Camelot."[6] The Public Broadcasting Act of 1967 closely followed the Carnegie Commission's recommendations.[7]

Structure

The public broadcasting system currently consists of three components: (1) noncommercial educational television and radio stations licensed by the Federal Communications Commission (FCC);[8] (2) national networks—the Public Broadcasting System (PBS) and National Public Radio (NPR)—that commission, aggregate, and sometimes themselves produce (as in the case of NPR) programming; and (3) the Corporation for Public Broadcasting (CPB), a private nonprofit corporation governed by federally appointed board members for the purpose of funneling funds from federal appropriations to the national networks, producers, and the stations.[9] The goal of CPB is to "facilitate the development of, and ensure universal access to, noncommercial high-quality programming and telecommunications services" which it does "in conjunction with noncommercial educational telecommunications licensees across America."[10] PBS and NPR are funded by their member stations and by CPB, but do not receive federal funding directly.

PBS, unlike the commercial broadcast networks, does not own stations, or have affiliation agreements that obligate stations to carry national network programming. Rather, local public television stations purchase PBS programming, support the network through membership fees, and have representatives on its board. The local stations thus control their own schedules and strongly influence PBS's direction. NPR is similar, although NPR, unlike PBS, produces much of its own programming, while PBS aggregates and brands programming produced by member stations and independent producers. Public broadcasting is funded by a combination of an annual federal appropriation, federal grants for programming and/or infrastructure, state and local funding, and private funding. In 2005, total federal revenue was just under 20 percent (annual appropriation distributed through CPB of almost $400 million or 16.3 percent and federal grants of $66 million or 2.8 percent). State and local government funds constituted about 25 percent of the funding, with the rest coming from corporate grants and donor funds.

Another form of subsidy that public broadcasting receives is a spectrum reservation. Radio and television frequencies are reserved for noncommercial operation in every local market. There are approximately 360 noncommercial television stations and ten times as many noncommercial radio stations (not all of these receive federal funds). Local stations often have overlapping coverage so that in any given market, a consumer may be able to access a handful of public stations, and there are multiple stations licensed to the largest markets. Not all noncommercial stations carry the national PBS program service, but in some markets, more than one station carries the service, resulting in duplicative programming in that market. All of these stations are completing digital conversions at a cumulative price tag of about $1.8 billion. Digital stations are able to use their television frequencies to provide multiple streams of programming and have begun to roll out multicast channels that focus on arts, children's, foreign language, and news and public affairs programming.

Public broadcasting institutions are familiar and, according to polls, highly valued fixtures of civil society. And yet it is not always clear, even to public broadcasting supporters, what purpose these institutions and their products serve. At the most general level, public broadcasting is expected to provide alternatives to commercial media products and support democratic aspirations for diverse and universally available speech products.[11] Where the market fails to produce high quality (and noncommercial) children's programming, public broadcasting is expected to fill this void. Where the market fails to deliver arts programming, or even live arts in rural areas, public broadcasting is expected to step in. And where the market is characterized by consolidated media companies that no longer have strong ties to the local communities they serve, public broadcasting is expected to sustain these ties. In all cases, public broadcasting exists to deliver products and services with an eye to meeting the needs of society and its citizens, rather than merely gratifying consumers.

At the same time that public broadcasting is supposed to supplement the market, it is also expected to reflect existing audience preferences for particular kinds of media products—the very task at which the market excels. If public broadcasting invests too heavily in programming that is not widely consumed, it risks irrelevancy. This fear makes public broadcasting institutions, although not reliant on advertising support, often just as mindful of program ratings as are their commercial brethren. And yet, it is difficult to justify public support for a service that uses market measurements as a gauge of value and guide to development. The attempt to develop large audiences, while at the same time targeting underserved niches, presents a contradiction in the mission of public broadcasting that has drawn fire from public television's critics.[12]

Nowhere in the Public Broadcasting Act or in the charters of the public broadcasting institutions is there a clear mission statement for public broadcasting or public media. Mission statements exist. For example, the

PBS Members' Mission Statement of 2004 states that PBS's mission is to "[c]hallenge the American mind; inspire the American spirit; preserve the American memory; enhance the American dialogue; promote global understanding." But these aspirations say little about the relationship between public broadcasting and the market or the role of public broadcasting in a tumultuous media environment.

Controversies

Partly because of uncertainties about the desired role of public broadcasting, the system is beset by perennial controversies over funding and content. Every year, when it comes time to appropriate funds for CPB, there are calls to "zero out" funding for public broadcasting on the one hand, or to move away from annual appropriations to a more permanent and sustainable trust fund model on the other.[13] As part of these funding controversies, and often independent of them, there are disputes over public broadcasting content. These disputes usually turn on whether public broadcasting entities have satisfied the statutory exhortation (it is not quite a requirement) that they advance "objectivity and balance."[14] The most frequent accusations are that public broadcast programming is too liberal, failing to give voice to conservative perspectives, and too mainstream, failing to give voice to minority or marginal perspectives. Underlying these controversies are fundamental disagreements about the justification for public broadcasting and more generally for public media.

Fundamentals

Opposition to continued funding for public broadcasting typically takes two forms. At the most general level, there are those who oppose governmental involvement in the production and distribution of media content. They view the First Amendment's command that government shall not abridge freedom of speech to mean that government should desist from supporting the creation of speech. This negative conception of the First Amendment places speech production in the same category as speech censorship. The idea is that the use of government resources to encourage speech, just as the use of government power to discourage speech, potentially distorts public discourse.[15]

A second strain of opposition to public broadcast funding is specific to the circumstances of today's media environment in which there is abundant niche and noncommercial content.[16] Even among those who do not categorically oppose government subsidies for speech, some believe that the time for media subsidies has passed. Public television was created for a media environment dominated by three large broadcast networks. Programming was limited and generally tailored to mass tastes, with little programming targeted to niche audiences. It was the job of public broadcasting to serve these "unserved and underserved" audiences.[17] Beginning in the 1980s, cable channels began to provide niche programming. Discovery and Nickelodeon, among others, sought to provide roughly the same genres that public television had pioneered. In the face of this new abundance, public broadcasting critics began to argue that whatever need once existed for public media subsidies no longer did.

Defenders of public broadcasting counter these critiques with arguments that are passionate, if not always precise. On the general question of government support for speech, public broadcasting's friends draw on First Amendment traditions that treat the free speech clause as a command for positive governmental action as well as governmental restraint. According to these traditions, where the private sector either inhibits or fails to provide for robust speech opportunities, the government is obligated to step in to enlarge the sphere of free speech.[18] Thus, government subsidies for media that are designed to increase the diversity and reach of speech are friendly to, if not required by, First Amendment values. This view of governmental responsibilities with respect to public discourse is part of a larger progressive perspective on the role of government in shaping civil society and the relationship between markets and the public good. It is thus inevitable that the fortunes of public broadcasting are tied more generally to the political appeal of governmental activism.

With respect to the need for public media to supplement the market, public broadcasting's supporters reject the notion that media markets are now capable of providing the kind of diversity and reach that a robust democracy requires. The market failure argument in support of public media is no longer as simple as it once was—namely, that the scarcity of broadcast channels yields nothing but programming catering to mass tastes and neglects entire programming genres and audiences. Today, it takes on two additional postulates: (1) it is necessary to look beyond genre to assess whether or not distinct audience interests are being served; and (2) the media environment, although radically different than it was thirty years ago, remains dominated by a handful of large companies (content providers, television and broadband service providers, and search engines) whose profit orientation often prevents them from providing media content that is needed and not otherewise provided even by the burgeoning noncommercial contributors to cyberspace.

With respect to genre, opponents of public broadcast funding contend that the stalwart productions of public broadcasting are now duplicated to a large extent on outlets like the History Channel, Nickelodeon, HBO, and independent film channels on cable and the Internet. Supporters of continued funding for public broadcasting, on the other hand, assert that it is a mistake to equate similarity of genre with similarity of content. Even if commercial media provide programming within the same genre as public media, they say, the public media offerings are better, as borne out by opinion polls showing, for example, that "most Americans believe that public television provides high-quality programming that is more trustworthy, in-depth and less biased than any major commercial news network."[19] Other measures of value include the disproportionate share of awards that public television earns for its documentary, children's and arts programs, and the resources that public media are willing to invest in programming in order to maintain quality standards.

The most obvious difference between public media and commercial media offerings of the same genre, of course, is that public media programming is noncommercial. The extent to which public broadcasting remains noncommercial, notwithstanding its reliance on corporate underwriting support and associated promotions, is disputed. It is, however, safe to say that even where the sponsorship announcements for noncommercial programming look much like commercials, they rarely interrupt the programming and are therefore less obtrusive. More importantly, the organizational differences between commercial and noncommercial media impact the programming they produce. One of the most frequently noted constraints on commercial media content is the pressure that large publicly traded companies have to satisfy the short-term earnings expectations of shareholders. This pressure tends to reduce the willingness of companies to experiment with new forms or to support programming that does not quickly attract an audience.[20] Because public broadcasting is not subject to these pressures, there may be a greater willingness to experiment with programming that is not immediately "successful" and to invest in programming that may never be successful by commercial standards, but that nevertheless benefits society.[21]

An increasingly common critique of public broadcasting looks not to commercial television but to amateur and other noncommercial online media. It should be a source of considerable concern for public broadcasting institutions that many media critics who have been vigorous public broadcasting supporters are now more focused on exclusively online activities. In the online environment, the public interest concerns tend to be more structural than content-related. Public interest advocates are focused on ensuring that digital networks remain open to diverse and independent content providers (what has become known as "network neutrality") and that the law permits the creative manipulation of intellectual property. Many such advocates believe that podcasts, amateur video, collaboratively produced investigative reports, and other uniquely web-based content are important supplements to, and perhaps even substitutes for, public television content. Even more than the producers of noncommercial television, participants in the online media community can freely experiment, speak to niche audiences, create new genres, and produce for unpopular ones.

The limitations of noncommercial amateur productions and the continuing role for professionally produced media, either in television or the online environment, must be better understood and articulated. At first blush, there seem to be two principal limitations on the ability of online amateur media to substitute for public media productions.

The first is that the professional norms and regulations that shape public television do not control amateur online production. To receive federal funding, noncommercial television productions must comply with limitations on commercial sponsorship. Moreover, developed professional norms and regulations force disclosure of commercial and other interests that might influence public television programming. In the online world, by contrast, it is not clear to what extent commercial interests permeate productions that seem to be noncommercial. The owner of any website that displays advertising, for example, may tailor content to attract more advertising. Even bloggers and other amateur content providers that do not accept advertising may be paid, or otherwise motivated, to endorse certain products and services without disclosing such influence.[22]

Second, amateur productions will not always be appropriate substitutes for professional media content. The popularity of video sharing sites that rely heavily on amateur productions, such as YouTube, shows that amateur productions may serve tastes and constituencies underserved by mainstream media. Indeed, notable contributions have been made in the form of collaborative amateur productions, such as wikis and citizen journalism projects, in which dispersed individuals join forces to produce information that no professional team could amass.[23] Nevertheless, not all forms of production are amenable to such collective efforts. A one-hour public television documentary costs between half a million and one million dollars.[24] This figure doubles when producers undertake to integrate their films with community action and education, as PBS did with Bill Moyers's 2002 documentary, *On Our Own Terms*, about humane dying.[25] Other kinds of less resource-intensive documentaries are available. Indeed, *Frontline* itself, "public television's flagship public affairs series,"[26] is soliciting and featuring such work.[27] But these alternatives rarely provide the same kind of sustained, serious and accurate reporting as *Frontline*'s long form documentaries do. In general, there is a growing shortage of this kind of resource-intensive investigative journalism that was once a staple of the large daily newspapers.[28] It is in this area in particular that public media has the potential to serve otherwise underserved needs in the digital era.

In sum, while it is impossible to predict just how digital media will evolve and what gaps will remain, it is probable that neither the market nor non-commercial amateurs will deliver the full array of socially desirable media products and services. Ofcom, the British broadcast regulator, concluded in its study of broadcasting in the digital era that public service media will continue to be important even as media markets are better able to deliver the kinds of products that consumers desire. This is because what people demand as consumers will not meet "all of [their] needs as citizens."[29] This distinction between media as a mere consumer product and media as an instrument of democratic exchange and growth is fundamental to the theory behind public media funding.

Forms of Support

In addition to the controversies over the justifications for public broadcasting support, there are controversies surrounding the particular forms that support should take. In the United States, most governmental support for public broadcasting comes in the form of cash appropriations. Another, less widely recognized, form of support is relief from ordinary copyright liability.

The producers of public media programs, like all producers, must clear copyrights to program content. In many cases, particularly in the case of documentary works, the amount of content that public media producers must clear is unusually large because favorite public media genres like documentaries require archival footage and recordings. As part of the Copyright Act rewrite of 1976, Congress provided public broadcasters with several special copyright benefits out of concern that they lacked the means to secure rights clearances through market negotiations. The two most important rights that public broadcasters have are: (1) the right to use sound recordings without permission or payment in educational television and radio programs, so long as the programming is not "commercially distributed,"[30] and (2) a compulsory license to use "published non-dramatic musical works and published pictorial, graphic, and sculptural works" subject to payment of royalties set by a copyright royalty arbitration panel.[31]

Technological and business changes have rendered these copyright provisions less and less useful. Although their scope is not entirely clear, they seem to provide relief only for broadcast purposes. Since most public television content is now transmitted online or through other media, in addition to being broadcast, public broadcasters cannot generally rely on the statutory provisions. Moreover, even when the provisions do apply, their subject matter limitations do not conform to the kinds of content that public broadcasters typically use. Public broadcasters complain that they have great difficulty obtaining the appropriate rights bundle for new projects and, more importantly, that they cannot clear the rights to use preexisting public broadcasting content in new ways. A case in point is the award-winning civil rights documentary *Eyes on the Prize*, which fell out of circulation because the producer could not clear the rights to the music for additional broadcasts and other uses.

The restrictions on their rights to copy, perform, and transmit content also clearly limit the ability of public broadcasters to make their content freely available to the public once it has been transmitted. The BBC has launched a creative archive to provide free digital content to the public. It makes thousands of audio and video clips available to the public for noncommercial viewing, sharing, and editing.[32] American public television has made similar efforts through a project called the Open Media Network, but these efforts on both sides of the Atlantic are hampered by rights clearance problems.

At the same time that public broadcasters would like to see more robust access to copyrighted works, copyright owners question why public broadcasters should receive any special consideration in their exploitation of copyrights. Rightsholders argue that the use of copyrighted works, such as music or video clips, is a cost of business much like the use of electricity and water.

This controversy over whether public broadcasters should retain special copyright privileges and what their contours should be focuses heavily on the fundamental question of whether public broadcasting remains a vital part of the media landscape. For the reasons suggested above, public media does and will continue, in some form, to serve a unique function in our media environment. But that function must be better articulated and the public media institutions that discharge it must be reconfigured to operate more effectively in the digital age.

Public Media 2.0: Proposals for Reform

Public media remains necessary. Investments in public media help to support programming and services that the market will not and that nonmarket participants (e.g., amateurs) cannot. But the critics of public broadcasting are right to point out that the market failure justification for public media has not been specific enough. Exactly what kinds of media products does the market fail to deliver and, accordingly, what kinds of corrections ought the government to support? Moreover, beyond market failure, what is the role of public media in relation to democratic engagement? That is, what kinds of media products and services are worthy of public support, not because consumers demand them, but because, like art museums and libraries, they serve democratic aspirations?

These questions about the role of public media require sustained examination, possibly in the form of a new Carnegie Commission that can systematically survey the media landscape and identify the kinds of noncommercial services and content most needed to support a robust public discourse.

Whatever content and services public media ultimately provides in the long term, the following structural changes need to be made in the short term to support public media in the digital era: (1) public media funding needs to be separated from the broadcast platform; (2) the sphere of entities eligible for public media funding needs to be widened; and (3) copyright laws need to be revised to better reflect the realities of content usage today.

Redefining the Medium

Public broadcasting entities have gone a long way in recent years to diversify their offerings. PBS and local stations now have significant presences on the web and on other digital distribution platforms, where they stream programming, provide teacher guides and other educational material, post extensive historical and other program-related materials, and provide interactive tools and experiences, along with many other activities. "Broadcasting" is thus a very incomplete description of what entities that receive public broadcast funding actually do. As the amount of non-broadcasting activity increases, along with the ratio of broadcast to non-broadcast activity, it will be more accurate to think of "public broadcasting" as the media content and services that are provided by public broadcasting entities, no matter how this content is distributed or what form it takes.

With this transition from broadcasting to other delivery platforms and media formats, the question naturally arises: Why should public funding go to support broadcast infrastructure and stations when much of what these entities do is not broadcasting? And even where broadcasting is the central activity of these entities, why should public media funding be channeled to broadcasting? Although broadcasting remains an important method of distributing video programming, more than 85 percent of the public receives television programming through non-broadcast media. Hence, there is a growing mismatch between the structure of public media funding, which so strongly supports the broadcasting medium, and the way in which media products are actually delivered.

The current broadcast-centric system ought to be restructured so that a smaller percentage of government funding goes to broadcast station operations and facilities. One way to do this, as discussed below, is to revise the Public Broadcasting Act to enlarge the pool of entities eligible to receive funds. Unless the total pool of public media funding were to increase, broadcast station funding would have to fall. Whatever the political feasibility of increased funding, which has never been great, the case for strengthening support of public media must include a systematic study of media market failures in the context of democratic goals for an informed and active citizenry. Such a study could tell us, for example, whether resources now devoted to arts programming would be better spent on science programming or whether new funding is required for noncommercial online tools, such as search and social networking.

Even if public media funding were to increase, existing funding patterns need to be revised. Under the law as it now stands, multiple noncommercial television stations in any given broadcast market are eligible for federal funding, and every market has at least one station. Each must support staff and transmission equipment, and many stations also maintain production facilities. It is not only the infrastructure, which may be redundant, but also the programming. Most noncommercial television stations transmit the PBS-branded National Program Service, which they supplement to various degrees with other programming. To the extent that overlapping stations transmit distinctive programming, it may now be possible to aggregate that programming on a single station. Digital television enables stations to transmit multiple program streams in place of the single analog stream. In smaller television markets, where the population cannot support the full array of commercial networks, some television stations maintain dual affiliations and transmit programming streams from two networks. The same kind of sharing should be possible for the transmission of noncommercial programming, with one station absorbing the programming from formerly independent stations on its multiplex channels.

Reducing the number of stations in the system would free up federal dollars for other public media activities. The CPB "community service grants" that go to support public television station operations range from about $500,000 for a station in Cocoa, Florida, to more than $12 million for each of the largest stations in New York City and Los Angeles.[33] This does not include other annual CPB grants and special federal outlays for such purposes as station conversions to digital television facilities, which in 2006 totaled $32.7 million.[34] In addition, stations receive significant amounts of private funding and may receive state funds.

This is not to say that the public media system should be divorced from broadcasting. Broadcasting remains the sole broadband medium that is available virtually everywhere and for free. Broadcasters have other advantages relative to alternative media. Because they are physically located within a community and have longstanding ties to the community, broadcasters may be especially well-informed and sensitive to local issues and tastes. This local orientation often results in local programming and the development of local production talent. The value that broadcasting provides may justify maintaining at least one broadcast station in every television market but not more than one. And in some markets, there may be alternative forms of local infrastructure and commitment, as well as alternative ways to develop human capital, so that sustaining a local noncommercial broadcast station is less crucial. In many ways, the task of closing noncommercial stations may be like the task of closing military bases. Every community would like to keep its base for the benefits it provides, but the system as a whole requires painful streamlining.

Redefining Grantees

The bulk of federal funds for public media are channeled through broadcast stations and made directly to independent television producers. While these stations and producers typically include an online component in their media productions, they are principally focused on the television medium and on the delivery of content to passive audiences. In 1967, when broadcasting constituted the only form of electronic mass media, this made sense. It makes much less sense today when content producers can create for many media platforms and the audience can interact, and itself recreate, the content that it consumes.

There are two kinds of public media functions needed in the digital era and two possible models to sustain them. One function is the one that public media has always played: the provision of media content that supports citizenship in a democracy. Such content need have nothing to do with broadcast television, but might include blogs, podcasts, streaming, and all other forms of electronic media. Grantees of federal funds should not have to tie their works to television projects or otherwise produce in partnership with, or distribution on, broadcast television. Public broadcaster grantees currently struggle with how to adapt their models of production to the "participatory and social media tools" that are now available and that "allow the public to submit content and engage with programming."[35] This struggle raises questions about how much control public media professionals should exercise over the content that they sponsor, aggregate, and "produce." The rise of a new class of grantees of public media funding from outside the public broadcasting world could ease—and enlighten—this struggle by showcasing alternative methods of content production. Grantees who are starting from scratch, without the traditions of public broadcasting, will navigate the professional-amateur divide in very different ways from public broadcasting professionals.

The second function that public media should serve in the digital era is different from content production and quite new: to provide a noncommercial alternative to commercial search and aggregation. In today's media world, the number of content options has far outgrown the ability of an individual to take advantage of even a small fraction of new products and services. In *Beyond Broadcast: Expanding Public Media in the Digital Age*, the Center for Digital Democracy provides examples of the thousands of blogs, video-sharing sites, and Internet radio sites that take on some of the challenges public broadcasting has long assumed.[36] Most of these providers struggle to find an audience and are therefore of questionable relevance to the public media goal of forging shared experiences and citizen engagement. Those who guide individuals to content through such tools as search engines, online indexes, and recommendations have as much influence over media consumption today as do the producers themselves. These guides are the search engines and other services that channel attention based on a user's affinity group, past preferences, or various commercial interests. Given the centrality of the navigation function in an impossibly crowded media field, public media could play an important role in guiding attention to content that satisfies the needs of citizenship.

This may be the highest and best purpose of the august institutions of public broadcasting, especially PBS, which have built up brand loyalty and trust over so many decades. How these two functions—the creation of noncommercial media content and navigation tools—are supported is a question that requires new thinking. One possibility is to dismantle the current structure of public broadcast funding, overhaul the Public Broadcasting Act, and make the funding of public media simply a grant-giving project of the kind that the National Endowment for the Humanities undertakes. Under this model, broadcast stations would apply for grants, as would video bloggers, citizen journalists, and many others. This model has the advantage of removing some of the cumbersome and expensive bureaucracy that has accumulated in institutions like CPB. However, it has several disadvantages, not least of which is the political difficulty of scrapping the existing system of public media funding and starting anew.

Another disadvantage of a simple grant procedure is that it is not conducive to the building and maintenance of a nationwide system of public telecommunications. As part of a system, rather than just a collection of individual efforts, public broadcasting institutions are engaged in a nationwide effort to develop expertise, thematic concentrations in programming, a network of shared content, and nationwide telecommunications (broadcast) infrastructure support. A system of public media entails redundancy, as discussed above, but it also provides the benefits of coordinated effort.

Would it be possible to expand PBS membership to include not only public broadcast stations but also independent, noncommercial media producers active in any medium? Would it be possible to change the function of CPB so that it supports a system of public media that includes a wide variety of noncommercial grantees? Alternatively, should these institutions, or ones like them, exist alongside a separate mechanism to disburse federal funds for noncommercial media production and navigation? The answers to these questions will depend on the willingness of the existing public broadcasting institutions to change and the political will to change them.

Whatever formula is used to move the system toward new kinds of producers and media products, there should be one constant: All grantees should have to commit themselves to a noncommercial model. They should have to be organized as nonprofit organizations or individuals, and federal funds should be tied to advertising-free products and services. This noncommercial commitment is, in the end, the hallmark of public media and should remain at its core.

Redefining Support

In 2008, NPR launched a new service that allows users to access a wide array of NPR content, including audio from most of its programs dating back to 1995, as well as text, images, and other content from NPR and its member stations. In all, at the time of launch, there were more than 250,000 stories available for personal and noncommercial use.[37] Providing unrestricted noncommercial access to archival content is one of the most important contributions that public media can make to the public informational sphere. Especially at a time when commercial media providers are using their copyrights to restrict access to historically or culturally significant content, public media entities have a special role to play in preserving public access to past programs

Unfortunately, public broadcasters—and public television, in particular—have been unable to make many important programs available online, on DVD, or even on broadcast television due to rights restrictions. The special copyright exemptions and licenses discussed above that were supposed to facilitate the distribution of programming are too outdated to address the kinds of distribution now desired. Moreover, none of these provisions would apply to new public media grantees who are unattached to broadcast stations. The copyright laws should be revised so that federal grantees of public media funding have access to content on reasonable terms and can distribute public media content across all platforms.

There is another problem with the public broadcasting copyright provisions, beyond the fact that they are technologically obsolete: they say nothing about the obligations of public broadcasters to permit access to the content they create with the benefit of special copyright exemptions and licenses. Any entity that receives the benefit of special copyright laws should be required to return that benefit to the public in the form of generous permissions for follow-on creativity. That is, an individual should not only be able to access archival content from a public media entity but should be free to incorporate reasonable portions of that content into new noncommercial productions. In this way, there is a reciprocity of copyright. The creative community must accept reduced copyright protection for works that are incorporated into public media content but can expect increased access to and use of that content when it is released. In sum, the copyright law should be modified to ensure that public media producers have access to video, audio, and graphic inputs on reasonable terms and that the public in turn has access to the content thereby produced.

The mission of public media should remain in the future, as it has been in the past, to nurture new talent, support a diversity of voices, provide noncommercial media content and experiences that are important for social flourishing, and ensure access to these products and services for all Americans. The public media output that is called for, and the entities and individuals that provide it, need to change in the digital age. New forms of media production, new capabilities for media interaction, and market evolution require a new openness to models of public media. In addition, it must be made clear that the value of public media should be measured not by commercial ratings but by criteria of "public value." In other words, what is new in what public media has provided, and how have these productions and tools created value for the public? This chapter has provided some ideas for how public media ought to evolve, but empirical work is needed to help articulate the mission of public media with more specificity and to set appropriate funding priorities. In particular, we need to know where there are shortcomings in commercial offerings and what form of support is needed for noncommercial media.

Notes

1. Reform proposals with a good understanding of new media and the role of independent media can be found in Center for Digital Democracy, "Beyond Broadcast: Expanding Public Media in the Digital Age" (1 February 2006), www.democraticmedia .org/issues/public_media/beyond_broadcast (28 July 2008).

2. *A Public Trust: The Report of the Carnegie Commission on the Future of Public Broadcasting* (New York: Bantam Books, 1979), 33–35.

3. *The Report and Recommendations of the Carnegie Commission on Educational Television: Public Television, A Program For Action* (New York: Harper & Row, 1967).

4. The Carnegie Commission hoped for noncommercial programming that would "deepen a sense of community in local life ... show us our community as it really is ... bring into the home meetings ... where people of the community express their hopes, their protests, their enthusiasms, and their will." *Public Television, A Program For Action*, 92–99.

5. *Public Television, A Program For Action*, 3 (finding that "a well-financed and well-directed educational television system, substantially larger and far more pervasive and effective than that which now exists in the United States, must be brought into being if the full needs of the American public are to be served").

6. Public Broadcasting Policy Base, "E. B. White's Letter To Carnegie I," Letter from E. B. White, to Stephen White, Assistant to Chairman, Carnegie Commission (26 September 1966), www.current.org/pbpb/carnegie/EBWhiteLetter.html (28 July 2008).

7. 47 U.S.C. § 396(a)(5) (2000) (providing that to further the general welfare, noncommercial television should be "responsive to the interests of people both in particular localities and throughout the United States, [and] which will constitute an expression of diversity and excellence").

8. See, e.g., 47 C.F.R. § 73.621 (2000) (a noncommercial educational television station will be licensed "upon a showing that the proposed stations will be used primarily to serve the educational needs of the community; for the advancement of educational programs; and to furnish a nonprofit and noncommercial television broadcast service").

9. 47 U.S.C. § 396 (2000) (authorizing the establishment of a nonprofit Corporation for Public Broadcasting to funnel federal funds to noncommercial television and radio stations and producers).

10. www.cpb.org/aboutcpb/goals/.

11. Willard D. Rowland Jr., "The Institution of U.S. Public Broadcasting," in *Public Television in America*, ed. Eli M. Noam and Jens Waltermann (Germany: Bertelsmann Foundation, 1998), 14.

12. Chris Johnson, "Federal Support of Public Broadcasting: Not Quite What LBJ Had in Mind," 8 *CommLaw Conspectus* 135 (2000): 138–40 (criticizing public television for political bias and a failure to garner a larger audience); Howard White, "Fine Tuning the Federal Government's Role in Public Broadcasting," 46 *Fed. Comm. L.J.* 491 (1994): 501–3, 513 (discussing congressional attempts to eliminate funding for public television and criticizing public broadcastings' overreliance on its most popular programming).

13. "Completing the Digital Television Transition: Hearing Before the Senate Comm. on Commerce, Sci. and Transp.," 108th Congress (2004) (testimony of John M. Lawson, president and CEO, Association of Public Television Stations), commerce.senate.gov/hearings/testimony.cfm?id=1220&wit_id=3514 (28 July 2008).

14. 47 U.S.C. § 396(g)(1)(A) (2000); Ken Auletta, "Big Bird Flies Right," *New Yorker*, 7 June 2004, 42 (reporting on political pressure exerted on PBS for allegedly left-leaning programming).

15. See, e.g., Statement of David Boaz, Executive Vice President, Cato Institute, before the Committee on Appropriations Subcommittee on Labor, Health and Human Services, Education, and Related Agencies, U.S. Senate, 11 July 2005, "Ending Taxpayer Funding for Public Broadcasting" ("When government brings us the news—with all the inevitable bias and spin—the government is putting its thumb on the scales of democracy").

16. Ellen P. Goodman, "Media Policy Out of the Box: Content Abundance, Attention Scarcity, and the Failures of Digital Markets," 19 *Berkeley Technology Law Journal* 1939 (2004).

17. 47 U.S.C. § 396(a)(6) (2000).

18. Cass R. Sunstein, *Democracy and the Problem of Free Speech* (New York: Free Press 1995), 18–19

19. James Barksdale and Hundt, *Digital Future Initiative: Challenges and Opportunities for Public Service Media in the Digital Age* (15 December 2005), 23.

20. Robert W. McChesney, *The Problem of the Media: U.S. Communication Politics in the Twenty-First Century* (New York: Monthly Review Press, 2004)

21. Meredith C. Hightower, "Beyond Lights and Wires in a Box: Ensuring the Existence of Public Television," 3 *Journal of Law & Policy* 133, 137 (1994) (noncommercial television may be a forum for programming that takes creative risks).

22. Jack Neff, "P&G Relies on Power of Mommy Bloggers; Giant Calls Them the 'New Influencers,'" *Advertising Age*, 14 July 2008.

23. Yochai Benkler, *The Wealth of Networks* (New Haven, CT: Yale University Press, 2006), 219–55 (describing collaborative production of Internet media); Dan Hunter and Gregory F. Lastowka, "Amateur-to-Amateur," 46 *William & Mary Law Review* 951 (2004).

24. Edward Nawotka, "TV Documentary Chornicles Indies' Challenges," *Publishers Weekly* 255:24 (16 June 2008) (estimating typical budget for an hour-long PBS documentary at $600,000); Stephen Smith, "What the Hell is a Radio Documentary?," *Nieman Report* 55:3 (31 December 2001) (estimating public television documentary budgets to be between $100,000 and over $1 million).

25. Ellen P. Goodman, "Media Policy Out of the Box: Content Abundance, Attention Scarcity, and the Failures of Digital Markets," 19 *Berkeley Technology Law Journal* 1389, 1469 (2004).

26. *Frontline*, www.pbs.org/wgbh/pages/frontline/us/.

27. *Frontline*, www.pbs.org/wgbh/pages/frontline.

28. Lili Levi, "In Search of Regulatory Equilibrium," 35 *Hofstra Law Review* 1321, 1326 (2007) (describing the economic pressures that have led to a reduction in investigative journalism).

29. Ofcom review of public service television broadcasting phase 3 (8 February 2005), 2.32

30. 17 U.S.C. § 114(b) (2006).

31. 17 U.S.C. § 118 (d) (2006). In addition, of course, public broadcasters can and do rely on the fair use doctrine when using content.

32. BBC, "Building Public Value: Renewing the BBC for the Digital World at 60–63" (June 2004), www.bbc.co.uk/foi/docs/bbc_constitution/bbc_royal_charter _and_agreement/Building_Public_Value.pdf, accessed 28 July 2008.

33. Corporation for Public Broadcasting, 2006 Annual Report, CPB 2006 Grants and Allocations.

34. www.cpb.org/aboutcpb/finacials/funding.

35. Center for Social Media, Rapporteur Report, "Beyond Broadcast: Reinventing Public Media in a Participatory Culture" (12–13 May 2006), centerforsocialmedia .org/documents/BeyondBroadcastRapporteurReport.pdf (28 July 2008).

36. Center for Digital Democracy, "Beyond Broadcast."

15

Creating a Media Policy Agenda for the Digital Generation

Kathryn Montgomery

THE RAPID GROWTH OF THE INTERNET AND proliferation of digital technologies are creating a powerful new media culture. Young people are in many ways the defining users of this new culture, the quintessential "early adopters" of new technology, eagerly embracing a host of digital tools, integrating them into their daily lives, and forging a new set of cultural practices that are quickly moving into the mainstream. They are especially avid users of Web 2.0 participatory media—MySpace, YouTube, Facebook, and the like. Social networking sites are among the fastest-growing platforms, particularly among young people. Facebook grew 125 percent in a single year and now reports more than fifty-seven million users.[1] MySpace recently boasted having seventy-two million unique U.S. monthly visitors to its popular site.[2]

Digital media are also playing an increasingly important role in the socialization of youth. The features of interactive media are especially appealing to young people because they tap into such key developmental needs as identity exploration, self-expression, peer relationships and independence. A study by Forrester Research found that youth incorporate digital media into their lives at a faster rate than any other age group. "All generations adopt devices and Internet technologies, but younger consumers are Net natives," one of the report's co-authors explained to the press. They don't just go online; they "live online."[3]

The public policy debate over children and new media continues to be dominated by Internet safety, fueled by persistent fears about pornography and predators.[4] For more than a decade, policymakers at the federal and local levels have launched dozens of efforts aimed at protecting children from these Internet harms.[5] Recently, the attorneys general of forty-nine states and the District of Columbia have been focusing intense efforts on MySpace, Facebook, and other popular social networking platforms, eliciting a series of agreements with the companies to add safety features.[6] AOL, AT&T, Facebook, Google, Microsoft, MySpace, Yahoo, and other media corporations recently partnered with Harvard's Berkman Center for Internet and Society to create a new Internet Safety Task Force.[7]

This ongoing public focus on Internet safety—driven by the media—has diverted attention away from a broader understanding of the role of digital media in the lives of young people. The transition to the Digital Age provides us with a unique opportunity to rethink the position of children in the media culture, and in society as a whole. While in the past, the focus was primarily on seeing children and youth as passive recipients of media *content*, the new media system enables young people to be much more active participants and co-creators of content. Many have eagerly embraced the web as an electronic canvas to showcase their writing, music, artwork, and other creations to the infinite audiences of cyberspace. Indeed, a growing body of literature documents how children, teens, and young adults are seizing a host of new digital tools—from blogs to mobile phones to social networks—to mobilize young voters, launch activist campaigns, and orchestrate congressional letter-writing efforts.[8] As they come of age in this new digital media environment, the values, behaviors, and practices they adopt will carry with them into adulthood, helping to shape the next generation of media and its relationship to the public.

As was the case with earlier media technologies, whether the Internet fulfills its potential will be determined not only by technological advances but also by political and economic forces. As a public medium, the Internet is really only a little more than a decade old. Its dramatic growth during that period parallels the rapid penetration of television a half-century ago. Like television, the Internet has brought about enormous societal changes, many of which are just being understood. But this new medium is by no means static. The Internet as we know it is undergoing a fundamental transformation. A new "dot-com boom" is underway, and it is fueling a resurgence of the digital marketplace while triggering dramatic consolidation and reconfiguration in the communications, media, high-technology, and advertising industries. Venture capitalists are spending billions of dollars to fund new "Web 2.0," startups, invest in next-generation content and services, and perfect the interactive advertising business models that are quickly becoming state-of-the-art.[9] More and more U.S. households are adopting high-speed Internet connections through cable or DSL, and mobile technologies are swiftly taking hold throughout the population, moving us further into the multiplatform broadband era and creating a digital media system that is increasingly portable, participatory, and ubiquitous.

Children and adolescents are positioned at the epicenter of this booming new digital marketplace, considered, as they are, a highly lucrative target market of "digital natives" setting trends for the future. Already, U.S. children under twelve spend some $18 billion annually, a total that is projected to reach $21.4 billion by 2010. Families, moreover, spend more than $115 million on consumer goods for children annually.[10]

A large youth marketing research infrastructure—composed of leading global corporations, advertising agencies, trend-analysis companies, and digital strategists—is engaged in ongoing, large-scale efforts to study how children and adolescents are interacting with new media, making today's generation of young people the most intensely analyzed demographic group in the history of advertising.[11] While academic scholars are just beginning to explore seriously the relationship between young people and new media, the market research industry continues to outpace them, employing an increasingly diverse array of specialists in sociology, psychology, and anthropology to explore youth subcultures and conduct motivational research. Marketers are keeping very close tabs on how young people interact with new media, cultivating relationships with them in order to develop new content and services that serve their needs and interests and create more effective vehicles for targeting them. Consequently, marketing and advertising have become a pervasive presence in youth digital culture.

The forces of the market are profoundly shaping the next generation of interactive technologies. Decisions made in the next few years—by industry and by policymakers—will have a far-reaching impact on how the twenty-first-century media system socializes young people into two key roles—citizens and consumers.

This chapter will focus on creating a framework of consumer safeguards for children and adolescents in the growing digital marketplace. I will first describe some of the major trends and practices that are shaping the new interactive market and discuss their implications for children and adolescents. I will then briefly review the history of children's advertising and marketing policy in the United States. I will then address two especially urgent issues—food marketing and privacy policy—in which prompt intervention could have the most significant and long-term impact on young people. Finally, I offer some suggestions for creating a broader policy agenda on behalf of children and youth in the new media.

The Digital Marketing Ecosystem

The expansion of digital media in children's lives has created what the industry calls a new "media and marketing ecosystem" that encompasses mobile devices, broadband video, social networks, instant messaging, video games, and virtual three-dimensional worlds. The forms of advertising, marketing, and selling that are emerging in the new media are distinct from the more familiar forms of commercial advertising and promotion on children's television. One of the buzzwords in contemporary digital marketing is the "360 strategy," designed to take advantage of young peoples' constant connectivity to technology, their multitasking behaviors (e.g., text messaging on tiny keyboards while simultaneously watching television), and the fluidity of their media experiences. Marketers are not just tapping into these new patterns but also actively cultivating and promoting them for their own purposes by creating synergistic, cross-platform campaigns designed to "drive" engagement from one medium to another, fostering ongoing relationships with brands. Thus, digital marketing increasingly permeates every aspect of children's lives, reaching and engaging them repeatedly wherever they are—in cyberspace, listening to music via a portable player, or watching television.

Behavioral profiling is another core tactic that companies employ to target teens, a lynchpin of many digital media campaigns. Marketers can compile a detailed profile of each customer, including demographic data, purchasing behavior, responses to advertising messages, and even the extent and nature of social networks. Employing a variety of new "measurement" tools, marketers and their advertising agencies can learn how individual users and very discrete groups respond to advertising and marketing. Offline and online databases can be joined, permitting almost a continuous focus group presence.[12]

Food and Beverage Marketers Target Youth

The food and beverage industry is playing a major leadership role in the new global digital marketing frontier, directing a number of major R&D initiatives to create the next generation of interactive advertising, much of it tailored specifically for young people. A study by the Berkeley Media Studies Group and the Center for Digital Democracy, released in May 2007, identified a panoply of new practices that major brands are using to target young people through digital media.[13] The following is only a brief snapshot of recent and current marketing efforts by some of the top fast food, soft drink, and snack food brands popular with children and teens, offering a glimpse into the variety of digital techniques that are quickly becoming state-of-the-art in the contemporary media environment.

Mobile marketing is one of the fastest growing advertising platforms for reaching young people, enabling companies to directly target users based on previous buying history, location, and other profiling data.[14] McDonald's conducted a mobile marketing campaign that urged young cell phone users to text-message to a special phone number to receive an instant electronic coupon for a free McFlurry. Youth were encouraged to "download free cell phone wallpaper and ring tones featuring top artists," and to e-mail the promotional website link to their friends.[15]

KFC (aka Kentucky Fried Chicken) used a high-pitched tone as a promotional "buzz" device for a recent "interactive advertising campaign." The Mosquito Tone was embedded in television commercials to launch KFC's new Boneless Variety Bucket. When inserted into the television commercial, the tones—too high-pitched for most adults to hear—were designed to attract the attention of young viewers and "drive" them to a website, where they could enter a contest to identify exactly where the tones could be heard in the advertisement in order to win $10 "KFC gift checks" redeemable for the new chicken meal at any KFC.[16]

Food and beverage companies have created their own online branded entertainment sites, seamlessly weaving a variety of interactive content with product pitches and cartoon "spokescharacters."[17] With the growth of broadband technology, these digital playgrounds have evolved into highly sophisticated "immersive" experiences, including entire programs and "channels" built around brands.[18] MyCoke.com, for example, offers a multitude of interactive activities to engage teens, including chat, music downloading and mixing, user-generated video, blogs, and its own currency. Coca-Cola worked with interactive marketing expert Studiocom (part of the WPP Group) to create Coke Studios, a "massive multiplayer online environment" where "teens hang out as their alter-identities, or 'v-egos.'"[19]

Marketers are also creating "viral videos" to promote their brands through peer-to-peer networks and video sharing services like YouTube. In some cases, the sponsoring company is identified, while in others, it is disguised. Wendy's, for example, placed several "commercials masquerading as videos" on YouTube, specifically designed to attract "young consumers." While Wendy's own corporate name was not connected to the intentionally humorous videos, users who watched them were sent to a special website for "Wendy's 99-cent value menu."[20]

In-game advertising, or "game-vertising," is a highly sophisticated, finely tuned strategy that combines product placement, behavioral targeting, and viral marketing to forge ongoing relationships between brands and individual gamers. Marketing through interactive games works particularly well for snack, beverage, and other "impulse" food products. Coca-Cola, Pepsi, Mountain Dew, Gatorade, McDonald's, Burger King, and KFC, for example, were the "most recalled brands" in an October 2006 survey of video game players.[21] Not only can marketers incorporate their brands into the storylines of popular games, they can also use software that enables them to respond to a player's actions in real time, changing, adding, or updating advertisements to tailor their message to that particular individual.[22] Sony partnered with Pizza Hut to build into its "Everquest II" video game the ability to order pizza. "All the player has to do is type in the command 'pizza,' and voila—Pizza Hut's online order page pops up," explained a trade article.[23]

History of Children's Advertising Regulation

The explosion in interactive marketing over the last decade comes amid minimal government and industry oversight. The safeguards that are currently in place offer very few protections for children against unfair and manipulative practices by digital marketers and virtually no protection at all for adolescents. In many other countries, children's advertising has been strictly regulated, especially in television, where government-run broadcasting systems have established restrictions and, in some cases, complete bans on television advertising aimed at this vulnerable group of consumers.[24] In the United States, however, advertisers have enjoyed considerable freedom to target children, with little interference from the government. In the 1970s, child advocacy and public health groups grew increasingly concerned that the growing number of television commercials promoting sugared cereals, snacks, and candies were harmful to children's dental health. Social science research documented the special vulnerabilities of young children to the powerful appeals of marketers.[25] Armed with this evidence, advocates petitioned both the Federal Trade Commission (FTC) and the Federal Communications Commission (FCC)— the two agencies that shared jurisdiction over broadcast advertising—to develop regulations for controlling television commercials.

The impact of these campaigns was mixed. Despite forceful industry opposition, the FCC passed a set of guidelines in 1974 to govern television advertising practices targeted at children twelve and under. The Children's Policy Statement limits commercial time in children's television programming and addresses a handful of particularly egregious commercial practices, such as host selling. Passage of the Children's Television Act in 1990 codified these time limits (twelve minutes per hour during weekday children's programming and ten and a half minutes on weekends), and extended them to cable television.[26] But advocates did not succeed in convincing regulators to restrict the growth of "program-length commercials," in which toy companies established economic tie-ins with children's programmers, their efforts to sway the FCC completely thwarted. When the agency launched a rulemaking procedure in 1978 to consider a ban on children's television advertising, the broadcast, advertising and food industries went directly to Congress and were successful in getting policymakers not only to stop the proceeding but also to weaken the powers of the regulatory agency.[27]

In response to the public controversy and pressure over children's advertising, the advertising industry established a self-regulatory body to deflect criticism, preempt any further regulatory attempts, and monitor industry compliance with the guidelines governing television commercials. The mission of the Children's Advertising Review Unit (CARU) is to ensure "truthful, non-deceptive advertising to children under the age of 12." The agency has tended to conduct its business narrowly, responding to public complaints about errant TV advertisers, but only within the limited framework of existing weak government rules.[28]

Consumer, health, and child advocacy groups have been able to institute some digital marketing safeguards for children. The Children's Online Privacy Protection Act (COPPA), enacted in 1998, was the first federal law to regulate children's privacy on the Internet, the result of an intense advocacy campaign launched by the Center for Media Education and other consumer and privacy groups.[29] That law gave the FTC the authority to develop and implement rules restricting commercial website operators' ability to collect "personally identifiable information" (e.g., e-mail, name, address, etc.) from children under the age of thirteen.[30] Under the law's safe harbor provision, self-regulatory organizations, including CARU, TRUSTe, and others, were allowed to develop their own guidelines and processes for enforcing the COPPA rules, as long as the FTC approved them in advance.[31]

With the transition to digital broadcasting, the FCC conducted a series of hearings and rulemaking procedures to consider how existing public interest obligations should be extended into the digital era. In 2003, the Children's Media Policy coalition—which included Children Now, the American Psychological Association, the American Academy of Pediatrics, and the National PTA—called on the commission to establish rules for governing interactive advertising on digital television.[32] As was the case with the earlier "kidvid" policy debates in the 1970s and 1980s, the debates leading up to the creation of the children's television digital rules were highly contentious. The television industry filed suit against the FCC's first set of rules, arguing that they were too strict; children's groups countered with their own suit, labeling the regulations too weak. Ultimately, after a series of negotiations between advocacy and industry representatives, a compromise settlement was hammered out and submitted to the FCC for approval. The outcome was a set of limited provisions on the amount and type of commercial content allowed on web pages whose links are displayed in children's commercials.[33]

As the digital marketing system continues to intrude further into young peoples' lives, U.S. regulations are ill-equipped to deal with its impact on children's health and well-being. While the rules for digital television advertising offer some modest protections for younger children against exploitive commercialization in interactive television, their scope remains limited by the weak and narrow regulations that have governed advertising on children's television. Furthermore, they apply only to television programs and their affiliated websites, not to the web itself. Though COPPA has forced many online marketers to curtail some of their data collection practices targeted at young children, it established no such protections for adolescents.[34]

Public Health and Personal Privacy

The next few years provide an important opportunity to develop commercial safeguards for children and teens, particularly in two key areas—public health and personal privacy. In both areas, policy debates and policymaking processes are already underway. But there is a strong need to ensure that any policies enacted will address the contemporary nature of digital marketing, as well as the segments of the child and adolescent populations in most need of protection.

The Impact of Digital Marketing on Children's Health

Childhood obesity has become a major epidemic in the United States. Experts have become increasingly alarmed by the dramatic rise in weight levels and associated illnesses among youth over the last thirty years.[35] According to research by the U.S. Department of Health and Human Services, the most overweight children in recent surveys are "markedly heavier" than those in previous studies. Obesity also disproportionately affects certain minority youth populations.[36] The health costs of these trends are staggering, both to individual children and to society at large.[37] If current trends continue, health experts warn, this generation of children may be the first in modern history that will not live as long as its parents.[38]

While experts have identified a host of economic, social, and environmental changes that have taken place during the last three decades that have combined to create the current health epidemic, there is a growing body of evidence that food and beverage advertising—particularly for "high-calorie, low-nutrient" products—has played a significant role in the disturbing shift in the overall nutritional intake of children and adolescents. Young people now consume high levels of saturated fat, sugars, and salt, and low levels of fruit and vegetables.[39]

The government is spearheading a number of initiatives aimed at addressing the role of food marketing in children's health. Under a direct mandate from Congress in 2004, the Centers for Disease Control and Prevention commissioned the Institute of Medicine to conduct a comprehensive study of the role of marketing in food consumption among children. A year later, the Institute released its report, *Food Marketing to Children and Youth: Threat or Opportunity?*, which found a direct connection between food and beverage marketing and children's dietary patterns.[40] The study's recommendations included issuing a strong warning to the food industry to change its advertising practices, mainly on television. No such recommendation was made about digital marketing practices.[41] The FTC and the U.S. Department of Health and Human Services have held a series of workshops with industry and consumer groups over the last several years, urging food and beverage companies to engage in more responsible production, packaging, and marketing practices.[42] Under congressional mandate, the FTC has issued subpoenas to a number of food and beverage and quick-service restaurant companies to provide data about their marketing practices, which it will be reporting back to Congress.[43] (Advocates have urged the FTC to include digital marketing within the scope of its investigation.) The FCC established a Task Force on Media and Childhood Obesity, composed of food and ad industry representatives, consumer groups, and health experts.[44] The emphasis at both of these regulatory agencies is to encourage better self-policing by the industry, rather than to propose new government rules to guide food marketing.

Amid this mounting public pressure, food manufacturers and media companies have launched a flurry of high-profile initiatives, including campaigns to promote health and fitness among children and changes in some of these industries' marketing practices.[45] Many of these efforts have garnered support and approval from public health professionals and federal regulators.[46] But while they are steps in the right direction, they are not enough. For example, the revised Children's Advertising Review Unit guidelines do include some provisions related to interactive marketing, but they are very limited and will most likely result in only minor alterations of online children's advertising. It is doubtful whether they will affect most of the new marketing strategies that have become state-of-the-art.[47]

One of the biggest weaknesses of the industry's self-regulation programs is that they apply only to advertising that is targeted exclusively at children twelve and under. The nutritional health problems facing America's young people, however, cannot be addressed by narrowly focusing attention only on the youngest segment of the youth population. The Institute of Medicine's comprehensive study was concerned with food consumption by all children, eighteen and under.[48] Adolescents may be even more at risk of consuming a high-calorie, low-nutrient diet than younger children. Teens spend more of their own money on food, make more of their food choices independently of their parents, and do more of their food consumption outside of the home. Food marketers can now target teens through a variety of new digital venues, completely bypassing any parental oversight.

The health crisis facing America's children and adolescents is not simply a matter of bad nutritional choices by individuals or families. It is part of a broad pattern of consumption that is affecting large segments of the youth population, and that will likely follow this generation into their lives as adults. We cannot afford to wait another decade to see if the rates of obesity and disease have risen further. Without meaningful systemic changes now, the risk to future generations may even be greater.

Protecting the Privacy of Youth Online

Contemporary digital marketing practices also seriously threaten young people's privacy. While COPPA offers some protective mechanisms for children below the age of thirteen, adolescents are completely left out of government policies and corporate self-regulatory programs. Consequently, they are now routinely subjected to some of the most extensive data collection and behavioral targeting in the current media environment.[49] For example, 360 Youth (part of Alloy Media + Marketing) promises marketers a "powerful and efficient one-stop-shopping resource" and access to more than thirty-one million teens, tweens, and college students. Its arsenal of advertising and marketing weapons includes "e-mail marketing strategy and implementation," viral applications, interactive and multiplayer games, and quizzes and polls. The company operates a stable of websites that serve as online data collection and youth marketing research tools, with clients that include Coca-Cola, Domino's Pizza, Frito-Lay, General Mills, Hershey, Kellogg's, Kraft, MTV, Nabisco, Paramount Pictures, Verizon Wireless, and Procter & Gamble.[50]

With more and more teens living their lives on MySpace, Facebook, and other social networking platforms, "social media marketing" has become one of the most important new venues for behavioral profiling. The ability to capture detailed data about youth behavior online explains why Rupert Murdoch's News Corp. (Fox TV) paid nearly $600 million to acquire MySpace in 2006. One trade publication, reporting on the high-profile deal, noted that "the digital gold inside of MySpace wasn't the number of users, but the information they're providing," including "demographic and psychographic data that Fox Interactive can use" to identify "the brand preferences of young people on the Web."[51] In addition to basic demographics, marketers can glean a wealth of "enormously rich" data—including personal relationships, ethnicity, religion, political leanings, sexual orientation, and smoking and drinking habits. MySpace offers marketers a sophisticated system of "hypertargeting" that monitors what members are saying on their profiles and combines that information with data on groups they belong to, age, gender, and friends, to offer advertisers more precise targeting opportunities.[52] Facebook, which began as a platform exclusively for college students, has recently opened itself up to everyone, attracting a large number of teenagers. Not surprisingly, outside advertising companies have zeroed in on Facebook's user base, taking advantage of arrangements in which Facebook gives third-party developers access to the profile data of users.[53]

These trends have sparked increasing concern from consumer and child advocacy groups, which have called upon regulators to investigate the growth of behavioral targeting and to develop effective safeguards, not only for youth, but for all consumers. In 2006, the nonprofit Center for Digital Democracy (CDD) and U.S. Public Interest Research Group (USPIRG) filed a complaint with the FTC, calling for "an immediate, formal investigation of online advertising practices," urging it specifically to investigate a set of new advertising initiatives at Microsoft.[54] The following year, CDD and USPIRG provided documentation of the growth of data collection and profiling practices aimed at adolescents on social networks, asking the FTC to address specifically the impact of new digital advertising practices on youth. In a separate filing in 2007, CDD, USPIRG, and the Electronic Privacy Information Center (EPIC) petitioned the FTC to block the merger of Google and DoubleClick unless it obtained meaningful privacy policies from the companies as part of a consent decree. Though the FTC ultimately approved the merger, it conducted several workshops on behavioral targeting, which helped raise interest in the issue among the press and in the policy arena.[55]

In December 2007, as a direct outcome of the consumer group petitions, FTC staff issued a set of proposed self-regulatory "Online Behavioral Advertising Privacy Principles," calling for public comments on a number of concerns raised in the public proceedings. Among the issues identified in the proposed principles were how to classify "sensitive" data and what measures companies should be required to take in handling such data. The FTC staff suggested that "[c]ompanies should only collect sensitive data for behavioral advertising if they obtain affirmative express consent from the consumer to receive such advertising." In addition to medical information, sensitive data could include "children's activities."[56]

In response to renewed government attention to privacy concerns, a few individual companies, as well as industry-wide organizations, have developed new self-regulatory guidelines. Both Facebook and MySpace, for example, have made some alterations in their privacy policies.[57] The Network Advertising Initiative (NAI) has proposed revisions to its self-regulatory guidelines that would prohibit behavioral targeting of children under the age of thirteen.[58]

While these are steps in the right direction, neither the industry nor the FTC has addressed the special privacy issues concerning adolescents raised by these new behavioral targeting practices. Many teens go online to seek help for their personal problems, to explore their sexual identity, to find support groups for handling emotional crises in their lives, and, sometimes, to talk about things they do not feel comfortable or safe discussing with their parents. Yet this increased reliance on the Internet subjects them to wholesale data collection and profiling. The unprecedented ability of digital technologies to track and profile individuals across the media landscape, and to engage in "micro" or "nano" targeting, puts these young people at special risk of having their privacy compromised.

As a coalition of prominent child advocacy and health groups explained in an April 2008 filing with the FTC: "Although adolescents are more sophisticated consumers than young children are, they face their own age-related vulnerabilities regarding privacy."[59] The prevailing formula embraced by industry and endorsed by regulators is rooted in the concept of "notice and choice." It is based on the expectation that consumers will read the privacy policies that online companies post on their websites, and if they do not like the terms, they will "opt out." But most privacy policies offer no real choice; instead, they are presented as "take-it-or-leave-it" propositions. Surveys have shown that most adults don't read, nor can they readily understand, the often confusing, technical legalese that characterizes these policies.[60] For underaged youth, these challenges are further complicated. As the children's coalition filing points out, "teenagers, who have less education and are less likely to make the effort to read privacy policies," are "less willing to forgo learning about or protecting against behavioral advertising practices . . . in order to move quickly and freely access Web sites and socially interact." Social networks have created privacy settings that create a false sense of security for teens. While young people may believe they are protecting their privacy, they remain totally unaware of the nature and extent of data collection, online profiling, and behavioral advertising that are becoming routine in these online communities. Finally, as the children's coalition filing pointed out, "[m]any areas of the law recognize that minors are at a disadvantage when it comes to reading, understanding, and consenting to legal documents. For instance, a common law doctrine in contract law makes agreements that minors enter into 'voidable'—that is, because minors cannot consent to contracts as meaningfully as adults can, they may cancel any contracts they enter into."[61]

Clearly, government has a role to play in protecting adolescents' privacy. The proposals presented by the coalition of children and health groups, all of which would be within the agency's current statutory authority, would be an appropriate and necessary initial step for the FTC to take. These would include adopting, as part of the industry's voluntary guidelines, a definition of "sensitive data" to include "the online activities of all persons under the age of eighteen," and prohibiting "the collection of sensitive information for behavioral advertising purposes." The groups have also called on the FTC to monitor "whether the industry is following these voluntary guidelines, and, if they are not, initiate a rulemaking proceeding to prohibit the collection of data concerning the activities of persons under the age of eighteen for behavioral advertising purposes."[62]

Even younger children may not be fully protected against the privacy threats posed by the latest generation of behavioral targeting practices. Although the FTC children's privacy rule, which went into effect in 2000, predated the emergence and growth of today's data collection and profiling techniques, it was designed to adapt itself to changing industry practices. "Using persistent identifiers (such as customer numbers held in cookies) to collect information to send individual children highly targeted ads," explains the children's coalition filing, "clearly fits within part (F) of the statutory definition of 'personal information,' even absent combination with a child's name, e-mail address, etc."[63] Thus, the coalition is urging the commission to revisit and clarify its COPPA rule to ensure that it addresses the most recent changes in industry practices and will continue to protect children under the age of thirteen in the expanding digital media marketplace.

Promoting the Healthy Development of Children and Youth

We have a relatively brief period in which to create policies and marketing standards that could help guide the development and growth of the digital media culture for the twenty-first century. The dramatic changes in media distribution and advertising technologies require a comprehensive and systematic approach. An overall goal should be to create a media system that promotes the healthy development of children and youth. Regardless of their recent public commitments, the food, advertising, and media industries cannot be expected to develop adequate consumer protections on their own. Self-regulation is always reactive. Adjustments are made to certain controversial practices in order to placate critics, deflect pressure, and preempt government regulation. But when pressures have subsided, and the public spotlight has been diverted elsewhere, the concern is that industry policing may be relaxed. When the potential for profit-making is great, as it is in the children and teen market, these industries are likely to return to business as usual mode or devise new practices to circumvent public scrutiny. Industry self-regulation will only work if it is developed and implemented in the context of strong governmental and public oversight. The responsibility will, therefore, fall on government, educators, health professionals, child advocates, and consumer groups to monitor closely the emerging practices in contemporary marketing and to develop interventions that can effectively minimize the harm that any of these practices may have on America's children.

Several steps should be taken in the short term to enable the United States to move toward a fair and equitable media and marketing system for children and youth. The appropriate congressional committees should hold hearings on contemporary digital marketing practices targeted at children and adolescents. The FTC, the FCC, and Congress should work together, along with the industry and the public health and child advocacy communities, to develop a new set of rules governing digital marketing to children. New regulations must take into account the full spectrum of advertising and marketing practices across all media, and apply to all children, including adolescents. Particular attention needs to be paid to how food and beverage products are promoted. Among the areas of special focus should be the following: requirements for full disclosure of data collection practices, including so-called nonpersonally identifiable information, targeted at children and adolescents; restrictions on personal profiling and behavioral targeting aimed at individuals under the age of eighteen; and restrictions on certain practices that may be deceptive, such as "viral videos" and other forms of stealth marketing that do not disclose, at the outset, the companies behind the campaigns.

The Internet and other new digital technologies hold great promise for youth, particularly for education, community-building, political involvement, and civic engagement. Therefore, marketing policies should only be a small part of a much broader media research and policy agenda. Among the issues that must be addressed are universal access to broadband, E-Rate policies, funding for noncommercial platforms, and support for education and training. If our goal is to have a generation that can help the country tackle it most pressing problems, then we need to provide it with a media environment that will help its members become effective contributors to our society and our democracy.

Notes

1. Jon Fortt, "Nielsen: Facebook Growth Outpaces MySpace," CNNMoney.com, 15 November 2007, bigtech.blogs.fortune.cnn.com/2007/11/15/nielsen-facebook -growth-outpaces-myspace/ (25 June 2008).

2. Michael Arrington, "Facebook No Longer the Second Largest Social Network," TechCrunch, 12 June 2008, www.techcrunch.com/2008/06/12/facebook-no-longer -the-second-largest-social-network (25 June 2008).

3. Karen Brown, "Study: Young Adults Snapping Up New Tech," *Multichannel News*, 31 July 2006, www.multichannel.com/article/CA6357818.html?display=Breaki ng+News (25 June 2008).

4. Marjorie Heins, *Not In Front of the Children: "Indecency," Censorship and the Innocence of Youth* (New York: Hill and Wang, 2001); Kathryn C. Montgomery, *Generation Digital: Politics, Commerce, and Childhood in the Age of the Internet* (Cambridge, MA: MIT Press, 2007), 35–66.

5. The Deleting Online Predators Act of 2006, introduced by Representative Mike Fitzpatrick (R-PA), would have amended the Communications Act of 1934 to require schools and libraries that receive federal E-Rate funding for Internet access to protect minors from online predators when using social networks and chat rooms by prohibiting minors' unsupervised use of such services. After wining approval in the House by a 410 to 15 margin, the bill was introduced in January 2007 in the Senate, where it died in committee. Congressional leaders called on the Federal Trade Commission in 2006 to issue a national consumer alert about MySpace and other social networking sites, charging that such sites have become a "virtual hunting ground" for predators. "Reps. Kirk, Wolf Warn of Pedophiles Operating on Top Internet Site: MySpace.com," U.S. Federal News Service, 13 April 2006, Washington, DC.

6. Karen Friefeld, "MySpace to Act Against Predators," *Washington Post*, 15 January 2008.

7. Berkman Center for Internet and Society, "The Berkman Center Announces Formation of Internet Safety Task Force to Identify and Develop Online Safety Tools," press release, 28 February 2008, cyber.law.harvard.edu/newsroom/Internet_Safety _Task_Force (25 June 2008).

8. See, for example, W. Lance Bennett, ed., *Civic Life Online: Learning How Digital Media Can Engage Youth* (Cambridge, MA: MIT Press, 2007); Morley Winograd and Michael D. Hais, *Millennial Makeover: MySpace, YouTube, and the Future of American Politics* (Piscataway, NJ: Rutgers University Pres, 2008); and Fadi Hirzala, "The Internet and Democracy: Participation, Civics, and Politics," *Javnost-The Public* 14, no. 2 (2007): 83–96, www.javnost-thepublic.org/media/datoteke/Pages_hirzalla_2-07-4.pdf (25 June 2008).

9. Center for Digital Democracy and U.S. PIRG, filing with the Federal Trade Commission concerning "Online Behavioral Advertising Principles," 11 April 2008, www.democraticmedia.org/files/FTCfilingApr08.pdf (25 June 2008). See also Piper Jaffray Investment Research, *The User Revolution: The New Advertising Ecosystem and the Rise of the Internet as a Mass Medium* (Minneapolis, MN: Piper Jaffray, 2007).

10. "U.S. Kids Spent $18 Billion Last Year, While Parents Spent $58 Billion Just to Feed Them," PR Newswire, 26 May 2006, www.commonsensemedia.org/resources /commercialism.php?id=6 (25 June 2008).

11. For a longer discussion of these trends, see Montgomery, *Generation Digital*, chapter 2.

12. See, for example, Donna Bogatin, "Nielsen to Track Digital Consumer with 'Anytime Anywhere' Media Measurement," ZDNet.com, 16 June 2006, blogs.zdnet .com/micro-markets/?p=130 (28 March 2007).

13. Jeff Chester and Kathryn C. Montgomery, "Interactive Food & Beverage Marketing: Targeting Children and Youth in the Digital Age," Berkeley Media Studies Group, May 2007, www.digitalads.org/documents/digiMarketingFull.pdf (21 October 2007).

14. "Solutions for Mobile Operators," JumpTap, www.jumptap.com/solutions _mob_adinv.aspx (28 March 2007).

15. Amy Johannes, "McDonald's Serves Up Mobile Coupons in California," *PROMO Magazine*, 26 October 2005, promomagazine.com/incentives/mcds_coupons_102605 (viewed 26 March 2007).

16. Nina M. Lentini, "KFC Airs Ring Tone Ad Aimed At Those Who Can Hear It," *Marketing Daily*, 12 April 2007, publications.mediapost.com/index .cfm?fuseaction=Articles.showArticle&art_aid=58606; KFC Corporation, "KFC Makes Noise with New Interactive TV Advertising," press release, 11 April 2007, www.prnewswire.com/cgi-bin/stories.pl?ACCT=109&STORY=/www/story/04-11 -2007/0004563459 (both viewed 17 April 2007).

17. For a description of some of the current branded entertainment sites food companies have created for children, see Elizabeth S. Moore, *It's Child's Play: Advergaming and the Online Marketing of Food to Children* (Menlo Park, CA: The Henry J. Kaiser Family Foundation, 2006), www.kff.org/entmedia/upload/7536.pdf (26 March 2007).

18. Felipe Korzenny, Betty Ann Korzenny, Holly McGavock, and Maria Gracia Inglessis, "The Multicultural Marketing Equation: Media, Attitudes, Brands, and Spending," Center for Hispanic Marketing Communication, Florida State University, 2006, 6, hmc.comm.fsu.edu/FSUAOLDMSMultiMktg.pdf (12 March 2007).

19. Betsy Book, "Advertising & Branding Models in Social Virtual Worlds" (presentation to the American Association for the Advancement of Science, 19 February 2006), available as a PowerPoint download at www.virtualworldsreview.com (viewed 30 March 2007). See description of Coca-Cola's Coke Studios at Studiocom, www.studiocom.com/public/site/home.html (2 April 2007); "Youniversal Branding"; "Cokestudios," MyCoke.com, www.mycoke.com/home.html?tunnel=cokestudios&sec tion=16 (17 April 2007); and "Coke in the Community," *Brand Strategy*, 5 February 2007. See also James Harkin, "Get a (Second) Life," FT.com, 17 November 2006, www.ft.com/cms/s/cf9b81c2-753a-11db-aea1-0000779e2340.html; "Yes Logo," New World Notes, 6 April 2006, nwn.blogs.com/nwn/2006/04/yes_logo.html; "Second Life: Coke Machine," Brands in Games, 15 February 2006, www.vedrashko.com /advertising/2006/02/second-life-coke-machine.html (all viewed 31 March 2007).

20. "The Bureau for Better Value," MySpace.com, profile.myspace.com/index

.cfm?fuseaction=user.viewprofile&friendid=14551144; Lisa Bertagnoli, "Wendy's Hits A YouTube Nerve," *Marketing Daily*, 27 October 2006, publications.mediapost.com/index .cfm?fuseaction=Articles.showArticle&art_aid=50292 (both viewed 29 March 2007).

21. "Coke, Nike Are Tops In Video Game Ads: Study," *PROMO Magazine*, 10 November 2006, promomagazine.com/research/other/brands_videogame_study _111006/index.html (30 March 2007).

22. Microsoft, "Microsoft to Acquire In-Game Advertising Pioneer Massive Inc.," press release, 4 May 2006, www.microsoft.com/presspass/press/2006/may06/05 -04MassiveIncPR.mspx (29 March 2007); John Gaudiosi, "Google Gets In-Game with Adscape," *The Hollywood Reporter*, 20 March 2007, www.hollywoodreporter.com/hr /content_display/business/news/e3i898ca0de1754206ae43bdbc6ee2d9ffd (30 March 2007); Mike Shields, "In-Game Ads Could Reach $2 Bil," *Adweek*, 12 April 2006, www. adweek.com/aw/national/article_display.jsp?vnu_content_id=1002343563 (30 March 2007).

23. Annette Bourdeau, "The Kids are Online," *Strategy*, 1 May 2005.

24. Patti M. Valkenburg, "Media and Youth Consumerism," *Journal of Adolescent Health* 27S (2000): 52–56.

25. Dale Kunkel, "Children and Television Advertising"; Dale Kunkel and Brian Wilcox, "Children and Media Policy," in *Handbook of Children and the Media* (Thousand Oaks, CA: Sage Publications, 2001), 375–94, 585–604.

26. Dale Kunkel, "The Implementation Gap: Policy Battles About Defining Children's Educational Programming," *Annals of the American Academy of Political and Social Science* 557 (1998): 39–53; Dale Kunkel, "Crafting Media Policy: The Genesis and Implications of the Children's Television Act of 1990," *American Behavioral Scientist* 35 (1991): 181–202; and Barry Cole and Mal Oettinger, *Reluctant Regulators* (Reading, MA: Addison Wesley, 1978), 243–88. See also Michael Pertschuk, *Revolt Against Regulation: The Rise and Pause of the Consumer Movement* (Berkeley: University of California Press, 1982).

27. Kunkel and Wilcox, "Children and Media Policy"; Dale Kunkel, "The Role of Research," *Science Communication* 12, no. 1 (1990): 101–19.

28. Angela Campbell, "Self Regulation and the Media," *Federal Communications Law Journal* 51 (1999): 711–71.

29. As president of the Center for Media Education, the author spearheaded the campaign that led to the passage of the Children's Online Privacy Protection Act.

30. "How to Comply with The Children's Online Privacy Protection Rule," Federal Trade Commission, www.ftc.gov/bcp/conline/pubs/buspubs/coppa.shtm; "Children's Online Privacy Protection Act of 1998," Federal Trade Commission, www.ftc.gov/ogc /coppa1.htm (both viewed 28 March 2008).

31. Center for Media Education, "Legislative Alert: S.2326 Children's Online Privacy Protection Act of 1998," n.d., author's personal files.

32. The Center for Media Education was also one of the commentators in this proceeding, calling for digital marketing safeguards. At the closing of CME in 2003, the Children's Media Coalition took over leadership on this issue. The author has continued to work closely with that coalition.

33. See Dale Kunkel, "Kids Media Policy Goes Digital: Current Developments in Children's Television Regulation," in *The Children's Television Community: Institutional, Critical, Social Systems, and Network Analyses,* eds. J. Alison Bryant and Jennings Bryant (Mahwah, NJ: Lawrence Erlbaum Associates, 2006).

34. For a case study of the campaign that led to the Children's Online Privacy Protection Act, as well as an assessment of its impact, see chapter 4, "Web of Deception," in Montgomery, *Generation Digital.*

35. Institute of Medicine of the National Academies, *Preventing Childhood Obesity: Health in the Balance,* Report Brief, September 2004, www.iom.edu/Object .File/Master/25/858/Childhood%20Obesity%204-pager-fix%20for%20web%20pdf. pdf (26 March 2007).

36. "Childhood Obesity," U.S. Department of Health and Human Services, aspe .hhs.gov/health/reports/child_obesity (2 April 2007).

37. American Academy of Pediatrics Committee on Nutrition, "Prevention of Pediatric Overweight and Obesity," *Pediatrics* 112, no. 2 (August 2003): 424–30, aappolicy .aappublications.org/cgi/content/full/pediatrics;112/2/424 (26 March 2007).

38. "Obesity Threatens to Cut U.S. Life Expectancy, New Analysis Suggests," press release, U.S. Department of Health and Human Services, 16 March 2005, www.nih.gov /news/pr/mar2005/nia-16.htm (10 December 2006).

39. See Juliet B. Schor and Margaret Ford, "From Tastes Great to Cool: Children's Food Marketing and the Rise of the Symbolic," *Journal of Law, Medicine & Ethics,* Spring 2007, www.blackwell-synergy.com/doi/pdf/10.1111/j.1748-720X.2007.00110 .x?cookieSet=1 (26 March 2007). As the authors write: "The increase of marketing to children has coincided with significant deterioration in the healthfulness of children's diets, higher caloric intake and a rapid increase in rates of obesity and overweight." See summary of studies in Institute of Medicine, *Food Marketing to Children and Youth: Threat or Opportunity?* (Washington, DC: The National Academies, 2005).

40. The National Academies, "Food Marketing Aimed at Kids Influences Poor Nutritional Choices, IOM Study Finds; Broad Effort Needed to Promote Healthier Products and Diets," press release, 6 December 2005, www8.nationalacademies.org /onpinews/newsitem.aspx?RecordID=11514 (26 March 2007).

41. *Food Marketing to Children and Youth,* "Executive Summary," 15, books.nap .edu/openbook.php?record_id=11514&page=1 (26 March 2007).

42. Federal Trade Commission, "FTC, HHS Release Report on Food Marketing and Childhood Obesity," press release, 2 May 2006, www.ftc.gov/opa/2006/05 /childhoodobesity.htm (26 March 2007).

43. "FTC, HHS Release Report on Food Marketing and Childhood Obesity: Recommends Actions by Food Companies and the Media," press release, 2 May 2006, www.ftc.gov/opa/2006/05/childhoodobesity.htm (1 April 2007). According to an announcement published in the *Federal Register,* the FTC "will seek data regarding, among other things: (1) the types of foods marketed to children and adolescents; (2) the types of measured and unmeasured media techniques used to market products to children and adolescents; (3) the amount spent to communicate marketing messages in measured and unmeasured media to children and adolescents; and (4) the amount of commercial advertising time in measured media directed to children and

adolescents that results from this spending." FTC, "Commission Seeks Public Comments on Food Marketing Targeting Children Commission Seeks Public Comments on Food Marketing Targeting Children," press release, 18 October 2006, www.ftc. gov/opa/2006/10/fyi0666.htm (1 April 2007).

44. Federal Communications Commission, "Task Force on Media & Childhood Obesity," www.fcc.gov/obesity (26 March 2007).

45. Bruce Mohl, "Activists Look to Sue Over Cartoons in Cereal Ads: State May Become Battleground in War on Childhood Obesity," *The Boston Globe*, 19 January 2006, www.boston.com/business/healthcare/articles/2006/01/19/activists_look_to _sue_over_cartoons_in_cereal_ads (26 March 2007).

46. Chester and Montgomery, "Interactive Food & Beverage Marketing: Targeting Children and Youth in the Digital Age," 11–12.

47. For example, when the new guidelines were announced, several food company representatives told the *Washington Post* that they were already abiding by the principles outlined. Annys Shin, "Ads Aimed at Children Get Tighter Scrutiny," *Washington Post*, 15 November 2006, www.washingtonpost.com/wp-dyn/content/article/2006/11/14 /AR2006111401245.html (1 April 2007).

48. The IOM report examined a range of studies, concluding that "children and youth consume a large proportion of their total calories from foods and beverages that are of high-calorie and low-nutrient content." Institute of Medicine, *Food Marketing to Children and Youth*, 53.

49. Center for Digital Democracy and U.S. PIRG, "Supplemental Statement in Support of Complaint and Request for Inquiry and Injunctive Relief Concerning Unfair and Deceptive Online Marketing Practices" (filing with the Federal Trade Commission), 1 November 2007, democraticmedia.org/news_room/press_release /FTCSupplementalFiling (18 January 2008).

50. "About 360 Youth," 360 Youth, www.360youth.com/aboutus/index.html (21 July 2005). Its 2005 form 10-K says the company has acquired a database of "31 million generation Y consumers."

51. Shankar Gupta, "Fox Exec: User Info Most Valuable MySpace Asset," *Online Media Daily*, 9 June 2006, publications.mediapost.com/index.cfm?fuseaction=Articles .san&s=44303&Nid=20848&p=198625 (28 March 2007).

52. Mark Walsh, "MySpace's 'HyperTargeting' Ad Program Off To A Strong Start," *Online Media Daily*, 4 December 2007, publications.mediapost.com/index .cfm?fuseaction=Articles.showArticleHomePage&art_aid=72037 (25 June 2008).

53. Facebook plans ultimately to automate this process. "Under the plan," according to *Advertising Age*, "Facebook would create an automated system that uses a member's profile information to direct relevant text advertising messages to the user's news feed. . . . Advertisers already are able to put messages into users' news feeds, the default news section that lets members know what their friends are up to. But these 'sponsored stories,' which can be text, graphical or click-to-play video ads, are expensive; the price tag limits them to mostly large brand marketers who have six-figure budgets to spend with Facebook's sales staff. An automated system could open up Facebook to smaller, more niche-targeted marketers, much as Google's system has done." Abbey Klaassen,

"Facebook vs. Google's AdWords: Social Net's Automated System Appeals to Small, Niche-Serving Marketers," *Advertising Age*, 27 August 2007.

54. Center for Digital Democracy, "Consumer Groups Call for FTC Investigation of Online Advertising, Consumer Tracking and Targeting Practices," press release, 1 November 2006, democraticmedia.org/news_room/press_release/FTC_online_adv2006. Copies of both the 2006 and 2007 CDD and U.S. PIRG FTC filings are available at democraticmedia.org/news_room/press_release/FTCSupplementalFiling (both viewed 25 June 2008). The author, formerly a CDD board member, continues to consult and collaborate with the organization.

55. Dawn Kawamoto and Anne Broache, "FTC Allows Google-DoubleClick Merger to Proceed," CNetNews.com, 20 December 2007, news.cnet.com/FTC-allows-Google -DoubleClick-merger-to-proceed/2100-1024_3-6223631.html. The FTC subsequently convened a town hall meeting on mobile marketing, "Beyond Voice: Mapping the Mobile Marketplace," on 6–7 May 2008, www.ftc.gov/bcp/workshops/mobilemarket (both viewed 25 June 2008).

56. "FTC Staff Proposes Online Behavioral Advertising Privacy Principles," 20 December 2007, Federal Trade Commission, www.ftc.gov/opa/2007/12/principles.shtm (15 January 2008).

57. Rhonda Evans, "Facebook Implementing Safeguards To Protect Young Users," Digtriad.com, 17 June 2008, www.digtriad.com/news/local/article.aspx?storyid=1031 76&catid=57; Steve O'Hear, "MySpace Makeover Announced," ZDNet.com, 13 June 2008, blogs.zdnet.com/social/?p=522 (both viewed 25 June 2008).

58. "The Network Advertising Initiative's Self-Regulatory Code of Conduct for Online Behavioral Advertising," Draft: For Public Comment, National Advertising Initiative, www.networkadvertising.org/networks/principles_comments.asp (15 January 2008).

59. Institute for Public Representation (on behalf of the American Academy of Child and Adolescent Psychiatry, the American Academy of Pediatrics, American Psychological Association, Benton Foundation, Campaign for a Commercial Free Childhood, Center for Digital Democracy), filing with the Federal Trade Commission concerning "Online Behavioral Advertising Principles," 11 April 2008, 6, www.democraticmedia .org/files/Children%27s%20Advocacy%20Groups%20%20Behavioral%20Advertising %20Comments%20FINAL.pdf (15 June 2008).

60. Institute for Public Representation FTC filing, 8.

61. Institute for Public Representation FTC filing, 9.

62. Institute for Public Representation FTC filing, 13.

63. Institute for Public Representation FTC filing, 13.

16

Race and Media

Several Key Proposals for the Next Administration

Leonard M. Baynes

Introduction

F OR THE PAST EIGHTEEN YEARS, COMMUNICATIONS experts have been saying that we are heading toward a multichannel, broadband-centric world that will cure all that ails the media. We all can be part of this process, they say, and affect real change by participating in the public discourse. On many levels, the media landscape is changing: Internet, computer, and broadband technology access is on the rise, as is the number of bloggers, YouTube videos, and social networking sites like Facebook. Many people of color are taking advantage of this new technology, with many websites that target their interests and tastes. Still, many people of color are still not digitally connected, and these new technological platforms cannot take the place of diverse ownership and content in the traditional broadcast media. This chapter examines and analyzes the media market for people of color and concludes that there is a separate media market for people of color, which, in the short term, requires policymakers to think about ways to increase minority ownership in traditional media as well as other programs that would help minority-owned broadcasters overcome existing capital market constraints. This chapter also proposes amending the Communications Act to ban racist and stereotypical hate speech. In the long term, policies are also needed that increase minority access to broadband technologies as well as policies that continue to guarantee minority-owned businesses access to capital.

There is Not One Ubiquitous Media Market

Although Internet penetration has reached 73 percent among American adults,[1] significant segments of the population still have no access to this technology. Only 40 percent of Americans with less than a high school education use the Internet, and 53 percent of Americans living in households with less than $30,000 a year in income go online.[2] It is believed that the digital divide will remain difficult to bridge,[3] and some Americans may choose to never participate in the broadband era.[4] Recent studies show that only 55 percent of the population has broadband access at home,[5] and among African Americans, home broadband access growth has slowed, with only 43 percent having it available.[6] In fact, around 60 percent of all American dial-up users say that they are not even interested in broadband.[7] According to the study *Broadband Internet Access Among Latinos: Status, Issues and Opportunities*, conducted by the Tomás Rivera Policy Institute at the University of Southern California, the lower broadband penetration rates of Latinos/as and African Americans may cost suppliers of the technology between $58 million and $74 million in foregone monthly revenues.[8] English-speaking Latinos/as use cell phones to access the Internet and to text message more often than African Americans and whites.[9] In fact, on a typical day, African Americans and Latinos/as are more likely to use mobile data and communications activities than whites.[10] Still, the percentage that do is well below 50 percent and they are more likely to use mobile services as a substitute for the telephone as the most prevalent use is text messaging—42 percent among Latinos/as and 34 percent among African Americans, as compared with 28 percent among whites.[11]

However, on a typical day, less than 5 percent of all racial groups are likely to watch a video on their mobile data and communications devices.[12] Similarly, only a small percentage of them are likely to use their mobile and communications devices to access the Internet for news, weather, sports, or other information.[13] The usage data suggest that users of these mobile data and communications devices do not use these devices as substitutes for television.

Traditional Broadcast Technologies Remain a Viable Market for Minorities

Despite the proliferation of new technologies in the media market, traditional broadcast television and radio are likely to remain viable product segments in the coming years. There has been a tendency to eulogize traditional media when major technological advancements in the field were made. Most of these eulogies turned out to be premature, since what generally happened was that the older technology remained and morphed into niche uses. AM radio still exists and has morphed into mostly talk radio despite the development of FM radio. Despite the development of television, AM and FM radio still exist and have found a niche audience in commuters, who listen to the radio in the car. Radio and television still exist despite the development of cable and satellite radio and television. And broadcast radio and television, as well as cable and satellite television, are likely to continue to exist despite the development of broadband technologies.

It is important to bear in mind that each media segment is a separate product market. The Federal Communication Commission (FCC) has lost sight of traditional economic and antitrust analysis when evaluating these different media product markets. Instead, in its ownership proceedings, it has relied on the media content offered by the Internet and cable technologies to offset broadcast concentration resulting from deregulation. As such, it has come to treat the submarkets—broadcasting, Internet, cable, and DBS—as one broad market in which media consumers can readily substitute one media technology for another.[14] This analysis has been detrimental to media consumers of color.

Brown Shoe v. the United States

In *Brown Shoe v. the United States*,[15] the U.S. Supreme Court, invoking antitrust theory,[16] "found that product markets are to be determined by "the reasonable interchangeability of use or the cross-elasticity of demand between the product itself and substitutes for it. However, within this broad market, well-defined submarkets may exist, which, in themselves, constitute product markets for antitrust purposes."[17] The submarkets are determined "by examining practical indicia or public recognition of the submarket as a separate economic entity, the product's peculiar characteristics and uses, unique production facilities, distinct customers, distinct prices, sensitivity to price changes and specialized vendors."[18]

Media and Content Geared for Minorities Constitutes Separate Media Markets

Since African Americans and Latinos/as do not have the same access to the Internet and broadband that they do to broadcasting, many of them are unable to substitute these two media product lines. Even among those who are able to substitute Internet and broadband technologies for broadcasting, studies show that they use this technology differently than whites.[19] For non-English-speaking Latinos/as, the biggest challenge is the lack of Spanish-language content and the fact that English is the *lingua franca* in cyberspace. It is estimated that as many as 86 percent of Spanish-speaking households with a home computer do not use the Internet.[20] If prior patterns are any indication, media consumers of color are likely to remain a separate market in their use of broadband technology.

Another key factor in determining whether separate markets exist from the consumer standpoint is the interchangeability of general programming. The broadcast market for the minority audience is a separate submarket of the mainstream media. The media industry has long acknowledged and encouraged the growth of this separate market for consumers of color.[21] The media industry views minority-owned and formatted stations as a separate market. In surveying the popularity of radio stations formats, Airplay Monitor, a division of *Billboard Magazine*, includes a format called "R&B/Urban,"[22] which is geared to minority listening tastes.

The existence of this separate market also becomes clear when examining the different television viewing habits of African Americans and Latinos/as.[23] About ten years ago, African Americans and whites had two completely different lists of the top ten most watched television shows, with little or no overlap between them.[24] By contrast, in the 2006–2007 television season, seven of the top ten prime-time programs were the same for both African-American and white viewers.[25] The drop in the number of African-American themed shows over the past ten years could explain this change. Moreover, African Americans and Latinos/as watch more hours of television than others. African Americans watch 15.59 hours per week[26] and Latinos/as watch 17.17 hours of prime-time viewing per week.[27] By contrast, non-African-American households watch television 14.36 hours[28] and non-Latino/a households spend 13.21 hours per week in front of the small screen.[29] African Americans and Latinos/as also spend more hours watching television in the daytime and late at night and more hours listening to radio programs than others.[30]

Minority-owned and formatted stations perform differently and take into account different minority tastes and values. In 1987, the Congressional Research Service Study found that minority-owned radio stations provided programming more suitable to the needs of minority audience members.[31] The FCC's authorized studies have found that minority-owned and formatted radio stations provide distinct and significant programming that appeals more to minority audiences and focuses more on the minority community than majority-owned radio stations.[32] The former FCC chairman, Michael Powell, recognized that

> minority broadcast station owners, when compared with non-minority owners, provide more public affairs programming on events or issues concerning ethnic or racial minority audiences, are more likely to broadcast in languages other than English, are more likely to staff their stations with minority employees and are more likely to participate in minority-related events in their communities.[33]

These minority-owned and formatted stations have historically provided community and civic functions. African-American and Latino/a media have traditionally connected members of the minority community to one another by bridging economic and geographic barriers. For example, black radio has connected rural black communities to black communities in larger American cities.[34] In the 1940s, Washington DC's African-American DJ, Hal Jackson, used his shows "to organize charity drives and benefit concerts, and to lead protests and pickets that integrated whites-only restaurants" and shops.[35] After the assassination of Martin Luther King Jr., African-American DJ Petey Greene was able to use the radio to calm listeners down during the ensuing riots in Washington, DC.[36] African-American NFL Hall of Famer Willie Davis, president of All Pro Broadcasting, Inc., uses his radio stations to address social issues such as teen pregnancy, drugs, and education.[37] More recently, a number of Latino-owned and formatted stations have used their stations as platforms to organize immigration protests and rallies. Black radio was expected to play a major role in increasing voter turnout among African Americans in the recent election.[38]

The FCC has historically employed a variety of different policies and programs to encourage the development of this market, among them advocating the licensing of minority broadcast owners. Such policies suggest that the FCC considered minority broadcasting to be a separate market.[39]

At this time and in the near future, the Internet and broadband technologies are not and will not serve as substitutes for broadcast among minorities. Since minorities have less access to the Internet and broadband technologies, broadcast television, and radio, which reach 99 percent of the population and are consumed more frequently than Internet services by African Americans and Latinos/as still represent for them a valid separate market. But despite being accessible to all, the broadcast market still underserves minority audiences when it comes to content and ownership of media properties. Unfortunately, the FCC has not succeeded in correcting this situation. FCC policies have been woefully unsuccessful in developing and encouraging the growth of this separate market because the communications industry, capital markets, and advertisers have discriminated against minority broadcasters.[40]

People of Color are Underserved in the Traditional Broadcast Media

Majority Broadcast Entertainment Programming Fails to Provide Media Consumers of Color with Sufficient Diverse Content or Opportunities

Minority media consumers may look to majority broadcasters for diverse content, but, generally, to no avail. The commercial news and entertainment media have historically misrepresented or failed to cover members of minority groups.[41] People of color have also been woefully unrepresented both behind and in front of the camera. In the 1960s, the Kerner Commission and the Civil Rights Commission called the media to task for such failures. These failures and misrepresentations become more worrisome when considering that the share of African American and Latinos/as in the United States is expected to reach 50 percent of the population by the year 2042.

The media coverage of Hurricane Katrina and radio talk-show host Don Imus's use of racially defamatory language are two recent examples of the media's lack of sensitivity to audiences of color. In 2005, Americans were shocked by the tragic scenes of Hurricane Katrina they were viewing on television. This was the first time (or at least the first time in a long time) that many Americans had been exposed to the plight of poor people in their country, a disproportionate number being African Americans. But media coverage of the event was full of distortions. Two photographs that initially appeared on Yahoo's website stood out in particular. One had a caption that described black survivors as "looting" while another, which had white survivors caught in a similar situation, described them as "finding" provisions.[42] The media initially described the Superdome, where mostly black hurricane survivors huddled until they were rescued, as unsafe and a place where murder, rapes, and robberies were rampant. This biased coverage may have affected policy and hampered relief efforts. There seems to be little question that it was directly responsible for the National Guard being ordered to "shoot to kill" those whom they perceived as breaking the law in the aftermath of the hurricane. Later, when the *New Orleans Times Picayune* investigated what in fact took place at the Superdome, it discovered that many of the reports about criminal activities had been highly exaggerated.[43]

On 4 April 2007, during a discussion about the NCAA Women's Basketball Championship, radio talk-show host Don Imus described the Rutgers University women's basketball team players as "rough girls." After his executive producer Bernard McGuirk called them "hardcore hos," Imus used the terms "nappy-headed hos," to which McGuirk responded that the Rutgers women athletes and their opponents looked like the "jigaboos versus the wannabes" memorialized in the Spike Lee film, *School Daze*. After much protest and debate, Imus's contract was terminated, and he was taken off the air, although he has since returned.

These two events are representative. With Hurricane Katrina, the media failed to cover stories that affected real people until it was too late. When they finally did report the story, the people harmed were often blamed for the tragic events that ensued. Instead, the media should have used the opportunity to spark a serious discussion about poverty and lack of opportunity, resources, and preparedness for many people in this country. If this had happened, it may have been possible to avoid this disaster. The Don Imus incident exemplifies how African Americans, who are more likely to be covered in the sports realm, are often described in stereotypical and harmful ways.

News is not the only area in which the media have been remiss. The entertainment media have historically employed few minority actors, writers, and directors and provided little minority-focused content. The television schedule announced in fall 1999 included twenty-six then-new shows, none of which starred an African American or any other minority member in a leading role. Only few featured minorities in secondary roles. Civil rights and advocacy organizations, such as the NAACP and the National Council of La Raza protested this lack of diversity and ultimately prompted the major networks to establish mechanisms for addressing diversity issues. They seem to have been effective, since in 2005, the television schedule included considerably more diversity among new scripted shows. In fact, out of forty-three new shows introduced that year, thirty-two regularly featured Latino/a, African-American, or Asian-American actors.[44] Still, the 2007–2008 season saw only five performers of color in starring roles. To make matters worse, the merger of the WB and UPN networks into the combined CW network has led to the elimination of almost all of the minority-centric programming that characterized the original networks. In fact, the increase in the number of minority actors in recent years has mostly been in supporting roles.[45] All this raises further questions about the complex role of minority characters and about whether television narratives are focused enough on minorities.

There are Very Few Minorities Behind the Camera

A study by the Ralph Bunche Center for African American Studies at the University of California Los Angeles (UCLA) suggests that much more effort needs to be made behind the television camera. The study found that less than 10 percent of all television writers are members of racially diverse groups. There is also an earnings gap: white writers earn on average $118,367 a years, while minority writers earn only $83,334 a year.[46] Writers from racially diverse backgrounds often work exclusively on minority-themed sitcoms. As a consequence, when these shows are canceled, employment opportunities for minority writers disappear. The lack of diversity among writers of non-minority-centered television shows may preclude cultural themes from being woven into the fabric of these shows.

Very Few Minority Owned Broadcast Media Exist to Provide Diverse Sufficient Diverse Content

Only 3.15 percent of television broadcast stations are minority owned[47] and only 5.87 percent are women-owned.[48] African Americans own only 0.6 percent and Latino/as own only 1.25 percent of all television stations.[49] Minority radio station owners constitute only 7.7 percent of all full-power commercial broadcast radio station owners, while women make up only 6 percent.[50] A study conducted by Free Press, the Washington, DC–based advocacy group, shows that minority-owned stations thrive in competitive and unconcentrated markets but face considerable challenges in consolidated markets. Easing up on concentration and cross ownership rules is likely to make the broadcast media more concentrated and, therefore, jeopardize the future of small minority-owned broadcasters. Consolidation is likely to make it more difficult for small entrepreneurs of color to obtain FCC licenses and enter the broadcast market[51] because the cost of buying a station has skyrocketed in the wake of media mergers.

All broadcast television networks are majority owned.[52] No minority-owned broadcast television networks exist today.[53] In fact, minority-owned television stations comprise only "5 of the 845 'big four' network-affiliated stations, or 0.6 percent of the total."[54] This represents a 62 percent decline since 2006, when minorities owned thirteen "big four"–affiliated stations.[55] A recent FCC-sanctioned study points to a 27 percent decline in the number of minority-owned broadcast stations across all markets.[56] In markets where rules have been relaxed and greater media concentration has resulted, there has been a 39 percent decrease in minority ownership. There are very few minority-owned cable companies. Viacom owns Black Entertainment Television (BET), and Comcast holds a substantial stake in TV One,[57] a new cable/satellite television network, programming primarily to African-American adults. The Spanish-language cable network Univision may be the only one that is "minority-owned."[58]

Minority-Owned Stations Face Discrimination

In 1995, the U.S. Supreme Court decided in *Adarand v. Pena* to raise the standard of review for race-based affirmative action programs. After this decision, the FCC abandoned its affirmative action programs[59] and converted almost all of its previous race-based programs into race-neutral ones. For example, in the auction process, instead of giving bidding credits to minority-owned businesses, the FCC decided to give them to small and/or new businesses. About this time, it also commissioned several market barrier entry studies to determine whether minority broadcasters faced discrimination. These studies found that in gaining (and operating) their licenses, many of these minority-owned licensees faced discrimination in the capital markets, as well as from advertisers and other members of the communications industry.[60]

In *Discrimination in Capital Markets, Broadcast/Wireless Spectrum Service Providers and Auction Outcomes*, William D. Bradford shows that loan applications submitted by minority-owned broadcast firms were less likely to be approved than those submitted by non-minority firms.[61] These same minority borrowers also "paid higher interest rates on their loans" than non-minority firms.[62] Bradford concludes that "[w]hen there is capital market discrimination, minorities will be capital constrained and less likely to qualify for any auction and less likely to win auctions."[63]

An FCC-commissioned study undertaken by KPMG, the accounting firm, found that the hearing selection process allowed many majority broadcasters to discriminate against minority broadcasters. In awarding licenses, the FCC favored "minority fronts" over real minority ownership.[64] As a consequence, despite the FCC's minority affirmative action program, minority ownership remained stagnant, and a minority owner had less of a chance of winning a license than did a non-minority owner.[65] Initial applications for a license comprised of a high proportion of minorities were more likely to be challenged and less likely to remain a singleton applicant.[66] In fact, the FCC awarded licenses to 74 percent of non-minority initial applicants who never competed in a comparative hearing, while only 35 percent of minority initial applicants "had the same non-competitive outcome."[67]

Another FCC-commissioned study, this one on advertising, underscores the discriminatory practices of broadcast advertisers.[68] It found, for example, that advertisers refused to advertise on minority-owned stations or on stations with substantial minority audiences—a practice known as "no urban/ Spanish dictates."[69] In the event that they did advertise on these stations, the study found that they would require substantial rate discounts. This practice was known as "minority discounts."[70] The study found that about 90 percent of minority broadcasters had encountered the "no urban/Spanish dictates."[71]

In addition, the study found that minority-formatted radio stations earned "less revenue per listener" than stations broadcasting general market programming.[72] Minority-owned stations also earned "less revenue per listener" than majority broadcasters owning a comparable number of stations nationwide. The minority broadcasters estimated that the "no urban/Spanish dictates," along with the "minority discounts," reduced revenues for these stations by 63 percent.[73] Given that minority-formatted and -owned stations in certain urban markets have larger audiences than other stations, these findings show that minority-formatted and -owned stations earn less advertising revenue per listener than do other radio stations. This is particularly devastating in an industry where profit maximization depends on the quantity and the price of commercials sold.[74] Indeed, advertising revenue is the primary asset of any broadcast company.

After these studies were released, the FCC conducted several hearings and appointed a diversity committee to investigate the matter. It finally took action on December 18, 2007, when it circulated several race-neutral proposals. This chapter will analyze and critique the effectiveness of these proposals, as well as recommend a proposal that would improve minority content.

Increase Minority Ownership, Access, and Representation

Proposed Solutions

On December 18, 2007, the FCC released the Report and Order and Third Further Notice of Rulemaking, which adopted nondiscrimination rules for market transactions and advertising. At the same time, it acknowledged discrimination in the industry. While the rules barring discrimination are forward looking, policies that remedy the harm minorities have suffered from discrimination in the past are needed as well. The best way to fix underrepresentation is with race-conscious programs, which would invoke strict scrutiny, requiring the government to show that there is a compelling governmental interest and that they are narrowly tailored. Indeed, race-neutral means should be used first in order to address underrepresentation, unless they are unsatisfactory. After thirteen years of studying minority underrepresentation, the FCC has gathered enough data that demonstrate how race-neutral allocation mechanisms of the past, which have focused exclusively on small businesses, have failed.

The FCC Report and Order and Third Further Notice of Rulemaking, which instituted several race-neutral remedies designed to increase minority ownership is therefore insufficient. Some of the proposals are regulations that the FCC previously employed in a race-conscious way, among them the distress sale policy and its "grandfather" provisions that allowed the transfer of grandfathered stations that violated new local media ownership rules. In this Report and Order, the FCC defined an "eligible entity" as a small business that fits the definition provided by the Small Business Administration (SBA). According to this definition, a small business is a television broadcasting station that has no more than $13 million in annual revenues and a radio broadcasting entity that has no more than $6.5 million in annual revenues.[75] The SBA considers the revenues of the parent corporation and any affiliates of the eligible entity in making an assessment of whether it meets this definition. In addition, the eligible entity must satisfy the following "control test":

> The eligible entity must hold (1) 30 percent or more of the stock/partnership shares and more than 50 percent voting power of the corporation or partnership that will hold the broadcast license; or (2) 15 percent or more of the stock/partnership shares and more than 50 percent voting power of the corporation or

partnership that will hold the broadcast licenses, provided that no other person or entity owns or controls more than 25 percent of the outstanding stock or partnership interests; or (3) more than 50 percent of the voting power of the corporation if the corporation that holds the broadcast licenses is a publicly traded company.[76]

The FCC's decision to adopt race neutral rules was meant to avoid what it sees as "constitutional difficulties." Regarding the question whether it should adopt a race-conscious definition of "eligible entity" it sent out for further comment.

It is my view that the FCC should include "socially and economically disadvantaged" businesses in its definition of eligible entities. The SBA defines "socially and economically disadvantaged businesses" as small businesses that are at least 51 percent owned and controlled by a socially and economically disadvantaged individual or individuals. Members of racially diverse minority groups are presumed to qualify. Other individuals need to provide evidence that they are disadvantaged to qualify.

Indeed, thirteen years of FCC studies should have already served as substantial evidence that the time has come to reintroduce race-sensitive policies.

Secondary Market Solutions to Increase Minority Ownership

Complicating the remedies available is the limited spectrum available for the FCC to auction. As a result, much of the effort to diversify media ownership has to focus on the sale of broadcast licenses in secondary markets, and it is, therefore, important to encourage majority-owned owners to sell to small, minority, and women owners.

Bring Back and Expand the Minority Tax Certificate Program

My first proposal is to revive the FCC's Minority Tax Certificate Program—a program repealed in 1995 by Congress in an anti-affirmative action backlash. During the fifteen years that it was in effect, members of minority groups acquired 288 radio stations, 43 television stations, and 31 cable systems.[77] "According to a study by the National Association of Black Owned Broadcasters, the vast majority of major-market minority broadcasters used tax certificates to attract initial investors, to purchase a broadcast station or to sell a broadcast property to another minority."[78] It is estimated that the minority tax certificate broadcast stations made up about two-thirds of all minority-owned stations.[79]

Through the tax certificate program, sellers were allowed to defer tax payments, thereby encouraging the sale or investment in minority-owned and controlled broadcast and cable companies. The minority companies would then be able to use the expected tax savings of the seller to negotiate a reduction in the purchase price.[80]

Besides the anti–affirmative action backlash of the 1990s, there is an oral history claiming that the primary reason for the repeal of the program was Congressional outrage at Viacom's plan to sell its cable systems to a minority-led group for $2.3 billion and to use the tax certificate program to defer $400 million in federal taxes and as much as $200 million in state taxes.[81] Some members of Congress charged that the program provided unjustified tax breaks to millionaires.[82]

Congressmen Bobby Rush (D-IL) and Charles Rangel (D-NY) have introduced two separate bills to reinstitute the program. Rush's bill (H.R. 600) defines an eligible purchaser as "any economically and socially disadvantaged business as designated by the Secretary of the Treasury using specified criteria." Rangel's bill (H.R. 3003) defines the eligible purchaser as a small business with net assets not exceeding $30 million and average taxable income for the preceding two taxable years not exceeding $10 million.

Both bills attempt to deal with the Viacom problem by limiting the amount of taxes that can be deferred. Rangel's bill (H.R. 3003) would permit a taxpayer to defer up to "$50 million of the gain from the sale of the assets or stock of a telecommunications business to certain small businesses that own 10 or fewer broadcast stations." The bill also "limits to three the number of such purchases by any qualifying small business and requires the recapture of such deferred gain for any telecommunications business resold within five years." Rush's bill (H.R. 600) permits the "exclusion from gross income of 50 percent of the gain from the sale or exchange of stock, held for more than five years, in an eligible purchaser engaged in a telecommunications business."[83]

Both bills broaden the tax certificate program to include other telecommunications businesses (besides broadcast). Rush's approach, which targets socially and economically disadvantaged businesses (not just minority-owned businesses), would be more effective in remedying difficulties experienced by minority owners in raising capital. This tailoring would guarantee that those businesses most affected by capital market discrimination are offered a targeted remedy that would allow the majority seller to provide the minority buyer with access to capital through the tax certificate program. A minority tax certificate program would be constitutional for several reasons. First, as mentioned above, several FCC-commissioned studies have shown that minority-owned broadcasters are discriminated against in the capital markets. This finding is supported by many other studies of other industries, which have found that minority-owned businesses tend to face this particular form of discrimination. Second, it would be the U. S. Congress, through legislation, that would reenact the tax certificate program. Section 5 of the Fourteenth Amendment stipulates that "[t]he Congress shall have power to enforce, by appropriate legislation, the provisions of this article,"[84] thereby giving Congress the power to combat discrimination. This congressional power to establish race-conscious programs has been diminished by the Supreme Court's *Adarand* decision to those circumstances when the Congress has demonstrated a compelling governmental interest and has a narrowly tailored remedy.

In short, a reenacted tax certificate program for socially disadvantaged businesses would pass muster because there is substantial evidence that minority-owned broadcast businesses face capital market discrimination, and this program directly addresses this problem since experience shows that race-neutral programs have not worked, reinstituting race-sensitive programs would appear to be the better alternative.

Bring Back the Distress Sale Policy

The FCC should also reinstitute the distress sale policy and apply it to socially and economically disadvantaged businesses. The distress sale policy permitted "a licensee whose license has been designated for revocation hearing, or whose renewal application has been designated for hearing on basic qualifications issues, to assign its license prior to commencement of the hearing to a minority controlled entity" at a price that is substantially below its fair market value. In its December 18, 2007 Report and Order, the FCC established a distress sale market for licensees who were in danger of losing their licenses.

The distress sale policy was created only for potential minority owners, but after *Adarand v. Pena*, the FCC failed to implement this policy fearing it was unconstitutional. The FCC has since advocated reintroducing the policy and applying it to small businesses. Since studies commissioned by the FCC have shown that minority-owned broadcasters were victims of discrimination, it should not be opposed to extending this policy to socially and economically disadvantaged businesses. Like the Congress's power to reenact the tax certificate program, the FCC's power to establish race-based programs has been restricted by the Supreme Court's *Adarand* decision to those circumstances when the FCC has demonstrated a compelling governmental interest and has a narrowly tailored remedy. A distress sale policy specifically designed for socially disadvantaged businesses would pass muster because there is substantial evidence that minority-owned broadcast businesses face capital market discrimination. The distress sale policy addresses this problem by creating a market for minority-owned broadcasters exclusively for those stations that are on the verge of losing their licenses, a narrowly tailored policy.

The position of the courts has been that programs designed to remedy past discrimination cannot continue indefinitely. As such the FCC would need to monitor both these programs closely to see what effect they are having on discrimination. In this way, it could also ensure that these programs and policies pass constitutional muster.

Have the SBA Guarantee Loans to Small Telecommunications Businesses

The FCC Market Barrier Entry studies show that minority-owned telecommunications businesses often are turned down for loans or obtain them on less favorable terms than white-owned telecommunications businesses. Several minority and women owners who took part in the FCC Market Entry Barrier anecdotal study, *Whose Spectrum is it Anyway?*, explained that regional and local banks had no experience providing loans to broadcast businesses and were, therefore, reluctant to provide them.

The Rangel bill (H.R. 3003) addresses this problem by giving the administrator of the SBA the power "to guarantee any loan made to a qualified business for the purchase of assets or stock described in section 1071(c) of the Internal Revenue Code of 1986 (relating to qualified telecommunications sale)." The Rangel bill also deals with the repercussions of the Nextwave bankruptcy that left FCC licenses held up in limbo during a bankruptcy by providing that the SBA administrator "not guarantee any loan under subsection (a) unless such loan provides that any license issued by the Federal Communications Commission to the borrower shall be returned and forfeited by the borrower immediately upon a finding by the Administrator that such borrower is in default under such loan." This proposal should also broaden the opportunities for minority-owned businesses to acquire FCC licenses.

Retention of Minority-Owned Stations

Once the number of minority-owned broadcasters grows, it is imperative that they remain viable. To this end, both the Rush and Rangel bills require minority-owned businesses to retain the media property for five years or else forfeit the deferred capital gains tax. This provision should ensure that "real" minority owners buy the property and not "fronts." The problems that confront minority-owned media companies revolve around access to capital, advertising discrimination and media consolidation, which makes the markets more monopolistic. The Rangel bill (H.R. 3003), which allows the SBA to guarantee loans to small telecommunications businesses, should ensure a more steady flow of capital to all small telecommunications businesses, including those that are minority-owned. In its recent order, the FCC acknowledged the existence of advertising discrimination against minority-owned broadcasters and required broadcasters, when renewing their licenses, to certify that "their advertising sales and contracts contain nondiscrimination clauses that prohibit all forms of discrimination."[85] Still, the FCC refused to include specific language in the contracts that would prohibit "no urban/no Spanish dictates"[86] on First Amendment grounds.

This advertising nondiscrimination provision may be ineffective, as it lacks monitoring and enforcement mechanisms. Hence, when implementing this provision, the FCC must be vigilant about monitoring the advertising dollars that flow into minority-owned and majority-owned stations, and measures should be taken against advertisers who discriminate against minority-owned broadcasters and minority-formatted stations. The FCC should partner (and coordinate) with the U.S. Department of Justice in this effort, and it should strip broadcasters of their licenses when they are found to aid and abet this form of discrimination. Given that advertising is the lifeblood of these stations, the FCC should coordinate with the other branches of government to encourage their advertising on minority-owned stations.

The FCC should also be looking for ways to promote small broadcast owners. For example, it should refrain from policies that cause media consolidation. Media consolidation generally puts small broadcasters in a difficult spot, because they are not able to sell advertising across a variety of media platforms and markets. The FCC needs to come back to its historic position of encouraging diversity of voices through disparate and far-ranging ownership. These small broadcaster-friendly policies will also help minority-owned broadcasters who tend to be small owners.

Make Nonstereotypical Portrayals and Diversity of Media Content Core American Value

What emerged from the Don Imus incident is that, unlike cases of indecency involving sexually explicit images or excretory functions, there is currently no legal or regulatory recourse against racially indecent speech on the broadcast airwaves. In fact, FCC Chairman Kevin Martin insisted that the Imus incident was not covered by the indecency rules,[87] despite claims to the contrary.

Section 1464 of the Communications Act states that: "Whoever utters any obscene, indecent, or profane language by means of radio communication shall be fined under this title or imprisoned not more than two years, or both."[88]

The FCC notice provides:

> Indecency findings involve at least two fundamental determinations. First, the material alleged to be indecent must fall within the subject matter scope of our

indecency definition—that is, the material must describe or depict sexual or excretory organs or activities. Second, the broadcast must be patently offensive as measured by contemporary community standards for the broadcast medium. In applying the "community standards for the broadcast medium" criterion, the Commission has ruled that the standard is not a local one, but rather is that of an average broadcast viewer or listener and not the sensibilities of any individual complainant. In determining whether material is patently offensive, the full context in which the material appeared is critically important. It is not sufficient, for example, to know that explicit sexual terms or descriptions were used, just as it is not sufficient to know only that no such terms or descriptions were used.[89]

No other Communications Act provision specifically addresses hate speech over the airwaves, and the provisions that deal with nondiscrimination and diversity are not as robust as they could be.

In 1996, Congress amended section 151 of the Communications Act to include a provision barring "discrimination on the basis of race, color, religion, national origin, or sex." Section 151 now reads:

For the purposes of regulating interstate and foreign commerce in communication by wire and radio so as to make available, so far as possible, to all people of the United States, *without discrimination* on the basis of race, color, religion, national origin, or sex, a rapid, efficient, Nation-wide, and worldwide wire and radio communication service with adequate facilities at reasonable charges for the purpose of national defense, for the purpose of promoting safety and life and property through the use of wire and radio communication, and for the purpose of securing a more effective execution of this policy by centralizing authority heretofore granted by law to several agencies and by granting additional authority with respect to interstate and foreign commerce in wire and radio as the "Federal Communications Commission," which shall be constituted as hereinafter provided, and which shall execute and enforce the provisions of this Act. [90]

Section 254(b) of the Communications Act provides the following:

(b) NATIONAL POLICY.—In carrying out subsection (a), the Commission shall seek to promote the policies and purposes of this Act favoring diversity of media voices, vigorous economic competition, technological advancement, and promotion of the public interest, convenience, and necessity.

But it relates only to the requirement for periodic market entry barrier studies "identifying and eliminating, by regulations pursuant to its authority under this Act (other than this section), market entry barriers for entrepreneurs and other small businesses in the provision and ownership of telecommunications services and information services."

The Communications Act's indecency provisions need to be amended. In most of the developed world, racist hate speech is outlawed.[91] The United States should join the rest of the world and "take affirmative responsibility for protecting the atmosphere of mutual respect against certain forms of vicious attacks."[92] The proposed statute would make diversity of media voices a core value and require that every action that the FCC takes is evaluated in the context of its effect on diversity of media ownership and media voices.

The proposed amendment to the Communications Act should state that as the United States is a multicultural nation, which has in the past discriminated against underrepresented and insular groups, it now affirms diversity as a core value that should be promoted through:

(1) Diversity of media ownership and media voices. The FCC should have the authority to take diversity into account in its decision making regarding media ownership in the hope of promoting a variety of different voices;

(2) Broadcasters must work to safeguard, enrich, and strengthen the diversity of the United States and its territories;

(3) No broadcaster should air any abusive comment or abusive pictorial representation that, when taken in context, tends or is likely to expose an individual or a group or class of individuals to hatred or contempt on the basis of race, national or ethnic origin, color, religion, sex, sexual orientation, age, or mental or physical disability;

(4) Broadcasters should ensure that the on-screen portrayal of all minority groups is accurate, fair, and nonstereotypical.

These changes would encourage media to promote the individual human dignity of all people, and prevent coverage that makes reference to religion, race, color, ethnic origin, or gender in an insensitive manner. This provision is more reactive than affirmative.

For First Amendment purposes, the Supreme Court has historically treated broadcast media differently than the print media.[93] The government owns the frequencies and distributes this valuable government resource to private individuals to use.[94] As part of this grant, licensees have certain obligations in their use of this government resource.[95] Because of the nature of the license, the grant, and the dearth of frequencies, the Supreme Court has held that a broadcast licensee does not have a constitutional right to hold a license or to monopolize a radio frequency to the exclusion of fellow citizens. As a fiduciary holding the license is in public trust, and a licensee may be required to share its frequency with others. The Supreme Court has stated that both broadcasters and the public have First Amendment rights that must be balanced when the government seeks to regulate access to the radio spectrum.[96] In fact, the Supreme Court has held that "it is the right of the viewers and listeners, not the right of the broadcasters, which is paramount. It is the right of the public to receive suitable access to social, political, esthetic, moral and other ideas and experiences which is crucial here."[97] An essential goal of the First Amendment is to achieve "the widest possible dissemination of information from diverse and antagonistic sources."[98] In Pacifica Foundation, the Supreme Court found that the FCC did not violate the First Amendment in issuing a warning to a radio station that had broadcast indecent materials.[99] The Supreme Court stated that "patently offensive, indecent material presented over the airwaves confronts the citizen, not only in public, but also in the privacy of the home, where the individual's rights to be left alone plainly outweigh the First Amendment rights of the intruder."[100] In essence, the court found that the words were protected but were broadcast at the wrong time of day.[101] All-white television images and negative minority stereotypes are equally disturbing. Viewers are exposed to them before they may realize what they are seeing. These stereotypes are as intrusive as indecent materials.

The Longer Term Future: Ubiquitous Broadband

For people of color to have more access and content in the new world of ubiquitous broadband, two types of policies need to be implemented. The first type would bolster demand. This would include setting a goal of achieving ubiquitous broadband in the next ten years, and it needs to include more robust measures for increasing access among low-income consumers in the home, school, libraries, work, and in remote places. The FCC should extend its Link-Up and Lifeline policies, which currently cover telephone service, to broadband. These policies could then provide low-income consumers with discounts when purchasing computers and broadband service. Making broadband technologies universal would provide African Americans and Latino/as with greater access and create a bigger demand for minority-focused content. Among other measures that need to be taken in this context are training people in computer literacy skills.

The second type of policy would bolster supply. Smaller content providers will have to access and reach audiences through broadband. Underserved audiences will be more easily able to reach their minority producer's content without going through a mediator. To ensure that minority broadband entrepreneurs who have designed minority content will be able to reach their intended audiences (and their audiences will be able to reach them), network neutrality should maintained and "Internet users should be able to access any Web content they choose and use any applications they choose, without restrictions or limitations imposed by their Internet service provider."[102] This neutrality will allow minority broadband content providers to provide full access to minority consumers without any interference from the broadband operators.

There will still be media owners and producers who have access to bigger audiences. Many of them may be the same big media owners of today who will have extended their reach to other communications platforms, like broadcast, cable, satellite, and the Internet. It is important that there be diversity among them, and for that reason, we need to enforce the minority tax certificate program, the distress sales policies, anti-discrimination policies, and SBA guarantees of loans. Both the Rangel and Rush bills extend the minority tax certificate program to non-broadcast companies, so that they can provide tax breaks to majority media companies that sell to minorities. This should help increase the number of minority media properties. The tax certificate program for digital content should work the same way it has been proposed in the context of broadcasting by compensating minority businesses' that are experiencing capital constraints.

Conclusion

The images presented in the mainstream news and the entertainment media affect how people of color are viewed. It is, therefore, imperative that we have real solutions to ameliorate negative representation of minorities by increasing minority representation and changing longstanding economic conditions barring minorities from acquiring a representative share of media outlets. In terms of minority media ownership, the next administration should bring back the tax certificate and the distress sale policy and extend them to socially and economically disadvantaged businesses. The SBA should have the power to guarantee loans for small telecommunications businesses. The Communications Act needs to be amended to make diversity a core value, and FCC regulations should prohibit racist and stereotypical speech on the airwaves. In addition, measures must be taken to increase minority access to broadband technology, maintain network neutrality and provide capital to these new minority entrepreneurs developing an online presence.

Notes

1. Mary Madden, "Data Memo, Internet Penetration and Impact," *Pew Internet and American Life*, 3, www.pewinternet.org/pdfs/pip_internet_impact.pdf (April 2006).

2. Madden, "Internet Penetration," 4.

3. Janna Quitney Anderson and Lee Rainie, "The Future of the Internet II," *Pew Internet and American Life Project*, 10, news.bbc.co.uk/2/shared/bsp/hi/pdfs/22_09 _2006pewsummary.pdf (24 September 2006).

4. Anderson and Rainie, "The Future," 58.

5. John B. Horrigan, "Home Broadband Adoption 2008," *Pew Internet and American Life Project* 1, www.pewinternet.org/pdfs/PIP_Broadband_2008.pdf (July 2008).

6. Horrigan, "Home Broadband," 2.

7. Horrigan, "Home Broadband," 10.

8. Waldo López-Aqueres, and Elsa Macias, "Broadband Internet Access Among Latinos: Status, Issues and Opportunities," 10, www.trpi.org/PDFs/BBDaccess.pdf (2004).

9. John Horrigan, "Mobile Access to Data and Information," *Pew Internet and American Life Project* (2008) www.pewinternet.org/pdfs/PIP_Mobile.Data.Access.pdf.

10. Horrigan, "Mobile Access," 4.

11. Horrigan, "Mobile Access," 4.

12. Horrigan, "Mobile Access," 4.

13. Horrigan, "Mobile Access," 4.

14. Horrigan, "Mobile Access," 4.

15. 370 U.S. 294 (1962).

16. 15 U.S.C. § 18. Section 18 provides:

> No corporation engaged in commerce shall acquire, directly or indirectly, the whole or any part of the stock or other capital of another corporation engaged also in commerce, where in any line of commerce in any question in any section of the country, the effect of such acquisition may be substantially to lessen competition, or to tend to create a monopoly.

17. 370 U.S. 325.

18. 370 U.S. 325.

19. Mary Madden, "America's Online Pursuits: The Changing Picture of Who's Online and What They Do," *Pew Internet and American Life Project*, 24, www.pewinternet .org/pdfs/PIP_OnLine_Pursuits_Final.PDF (2003).

20. López-Aqueres and Macias, "Broadband Internet Access Among Latinos," 14.

21. H. Peter Nesvold, "Communication Breakdown: Developing an Antitrust Model for Multimedia Mergers and Acquisitions," *Fordham Intellectual Property Media & Entertainment Law Journal* 6 (1996): 781 (noting that the appropriate market definition for media depends on its reasonable interchangeability with other media products).

22. Frank Ahrens, "Black Radio Edges Out Other Stations, Hip-Hop, R&B, Oldies Rise to No. 2 Spot in Cities," *Washington Post*, 19 November 1999, C1.

23. James Sterngold, "A Racial Divide Widens on Network TV," *New York Times*, 29 December 1998, A1.

24. Stergold, "A Racial Divide Widens on TV," A1.

25. "African-American TV Usage and Buying Power Highlighted By Nielsen" (27 October 2007), www.nielsen.com/media/2007/pr_071018a.html.

26. Nielsen, "African American Television Usage: Primetime," www.nielsenmedia .com/ethnicmeasure/african-american/03-04_AAPrimetime.htm.

27. Nielsen, "Hispanic Television Usage: Primetime," www.nielsenmedia.com /ethnicmeasure/hispanic-american/hispprimetime05.htm.

28. Nielsen, "African American Television Usage: Primetime," www.nielsenmedia .com/ethnicmeasure/african-american/03-04_AAPrimetime.htm.

29. Nielsen, "Hispanic Television Usage: Primetime," www.nielsenmedia.com /ethnicmeasure/hispanic-american/hispprimetime05.htm.

30. "Radio Advertising Bureau Radio Marketing Guide and Factbook," www.rab .com/public/MediaFacts/2007RMGFB-150.pdf.

31. Congressional Research Service, *Minority Broadcast Station Ownership and Broadcast Programming: Is There a Nexus?* (1988).

32. Christine Bachen et al., "Diversity of Programming in the Broadcast Spectrum: Is There a Link Between Owner Race or Ethnicity and News and Public Affairs Programming?" 26 (1999) (FCC Santa Clara University Report), www.fcc .gov/opportunity/meb_study; Jeffrey Dubin and Matthew L. Spitzer, "Testing Minority Preferences in Broadcasting," *Southern Califonia Law Review* 68 (1995): 841, 869. Merely increasing the number of radio stations in a market failed to increase the amount of minority programming; Peter Siegelman and Joel Waldfogel, "Race and Radio: Preference Externalities, Minority Ownership, and the Provision of Programming to Minorities," www.fcc.gov/ownership/roundtable_docs/waldfogel-c.pdf (October 2001).

33. John McCain and Michael K. Powell, "Clear Signal, Static Response," *Washington Times*, washingtontimes.com/op-ed/20040302-085047-6972r.htm (3 March 2004).

34. LaVonda Reed-Huff, "Radio Regulation: The Effect Of A Pro-Localism Agenda On Black Radio," *Washington & Lee Journal of Civil Rights & Social Justice* 12 (2006): 97.

35. Marc Fisher, "Black Radio Today: Where Are the New Petey Greenes?," *Washington Post*, 21 July 2008, blog.washingtonpost.com/rawfisher/2007/07/black_radio _today_where_are_th.html.

36. Voa News: "'Talk To Me' Highlights Career Of Popular D.C. Radio Personality," *US Federal News*, 30 July 2007.

37. Tannette Johnson-Elie, "NFL Legend Sure of Ability to Serve on Many Boards," *Milwaukee Journal & Sentinel*, 3 March 2004.

38. Jim Rutenberg, "Black Radio on Obama Is Left's Answer to Limbaugh," *New York Times*, 27 July 2008, A1.

39. Leonard M. Baynes, "Life After Adarand: What Happened to the Metro Broadcasting Diversity Rationale for Affirmative Action in Telecommunications Ownership?," *University of Michigan Journal of Law Reform* 33 (1999/2000): 87, 128.

40. Leonard M. Baynes, "Making the Case for a Compelling Governmental Interest in Broadcast Media Ownership," *Rutgers Law Review* 57 (2005): 235.

41. Leonard M. Baynes, "WHITEOUT: The Absence and Stereotyping of People of Color by the Broadcast Networks in Prime time Entertainment Programming," *Arizona Law Review* 45 (2003): 293.

42. Neil Carlson, "Rethinking the Discourse on Race: A Symposium on How the Lack of Racial Diversity in the Media Affects Social Justice and Policy," *St. John's*

Journal of Legal Comment 21 (2007): 581 (ed. Leonard M. Baynes), www.stjohns.edu/media/3/fe444f7c26664e8291c65d37bd4bd3e8.pdf.

43. Brian Thevenot and Gordon Russell, "Rape. Murder. Gunfights," *New Orleans Times Picayune*, 26 September 2005, A1.

44. Suzanne C. Ryan, "It's Prime Time for Improved Racial Diversity," *Boston Globe*, 15 September 2005, E1.

45. Greg Braxton, "White Still a Primary Color," *Los Angeles Times*, 6 June 2007, 1.

46. Richard Verrier, "White Male Writers Dominate Hollywood Film, Television Jobs," *Miami Herald*, 5 June 2007, C5.

47. Department of Commerce, Minority Commercial Broadcast Ownership Overview, www.ntia.doc.gov/reports/97minority/overview.htm.

48. S. Derek Turner and Mark Cooper, "Out of The Picture: Minority & Female TV Ownership in the United States," available at www.freepress.net/files/otp2007.pdf (Free Press) (2007).

49. Turner and Cooper, "Out of the Picture," 2.

50. S. Derek Turner, "Off the Dial: Female and Minority Radio Station Ownership in the United States," www.stopbigmedia.com/files/off_the_dial.pdf (Free Press) (2007), 4.

51. Ivy Planning Group LLC, Federal Communications Commission, "Whose Spectrum Is It Anyway? Historical Study of Market Entry Barriers, Discrimination and Changes in Broadcasting and Wireless Licensing 1950 to Present," 47–52, purl.access.gpo.gov/GPO/LPS7938 (December 2000).

52. Turner and Cooper, "Out of The Picture," www.freepress.net/files/otp2007.pdf, 4.

53. U.S. Department of Commerce, Changes, "Challenges and Charting New Courses: Minority Commercial Broadcast Ownership in the United States," 66 (December 2000).

54. Turner and Cooper, "Out of the Picture," 29.

55. Turner and Cooper, "Out of the Picture," 4.

56. Allen S. Hammond IV, "The Impact of the FCC's TV Duopoly Rule Relaxation on Minority and Women Owned Broadcast Stations 1999–2006," 56, fjallfoss.fcc.gov/edocs_public/openAttachment.do?link=DA-07-3470A9.pdf.

57. "Minority Ownership," Hear us Now, www.hearusnow.org/mediaownership/20/.

58. "Minority Ownership," Hear us Now, www.hearusnow.org/mediaownership/20/.

59. Baynes, "Life After Adarand," 87.

60. Baynes, "Making the Case," 235.

61. Baynes, "Making the Case," citing William D. Bradford, "Discrimination in Capital Markets, Broadcast/Wireless Spectrum Service Providers and Auction Outcomes," v (5 December 2000), www.fcc.gov/opportunity/meb_study/capital_market_study.pdf.

62. William D. Bradford, "Discrimination in Capital Markets Broadcast/Wireless Spectrum Service Providers and Auction Outcomes," v.

63. Bradford, "Discrimination in Capital Markets," v.

64. Bradford, "Discrimination in Capital Markets," v.

65. Bradford, "Discrimination in Capital Markets."

66. Bradford, "Discrimination in Capital Markets."

67. Bradford, "Discrimination in Capital Markets."

68. Kofi Ofori, "When Being No.1 Is Not Enough: The Impact of Advertising Practices on Minority-Owned & Minority-Formatted Broadcast Stations," 13 (January 1999), www.fcc.gov/Bureaus/Mass_Media/Informal/ad-study/adstudy01.pdf.

69. Ofori, "When Being No. 1 Is Not Enough," 25.

70. Ofori, "When Being No. 1 Is Not Enough," 25.

71. Ofori, "When Being No. 1 Is Not Enough," 13.

72. Ofori, "When Being No. 1 Is Not Enough," 13.

73. Ofori, "When Being No. 1 Is Not Enough," 13.

74. Deborah M. Wilkerson, "Power Beyond the Remote Control," *Black Enterprise*, December 1996, 76.

75. 13 C.F.R §§ 121.210, 121.103, 121.105.

76. 2002 Biennial Review Order, 18 FCC Rcd at 13811, P489.

77. Erwin Krasnow, "A Case for Minority Tax Certificates," *Broadcast & Cable*, 15 December 1997, 80.

78. Krasnow, "A Case for Minority Tax Certificates," 80.

79. Financial Issues Subcommittee Recommendation to the Federal Communications Commission's Advisory Committee on Diversity for Communications in the Digital Age Recommendation on a Tax Incentive Program (25 May 2004) www.fcc.gov /DiversityFAC/adopted-recommendations/TaxIncentiveProgramRecommend.doc.

80. Krasnow, "A Case for Minority Tax Certificates," 80.

81. Mark Bobichaux, "A Cable Empire that Was Built on a Tax Break," *Wall Street Journal*, 12 January 1995, B1.

82. 141 Cong. Rec. §4551, §4559 (daily ed. 24 March 1995) (statement of Senator Dole).

83. H.R. 600, thomas.loc.gov/cgi-bin/query/z?c110:H.R.600.

84. U.S. Constitution, 14 Amendment § 5.

85. FCC Report and Order and Third Further Notice of Proposed Rulemaking P49 (2008).

86. 2002 Biennial Review Order, ¶ 489.

87. "The Buzz," *Newsday*, 18 April 2007, A15.

88. 18 U.S.C. §1464.

89. FCC Industry Guidance on the Commission's Case Law Interpreting 18 U.S.C. §1464 and Enforcement Policies Regarding Broadcast Indecency 66 FR 21984-02 (2001).

90. 47 U.S.C. § 151.

91. Adam Liptak, "Unlike Others, U.S Defends Freedom to Offend Speech," *New York Times*, 12 June 2008, A1.

92. Liptak, "Unlike Others" A1.

93. *FCC v. National Citizens Committee*, 436 U.S. 775, 779 (1978) (upholding FCC ban on cross ownership of broadcast stations by newspapers in the same market because there is no "unabridgeable First Amendment right to broadcast comparable

to the right of every individual to speak, write, or publish"); *Red Lion Broadcasting Co. v. FCC*, 395 U.S. 367 (1969) (finding the fairness doctrine, which required the broadcaster to cover both sides of a controversial issue, constitutional; but compare *Miami Herald Co. v. Tornillo*, 418 U.S. 241 (1974) (finding Florida "right to reply" statute unconstitutional to newspapers)).

94. *Red Lion Broadcasting Co. v. FCC*, 395 U.S. 367; see also *Turner Broadcasting System, Inc.*, 512 U.S. at 637–38 (1969).

95. *FCC v. Pacifica Foundation*, 438 U.S. at 726 (1978).

96. *Columbia Broadcasting System, Inc. v. Democratic National Committee*, 412 U.S. 94, 102–3 (1973).

97. *Red Lion*, 395 U.S. at 390.

98. *National Citizens Committee For Broadcasting*, 436 U.S. 779 (quoting Associated Press, 326 U.S. at 20).

99. *Pacifica Foundation*, 438 U.S. at 750–51.

100. *Pacifica Foundation*, 438 U.S. at 748.

101. *Pacifica Foundation*, 438 U.S. at 726; *Action for Children's Television v. FCC*, 58 F. 3d 654 (DC Cir. 1995), cert. denied, 116 S. Ct. 701 (1996).

102. "Keep the Internet Free and Open," Common Cause, www.commoncause.org /site/pp.asp?c=dkLNK1MQIwG&b=1234951 (last visited 2 July 2008).

Index

360 strategy, 284
360 Youth, 290

access. *See* broadband access; Internet access
Adarand v. Pena, 308, 313
adolescents: media advertising and nutritional health, 289–90; online video viewing, 129n16; privacy online, 292. *See also* youth
"advanced services," 205
advertising: consumer movements and, 48; discriminatory practices directed at minorities, 309; Internet video and, 135n83; targeting of youth, 283. *See also* children's advertising; marketing
advocacy groups, 37
affirmative action programs, 308, 309
African Americans: Internet penetration and, 18; mobile communications services and, 302; ownership of broadcast media, 307; television use, 304
age, Internet penetration and, 18
Airplay Monitor, 304

a la carte programming, 118
Alaska, 249, 255
Alaska Federal Health Care Access Network (AFHCAN), 249
Alloy Media + Marketing, 290
All Pro Broadcasting, Inc., 305
Alltel, 163n6
American Broadband for Communities Act, 232
Ameritech Corp., 90, 102n24
AM radio, 302–3
analog television, 114
"anchor tenants," 251
anti-trust law, 303
"any stream to any screen," 114
Apple iPhone, 158, 161, 165n16
arbitrators, 97
AT&T: "deep packet inspection," 119; digital video services, 110; dominant position in the MRS market, 159; entry into cable, 90; MCI's access to network of, 60; mergers and, 218n2, 218n3; revenues, 111; service to rural regions, 204; structural separation, 59; "three-screen strategy," 113–14; universal service and, 182, 205;

About the Contributors

Marvin Ammori, J.D., is an assistant professor of law at the University of Nebraska, Lincoln, College of Law. After graduating from Harvard Law School, Professor Ammori practiced at a corporate law firm in Chicago, primarily litigating intellectual property disputes. Subsequently, he held a research fellowship at Yale Law School, with its Information Society Project. He then served for two years as a staff attorney at the Institute for Public Representation, a public interest law clinic at Georgetown University Law Center that handles significant legal matters of broad public importance. Professor Ammori handled matters involving free speech and media regulation before appellate courts, the Federal Communications Commission, and Congress, including the leading public policy debates in media policy, including broadcast ownership limits, network neutrality, children's media rules, and other rules. He spent the 2007–2008 year as general counsel of Free Press, the nation's leading media reform organization, working on several campaigns concerning open internet initiatives, wireless policy, and access for all Americans to high-speed internet.

Leonard M. Baynes, J.D., M.B.A., is professor of law and the inaugural director of the Ronald H. Brown Center for Civil Rights and Economic Development at St. John's University School of Law. Professor Baynes received his B.S. from New York University and J.D./M.B.A. from Columbia University. He is a nationally recognized communications law scholar, specializing in race and media issues. While on leave of absence and sabbatical, from 1997 to 2001, Professor Baynes worked for then-FCC chairman William E. Kennard as a scholar-in-residence at the Federal Communications Commission, where he served as a member of the Opportunity Team and worked on minority access and ownership issues. In 2004, Professor Baynes served as an expert witness at the FCC Federal Advisory Committee for Diversity in broadcast ownership. In 2005, the Ford Foundation awarded Professor Baynes a $50,000 grant to organize a conference on race and media diversity titled "Rethinking the Discourse on Race: A Symposium on How the Lack of Racial Diversity in the Electronic Media Affects Social Justice." In 2006, the Ford Foundation also awarded a $10,000 grant for Professor Baynes to lead a ten-person delegation of media diversity scholars to the National Media Reform Conference in Memphis, TN. Also in 2006, the Minority Media & Telecommunications Council (MMTC) inducted Professor Baynes into its hall of fame. Professor Baynes has written over twenty-five law review articles on race/racism and the law, corporate law, communications law, or the intersection of the three.

Rob Frieden, J.D., holds the Pioneers Chair in telecommunications at Penn State University. Professor Frieden is a leading analyst in the field of telecommunications and Internet infrastructure and has authored many comprehensive works on international telecommunications, cable satellite television, and communications law. His book contributions included coauthorship of "All About Cable and Broadband," a treatise on law and policy, and *Managing Internet-Driven Change in International Telecommunications*, a comprehensive primer. Prior to joining Penn State, Frieden was deputy director, international relations, Motorola Satellite Communications, Inc., where he managed the regulatory and international liaison efforts for Motorola's IRIDIUM low earth orbiting satellite project. He has held senior level policy making positions in government and worked in the private sector as an attorney. Frieden has served on several telecommunications and trade delegations and has authored numerous articles and papers that have appeared in law reviews, trade journals, and proceedings of major conferences. He is a frequently invited speaker to forums hosted by organizations such as the American Bar Association, the Annenberg-Washington Program, the International Telecommunication Union, the United Nations, and the World Bank.

Ellen P. Goodman, J.D., is professor at Rutgers University School of Law, Camden. Professor Goodman specializes in the law of information technology, including telecommunications, advertising media, and intellectual property. She has been an expert panelist before the National Science Foundation, the Federal Communications Commission, the Brookings Institute, and the Aspen Institute, as well as other policy and academic audiences. Professor Goodman has been a visiting associate professor at the University of Pennsylvania Law School and a visiting scholar at the University of Pennsylvania

Wharton School of Business. Prior to joining the faculty at Rutgers in January 2003, Professor Goodman was a partner in the law firm of Covington & Burling LLP with a practice in information technology law. Professor Goodman graduated from Harvard College and Harvard Law School, and clerked for the Honorable Norma L. Shapiro in the Eastern District of Pennsylvania.

Heather E. Hudson is professor of communications technology management in the School of Business and Management at the University of San Francisco. Her work focuses on both domestic and international topics concerning applications of ICTs for socioeconomic development, regulation, and policy, including universal service and other strategies to extend affordable access to new technologies and services. Dr. Hudson has planned or evaluated communication projects in Alaska, northern Canada, and more than fifty developing countries and emerging economies. She has also consulted for the private sector, government agencies, consumer and indigenous organizations, and international organizations. She is the author of numerous articles and several books, including *From Rural Village to Global Village: Telecommunications for Developing in the Information Age, Global Connections: International Telecommunications Infrastructure and Policy, Communication Satellites: Their Development and Impact,* and *When Telephones Reach the Village,* and coauthor of *Electronic Byways: State Policies for Rural Development through Telecommunications,* and *Rural America in the Information Age.* Professor Hudson has been a Sloan Foundation Industry fellow at Columbia University's Institute for Tele-Information, has held a Fulbright Asia/Pacific Distinguished Lectureship, and has been an honorary research fellow at the University of Hong Kong and senior fellow at the Centre for International Research on Communication and Information Technology (CIRCIT) in Australia and the East/West Center in Hawaii.

Krishna Jayakar, Ph.D., is associate professor of communications at Penn State University. Professor Jayakar's research interests include telecommunications policy, intellectual property rights, and media economics. His research has been published in many journals, including *Communications Law and Policy, Telecommunications Policy, Info, Journal of Media Economics,* and *The Information Society.* His papers have been presented at numerous academic conferences, with several winning top honors in paper competitions. Professor Jayakar served as the head of the media management and economics division of the Association for Education in Journalism and Mass Communication (AEJMC) for 2006–2007. Previously Dr. Jayakar worked at the Ministry of Information and Broadcasting of the government of India, where he authored reports on mass media policy.

Robert W. McChesney, Ph.D., is the Gutgsell Endowed Professor, Department of Communication, University of Illinois at Urbana–Champaign. In 2002, Dr. McChesney co-founded Free Press, a national media reform organization and served as its president until April 2008, when he stepped down to devote more time to other interests. McChesney also hosts the "Media Matters" weekly radio program every Sunday afternoon on NPR-affiliate WILL-AM radio. McChesney has written or edited seventeen books. McChesney's most recent book is *The Political Economy of Media: Enduring Issues, Emerging Dilemmas,* the companion volume to *Communication Revolution: Critical Junctures and the Future of Media* (2007). In 2008, McChesney's 1999 book *Rich Media, Poor Democracy* was awarded the ICA Fellows Book Award, which recognizes books that "have made a substantial contribution to the scholarship of the communication field, as well as the broader rubric of the social sciences, and have stood some test of time." His work has been translated into eighteen languages.

Kathryn Montgomery, Ph.D., is professor in the School of Communication at American University. Dr. Montgomery joined American University with more than twenty-five years of experience in both the nonprofit field and academe. For twelve years, she was president of the DC-based Center for Media Education (CME), which she co-founded in 1991. During her tenure at CME, Montgomery's research, publications, and testimony helped frame the national public policy debate on a range of critical media issues. She led a coalition of child advocacy, health, and education groups in a series of successful advocacy campaigns, leaving behind a legacy of policies on behalf of children and families. They include a FCC rule requiring a minimum of three hours per week of educational/informational television programming for children, a content-based ratings system for TV programs, and the first federal legislation to protect children's privacy on the Internet. Before moving to Washington, DC, Montgomery was a media studies professor at California State University, Los Angeles, and at the University of California, Los Angeles. She is the author of *Target: Prime Time—Advocacy Groups and the Struggle over Entertainment Television* (1989)—named "Outstanding Academic Book of 1989–1990" by *Choice Magazine.* Her most recent book is *Generation Digital: Politics, Commerce, and Childhood in the Age of the Internet* (2007). She received her Ph.D. in motion pictures and television from UCLA.

Philip M. Napoli, Ph.D., is associate professor of communications and media management and director of the Donald McGannon Communication Research Center at Fordham University. Dr. Napoli's research focuses on media institutions and media policy. He is the author of the books *Audience*

Economics: Media Institutions and the Audience Marketplace (2003) and *Foundations of Communications Policy: Principles and Process in the Regulation of Electronic Media* (2001) and the editor of *Media Diversity and Localism: Meaning and Metrics* (2007). His work has been published in academic journals such as *Telecommunications Policy, Communication Law & Policy,* the *Journal of Communication,* the *Policy Studies Journal,* and the *Harvard International Journal of Press Politics.* Dr. Napoli's work has been supported by organizations such as the Ford Foundation, the National Association of Broadcasters, the Phoebe Haas Charitable Trust, the Benton Foundation, and the National Association of Television Programming Executives. He has testified before Congress and the Federal Communications Commission on media policy issues and has been interviewed for a number of media outlets, including the *Los Angeles Times,* the NBC *Nightly News,* the *Baltimore Sun,* the *Chicago Tribune,* and *Rolling Stone.* Dr. Napoli previously held academic appointments at Rutgers University and Boston University.

Jon M. Peha is professor in the Department of Engineering and Public Policy and the Department of Electrical and Computer Engineering and associate director of the Center for Wireless and Broadband Networking at Carnegie Mellon University. His research spans technical and policy issues of computer and telecommunications networks. This has included spectrum, broadband Internet, wireless networks, video and Voice over IP, communications for emergency responders, universal service, secure Internet payment systems, e-commerce, and network security. He frequently consults for industry and government agencies around the world. Dr. Peha has addressed telecom and e-commerce issues on legislative staff in the U.S. Congress, and helped launch a U.S. government interagency program to assist developing countries with information infrastructure. He has also served as chief technical officer of three high-tech start-ups, and as a member of technical staff at SRI International, AT&T Bell Laboratories, and Microsoft. Dr. Peha is a congressional fellow of the IEEE and a diplomacy fellow of the AAAS. He holds a Ph.D. in electrical engineering from Stanford University.

Amit M. Schejter, Ph.D., is assistant professor of communications and co-director of the Institute for Information Policy at Penn State University. His research focuses on identifying regulatory responses to technological change, highlighting social inequalities and communication distortions created by them, and prescribing theoretically informed approaches to policymaking that enhance fairness and equality. His studies have been widely published in both communication and law journals, cited in congressional and Knesset hearings and have dealt with the challenges raised by television, cable, the

Internet, mobile phones, and digitization in Israel, the United States, Korea, the European Union, and across wide international comparative settings. His background includes a decade of holding senior executive positions in the telecommunication industry in Israel, including general counsel for Israeli public broadcasting and vice president of Israel's largest mobile operator. In addition, he served on and chaired a variety of public committees, counseled media and telecommunication entities in Israel and the Palestinian Authority, and held the post of assistant professor at Tel Aviv University. His books include *The Wonder Phone in the Land of Miracles* (co-authored with Akiba Cohen and Dafna Lemish, 2008) and *Muting Israeli Democracy* (forthcoming).

Jorge Reina Schement, Ph.D., is professor and dean of the School of Communication, Information and Library Studies, at the State University of New Jersey, Rutgers. Schement's research and scholarship address issues in the areas of information policy, global telecommunications, the social aspects of the information age, Spanish-language media, and information-consumer behavior. More specifically, he has focused on the social and policy consequences of the production and consumption of information, with a special interest in policy as it relates to ethnic minorities. He is a faculty fellow of the Columbia Institute for Tele-Information. He has served on the editorial boards of seven academic journals and is editor-in-chief of the *Macmillan Encyclopedia of Communication and Information*. Schement has been an associate editor of the *Information Society* and an editor of the *Annual Review of Technology* for the Aspen Institute. He has held positions at Penn State, Stanford University, the University of Texas at Austin, the Annenberg School for Communication at the University of Southern California, and the Graduate School of Library and Information Studies at UCLA. He has been a Ford Foundation Fellow and a Fulbright Senior Research Fellow at the University of Helsinki. In 1994, Schement served as the director of the Federal Communications Commission's Information Policy Project. He is the author or editor of ten books, with two additional volumes in preparation, one hundred articles and reports, multiple other papers and presentations, and a substantial list of corporate and foundation grants.

Sharon L. Strover, Ph.D., is chair and Philip G. Warner Regents Professor in the Department of Radio-Television-Film and director of the Telecommunications and Information Policy Institute at the University of Texas. Dr. Strover heads the national Telecommunications Panel for the Rural Policy Institute, a national, multi-university think tank devoted to rural issues. She has worked with the Federal Communication Commission on technology needs and state and local telecommunications applications, participated in advisory panels for the U.S. Office of Technology Assessment and the Federal Trade Commission, and was subcommittee chair for the State of Texas's investigation of the U.S.-Mexico Free Trade agreement (later NAFTA). The recipient of numerous grants and contracts in the telecommunications field, she has worked with several foundations and state agencies around the country on networking and telecommunications policy issues. Dr. Strover codirected a three-year Ford Foundation study of telecommunications and rural areas and collaborated on the book *Electronic Byways*, examining state telecommunications applications and policy. Her recent work has appeared in *Government Information Quarterly*, *Telecommunications Policy*, and *The Information Society*, among other journals, and previously she coedited two other books examining telecommunications in urban and rural regions. She currently sits on the editorial boards of six journals.

Andrea H. Tapia, Ph.D., is assistant professor of information sciences and technology, and affiliate assistant professor in the Department of Labor Studies and Industrial Relations at Penn State University. Dr. Tapia completed her Ph.D. in sociology at the University of New Mexico and a postdoctoral fellowship at the University of Arizona before coming to Penn State. The U.S. National Science Foundation, the U.S. Department of Defense, the United Nations, and Penn State's Schreyer's Honors College have funded Dr. Tapia's work, which has appeared in *The Information Society*, *Government Information Quarterly*, *Database for Information Systems Research*, *The Communications of the ACM*, *Science Technology and Human Values*, and *Information Technology and People*.

Richard D. Taylor, J.D., Ed.D., is the Palmer Chair and professor of telecommunications studies and co-director of the Institute for Information Policy at Penn State University. Dr. Taylor has directed major research projects and published widely on the implications of investment in information technology on economic development in the Asia Pacific region. He has some thirty-five years of experience in the telecommunications field. His scholarly work has primarily been in understanding the impact of investment in information technologies. In 2002, he was honored by appointment as an IBM faculty partner for his work in the area of information metrics. He is coauthor of the book, *Technology Parks of the Asia Pacific: Lessons for the Regional Digital Divide* (2003), sponsored by the Ford Foundation. He has been a speaker at academic, governmental, legal, and corporate meetings in the telecommunications, cable television, broadcasting, and publishing industries, as well as a consultant to nonprofit groups, including regulators, educators, and librarians. He has organized and chaired a number of major conferences on topics relating to information technology and development and electronic commerce. Prior to joining the faculty at Penn State in 1989, he was vice president and corporate counsel for Warner Cable Communications, and from 1993 to 1998 was an outside member of the Board of PrimeStar Partners, Ltd., a satellite television broadcasting company.

Ernest J. Wilson III, Ph.D., is the Walter Annenberg Chair in Communication and dean of the Annenberg School for Communication at the University of Southern California. Dr. Wilson's scholarship focuses on the convergence of communication and information technology, public policy, and the public interest. He is also a student of the "information champions," who are leaders of the information revolution around the world. His current work concentrates on the politics of global sustainable innovation in high-technology industries, on China-Africa relations, and the role of culture in U.S. national security policy. In addition to his most recent books—*The Information Revolution in Developing Countries* and *Negotiating the Net in Africa*—Dr. Wilson coedits the MIT Press series The Information Revolution and Global Politics and an MIT journal, *Information Technologies and International Development*. Nominated by President Bill Clinton, Dr. Wilson is the ranking senior member of the board of directors of the Corporation for Public Broadcasting. President Bush reappointed him to the CPB board in 2004. Prior to his appointment at USC Annenberg, Dr. Wilson was a senior research scholar at the University of Maryland, College Park, holding a joint appointment as professor in the Department of Government and Politics and in the Department of African-American Studies.